BEYOND

CIVIL

SOCIETY

BEYOND

CIVIL

SOCIETY

Activism, Participation, and
Protest in Latin America

SONIA E. ALVAREZ · JEFFREY W. RUBIN · MILLIE THAYER

GIANPAOLO BAIOCCHI · AGUSTÍN LAÓ-MONTES · EDITORS

Duke University Press   Durham and London   2017

© 2017 DUKE UNIVERSITY PRESS. All rights reserved
Printed and bound by CPI Group (UK) Ltd, Croydon, CR0 4YY
Text design by Courtney Leigh Baker
Cover design by Matthew Tauch
Typeset in Garamond Premier Pro and Din by Westchester Publishing Services
Library of Congress Cataloging-in-Publication Data
Names: Alvarez, Sonia E., [date]–editor. | Rubin, Jeffrey W., editor. |
Thayer, Millie, editor. | Baiocchi, Gianpaolo, [date]–editor. | Laó-Montes,
Agustín, editor. | Escobar, Arturo, [date]–writer of the foreword.
Title: Beyond civil society : activism, participation, and protest in
Latin America / Sonia E. Alvarez, Jeffrey W. Rubin, Millie Thayer,
Gianpaolo Baiocchi, and Agustín Laó-Montes, editors ; [foreword by Arturo Escobar].
Description: Durham : Duke University Press, 2017. | Includes
bibliographical references and index.
Identifiers: LCCN 2016056545 (print) | LCCN 2017004586 (ebook)
ISBN 9780822363071 (hardcover : alk. paper)
ISBN 9780822363255 (pbk. : alk. paper)
ISBN 9780822373353 (e-book)
Subjects: LCSH: Political participation—Latin America. | Political activists—
Latin America. | Social movements—Latin America. | Democracy—
Latin America. | Pressure groups—Latin America. | Political culture—Latin America.
Classification: LCC JL966 .B496 2017 (print) | LCC JL966 (ebook) |
DDC 322.4098—dc23
LC record available at https://lccn.loc.gov/2016056545

Cover art: JR, *Action dans la Favela Morro da Providência, Arbre, Lune, Verticale, Rio de Janeiro, 2008*. Courtesy of jr-art.net.

Contents

Part IV.
Movements, Regimes, and Refoundations

Foreword

ARTURO ESCOBAR

This is a comprehensive and ambitious tome, an "anthology" of a field at its best. It was easy to name this field when it was emerging, sometime in the 1980s, in both Latin American and U.S.-based Latin Americanist scholarship. "Back then," we called it, simply, "social movements theory and research." The field has grown more complex ever since, as the social, cultural, and political processes it seeks to name, and the struggles themselves, became more complex—less bounded, less neatly oppositional, more massive in some cases but fragile in others, and certainly more resistant to theory. Out of this messiness and complexity, but also and fundamentally out of the continued and ever renewed commitment to understanding them and to contribute to the struggles for change, there arose, over the past decade, the incredibly diverse but coherent set of inquiries, categories, and empirical research that make up this compelling volume. "Beyond Civil Society" serves as a shorthand for this emergence.

To appreciate what has changed, it might be useful to go back and trace a bit of the genealogy of the collective research program of which this volume forms part. In the mid-1980s, Sonia Alvarez and I organized a Latin American social movements research group at the University of California, Santa Cruz. From the outset, the group's project maintained a balance on many fronts: gender, for sure, but also perspectives (Latin American versus Euro-American), age, discipline, and geographical coverage. This explicit balance fostered a richness of perspectives that has remained a feature of the various collaborative projects ever since. It also bridged paradigms, examining simultaneously what had remained separate aspects in social movements' research, namely, their role in constituting identities, their strategies to pursue social change, and their contributions to democracy and alternative visions of development. This three-pronged approach was reflected in the book's full title: *The Making of Social Movements in Latin America: Identity, Strategy, and Democracy* (1992).

About 1994, Sonia and I undertook a follow-up collective project with Brazilian political scientist Evelina Dagnino. This time our shorthand organizing rubric was the need to explore simultaneously the cultural dimensions of the political and the political dimensions of the cultural. The increasing popularity of cultural studies in both the United States and Latin America, fostered by the influence of poststructuralism, was an important driving factor in our work, besides trends in anthropology, political science, and feminist theory. We all read influential chapters from the best-known cultural studies reader of the decade (*Cultural Studies*, edited by Larry Grossberg and Cary Nelson, which we affectionally called "The Brick" because of its size). After several conferences and work meetings in Brazil and the United States, the new project crystallized in the volume *Cultures of Politics/Politics of Cultures: Re-visioning Latin American Social Movements* (1998), also published in Spanish and Portuguese.

Over the course of the 2000s, the research agendas of the editors and a number of contributors to this volume intersected in creative, always productive ways with my own, with one another, and with other intellectual-activists committed to developing engaged, forward-looking theories about activism, participation, and protest. In the early 2000s, for instance, Sonia and I collaborated in two other projects. The first, entitled "Women and the Politics of Place" (WPP), ran for over five years, coordinated by Australian feminist historian Wendy Harcourt and myself. The project brought together over twenty feminist participants from many regions of the world, working on struggles connecting place, gender, and politics. The approach highlighted the interconnections among body, environment, and the economy in place-based women's struggles. At around the same time, Gianpaolo Baiocchi, Agustín Laó-Montes, Sonia, and myself were involved with the World Social Forum (WSF) process, especially its first gatherings held in Porto Alegre. The agendas of Jeff Rubin and Gianpaolo also crossed paths in their related research on popular participation in that city. An anthology on the WSF with which I collaborated included a chapter by Sonia on feminist readings of the WSF (*The World Social Forum: Challenging Empires*, coedited by Jai Sen, Anita Anand, A. Escobar, and Peter Waterman) and was assembled in the same spirit as the present volume: it sought to theorize the process while actively contributing to the alter-globalization movements then under way. A parallel initiative involving Millie Thayer and Sonia brought together feminists from the Global South and the Global North and focused on the multiple translations among Latin American and Latina feminisms across the continent, resulting in the 2014 volume *Translocalities/Translocalidades*, coedited by Thayer and Alvarez, together with Claudia de Lima Costa, Verónica Feliu, Rebecca Hester, and Norma Klahn.

These multiple crossings provoked incredibly productive theoretical-organizational innovations—assemblages, one might say, of theories, grants, scholars, events, emotions, debates. Convened under several engaging rubrics—"On Protest," "Theorizing the Tahrir Moment," and "Beyond the Civil Society Agenda"—the most recent of the collective initiatives emerging from those intersections locates Latin American contemporary mobilizations transnationally and transculturally. It crystallized with the project "Beyond the Civil Society Agenda," an incredibly productive initiative out of which comes the present volume, coedited by a closely collaborating group that includes Sonia Alvarez, Jeffrey Rubin, Millie Thayer, Gianpaolo Baiocchi, and Agustín Laó-Montes.

Firmly anchored in the Amherst area, the group has been hard at work for close to a decade, resulting in a research network that includes nodes in Perú, Brazil, México, and Colombia, besides UMass Amherst, Chapel Hill, the Universidad Nacional Mayor de San Marcos, and other institutions, with over three dozen researchers and intellectual-activists participating. Many of them are included in this volume. Needless to say, the project's social context is quite different from that of the 1980s and 1990s: the so-called turn to the Left or Pink Tide that started in the continent with the election of Hugo Chávez in December 1998, and which seemed to become consolidated, for a time, as it involved a majority of countries in the region. While the wave of progressive governments appeared to make the interpretation of the collective mobilizations of the past fifteen years straightforward again—indeed, for some it called for a return to established Marxist analyses of progressive forces capturing the State—as chapter after chapter in this volume show this was hardly ever the case. True, a great deal of active participation by individuals and organizations has taken place within the ambit of the State and through the so-called Third Sector made up largely of nongovernmental organizations. Yet confrontational collective action continues to take place, sometimes with an intensity one might not suspect to be possible from a conventional Left perspective, as in the case of the most progressive regimes, such as Evo Morales's Bolivia and Rafael Correa's Ecuador.

Thus, as this anthology so perceptively envisions it, between the permitted forms of participation by the hegemonic "Civil Society Agenda" and the "uncivic activism" of many of the actual mobilizations within the larger social movement field, there emerged an entire range of forms of protest and mobilization by an incredibly diverse set of actors that seemed to call for a significant "reset" of the research agenda and a transformed interpretive framework and theoretical language. This was the challenge to which the research collective behind this anthology responded with great prescience. Above all, what they found, as vividly chronicled and constructively theorized in various chapters and case studies, was that contemporary mobilizations employ multiple strategies and emerge from numerous locations, deploy both civic and "uncivic" forms of protest, contest development and modernity while cleverly engaging with them, and function within gray zones that sometimes make it difficult to discern where they stand in the span between emancipation and democracy, order and disorder, liberalism and progressivism, radical inter-culturality and neoliberal multiculturalism, and society, the market, and the State.

A "softer" theory, if one wishes—and certainly not any "general theory" in the old-fashioned sense of the term—emerges from these inquiries, perhaps the only possible one given the complexities and ambiguities of the processes and actions at play. A forceful, and hopeful, concept identified by the authors is the need to "decolonize the Civil Society Agenda" in such a way that its most disabling effects on movements and protest become visible and can be acted upon. Given the intensification of brutal forms of extractivism and the aggressive counterattack by right-wing groups in the continent and in so many parts of the world (the reassertion of patriarchal, racist, sexist, homophobic, and intensely capitalist agendas), a clarification of what is at stake socially, politically, and culturally in the world at present is essential for maintaining alive the dream of social justice and of a kinder, gentler world. As this book so incisively puts it, finding a new balance of forces that could make this goal again feasible might require novel and wiser strategies of "mixing and reshaping civic and uncivic spaces and practices" (from the introduction). This is a hopeful call, one for which we find a great deal of concrete ideas and proposals in the chapters that follow.

Preface and Acknowledgments

This collection is the product of sustained dialogues and transnational collaborations among scholars and intellectual-activists from the Global North and South who share an interest in developing critical theoretical approaches to the participatory institutions and mass-based movements that have proliferated in contemporary Latin America. Bringing together people working on each of these two forms of citizen engagement, our goal was to collectively interrogate received understandings of civic participation, movement activism, and political protest.

The dialogue that eventually resulted in this volume was officially launched at a two-panel plenary session, entitled "After Washington, Beyond Civil Society," during the International Congress of the Latin American Studies Association in 2007 in Montreal. Under the auspices of the Center for Latin American, Caribbean, and Latino Studies at the University of Massachusetts Amherst, we subsequently organized the Inter-University Consortium on Social Movements and 21st Century Cultural-Political Transformations, which was co-coordinated by the Programa Democracia y Transformación Global of the Universidad Nacional Mayor de San Marcos, in Lima, Peru. Our network set out to promote collaborative research into the expansion of civic participation through the Third Sector and governmental programs, on the one hand, and the increased visibility of less "civil-ized," more contentious collective action, on the other, which we dubbed the "Civil Society Agenda" and "Uncivic Activism," respectively.

Our Consortium—later "translated" by our Latin American partners as Coordinadora Interuniversitaria de Investigación sobre Movimientos Sociales y Cambios Político-Culturales—involved faculty and graduate students from research institutes at the University of Massachusetts (Amherst), Brown University, the University of North Carolina (Chapel Hill), Harvard University, the University of Puerto Rico (Río Piedras), Universidade Federal de Minas Gerais (UFMG-Brazil), Universidade Estadual de Campinas (Unicamp, Brazil), Universidad del Valle (Cali, Colombia), Universidad Nacional Mayor de San Marcos (Lima, Peru), and Universidad Nacional San Martín (Buenos Aires, Argentina), as well as over thirty members-at-large linked to civil society- and university-based research centers in the United States and in several other Latin American countries. Together, we worked to challenge the prevailing assumptions that guided the Civil Society Agenda by investigating the limits and possibilities of the wide variety of participatory schemas found throughout the Americas. At the same time, we explored what lessons seemingly "uncivic" activist practices might offer for promoting social justice and democratic innovation.

From the early to mid-2010s, the Consortium/Coordinadoras's work was furthered and expanded—both empirically and conceptually—by six transnational, interdisciplinary research teams that grew out of our initial debates: the Environment in 21st century Social Movements in Latin America and India; Social Movements and Political Institutions; "Sidestreaming" Feminisms; Political Research in Times of Crisis; Religion and Progressive Reform; and Civil Society Organizations' Pathways of Action. The teams met together and presented their research findings in a number of venues over the years, including panels at several Latin American Studies Association (LASA) Congresses, pre-LASA research meetings (including a workshop before LASA 2009 in Rio), and a variety of separate intragroup public events and working meetings held in various sites in different moments by each of the six collaborations. In addition, each of the groups presented their work at a second international public conference and activist-intellectual workshop of the whole Consortium/Coordinadora in Lima in May 2010.

We are pleased to say that a number of products beyond the present anthology came out of our collective theorizations, among them the sister volume to this book, emerging from the Lima meeting, *Movimientos sociales: Entre la crisis y otros saberes*, edited by Mar Quintanilla, Gina Vargas, and Raphael Hoetmer (Lima: Programa Democracia y Transformación Global; Universidad Nacional Mayor de San Marcos, 2012), and a special issue of *Latin American Research Review* on "Lived Religion and Lived Citizenship in Latin America's Zones of Crisis," edited by Jeffrey Rubin, David Smilde, and Benjamin Junge (vol. 49, 2014), produced by the research network that developed from our original Religion and Progressive Reform research collaboration, as well as a number of articles and essays.

The present volume, of course, very much grows out of the academic and political engagements, interests, and positionalities of its editors and contributors. Rather than attempt to represent all countries and subregions or the enormous array of themes and topics that could fit under the capacious rubric "Beyond Civil Society," from the outset we chose, instead, to solicit contributions from scholar-activists we knew to be engaged in critical thinking about vexing questions concerning activism, participation, and protest—the answers to which the conventional wisdom all too often treats as given. Because of the editors' and many of the contributors' specific scholarly and political commitments, there are some notable overrepresentations that readers will readily perceive with respect to places (Brazil) and issues (participatory budgeting, gender/feminisms).

Because all of us involved in this project are engaged scholars, sometimes deeply entangled in the processes that we analyze, this book, more than many, was shaped by the moment in which it was produced. It has always been our goal that our dialogue and debate across places help provide a framework to navigate puzzles and dilemmas confronting activists, a forward-facing analytic that is politically helpful. We believe the collection achieves that. But also we believe the book serves another purpose. Both the individual pieces and the anthology as a whole stand as a document about the concerns of the time, a moment between the euphoria of the World Social Forums and electoral victories of sympathetic governments of the mid-2000s and a later period, a few years later, when Occupy and Tahrir Square took world attention away from Latin America, right before strong political headwinds changed political contexts across the region. The essays here assembled offer an unflinching look at limits and possibilities that the Pink Tide afforded, and a window onto the kinds of choices activists were faced with. If anything, subsequent events only underscore the point made throughout and in various ways, that social gains enshrined in governmental programs have been fragile and that the choice of investing activist energies into civic spaces has real costs.

Significant energies have gone into the production of this volume, and we owe thanks to a number of folks. We are grateful to all of our contributors for their astute analyses and their gracious acquiescence to our multiple requests for revisions, updates, documents, and the like. We are also appreciative of other project participants, whose intellectual insights were of great value to our collective analytical process but whose essays we regrettably were unable to include in this volume: Luís Carlos Castillo, Liliana Cotto, Guillermo Delgado, Joseph Krupczynski, Edwin Quiles, Nora Strejilevich, Maristella Svampa, Luciana Tatagiba, Alejandro Velasco, and Brian Wampler. We are grateful to Wendy Wolford, Charlie Hale, and to colleagues at UMass Amherst, particularly Barbara Cruikshank, who provided incisive and useful feedback on earlier versions of the book's introduction and select chapters. We thank Arturo Escobar for his intellectual generosity and for the foreword. Our editors at Duke, Gisela Fosado and Valerie Millholland, also deserve our gratitude for their unwavering support for and encouragement of this project. Gloria Bernabe-Ramos, associate director of the Center for Latin American Studies at UMass Amherst (CLACLS) and various center staff over the years provided crucial logistical support for our work. Our graduate and undergraduate research assistants have been the backbone of this effort over time. We especially thank Martha Balaguera, Eric Sippert, Manuela Borzone, Julissa Frías Pérez, Amy Fleig, Casey Stephen, Niall Stephens, and Graciela Monteagudo.

Institutional support is essential to any project of this magnitude and duration. A grant from the Research Leadership in Action program of the Office of the Vice Provost for Research at UMass Amherst helped get our collaboration off the ground. The Ford Foundation provided generous support over a three-year period, underwriting the initial work of the collaborative research teams and partially subsidizing the Lima conference. The Leonard J. Horwitz Endowment afforded sustained support for research assistance, editorial sessions, and other essentials. Finally, CLACLS and the Programa Democracia y Transformación Global (PDTG) at the Universidad Nacional Mayor de San Marcos provided secure institutional homes for our collective effort.

Introduction

INTERROGATING THE CIVIL SOCIETY AGENDA, REASSESSING UNCIVIC POLITICAL ACTIVISM

SONIA E. ALVAREZ, GIANPAOLO BAIOCCHI, AGUSTÍN
LAÓ-MONTES, JEFFREY W. RUBIN, AND MILLIE THAYER

This anthology explores two faces of cultural-political struggles evident throughout Latin America today: the increased visibility of confrontational collective action, often represented as "uncivic," on the one hand, and the proliferation of civic participation through the so-called Third Sector and governmental programs, on the other. Both facets—which we refer to as "Uncivic Activism" and the "Civil Society Agenda," respectively—have profound policy and cultural implications for democratic politics, as well as social, racial, sexual, environmental, and gender justice.

From the Caracazo in Venezuela in 1989, to the massive Indian Uprising that took Ecuador by surprise in 1990, through the protests that brought the De la Rúa government in Argentina to its knees and the Bolivian Gas and Water Wars of the early 2000s that forced the resignation of two presidents, the panorama of social struggle changed dramatically at the turn of the twenty-first century. Involving an impressively broad array of nonstate actors that panorama spans novel forms of organizing among women, immigrants, indigenous and Afro-descendant peoples; innovative modalities of politics developed by the Movement of Landless Rural Workers (Movimento dos Trabalhadores Rurais Sem Terra, MST) and other mass protest movements in Brazil; Argentina's *piqueteros*; mobilizations against extractivism and dispossessive agribusiness in the Andean region and beyond; revitalized student protests in Chile, Mexico, and Puerto Rico; hip-hop and alternative media movements across the Americas; and multiscalar networks growing out of the World Social Forum.

The transformed twenty-first century political panorama also encompasses more than two decades of civil-society-based experiments in participation and the continentwide shift post-1998 toward Left and Center-Left governments, many of which advocated "participatory democracy."[1] This converged with what some have called the "neoliberalization of civil society"—the active promotion of civic participation by neoliberal governments and international financial institutions (IFIs) such as the World Bank and intergovernmental organizations (IGOs) such as the UN. This confluence constitutes what we refer to as the Civil Society Agenda: a hegemonic though contested set of normative and prescriptive assumptions about citizen participation that has deeply shaped the discourses and practices of both governments and social movements in the Americas.[2] That convergence may take an even more confounding form if the political U-turn toward a "post-neoliberal right," portended by elections in countries such as Argentina and Venezuela in the mid-2010s, were to spread to more countries in the region.

The Civil Society Agenda, we maintain, prescribes what actors operating in the space named civil society should do and how and to what end they should act and participate. The more unruly forms of activism listed above, by contrast, are often construed as uncivic when they are seen as transgressing the Civil Society Agenda's normatively charged participatory prescriptions.

This book thus promotes an unprecedented dialogue between two parallel streams of theorizing that heretofore have seldom intersected in scholarly research: more recent investigations of contentious twenty-first-century social movements and inquiries into civil society, civic participation, and democracy underway since the late 1980s–early 1990s. The collaborative research fomented by this project and now presented in this volume sets out to interrogate core assumptions prevailing on opposing sides of the contemporary debate about the relationship between social movements, civil society, and democracy. On the one side, hegemonic, liberal social science has often argued that unruly political action by "uncivic" society inherently threatens democracy, while "civic" civil society participation in governmental and intergovernmental institutions always enhances or expands it. Yet, as our case studies show, "participation" can subvert movements' agendas, discourage alternative forms of collective action, and channel movement energies into procedures and policies that do little to change the status quo or deepen democracy. As Cornwall's study of a Brazilian health council suggests (chapter 3), for instance, a vibrant site for citizen engagement can readily be transformed into an "empty space." In contrast, unruly political activism in countries such as Bolivia, Ecuador, and Peru played a key role in pushing neoliberal governments to loosen their grip on power, challenging dominant discourses, and creating new possibilities for the formerly excluded, as contributions by Lucero (chapter 15), Pallares (chapter 12), and Hoetmer (chapter 9) demonstrate.

Analysts less sanguine about liberal democracy often make the opposite assumption: that uncivic action always advances democracy, while "civilized" participation never does. Here, too, the record does not support their premises. In fact, forms and venues of activism do not map easily onto political outcomes. Certain locations and modalities of participation offered by dominant institutions such as the UN certainly pose greater risks of absorption into hegemonic agendas. However, as Laó-Montes suggests in his analysis of Afro-Latin American movements' participation in the Durban process (chapter 5), political openings may occur in these arenas as well. Feminists and other movements' activists sometimes have taken advantage of participatory policy spaces originally created as mere window dressing to advance autonomous agendas, as Alvarez notes in chapter 16. Then too, in-your-face street protest and direct action do not guarantee meaningful reform and democratic outcomes, and have been taken up, in recent times, for instance, by demonstrations calling for Dilma Rousseff's impeachment—if need be, by means of a "constitutional military coup"—and by other conservative forces displaced by the region's shift toward the Left demanding the reinstitution of systems of exclusion, as chapters by López Maya and Lander (chapter 13), Monteagudo (chapter 7), and Lucero (chapter 15) make clear.

In view of these complexities, one of the core goals of our project has been to question the reigning binary implicit in both the post-Washington Consensus's agenda for civil society and that of its critics. In doing so, we call on another set of categories, *lo permitido* and *lo no permitido*—the permissible, authorized, tolerated forms of activism and participation and their "other," the prohibited, unauthorized, intolerable (Hale 2002, 2006; Hale and Millamán 2006). Activism occurs in a wide range of modalities and venues, from roadblocks to World Bank advisory groups, any of which may be perceived as within or beyond the bounds of the permissible. The categories *permitido* and *no permitido*, in our usage, straddle the conventional civic-uncivic divide, *calling attention to actions and demands rather than actors and venues* that are deemed acceptable or unacceptable within the prevailing Civil Society Agenda—for example, making class-based claims in Participatory Budgeting is permissible, whereas making race- or gender-based demands is not, as Ben Junge shows in his chapter (chapter 4).

The chapters that follow demonstrate that it is not the space, place, or form in which citizen action unfolds that determines whether a given practice or discourse is permitido or no permitido, authorized or unauthorized. Rather than venues and political forms, the more important distinctions lie in the political effects of activism and its relationship to dominant discursive formations and constellations of power. Any given set of political practices may move in the direction of obscuring or unveiling inequality, reinscribing or transgressing relations of power and exclusion, reifying hierarchies or dismantling them. Clearly these are poles along a continuum with many shades of gray; movement effects may be contradictory, shifting, and difficult to discern. But, we argue, they are not harnessed to particular strategies or locations. Transgression can and does happen within institutions, and mass protest doesn't always have counterhegemonic effects or consequences. We seek to move beyond this binary to propose a new conceptual language and interpretative framework for thinking about social activism.

Second, our collective findings suggest that many, if not most, movements in Latin America today deploy multiple strategies and occupy distinctive locations at different moments. In contrast to the Left's earlier rejection of "bourgeois democracy," on the one hand, and the later euphoria over participatory budgeting and its offspring, on the other, we find that few twenty-first-century movements adhere to such certainties and most make use of a mix of strategies. The civic and its "other" are two facets of many of today's social movements, two faces of social change, which, we argue, often work effectively in concert (or in productive tension), as chapters by Rubin (chapter 11), Hoetmer (chapter 9), Pallares (chapter 12), Thayer (chapter 8), and Laó-Montes (chapter 5) make particularly clear.

Although our contributors illustrate that most social movements today regularly and sometimes simultaneously deploy both civic and uncivic practices and that activism and participation most often occupy a "gray zone" in between, many of the case studies collected here attest to the fact that, notwithstanding the conceptual utility of blurred boundaries, "Manichean divisions, when performed and objectified," remain "important social facts" with sometimes grave political consequences, as José Antonio Lucero insists in his contribution to this anthology (chapter 15; on gray zones, see Auyero 2007; Levi 1989). The often violent struggle in Bolivia between the "socials"— the largely indigenous and mestizo popular movements supportive of Evo Morales's government—and the "civics"—the more European-descendant, wealthier, and regionally centered secessionist opposition—Lucero maintains, very much takes place on the "well-trodden discursive borderlands of civilization and barbarism, with each side finding the other on the wrong side of the divide." Indeed, the middle- and upper-class opposition to several of today's leftist governments has politically appropriated the name "civil society" for itself, disdainfully relegating pro-government popular organizations to the status of barbaric, uncivilized "hordes," "rabble," and pejoratively racialized "mixed breeds" and "Indians" (see, especially, Fernandes 2010; García-Gaudillo 2003, 2007; Gottberg 2011; see also López Maya and Lander, chapter 13; Hoetmer, chapter 9; and Pallares, chapter 12, in this volume). In short, though movement practices and performances clearly oscillate within a civic-uncivic gray zone, we found it critical to retain the distinction—and several contributors use it in various formulations in their essays. Di Marco, chapter 6, refers to "uncivic, untamed identities" in the sense that they resist the policing of bodies and emotions; Monteagudo, chapter 7, analyzes "untamed" movements to reflect important social phenomena and analytically de- and reconstruct them.

Producing the Civil Society Agenda in Latin America

To better understand the representation of social struggles as permitido or no permitido, we need to retrace the genealogy of civil society in the Latin American region. To do so means, among other things, paying close attention to the academic literature, because more than many other domains, civil society is a social construct of scholars. Indeed, as Nira Wickramasinghe has warned, "So ubiquitous is the phrase 'civil society,' . . . that it is easy to believe that it has always been an existing entity, in the same way as the state or the market, in an ephemeral but nevertheless secure manner. This is because so many voices speak about it, name it, give it a shape and an aura of certainty, almost like Hannah Arendt's stray dog, whose chances of remaining alive increase once named" (2005, 459).

Despite the effusive way in which the concept has been deployed in academic, policy, and activist circles over the last three decades, the idea emerged relatively late in Latin America and was historically associated with Liberal elites. The independence movements of the 1800s in the region had strong anti-Liberal elements, and political Liberalism had a precarious existence in the political culture of the time. In the foundational text, *Facundo: Civilización y Barbarie* (1845), Domingo Sarmiento, the celebrated early Liberal Argentine thinker and statesman, famously contrasted cosmopolitan and Liberal Buenos Aires with conservative and backward Córdoba, and argued that the liberal project could advance only with the eradication of gauchos, Indians, and blacks.

For much of the twentieth century, organized expressions of collectivity came to be subsumed under a strong state that protected national interests. The rise of organized working classes and middle sectors in the early decades of the last century was often absorbed by national regimes through the granting of limited rights to narrowly demarcated groups. Thus, trade unions under Getúlio Vargas in Brazil, Juan Perón in Argentina, or the Partido Revolucionario Institucional (PRI) in Mexico became organized expressions of collective, "popular" interests that were part of corporatist strategies of ruling elites. While they contained an element of empowerment, these were officially sanctioned representations of class interests in which the "people" and the "popular" were consonant with state-led national projects. In the domain of activism, there was no mention of civil society as either a realm of sociability or a terrain of contestation at this point despite moments of opposition to national authoritarian projects.

Civil society did, however, appear prominently in Latin American oppositional discourse in the 1970s and 1980s as a central, if not *the* central, part of the political imaginary of social movements, as "a theoretical tool for political action" (Pearce 1997, 258; see also Weffort 1989, for an example of a foundational text in that tradition). The "double defeat" of both electoral and insurgent socialist movements had helped spur a search for alternative theoretical conceptualizations of new political subjects who emerged in opposition to military regimes (Castañeda 1993). As was also the case in much of Eastern Europe at the time, civil society appeared, from the Left, as a way to understand, and articulate, the experiences and projects of the "new social movements" and as a new path toward social transformation (Escobar and Alvarez 1992).

At this time, civil society was often used interchangeably with "the people," or the popular subject, invoked as a counterhegemonic force against the military state. In Brazil, for instance, for many movements, the state figured *centrally* both as a target and as a political horizon (see Avritzer, chapter 2 in this volume). Many movements that have sometimes been described as antistate were actually very much involved in the project of imagining *another* state at the same time as imagining *another* society and set of relationships (Evers 1983; Slater and Amerika Centrum voor Studie en Documentatie van Latijns 1985).

By the mid- to late 1980s and early 1990s, in contrast, Gramscian conceptions of civil society—as a contested terrain and not a purely virtuous one—had diffused throughout the region. Exemplified by Brazil's Workers' Party, much of Latin America's New Left turned away from Leninist practices and developed new relationships with the progressive church, emerging social movements, and middle-class "fellow travelers" linked to NGOs. By the early 1990s, the Left had taken a "local" and a "social" turn, and civil society was a prominent part of its discourse. It was imagined that a "new left, emanating from the plural, proliferating movements, could succeed where others had failed" (Castañeda 1993, 200). The Zapatistas couched their insurgent demands in terms of a complex Mexican civil society, and in Guatemala the Civil Society Assembly sought to mediate the end of the armed conflict, while in Mexico and Brazil heterogeneous civil societies spearheaded processes of democratization. Whereas the undifferentiated, militarized masses had been summoned to the barricades in the past, the Left now advocated the benefits of heterogeneous popular participation, framed in the language of a civil society that articulated, through struggle and internal negotiation, a counterhegemonic project.

The North Americanization of a Concept

In the 1990s and early 2000s, a different conception of civil society appeared, promoted by neoliberal Latin American elites, often at the urging of donors, IFIs and IGOs. International organizations were particularly prominent in fostering a "North American" conception of civil society instead of a Gramscian one. In this new lexicon of development and democracy, civil society now referred to "the art of association" (Fukuyama 2000), the place where an "I becomes a We" (Putnam 1995), an autonomous realm of citizen engagement where trust and solidarity emerge, outside of, but not necessarily in opposition to, the state. The language continued the same, but the attributions to the object "civil society" shifted. If, for Latin American movement activists, civil society had been a means to social transformation, now civil society *became* the social transformation. If before, civil society was born of social conflict to carry out contestation, now civil society was the *solution* to social conflict. And finally, if civil society was formerly understood as an explicitly political terrain, it now became the grounds for antipolitics.

While the neoliberal version of civil society has its roots in Alexis de Tocqueville, Domingo Faustino Sarmiento, and liberalism more generally, its immediate predecessor was mid-twentieth-century U.S. social science, and in particular Modernization Theory. As is well known, civil-izing social mobilization in backward societies was among the concerns that motivated scholars such as Talcott Parsons, Gabriel Almond, and Sidney Verba, and many others who were preoccupied with the cultural conditions that gave rise to democracy (such as Banfield 1958; Inkeles 1969). While pathological cultures and modes of association gave rise to uncivic backwardness, proper democratic association gave rise to trust, economic growth, and viable institutions. For instance, Edward Banfield (1958) purported to have found in the culture of southern Italy the "moral bases" of that "backward society" in its insistence on honor, "the favor," and asymmetrical relationships. He argued that certain cultures, where a peasant can "satisfy his aspirations by reaching out his hand to the nearest coconut," were incompatible with the requisites of democracy (1958, 8). Save for the dated language, the argument that "honor" favors asymmetry and corruption while more proper values promote democracy and development is essentially the same vision of civil society advocated by development agencies in the 1990s and 2000s, who, like Sarmiento, examined subaltern cultures to domesticate and civilize (when not annihilate) them.

The newfound interest in civil society can be traced back to a few prominent donor agencies and international institutions who understood it as a panacea for the problems of development. The Inter-American Development Bank held a meeting of governors in 1994 that concluded with a policy proposal, "Strengthening Civil Society," in which civil society building was promoted as a "basis of sustainable development and school for training responsible citizens committed to economic growth and the maintaining of democracy" (IDB 1994, cited in Pearce 1997, 267). The United States Agency for International Development (USAID) set up a Center for Democracy and Governance in 1994, and the New Partnership Initiative in 1995, which directly funded civil society organizations. The World Bank, which in 1989 had established an NGO unit, in 1995 renamed its "NGO liaison officers" as "civil society specialists" and began to invest more in projects carried out by local civil society organizations (Howell and Pearce 2001). By 1998, roughly *half* of all bank projects included a component that funded civil society organizations

(Bain 1999). Similarly, other bilateral and multilateral donors such as the Department for International Development (DFID) (UK), the Canadian International Development Agency (CIDA), the United Nations Development Programme (UNDP), and major foundations such as Ford, Kettering, Rockefeller, and MacArthur had all adopted the language of civil society by the mid-1990s.

Civil society thereby became a central component of the new development lexicon. This change resulted in part from the increased influence of reformers and progressives within global institutions (Bebbington et al. 2006; Cornwall 2004; see also Thayer, chapter 8, and Laó-Montes, chapter 5, this volume). But change was also propelled by the failure of Structural Adjustment Programs to provide benefits for the majority of populations or even actually promote development, and by the recognition that "state-dominated development has failed, but so will stateless development" (World Bank 2006, 25). There was then a shift toward *good governance*, or the idea that "the state itself does not inhibit development, but its manner of governance can" (Grindle 2004, 525). The development problematic at this time thus moved toward a focus on the *functioning* of institutions, and in particular whether they worked with "transparency," "accountability," and "efficiency." Civil society, now the privileged agent of development, became a sort of magic bullet to neutralize corruption and hierarchy, institutionalize human rights, and solve the problems of poverty and inequality, among many other laudable things (Hulme and Edwards 1997).

A wave of critical scholarship—looking largely at other world regions—has since challenged these assumptions, calling into question the emancipatory potential of civil society, its participatory prescriptions, and democratic possibilities. Scholars of South Asia and Africa in particular argue that civil society is part of a new rationality of government that calls forth an entrepreneurial citizen, self-regulation, responsibility for one's own problems, and nonconflictive partnerships with the state (see Chandhoke 2003; Chatterjee 2006; Cleaver 2001; Cooke and Kothari 2001; Comaroff and Comaroff 1999; Cornwall 2003, 2004; Encarnación 2003; Ferguson and Gupta 2002; Harriss 2002, 2005; Harris, Stokke, and Tornquist 2005; Leal 2007; Mohan 2001; White 1996; Williams 2004). As John Harriss has put it, "the [civil society] discourse has been quite deliberately apolitical, in a way that is ultimately supportive of neoliberal orthodoxy" (2002, 121). As the state pulled out of the realm of social policy, these "flexible" civil citizens were charged with shouldering the burden.

While neoliberal governments and international agencies have become some of the most important players in promoting the language of civil society and civic participation in Latin America, they have often done so through the intermediation of NGOs and civil society organizations with roots in social movements. The North Americanized and internationalized version of civil society shaped the programmatic plans of many NGOs and social movements throughout the region. Although many organizations sought to maintain their autonomy and political integrity, pragmatic searches for funding sometimes trumped their ideological commitments. And of course, local governments of the Left, notably Porto Alegre in the heyday of Participatory Budgeting in the early 2000s, promoted their participatory toolkits in international competitions, directly engaging international agencies, such as the Inter-American Development Bank (IADB) and the World Bank, with their own initiatives.

Evelina Dagnino, Alberto Olvera, and Aldo Panfichi designated this convergence as a "perverse confluence," "the encounter between, on the one hand, the democratizing projects that were constituted during the period of resistance to authoritarian regimes and continued in pursuit of a more profound democracy, and on the other, the neoliberal projects that installed themselves, with different rhythms and chronologies, as of the end of the 1980s. In effect, not only do both projects require an active and purposeful civil society, but they are based on the same references: the construction of citizenship, participation, and the very idea of civil society" (2006a, 16).

The Gramscian civil society vision propelled by leftist political parties and radical movements, though tempered by almost two decades of electoral successes in local governments, again achieved prominence and institutional weight in the 2000s and early 2010s in many national governments of the "Pink Tide" (for Brazil, see contributions by Avritzer, chapter 2; Baiocchi and Teixeira, chapter 14). So the Civil Society Agenda in Latin America came to be promoted by Left-of-Center local and national governments as well as by international agencies and Right and Center-Right regimes in the region—including postneoliberal ones, as we shall suggest in this chapter below—a complex reality that has made facile dismissals of all civic participation-as-neoliberal governmentality difficult to sustain. Critical discussion on civil society in Latin America must thus necessarily encompass USAID prescriptions as well as the Consejos Comunales in Venezuela's Bolivarian Revolution (see, especially, contributions by Baiocchi, chapter 1; Cornwall, chapter 3; and López Maya and Lander, chapter 13).

The inherent ambiguity of civil society is also evident in the articulation of rights claims. The social movements that mobilized Latin Americans in the 1980s, for instance, crystallized explicitly around claims for full citizenship.

In the context of the end of the Cold War and national transitions to civilian rule, they not only developed a vibrant and broad-based discourse of social justice, but frequently defended liberal rights-based claims as well. In the case of Brazil, Evelina Dagnino (1998, 50) refers to this as the new citizenship; its premise was "the right to have rights," and it lauded the invention of "new rights that emerge from specific struggles and concrete practices." Concurrently, donor agencies and Latin American NGOs moved away from need-based and service-driven approaches to emphasize "rights issues" and "rights-based development" (Molyneux and Lazar 2003, 1–6). Movements throughout the region, including emerging women's and indigenous counterpublics (Schild 1998; Yashar 2005), were "influenced by new global as well as local conceptions of individual and collective rights" (Eckstein and Merino 2001, 2).

Of particular concern to us are the ways these rights claims straddled the divide between the Civil Society Agenda and more expansive or transformative notions of rights. The literature often characterizes rights claims as *propositional* (as opposed to *oppositional*) to liberal-democratic versions of citizenship. However, while claiming rights from and dialogue with the state, activists often challenged the limits of representative democracy by calling for new participatory processes and expanded versions of conventional rights. In the case of Brazil, participatory reforms embedded in the Constitution and in subsequent progressive legislation were an expression of the demand for the deepening and expansion of the citizenship rights that emerged from urban movements of the 1980s and 1990s (Holston 2009).

And yet, citizenship and rights claims are profoundly ambiguous. Sometimes they imply minimalist liberal principles: individual claims divorced from collective or redistributive notions and separate from social justice, quite compatible with neoliberal discourses (Craske and Molyneux 2001).[3] Furthermore, the increase in political rights in the region was accompanied by a decline in social rights (Oxhorn 2003). Thus, like civil society, rights claims in and of themselves are neither transformative nor neoliberal.

Questioning the Civil Society Agenda

As a consequence of this equivocality, produced largely by the perverse confluence of neoliberal prescriptions and progressive aspirations for civic participation, there is today a renewed, vibrant, plurivocal, and messy debate about the Civil Society Agenda in Latin America. There are at least four competing interpretations of civil society. First the "infinite justice" position sees *in civil society itself* the utopian possibility of civil repair, as "conditions for emancipation are sometimes fostered within the structure of domination itself" (Alexander 2006, 416). The second position is that civil society has been co-opted. That is, civil society, as a realm of emancipatory possibilities was neoliberalized, depoliticized, bureaucratized, and so on (Petras 1997; Petras and Veltmeyer 2003, 2011). Yet this position, like the first, obscures the contestation inherent in civil society. A third position—somewhat less common in the context of Latin America—is that civil society itself is not what it seems or claims to be, a view exemplified by Partha Chatterjee (2006) and Inderpal Grewal (2005). In this account, civil society is a privileged realm of bourgeois citizenship, impervious to the claims of the popular classes or "the governed." There is a fourth perspective, one that many of us in this volume develop in different ways, that emphasizes the ambiguities of civil society: that civil society represents and misrepresents; civil society politicizes questions and depoliticizes them; that power runs through, and not against, civil society organizations. Democracy's ambiguity—in which it could be said that civil society is "a two-faced being, the bearer of both subjection to sovereign power and of liberties" (Agamben 1998, 125)—is played out in this arena.

Recognizing civil society's paradoxes is not the property of any particular theoretical tradition. Several recent studies highlight the contradictions and ambiguities that typify civil society dynamics in Latin America (see, especially, Rossi and von Bülow 2015). Some anthologies explore whether the various forms of participation we identify with the Civil Society Agenda challenge or complement institutions of representation based on electoral participation (Cameron, Hershberg, and Sharpe 2014; Selee and Peruzzotti 2009). Other even more skeptical voices focus instead on what Ariel Armony calls its "dark side," its nondemocratic face (2004). For Mark Goodale and Nancy Postero (2013), civil society is central to "subject making" in both neoliberal and post-neoliberal contexts, with radically differing effects. Studies of civil society in governments of the Pink Tide document the often strained collaborations and stress the multiple conflicts that surface between states and movements in that terrain. Especially in cases of radical "refoundation," "the civic" often has been colonized by mestizo and Euro-descendant, middle- and upper-class opposition forces (see, for example, Cannon and Kirby 2012; Prevost, Campos, and Vanden 2012).

For us, engaging civil society's ambiguities can best be achieved by combining Gramsci's original formulation of civil society as a terrain of both legitimation and contestation with the Foucauldian insight that any collective organization—even the most revolutionary we can imagine—is born of the operations of power (see also Alvarez, chapter 16 in this volume). As Michael

Hardt has written, this means facing the fact that "the institutions or enclosures of civil society . . . constitute the paradigmatic terrain for the disciplinary deployments of power in modern society" (1995, 31). Civil society disciplines subjects, regulates practices, and brings forth political rationalities, moving us beyond the notion that movements resist governmentality while states promote it.

Decolonizing the Civil Society Agenda

The language of decolonization is today deployed by many indigenous, Afro-descendant, and other activists in an effort to resist the disciplinary force of the Civil Society Agenda and demand profound changes in the state, the capitalist economy, and culture (see, especially, Daza, Hoetmer, and Vargas 2012). Decolonization is also invoked by governments, such as that of Evo Morales in Bolivia, which declares itself to be decolonizing and "depatriarchalizing" state, economy, and education as a government project (Chávez et al. 2011; Dangl 2010; Madrid 2008; Miñoso, Gómez Correal, and Ochoa Muñoz 2014; Paredes 2008; Postero 2010). Part of the language of scholarship as well as activism, decolonization today means more than overthrowing imperial rule and building independent postcolonial states. Scholars using this approach, such as Aníbal Quijano (2000a, 2000b), argue that postindependence Latin American nation-states reproduced and reconfigured hierarchies of class, race, ethnicity, and gender created in the colonial context. They maintain that global capitalist modernity itself rests on a modern/colonial matrix of power. The notion of the decolonial has come to be used to describe processes of self-affirmation of peoples whose cultures and identities have been marginalized, folklorized, and/or violently challenged by Western and creole elite hegemonic cultures. It is in this sense that theorists such as Orlando Fals Borda and Silvia Rivera Cusicanqui have long advocated the "decolonization of knowledge" and others, following Fanon, insist on the need to decolonize mind, self, and social relations (for a comprehensive overview of these debates, see, especially, Moraña, Dussel, and Jáuregui 2008).

The persistent use of the language of decolonization and liberation, instead of the language of civil society, by many Afro-descendant, indigenous, and other contemporary movements gives less centrality to "civil society" as a location and framework for politics. Afro-Brazilian feminists, for instance, mobilized a national effort in 2014–15 to stage the March of Black Women against Racism and Violence and for Living Well (*Marcha das Mulheres Negras 2015 contra o Racismo e a Violência e pelo Bem Viver*), clearly drawing inspiration from *Sumak Kawsay*, or "Buen Vivir," a guiding principle of decolonial struggles among indigenous movements and Bolivarian states such as Ecuador and Bolivia. At the same time, some Afro-descendant and indigenous leaders, organizations, and communities are now important components of the Civil Society Agenda, as clearly expressed in the notions of *indio permitido* and *negro escogido*.[4] Indeed, what has been called neoliberal multiculturalism is largely a product of and response to claims of rights, resources, and representation by Afro-descendants and indigenous movements (Hale and Millamán 2006; Hooker 2009; Lucero 2008; Mullings 2009; Richards 2004).

We contend that the relationships between subaltern interculturality and neoliberal multiculturalism are open, diverse, and indeterminate, depending on the political rationalities and historical projects at stake, as chapters by Hoetmer (chapter 9), Lucero (chapter 15), and Laó-Montes (chapter 5) make clear. The struggles, mobilizations, collective actions, and organizations of Afro-descendants and indigenous peoples that emerged in the era of neoliberal capitalist globalization can be productively analyzed through the lens of the coloniality of power by focusing on the coloniality of modern citizenship (i.e., de facto exclusion and second-class citizenship of ethnic-racial others), on the one hand, and on the patterning of subaltern spaces of social and cultural life as counterpublics for collective action and politics, on the other. Furthermore, decolonizing civil society involves recognizing forms of associational life beyond the conventional parameters of liberal democracy. Bolivian sociologist Luis Tapia (2006) argues, for instance, that practices and conceptions of self-government and egalitarian membership in the political community that characterize peasant-indigenous spaces in Bolivia constitute forms of democracy distinct from those developed in the Western liberal and neoliberal traditions.

However, while spaces of communitarian self-government may originate largely outside of the arena of the Civil Society Agenda, they often function simultaneously inside and outside of it; actors in these spaces engage selectively in a diversity of relationships with national and transnational institutions. As a result, movement efforts to decolonize the Civil Society Agenda deploy the same contradictory and heterogeneous set of strategies documented throughout this volume. For example, the Process of Black Communities (Proceso de Comunidades Negras, PCN) in the community councils of the Pacific region of Colombia articulates a project of decolonization as an alternative way of life, involving a grassroots sustainable practice of economic development grounded in community self-government, the cultivation of ancestral ways of life, and an active defense of Black cultural and ethnic-racial identity (Escobar 2008). This does not mean, however, that the PCN and the communities with which it works do not sometimes engage the Civil Society Agenda by participating in IGO-sponsored arenas, for instance, while remaining critical of their political rationality, economic practices, and cultural politics (see chapter 10, by Asher).

Mobs, Masses, and Movements:
The Civil Society Agenda's Constitutive Others?

If in some countries, such as Chile and Brazil, the late 1980s through mid-1990s are often portrayed as a time of NGO-ization and relative movement demobilization consequent to neoliberalism, in much of the rest of the region the past two-plus decades are often heralded (or decried) as a new mobilizational moment. Epitomized by mass protests against neoliberalism, confrontational direct-action tactics, and "mob actions" or (more approvingly) *pueblazos*, or uprisings against unpopular policies and politicians, contemporary activism often both defies conventional liberal democratic politics and challenges the parameters of lo permitido. If many of these mobilizations tend to lean toward the political Left, they also resist ready classification along a standard Left-Right spectrum, as many, if not most, bring ethnicity, race, gender, sexuality, generation, and other vectors of power and resistance onto center stage in their varied theaters of struggle.

Most overviews of early twenty-first-century movements in the region depict heterogeneous streams, when not torrents, of internally complex collective subjects (see Dangl 2010; Daza, Hoetmer, and Vargas 2012; Goodale and Postero 2013; Prevost, Campos, and Vanden 2012; Ross and Rein 2014; Silva 2009; Stahler-Sholk, Vanden, and Kuecker 2008a; Stahler-Sholk, Vanden, and Becker 2014; Svampa 2008; and Zibechi 2010, 2012), which we suggest were *produced* through two distinct sets of processes. First, the inequalities exacerbated by neoliberalism, and the targeted social programs it deployed to ameliorate the most nefarious effects of growing disparities, triggered unprecedented forms of mobilization among the unemployed (such as Argentina's *piqueteros*), pension-deprived retirees, the homeless, students, informal sector workers, and "poor women." Second, responding to the current *modelo extractivo-exportador* (extractive-export model), neoliberal multiculturalism's efforts to assuage or co-opt "the diverse," together with state doctrines of "citizen security," indigenous peoples, Afro-descendants, rural workers, the landless, or, more generally, the displaced and dispossessed also engaged in mass protest and other innovative modalities of unruly activism. The fruits of our collective research, featured in the ensuing chapters, offer vivid portrayals of a wide range of contestatory practices found throughout much of Latin America since the turn of the century, as well as, in some cases, documenting those same activists' simultaneous engagement with the Civil Society Agenda.[5]

As chapters by Monteagudo (chapter 7), Di Marco (chapter 6), Pallares (chapter 12), and Hoetmer (chapter 9), among others, suggest, the current surge in more unruly mobilization is characterized by a series of seemingly new features. The defense of territory, direct action, horizontalism, and forms of direct democracy such as the *asamblea* are said to typify many more recent movements (Svampa 2008, 78–79; also see, especially, Daza, Hoetmer, and Vargas 2012; Sitrin 2006, 2013, Sitrin and Azzellini 2014; Zibechi 2012). Organized labor and the (small landholding) peasantry have played a less prominent role than in decades past, and pride of place in many mobilizations has instead gone to what we could call the "*sin*-blank," without work, without rights, without culture, without roof, or without land; and perhaps also to the "trans-something," the transnational, the transgendered, the translocal, the transcultural. These denominations reflect a politics that responds to two significant political phenomena: accumulation by dispossession (Harvey 2005) and the challenge to rigid boundaries and essentialized identities, whether national, regional, or embodied.

In this scenario, marked by deprivations and border crossings, cultural interventions, the ludic, and literal and figurative performances have proliferated, heirs to the theatrical displays deployed by more militant sectors of gay and lesbian movements. A way of doing politics also practiced by early radical feminisms North and South, and subsequently taken up by the antiglobalization and autonomist-anarchist movements of the 1990s and 2000s, these ex-centric forms of politics typify today's public protests, flash actions (like Argentina's *escraches* or Chile's student movement kiss-ins and advocacy "marathons"), land occupations, road blockades, and bridge obstructions. Nearly all contemporary movements pursue translocal linkages and even the most geographically remote connect through multiple media, virtual, and multiscalar venues with their counterparts nationally, regionally, and globally, as several chapters also show (notably Thayer, chapter 8, and Laó-Montes, chapter 5). Most in the recent mobilizational surge also eschew hierarchy and preach horizontalism, while often espousing discourses of intersectionality, highlighting the interconnectedness of class, race, gender, sexuality, generation, and so on—even if those discourses seldom translate neatly into movements' quotidian practices (see, especially, Monteagudo, chapter 7).

The current wave of mobilization is often presumed to be the Civil Society Agenda's "other," the antithesis of the civic, professionalized NGOs and neighborhood associations that "opted into" the various official participatory spaces created in the late 1980s and 1990s. But as many of our chapters show, the boundaries between civil society and its presumptive other are less than precise; even the most defiant and confrontational among contemporary movements typically straddle the civic/uncivic divide, engaging in direct action in the streets and contestational forms of activism in a variety of arenas, including in civic spaces in civil society, political society, and the state, and beyond, in culture, the arts, the media, and the universities. Even the most NGO-ized actors and sectors of the 1990s sometimes openly and deliberately defied or even defiled the civic, as when seemingly civil-ized "blazer-feminists" from Latin America staged a highly disruptive and theatrical "escalator protest" against neoliberalism and inequality at the UN "civic celebration" of the Fourth World Congress on Women in Beijing.

Our contributors propose several broad-gauged concepts intended to capture the multiple ways in which the civic/uncivic coexist, almost always in conflict-inducing but sometimes productive tension, in much contemporary activism in Latin America. Thayer (chapter 8) extends the work of feminist theorists Rita Felski (1989) and Nancy Fraser (1997), conceptualizing counterpublics as internally heterogeneous oppositional spaces, constituted by relations among diverse collections of actors who engage with one another around the politics of issues such as race, class, gender, and sexuality.[6] In her chapter, participants in the feminist counterpublic—from rural Brazilian women, to urban NGO activists, to European donor agency staff members—not only cross national borders, but also transgress the indistinct boundaries between state and civil society, sanctioned contention, and impermissible political practices. What Laó-Montes (chapter 5) dubs the "field of Afro-Latin American politics" similarly emerged "with a variety of actors (state and societal), institutions, organizations, leaders, discourses and political cultures, and practices." He contends that in the process of constructing that field, "the borders between actors located in states, transnational institutions and movement organizations," between those inside and outside the Civil Society Agenda, became blurred (on "institutional activism," see Abers and Tatagiba 2015). In an effort to characterize the array of unruly activisms unleashed by the Argentine crisis of 2001, Monteagudo (chapter 7) develops the notion of a "field of politics by other means." Also focusing on twenty-first-century Argentina, Di Marco (chapter 6) analyzes the emergence of a Laclauian *pueblo feminista*, or "feminist people." She examines the "chains of equivalence" that transformed issues such as abortion rights and gay marriage into "empty signifiers," which articulated diverse forces such as unions and leftist parties into civic/uncivic political coalitions that included but moved beyond both "historic" and popular feminisms. And several contributors show that activist arenas that stretch beyond movements, conventionally understood, and across received notions of civic and uncivic, frequently extend beyond national borders as well.

Translocal and Transnational Movement Practices

Many if not most of activist spaces analyzed in this volume have transnational dimensions, at once objects of powerful "global" forces and participants in cross-border political relationships. We speak of these arenas as transnational to acknowledge the ongoing power of nation-states to construct distinctive political cultures and institutions, even as their borders are increasingly porous to incursions from elsewhere. The global, from our perspective, is not the disembodied fantasy of multilateral or corporate self-promotion, but is rather a construct of relations between multiple social actors, from the World Bank to the *piqueteros*, all with particular local histories, interests, and understandings of the world (Freeman 2001; Massey 1994; Thayer 2001, 2010; Tsing 2005). This relational approach challenges what Gibson-Graham (2006a) calls the "rape script" of inexorable domination by multinational capital, putting in its place a far less predictable and more contested view of how contemporary global processes play out. It offers space for the voices and bodies of the excluded in the construction of transnational, as well as local, politics.

Latin American activists have a long history of trespassing the boundaries between nation-states. World systems theorists argue that the Haitian revolution of 1791 was at the epicenter of the first wave of antisystemic movements and that it generated connections with other such movements within and beyond Latin America (Martin 2008). In the last decades of the nineteenth century, anarchist and socialist ideas brought by European immigrants spread outward from focal points like Argentina, Brazil, Chile, Uruguay, Mexico, and Cuba to labor movements in neighboring Latin American countries. Interregional connections were reflected in early efforts to organize continental workers' congresses and, post–World War I, regional labor confederations reflecting distinctive political orientations (Alexander 1965; Sacchi 1972; Spalding 1977). Also beginning at the turn of the twentieth century, women's movements reached across borders to form alliances, lobbying continental scientific meetings and organizing gatherings, such as the International Feminine Congress, held in Buenos Aires in 1910, and continuing through debates in organizations such as the Pan American Women's Union and at venues including the First Inter-American Women's Congress in Guatemala City in 1947 (Ehrick 1999; Miller 1990, 1991).

Transnational collaborations accelerated between the 1970s and 1990s, stimulated by UN conferences on women, population, human rights, and the environment, and facilitated by new developments in communications technology and other factors (Alvarez 1998; Antrobus 2004; Desai 2002; Friedman, Hochstetler, and Clark 2005; Vargas Valente 1996, 2003). Common experiences with authoritarian regimes in this era also helped foster connections among Latin American activists, many of whom met in exile in cities from Milan to Managua. These transnationalized sites served as fertile grounds for political imagination at a time when dictatorships were faltering and civilian rule was on the horizon. In these and other spaces, social movements and their scholarly supporters elaborated discourses about civil society as the counterweight to an oppressive state. The euphoric civil society discourse of the time reverberated between Eastern Europe and Latin America and traveled rapidly among activists in different parts of each region.

In the late twentieth century, activists faced increasingly transnationalized targets and venues. As multinational capital and neoliberal market discourses spread, as racist and ethnocentric forces made common cause, and as rightwing religious and secular movements made inroads into the United Nations and growing numbers of states in the region, the incentives for cross-border collaboration grew. The incursions of international mining conglomerates described by Hoetmer (chapter 9) and the aggressive International Monetary Fund (IMF) prescriptions for Argentina depicted by Di Marco (chapter 6) and Monteagudo (chapter 7) illustrate the dimension of the transnational challenges facing contemporary movements.

The ambitions of the Civil Society Agenda itself were, from its inception, transnational in scale, as were the aspirations of the institutions that oversaw its production and dissemination and monitored its implementation. It was a "civil-izing" mission, powerfully sponsored by the IFIs and the bilateral aid programs whose conditionalities produced streamlined states with a neoliberal and nominally multicultural, gender-friendly, race-sensitive, environmental, and democratic face (Bedford 2009; Cornwall, Harrison, and Whitehead 2007a; Goldman 2005; Lucero 2008). Governments and IFIs were joined by the private nongovernmental aid agencies who helped underwrite an expanding Third Sector and proliferating civic participation programs.

They also, on occasion, funded organizations that sought to advocate for or "empower" marginalized constituencies to act against the injustices intensified by shifting forms of neoliberal capitalism (Biekart 1999; Hulme and Edwards 1997). Flows of funding sometimes amplified those oppositional voices, facilitating access to new political spaces and supporting increasingly sophisticated strategies often aimed at civic engagement with dominant institutions. Discourses about racial, ethnic, gender, and other forms of injustice insinuated themselves into the state and international institutions, and transnational networks and alliances proliferated.

But there was a price to pay for this success. The power relations implicit—or explicit—in donor-grantee relationships promoted the reshaping of movement fields in Latin America (Alvarez 1999; Ewig 1999, Lebon 1996, 1998; Lind 2010; Murdock 2008; Thayer 2001, 2010). Aid agency staff insisted that their activist counterparts in the global South take on professionalized structures with hierarchies of authority as a means of guaranteeing "transparency" and "accountability" to donors who, in turn, were facing similar pressures from their own civil societies in the North (see chapter 8, by Thayer). A wave of NGO-ization ensued, transforming significant parts of the movement landscape (Alvarez 1999). Institutionalized movements found themselves navigating in a world of grant guidelines, evaluation criteria, and reporting requirements that threatened to circumscribe possibilities for radical critique and cross-class alliances, even as they fostered new opportunities for influencing the discourses and practices of power (Bickham Mendez 2005; Lebon 1996, 1998; Murdock 2008; Thayer 2010).

In the 1980s, transnational activist alliances began to multiply and take institutional as well as discursive form as they sought means to defend political autonomy, cultural survival, and economic sustainability. By the end of the twentieth century, *encuentros*, advocacy networks, and strategic campaigns linked movements in Latin America to one another, as well as to counterparts in other regions of the world (Alvarez et al. 2002–3; Brysk 2000; Keck and Sikkink 1998). These relationships gave a cross-border dimension to the discursive fields described earlier, organized around issues of race, ethnicity, gender, class, environment, and other issues.

The internal heterogeneity of these political spaces and the way they stretched across continents meant that they were characterized by differences and inequalities. The politics of their participants were diverse and debates were often fiercely contested, but such spaces played an important role in fostering discursive and strategic innovation, as well as mutual support and engagement among activists—as chapters by Thayer (chapter 8) and

Laó-Montes (chapter 5) amply document. If the Civil Society Agenda offered the seductions of power, these counterpublics provided a venue for elaborating alternative meanings and practices to disrupt the ostensibly "global" civic script (Gibson-Graham 2006). Their transnational dimension brought movements from widely divergent political contexts into contact with one another, whether at UN conferences, street demonstrations, World Social Forum gatherings, or in cyberspace. The alliances constructed within counterpublics, though sometimes fraught with tension, were also strengthened by the distinctive sets of discourses and other resources brought to the table by differently situated social actors.

Performing beyond the Binary

Culture and performance serve as mobilizational tools for activism and as key components of struggles over representation. Practices generally characterized as art or popular culture appear in our cases as reconfigured national symbols (Pallares, chapter 12), signs and memorials (Lucero, chapter 15), reworkings of black identity and cultural politics (Asher, chapter 10), performative nudity (Monteagudo, chapter 7), and collective ceremonies and women's pharmacies (Rubin, chapter 11). In the course of mobilizing people and representing struggles over power, these and other forms of political art and performance can create ruptures that momentarily confront us with unsettling information or suggest alternative paths of inquiry, "stopping time, or slowing it down ... to shatter the placid surface of the present" (Buck-Morss 1998, 22); they "interrupt," as Doris Sommer put it in her remarks at the conference that gave rise to this book (see also Sommer 2014, 4).

When cultural activism interrupts politics as usual, it can unsettle meanings, indeed the power relations out of which meanings are produced. For example, such quintessentially civic actions as those of participatory budgeting in Porto Alegre—typically described as a set of institutions, procedures, deliberations, votes, and outcomes (Abers 2001; Avritzer 2002; Baiocchi 2005a; Shah 2007; Wampler 2007b)—are shown to draw on alternative political discourses and gendered performances that resist the "participatory citizen" subjectivity that the Civil Society Agenda calls into being (Junge, chapter 4 in this volume). In rural Rio Grande do Sul, the Movement of Rural Women Workers creates *farmácias* or *casas* whose cultures of alternative medicine transgress norms of Western medicine, the body, and gender (Rubin, chapter 11 in this volume; see also Rubin and Sokoloff-Rubin 2013).

Awareness of the centrality of struggles over representation has both reflected and shaped on-the-ground practice in diverse counterpublics as they engage with and/or evade the Civil Society Agenda and challenge conventional understandings and practices of development (Asher, chapter 10; Hoetmer, chapter 9), gender (Di Marco, chapter 6; Thayer, chapter 8; Rubin, chapter 11), or race and ethnicity (Laó-Montes, chapter 5; Lucero, chapter 15; Asher, chapter 10). In the course of these cultural conflicts, participants cross disciplinary, professional, and political boundaries. Our chapters show how bodies become the imagery and sites of political activism: women revise health practices as they claim economic rights, and indigenous and popular classes reshape nationalist representations of themselves as embodied citizens in the process of challenging and/or toppling governments (Pallares, chapter 12; Hoetmer, chapter 9; and Lucero, chapter 15, this volume). Art and culture serve to foster these mobilizations and to envision future transformations. They offer a means to imagine reform, often in the long moments when change seems anything but likely. In several of the cases we examine, such as participatory budgeting and the rural women's movement in Brazil, cultural forms provide links between mobilization and formal politics, making the bridge between them fully lived and engaged (Rubin 2004).

As this volume shows, the room for maneuver in Latin America's democratic regimes and participatory mechanisms is limited, with their parameters perpetually shifting. At the same time, this room for maneuver, or as Brazilians would say, *jogo de cintura*—in which physical bodies are not disappeared and cultural imaginations have access to resources and networks—is the hard-won result of decades of mobilization and cultural production, in interaction with evolving regimes of neoliberal governmentality. Whereas Partha Chatterjee suggests that the "politics of the governed" (2006) happens apart from the institutions of democratic government and the actions of civil society, most of the activists described in this book have at least one foot in the Civil Society Agenda. They are engaged, in part, with a vision of "civic" civil society that transcends the Civil Society Agenda, or at least delivers on some of its promises. Others—such as radical *autonomistas* and young anarca-feminists—reject the Civil Society Agenda as inherently capitalist, colonialist, heteronormative, and patriarchal. Along this civic-uncivic continuum, unauthorized, contestatory claims—lo no permitido—assert themselves in multiple venues, through varied strategies, and in the voices of diverse actors. As Arturo Escobar has suggested, development, alternative modernities, and alternatives to modernity are unstable categories that interweave in the real time of political contestation (2008, 198).

As recently as the Summit of the Americas in 2014, it was possible to speak of a Left-of-Center consensus among Latin America's governments. At the time of this writing in early 2016, in contrast, a number of Left-of-Center governments have fallen, either through electoral means (Cristina Fernández de Kirchner in Argentina) or extra-electoral processes (Dilma Rousseff in Brazil, Fernando Lugo in Paraguay, Manuel Zevava in Honduras), with yet other Left-of-Center administrations in trouble and facing popular discontent (Daniel Ortega in Nicaragua, and Rafael Correa in Ecuador). It is possible that by the end of 2017 there will be a new cluster of right-leaning, U.S.-friendly, and pro-business governments in Latin America, shifting the center of geopolitical gravity in the region.

If the leftism of the Pink Tide was tempered by accommodation to domestic status quos and international pressures, the right-wing parties that seek to take their place do so with the blessings of international agencies and investors. These parties have been able to align middle-class resentment, elite interests, and financial institutions in broad pro-business political projects, with elastic notions of corruption and "special interests" as ideological underpinning. In power, it is likely that emboldened right-wing leaders will act aggressively to roll back hallmark redistributive policies, combining disregard for institutional protections and the rule of law with the criminalization of protest. However, in light of the political strategies and transformations described in the following chapters, this will be a deeply contested agenda.

What will be the role of social movements in these new scenarios? In the context of a rollback of both legal protections and moderate redistribution, activists will likely defend both the rule of law and the less-than-ideal social policies implemented by Pink Tide governments. At the same time, associations of the "civic" with anti-corruption and anti-leftist mobilizations will likely harden the divide between civic and uncivic modes of activism and provide an opening for more radical demands.

In this context, what new opportunities—or forms of exclusion—could emerge from the intersections between movements and institutions, the civic and the uncivic, described in this volume? As the following chapters will demonstrate, activists bring both developmentalist claims and alternative knowledges into public politics, mixing and reshaping civic and uncivic spaces and practices in the process. These mobilizations and strategies, marked by fluid, dynamic, and heterogeneous fields of contestation, were not contained by the governments of the Pink Tide, but rather overflowed their prescriptions and boundaries, opening new democratic spaces or extending existing ones in the process. They will not likely be contained by new governments of the Right or Left in the future.

NOTES

Many of the ideas with which we engage in this introduction emerged not only from our individual research trajectories, but through a series of study groups in which we read across our areas of expertise and ventured into new areas together. As different sections were initially drafted by one or another of us, we developed a lively method of collective discussion and revision that took on a lengthy and tempestuous life of its own. In our meetings, Sonia Alvarez proved extraordinarily adept as scribe, getting down with heroic speed, accuracy, and imagination the words and phrases that emerged out of our swirling conversations. Together we made grammatical and substantive sense out of our multiple angles of vision. What is often the case in joint authorship, but not always sufficiently noted, is deeply true in our case: the introduction, like the book of which it is a part, is a genuinely collective product.

1. On the region's shift to the political Left, often referred to as the Pink Tide, to denote the manifold gradations of Marxist red to social-democratic light pink, see Cameron 2009; Castañeda 2006; Grugel and Riggirozzi 2009; Lievesley and Ludman 2009; Levitsky and Roberts 2011; Prevost, Campos, and Vanden 2012; and Weyland, Madrid, and Hunter 2010. On inclusionary civil-society-based experiments since 2000, see Rubin and Bennett 2014.

2. On the "perverse confluence" of participatory and neoliberal political projects, see Dagnino, Olvera, and Panfichi 2006a; see also Alvarez 2001.

3. There is a parallel discussion about the international dimension of human rights. Some scholars such as Keck and Sikkink (1998) have argued that it is precisely the individual notions of rights that has made international advocacy—and real victories—possible, and emphasized new forms of engagement made possible by these international networks. Others have primarily seen in the field of human rights the export of ideas and expertise from the United States to the region (Dezalay and Garth 2002; Grewal 2005).

4. The notion of *indio permitido* comes from an argument for decolonization in Silvia Rivera's original formulation. For the notion of *negro escogido*, see Laó-Montes, chapter 5, this volume.

5. We did not set out to compile a country-by-country anthology that would attempt to represent the diverse panoply of today's mass mobilizations.

6. She also draws on scholars in sociology (Calhoun, 1992, 2002), communications (Asen 2002), and geography (Massey 1994).

Part I

INTERROGATING

THE CIVIL SOCIETY

AGENDA

Reflections on Brazil

Chapter 1

A CENTURY OF COUNCILS

Participatory Budgeting and the
Long History of Participation in Brazil

GIANPAOLO BAIOCCHI

A New Critical Juncture?

Latin America has become ground zero for citizen participation, a global destination for those interested in myriad new forms of citizen engagement. Quite apart from the so-called Pink Tide, whose governments *all* express commitments to participatory democracy, participation has featured centrally in governmental discourse throughout the region in national and local governments Right, Left, and Center. From Antanas Mockus's citizen consultations in Bogotá, to Bolivarian *consejos comunales*, to *foro ciudadanos* in Mexico, the "citizen" has come to occupy a central place in governmental planning. This has been especially true in the first decade of the 2000s. As ideas of New Public Management and minimal states have given way to Public Governance in the United States and Europe, in Latin America participatory democracy has decidedly moved from its social movement and leftist party roots to mainstream thinking, planning, and institutions. If radical urban planners under Salvador Allende served as inspiration to insurgent leftist political forces in Brazil, making forays into governance in the early 1980s, in the early 2000s an administrator in that region seeking to "involve citizens" would have a wide menu of choices of models and materials to choose from, including those by the prestigious national management programs as well as courses promoted by the U.S. Agency for International Development (USAID) and United Nations Development Programme (UNDP) or expert consultancies in the region.

As discussed in the introduction, part of the motivation for this volume has been to make sense of this turn of events, and many of the contributions here deal with the nuances of what this participation means, what it makes possible, and what it obscures. The contributions here all carefully chart a path between two poles. There is on one hand, a largely celebratory literature on citizen participation that takes for granted that participation, in itself, is democratizing, normatively desirable, and brings with it other components of "good governance" such as transparency and accountability. Cleaver argues that unconditional belief in participation is based on three postulates: "participation is intrinsically a 'good thing' (especially for the participants); a focus on 'getting the techniques right' is the principal way of ensuring the success of such approaches, and considerations of power and politics on the whole should be avoided as divisive and obstructive" (Cleaver 2001, 598). Critical scholars have taken this view to task for failing to address questions of power, inequality, and politics. But among critical scholars there is also by now a sentiment that participation, and participatory prescriptions in particular, are part and parcel of neoliberal governmentality. Because participation in government is seen as an alternative to conflictive mobilization and disruption, it is argued, it becomes part of a set of strategies that depoliticize conflicts and thus pave the way for ever-more-aggressive neoliberal reforms of the state. Pablo Leal, for example, in a piece that calls participation a "buzzword in the neo-liberal era," writes that "it is clearly more than coincidence that participation appeared as a new battle horse for official development precisely at the time of the shock treatment of Structural Adjustment Programmes (SAPs) inflicted on the underdeveloped world by the World Bank and the IMF" (Leal 2007, 543).

This turn of events (the adoption of participation by mainstream governance) and its appearance in the critical discourse (the direct association of participation with neoliberalism) are certainly puzzling when looked at in the context of the "long 1980s." Leaving aside the intention of some of the original participatory reformers in the 1980s who thought that participation in government was part of an incremental strategy of socialist takeover of the bourgeois state, the dominant position among critical scholars in the 1990s was that participatory experiments in Latin America were part of a process of colonization of the state by civil society actors who were intent on achieving social justice and empowerment, and for whom transparency and account-ability were important side benefits but by no means the central goal.

This chapter is an attempt to critically engage this juncture of events, a task that necessarily calls for a critical and careful genealogy of partici-pation and participatory prescriptions. The essay is about Brazil, and the particular participatory prescription it focuses on is participatory budgeting, one of the prescriptions that has taken on the widest appeal and probably gen-erated more conferences, consultancies, and dedicated institutions than any other single one. But similar investigations could no doubt be undertaken on the trajectories of the solidarity economy, citizen juries, users' councils, micro-credit schemes, gender budgeting, urban cooperatives, and fair trade, among many other traveling best practices that have achieved prominence since the late 1990s.

This essay "connects the dots" between the early invocations of citizen participation to the first moments of participatory budgeting and its later incarnations, paying specific attention to the institutional forms, ideas, and organized actors that have propelled—and transformed—the idea (Ong and Collier 2004). I am especially attentive to how participation emerges as what anthropologist David Scott (2004) has called a "problem-space." That is, "an ensemble of questions and answers around which a horizon of identifiable stakes (conceptual as well as political-ideological stakes) hangs" (2004, 5). Identifying a problem space means distinguishing the contours of debate and intervention, determining legitimate questions, and exploring the broader "context of rival views."

A Century of Councils

As the introduction of the volume intimates, the participation boom in Latin America of the late 1990s and early 2000s did not appear out of nowhere. Governments have involved citizens throughout the twentieth century, and there are at least two strands of participation in competing ideas of councils. One emphasizes incorporation and legitimacy, while the other emphasizes empowerment and transformation. The first is represented by workers' councils under populist regimes, which existed throughout the region. Councils were a place for invited participants to voice concerns directly to populist leaders; selected demands were incorporated into the body politic, legitimating both the regime and the particular demand. Davis, for example, describes the Consejo Consultivo de La Ciudad de México, which was established in the late 1920s as part of the corporative strategies of the ruling party in Mexico: "It was to be a body of politically appointed representatives with the official purpose of 'aiding' Mexico City's mayor in governing the capital. It had no legislative power, and its representatives were handpicked by the Calles-dominated PNR leadership. . . . representatives were selected who could vocalize the urban demands and redevelopment concerns of well-established constituencies in the capital . . . and from groups whose relatively high degree of mobilization or organization meant they could cause political problems if not incorporated" (67–68).

The other sort of council—emphasizing autonomy, empowerment, and transformation—is represented by the revolutionary councils in Cuba in the early days of the revolution, or in liberated zones under control of the Frente Farabundo Martí para la Liberación Nacional (Farabundo Martí National Liberation Front, FMLN) in the early days of the uprising, or in the idea of "popular councils" that appeared in Brazil in the 1970s under the influence of liberation theology and new leftist thinking. These neighborhood popular councils were created to "articulate the popular movement's demands" in permanent, autonomous fora. Here, the importance of participation in the council was to neither legitimate a regime nor incorporate participants or demands into it. It was a principally a movement-building space: a place of discussion that rendered different demands equivalent (so that different neighborhoods could act in concert, for example) and as a way to empower participants to act in the direction of transforming society.

The populist version and the revolutionary, or radical-democratic, versions of councils varied in their emphases on empowerment, self-regulation, and legitimation, but either version contained elements of all three. So even the workers' councils under Juan Perón contained an element of empowerment for workers. And the various revolutionary councils always had a strong element of self-regulation; the *Comités de Defensa de la Revolución* (CDRs) in Cuba, which existed in every block, were both the most local instance for citizen participation but were also instruments of self-regulation, serving to police crime, preserve neighborhood cleanliness, and root out counterrevolutionary activity. The distinguishing feature between the two types of councils is how they recognize and articulate demands, an insight indebted to Laclau's analyses (2005). In the populist version, the state demands political allegiance in exchange for the recognition of societal demands. The form of the interface between state and society may vary, but the *selective recognition* of certain actors according to political allegiance is the key feature. And the relationship between actors and the state is individual and direct. There is no equivalence possible between recognized actors and others. In contrast, revolutionary or radical democratic councils always emphasize the *horizontal and equivalent relationship* between various demands, which are then placed before the state. As I describe below, the appearance of a new participatory imaginary in Brazil in the 1970s and 1980s reflects the replacement, in the imagination of activists, of the populist version by the revolutionary one.

The "New" Social Movements and the New Participatory Imaginary

The contemporary idea of participatory governance in Brazil begins with the variety of new urban social movements in the 1970s that brought new visions of urban democracy and participation to Brazilian politics.[1] Central to this history is liberation theology. Often in the form of outside advisors, progressive clergy played an important role in providing assistance to neighborhood associations, from mimeographing flyers to running "discussion circles." As elsewhere in Brazil, these were often middle-class activists who moved into poor and working-class neighborhoods with the intent of supporting and politicizing local struggles. The well-known Ecclesiastic Base Communities (CEBS) were embryonic spaces for discussion and debate, dedicated to fomenting social change anchored in a vision of individual and collective consciousness-raising.

Neighborhood associations, of course, had existed in urban centers in Brazil for decades, some starting operations as early as in the 1930s, and many since the 1950s. These were often residents' associations, "Friends of the Neighborhood" or "Amigos do Bairro"-type organizations that had been started in close concert with, if not directly created by, politicians tied to local governments. In the city of Porto Alegre, for example, the first registered neighborhood associations were founded in 1945 at the urging of government officials. In exchange for political allegiance, municipal government offered urban improvements and social events, at one point sponsoring a municipal Olympics and a municipal congress for neighborhood associations, where a "diploma" in neighborhood leadership was handed out. In the mid-1950s, the local government created municipal councils, where representatives of neighborhood associations would be permitted to participate in decisions on the provision of social services. During the early years of the dictatorship (1964–85), the government first limited the activities of associations to purely social service functions, before relaxing restrictions and sometimes encouraging their formation. These tended to function very much like the populist councils—they served to legitimate the regime or local politicians and selectively recognized certain claimants, and emphasized a direct, vertical connection with authorities. The new participatory imaginary emerged in direct contrast to this vision, often through the work of activists who worked to transform existing associations.

A notable first experience, which would precede hundreds of others in Brazil in the next decade, was the Movement of Neighborhood Associations (Movimento de Associações de Bairro, MAB), in the Baixada Fluminense in Rio de Janeiro. The Baixada was then known in the Brazilian media as "the most violent place on Earth." The number and visibility of homicides in this region adjacent to Rio de Janeiro was then at a high point, with some months registering fifty homicides a month in this region of 2 million (J. Alves 1998). Death squads operated with immunity in the region, claiming as many as a hundred lives a year.

The movement was started in 1976 with the help of progressives within the local parish as an experiment in establishing a permanent forum for discussion of urban needs, bringing together representatives of several neighborhood associations in the district. Although many new associations had appeared in those years in Rio, many of them functioned in vertical relationships with authorities, with a marked "preference for direct contact" (Boschi 1987, 48), mediated through a neighborhood association president. The movement was organized in direct contradiction to those practices. At MAB meetings, members sought ways to organize these various associations into a common bloc that could make demands on city and state government (Jacobi 1987). After a diagnostic process, representatives from thirty-four neighborhoods gave the mayor a list of problems and demands in their areas, followed by a mobilization demanding public audiences and a process of accounting. In the years following, neighboring communities developed similar coalitions, leading to the formation of a statewide association of associations to make demands on state government. In 1979, the MAB was active in defending residents against evictions, and in 1981 it organized a march to city hall to give the mayor an open letter about the poor quality of public services. The movement continued to act throughout the 1980s and 1990s, creating a series of Community Health Councils, a "space of social control and popular demand-making," which in 1986 partnered with the National

Ministry of Health to promote "SOS Baixada" to combat dengue and other transmissible diseases.[2]

By the mid-1980s there were thousands of active neighborhood associations throughout the country working in this manner. Many were reimagined or reinvented "Friends of the Neighborhood" associations that had been closely tied to politicians or the regime that were now acting in novel ways, but many were new as well. They represented the work of community organizers in poorer communities as well as the perceived political opening as the dictatorship was coming to an end. In most communities these were tied to the search for "collective solutions for the lack of education, health facilities, sewage control, and transport" (M. Alves 1984, 78). They employed a mix of practices: contestatory claims-making, collective self-improvement and mutual assistance, and consciousness raising. Maria Helena Moreira Alves describes their efforts: "They mobilize the population to participate in collective work for the physical improvement of the area by organizing mutirões (group work) . . . or the renovating of shacks and homes. In addition, the population is organized by the associations to pressure the municipal or state government to provide better education, health care, or transport. Neighborhood associations engage in cultural activities, as well as with programs that include film clubs, theatre groups, music, and sports. . . . These play a crucial role in both informing the population and raising political consciousness" (1984, 79).

Nationally, movements for urban rights such as the Cost of Living Movement, the Housing Movement, and the Collective Transports Movement organized in the mid- to late 1970s. In demanding the recognition of new subjects, these movements proposed new forms of social relationships mediated by the state, as well as new relationships between civil society and the state, while emphasizing autonomy from manipulative government agencies and politicians, proceduralism, and democracy in decision making (Viola and Mainwaring 1987, 154). Similarly, many of the descriptions of the New Social Movements in Brazil in the late 1970s emphasize the importance of transforming the participants' own practices. Popular education, for example, often emphasized the transformation of subjects into rights-bearing citizens, who not only recognized oppression and knew how to defend themselves against police abuses but also pledged not to engage in clientelism or domestic abuse.

What is of note is that for a large number of movements, such as the MAB, the state figured centrally both as an object and as a limit of political horizon. Contrasting the so-called New Social Movements of Europe and of Latin America in the 1970s and 1980s highlights just how important the state was. Some New Social Movement scholars have gone so far as to characterize these movements in Europe as "post-materialist" and not aimed at achieving state power (Buechler 1995). The MAB and many of the Latin American New Social Movements (though sometimes overlapping in thematic area with European counterparts) were their mirror image: very "materialist" and very much aimed *at* the state.

Evelina Dagnino refers to this as "the new citizenship" that dominated Brazilian social movements in the 1980s and 1990s. Its premise was "the right to have rights," and it lauded the invention of "new rights that emerge from specific struggles and concrete practices." But central to the Brazilian, and Latin American, versions of citizenship imagined was a large role for the state. These new propositional practices of social movements were grounded in the ideologies of movements of the 1970s and 1980s, and while demanding dialogue with the state, they simultaneously challenged the limits of representative democracy by calling for participatory reforms and expanded versions of traditional rights.

From Movement to City Hall:
Participation in Government and the Abertura

If it was in the favelas of the large metropolitan areas of Brazil that the new movements claiming rights and services emerged, ideas about participation in government were also appearing from the government side in a few notable small towns. The otherwise conservative weekly newsmagazine *Istoé* ran, in 1980, the unusual story of an architect who, at thirty-two, became mayor of his small town of Lages (population 180,000) in 1977 in the southern state of Santa Catarina. This young reformer, whose election slogan had been "The Power of the People," had created a series of spaces for the population to decide and participate in the affairs of town governance, with the purpose of creating "participatory democracy, the utilization of local economic resources, and the search of alternatives to the use of petrol products" (*Istoé* 1980, 23). More inspired by "Small Is Beautiful" than by "Mao's Little Red Book," according to the magazine, Carneiro created a working system of local economic self-sufficiency and community participation.

While much of the participation revolved around an extensive mutual-assistance and rotating credit program, this eventually developed into a participatory structure of intervention in the municipal budget, with representatives of different communities voting on budget priorities for the year (H. Sousa and Ferreira 1991). According to Celina Souza, Lages was especially attractive to medium-sized administrations "because of the city's focus on small initiatives that were cooperatively implemented by the government and the community," though participation rates in the government schemes were modest, as were outcomes, with the possible exception of an emergency housing program (C. Souza 2001, 52). Nonetheless, as the Lages administration gained recognition, it received scores of "professors, politicians, liberal professionals, and students" interested in learning about, and later promoting, the city's participatory model (*Jornal de Santa Catarina* 1980), an island of possibilities in the middle of an authoritarian country. The book about the experience, *The Power of the People: Participatory Democracy in Lages* (M. Alves 1980), was widely circulated among urban activists and reformers of the time.

There were other short-lived and small-scale experiments in participatory governance in the late 1970s and early 1980s in Brazil that also served as reference points for later experiments.[3] The small city of Piracicaba, in São Paulo State, had an experiment in consultative budgeting in 1977 based on a series of community centers tied to each of the town's districts where priorities were discussed and sent on to city hall. Later, a "Citizens' Budget Committee" was created, where representatives of neighborhood associations participated (Castro 1988). In Boa Esperança, a town of 18,000 in Espírito Santo, Mayor Amaro Covre, also in the late 1970s, developed a more sophisticated neighborhood participatory system that granted the community a substantial amount of decision-making power as well as establishing permanent fora for deliberation on local problems. Although none of the three proved to be lasting experiments, they, and Lages in particular, became well-known examples for urban activists in the 1980s (Caccia Bava 1983; Caccia Bava 1995; H. Souza 1982). Common to all these experiences were the emphasis on self-help and mutual assistance as ways of lowering costs; the merit of these was to "create alternative ways to deal with people's most urgent needs through the development of quick and cheap initiatives" (C. Souza 2001, 159).

Civil Society Colonizes the State—Opposition Mayors after the Abertura

If a first moment in the emergence of the new political imaginary was the appearance of a radical-democratic logic in civil society participation in contradiction to a populist one, the next stage was taking that logic to the state. This became possible in the mid-1980s with a cohort of new opposition mayors, many of whom emerged from social movements. While state-level contests favored political machines and established powerful families, the first fully free municipal elections of 1985 and afterward opened space to many outsiders (Alvarez 1993). The constitutional reform of 1988 made significant forms of participation possible and codified some language about participation at the local level, partially as a result of the social movement and NGO activists who testified in Congress in the reform process (Shildo 1998). While many city governments evoked "participation" (Curitiba, Rio de Janeiro, Recife, and Salvador among others) by the late 1980s, it would be the Workers' Party (Partido dos Trabalhadores, PT) that would become known as the party of participation.

The PT in this period was representative of what some have called the "social turn" of the Left in Latin America, as well as a new focus on winning local as opposed to national arenas of governance (Castañeda 1993). The Workers' Party, which had won a *prefeitura* in the limited elections of 1982 in its "hometown" of Diadema, in São Paulo, elected two mayors (in Diadema and Fortaleza) in the next election, and then thirty-six in the contests of 1988, which brought roughly 10 percent of Brazilians under local PT administrations, "the greatest electoral advance for the Latin American left since Salvador Allende," in the words of one commentator (Hichenberger 1989). The experiences of 1986–89 in government of the PT in Diadema (qualified success) and Fortaleza (an unmitigated disaster) had shown administrators that governing would be a difficult task, but ideals about participation remained important elements in electoral programs. Claims from social movements that had backed the PT and strongly favored participation, an imaginary about participation from mythical places such as Lages, and leftist visions of people in power that invoked a wide variety of historical examples contributed to this program. Most of the proposals involved the creation of popular councils, or people's councils, where the organized population would mobilize and exert power over the administration. As an early version proposed, "In our vision, the Popular Councils constitute a virus infiltrated in the bourgeois political system that can continue to broaden its action and undermine the forces of this regime. In other words, it is an element not of reinforcement of the system, but of its destabilization in the long term. . . . Popular Councils are an indispensable strategy for social transformation" (Galletta 1989).

Despite good intentions, the administrations of the PT during 1989–92 were also generally not successful. Those in the PT's home state of São Paulo were voted out of office after only one term in 1992, often with acrimonious conflicts, in the period later described as the "shock with reality." All of the PT prefeituras of the time invoked participation in some way, but most had political difficulties, often with the PT's own base of support in movements and unions. A third of the mayors in question left the PT before completing their term, and another third did not manage reelection.

A central problem for administrators was how to make participation compatible with governance and reelection. In many instances, the combination of party-administration-movement that was imagined to happen within popular councils was unworkable and often led to difficulties. In these cases, councils tended to privilege organized movements, which proved politically costly for administrations in terms of elevating the demands of movements and reducing the legitimacy of the administration with the broader electorate. In São Paulo, for instance, the PT administration was caught between its base of support and this broader electorate, often coming under attack for listening to social movements sympathetic to the party. By the time of the administrations of 1993–96, however, administrators had found a solution in the form of a new pragmatism, in which social movements would not be privileged and participation would be open to all, but this participation would be directed in a format that would not produce disruption.

The FNPP and the Development of the "PT Way"

By the end of the 1980s, and the "second generation of popular administrations," there was a certain amount of experience accumulated about participatory reforms, but little systematic "theorizing." While the PT itself had created the National Department for the Discussion of Institutional Action in 1988 to coordinate plans of action for local-level victories, in 1990 a national forum was created, led by a small number of important NGOs, to meet and exchange experiences and ideas about participation: the National Forum on Popular Participation in Democratic and Popular Administrations (or the Fórum Nacional de Participação Popular, or FNPP). In it, participants from NGOs, from social movement organizations, from PT administrations, and from the academy debated the merits of various forms of participation, decentralizing local administration and increasing popular participation in decision making.

Early on in the FNPP, there was a debate between those who advocated "popular councils" and those who defended "institutional channels" of participation, such as participatory budgeting (PB). Some of the best-known examples of such innovations took place in Belo Horizonte, São Paulo, Porto Alegre, Santos, and Diadema under the Workers' Party. These ranged from self-help favela urbanization programs, innovative councils for oversight of public health clinics, and creative experiments with social service delivery. Partially informed by the experiences of the next few years, when several PT administrations failed, some spectacularly, and partially by the shifting of the composition of the forum, which by 1996 had become almost exclusively occupied by administrators from PT administrations, the forum settled on PB as a preferred prescription, and it became involved in tracking and disseminating PB practices.

Porto Alegre's model of participatory budgeting—which emerged out of a combination of experimentation, responses to external pressures, and a search for legitimacy in the absence of a reliable social movement base—became the model administration and the central point of reference for other PB experiments. First, it was successful in both delivering good governance and in garnering legitimacy. A range of research and indicators confirms that as innovation to governance and to municipal decision-making, PB has indeed been very successful.

In terms of legitimacy, the ability of the administration to consistently draw thousands of participants and to deliver results in a timely and transparent way became a bedrock of the administration, which kept local opposition at bay and carried out a number of ambitious reforms, such as introducing land-use taxes targeted at wealthier citizens that have funded many of the PB's projects. The political efficacy of the PB in Porto Alegre was in sharp contrast to several of the other PT administrations that self-destructed under political conflicts in the late 1980s and early 1990s.

One of the central differences of the "Porto Alegre Model" was what administrators describe as the "open format" for meetings, which emerged out of disappointment with civil-society-mediated forums early on. The original broad concern with increasing popular participation in government and with the "inversion of priorities" (reversing the traditional pattern of spending public monies in Brazilian cities that privileged wealthier areas) led to initial attempts to dialogue with organized civil society, the "natural allies" of a PT administration. This format of civil society representation was dominant in many other PT administrations and is the implicit formula of "council democracy" that guided Luiza Erundina's administration in São Paulo. Civil-society-mediated participation, however, was prone to political difficulties and crises of legitimacy, when PT administrators were caught between charges of "clientelism of the Left" (as seen by local media) when they met the demands of civil society, and "class treason" (as seen by their allies) when they did not. Open participation, or citizen participation (as opposed to civic participation), in the local forums that decided on the budget became a way for the administration to generate legitimacy for its redistributive platforms among the broader voting public as well as with allies. The other two important elements of the Porto Alegre Model are "self-regulation," that is, participants themselves decide on the rules of the process, and "self determination," that is, participants themselves decide on the whole of the capital (new investment) budget and not administrators. The net result in Porto Alegre was a transparent participatory system with broad participation from the city's poorer citizens that was widely perceived as legitimate and citizen-run, and that was successful at managing conflicts for demands.

The PB became widely recognized as central to the "PT formula" of combining redistribution with broad-based participation, and by the mid-1990s the PT had become more adept at solving certain endemic problems. The "PT Way of Governing" was one that combined social justice goals with transparency, broad participation, and effective governance, and it was on this basis that the PT expanded its electoral influence in municipal governments throughout the country in the late 1990s. Participation, far from being an instrument of destabilizing the bourgeois political system as had been imagined by some in the mid-1980s, became instead a central piece in a strategy of running government well. Good governance for the thinkers and activists of the PT, of course, meant something other than reducing deficits and improving the delivery of public services, but it certainly included those outcomes as well.

Participatory budgeting reforms were copied, and transformed in the process of being copied, throughout Brazil. Twelve cities introduced PB in 1989–92, thirty-six did so in 1993–96, 103 adopted PB in the 1997–2000 tenure according to surveys done by the FNPP, at least 150 did so in 2001–4, and close to 200 did so in the next period (de Grazia and Torres 2002). Most earlier experiments were associated with the PT, but an increasing number of other political parties have carried out PB in later years. Participatory budgeting was widely adopted throughout the country for a variety of reasons. Fundação Getúlio Vargas, Brazil's elite public policy institute, as well as NGOs such as Pólis, in São Paulo, were instrumental as well in documenting and promoting best municipal practices, and PB programs, alongside a bundle of other municipal best practices, were diffused in a period of intensive creativity and experimentation. A "How To" guide from FNPP, for example, extols the benefits of participatory budgeting in this version as a mix of good governance (transparency, increased resources; the reduction of clientelism), social justice (redistribution of resources), and civic goals (legitimacy, dialogue, cooperation, and solidarity). As Brian Wampler has noted, there are a range of motivations for administrators to pursue these types of projects, such as building a base of support, legitimating redistribution, increasing the awareness of the population, and increasing transparency (Wampler 2007).

Participatory budgeting became a global phenomenon in the late 1990s. In 1997 it was declared a "best practice" by the UNDP, and in 2001 it featured prominently in the Human Development Report. The United Nations Development Program funded a prominent network of cooperation and exchange for Latin American cities, the Urban Latin America (URB-AL) network, which later received EU funding and was central to dissemination of the idea (Allegretti and Herzberg 2004, 3). In much of the developing world, the World Bank became an important indirect promoter of PB projects, funding training, exchanges, and organizations to implement it. In Latin America in particular, USAID has also been very active in directly promoting PB. Two important elements were important for participatory recipes and blueprints to "jump" to the terrain of multilateral agencies—first, participation became seen as a technical fix, as described above, and second, development discourse was changing as were the roles and functions of national states, with lower levels of government attracting attention as strategic sites.

The success and diffusion of participatory budgeting took place alongside the growing interest in participation by multilateral agencies in the 1990s. In the 1980s, Structural Adjustment had become the order of the day, and participatory prescriptions were brought in line, as participation became also participation in the market and a means to implement, and soften, the impacts of adjustment. But the late 1990s were a different period of intense interest in the role of civil society and community-based development among development agencies. Part of this was no doubt due to the increased influence of reformers and progressives within these institutions who gained influence during this period (Bebbington 2005). But a part of this was also due to a shift in thinking that culminated with the recognition that Structural Adjustment had failed either to provide benefits to the majority of populations in question or even to actually promote development plus the recognition that "state-dominated development has failed, but so will stateless development" (World Bank 1997, 25). There was a shift, in other words, toward good governance, or the idea that "the state itself does not inhibit development, but its manner of governance can" (Grindle 2004, 525).

It is in this context, then, that participation comes to be valued as a complement to good local governance and as an alternative development prescription, as a means to "greater efficiency and effectiveness of investment and of contributing to processes of democratization and empowerment" (Cleaver 2001, 597). The World Bank decisively has begun to incorporate participatory methodologies and affirms its commitment to "promote participatory processes and stakeholder engagement at the project, program, and policy level" and increasingly adopts a language of participation and empowerment throughout its programs.

Participation as Good Governance:
The Diffusion of Participation in Brazil

Alongside the global take-up of participatory budgeting, the meanings attached to participatory democracy in Brazil have also changed considerably throughout the 1990s and later. The undeniable successes of participatory democracy in achieving governance goals had the effect of propelling participation to a range of institutions. Participation was decidedly mainstreamed, now as a tool of good governance. Not only did participatory budgeting continue to spread beyond PT and leftist-run cities throughout the late 1990s (reaching some 500 municipalities by the end of the decade), municipal councils on various aspects of service provision—health, social services, and education—became active in most municipalities. A study in 1999 found that the average municipality in Brazil had nearly five active councils (Braemer 2001). It could be said that by 2000, citizen participation was a central feature of government functioning in Brazil.

But the participatory imaginary originally born of the successful mix of social movement ideas and electoral fortunes embodied in the PT continued to evolve as participation became one of the principal pillars of the national PT administration under Luiz Inácio Lula da Silva, beginning in 2002. Under the banner of radical inclusion ("a country for all"), the national administration of the PT dedicated enormous institutional resources to the promotion of participation. It created or revived national councils on a variety of issues and instituted "national conferences" on many more. By 2010 there were sixty-eight active national councils on these various topics, and seventy-two national conferences were held in Brasilia, mobilizing over 5 million people.

And while the PT-led government has embraced participatory practices, these represented something quite distinct from earlier stages. Participation through national councils was often focused on implementation of the already-formulated policies. Critical reflections from these forums complain of the lack of effective decision-making power in participatory spaces. That is, time and again, conference resolutions that went directly against government policy or powerful economic interests did not get adopted as policy. Moreover, marquee policies such as the Bolsa Família (the income transfer program), and and the anticrisis economic measures of 2008 did *not* go through participatory spaces and ignored more progressive alternatives. In fact (as has been argued by a former head of the Ministry of Cities), the participatory spaces in Brazil do not discuss structural issues (such as transfers of funds to the financial sphere through the payment of interest on public debt, or decrease in social policy) by design (Maricato 2011).

Participation as Politics or Antipolitics?

To return to the questions that opened the essay, when we consider the genealogy of participatory budgeting it is clear that it represents the evolution of ideas about "participation in government" from something that could "defy" the status quo to something that could maintain, and improve, it. But the story is much more complicated than its "sanitization" by development agencies or neoliberalism in the abstract. First, the story is quite clear—the evolution of participatory budgeting as a privileged tool for the dual goals of good governance and redistribution was a result of the changing fortunes of the Workers' Party. As the party won its first administrations and its administrators embarked on the path of running administrations that delivered results and gained reelection, the calculus about the usefulness of different participatory strategies changed. And over time, in Brazil, participation more generally became mainstreamed into many aspects of government functioning. By the 2000s it was part of governmental common-sense. But it is important to remember that participation as something that enhances governance dates to discussions within the PT in the late 1980s and not a cabal of neoliberal development technocrats in the 2000s.

And if we go back further, the story is even more complicated and challenges the notion of the purity of civil society or that it occupies (or occupied) a privileged outside to the state's machinations. Civil society in Brazil, as in much of Latin America, has always aimed at the state with its claims and imaginations of what is possible. Unlike, perhaps, civil society organizations in liberal societies that have a stronger claim at "separateness" if not "autonomy," civil society in Brazil has often had ties with the state, if not direct origins in the state itself. In the period of transition to democracy, civil society's aims and wishes were squarely located with the state. The state did not just reach out and co-opt civil society with its participatory schemas; rather, it is the combination of a legacy of earlier versions of participation with the porousness of the state to outside activism that led to the creation of participatory schemas in the first place. And if we consider civil society itself carefully, what emerges is that self-regulation is central to its practices. From the MAB in the Baixada Fluminense to countless other organizations and groups, whether doing civic work, consciousness raising, self-help, or making claims on the state, the voluntary regulation of the activity of its members is a central axis of activity.

The long history of participation, and of participatory budgeting in particular, in Brazil is a clear story of the evolution of "governmentality from below" or "auto-governmentality" and subtle shifts as the technology travels across institutions and domains. Considering participatory budgeting as a form of governmentality is closer to the original deployment of the concept than analyses that associate it exclusively with the state and reminds us that the concept is supposed to elucidate the way that empowerment is laden with regulation instead of the opposition of regulation to empowerment (Kruikshank 1999).

That said, the critical juncture facing activists is in some ways a return to an earlier period when governments encouraged the creation of associations and councils in order to legitimate its rule. But even in this earlier period, when the populist version of councils that emphasized the selective recognition of some demands was dominant, there was instability. Just as workers' councils eventually led to new forms of unionism, traditional neighborhood associations gave way in many instances to other forms of association that were premised on seemingly radical principles of equality and equivalence. Today, the version of participation that dominates both governmental discourse in Brazil and discourse among international traffickers of participatory blueprints incorporates elements of the radical-democratic and revolutionary councils, which emphasize equivalence and inclusion, even if they have given up ideas of social transformation and popular empowerment. Setting aside, for a moment, the question of whether this explosion of participation without empowerment makes for effective public policy, we should be attentive to the possibility that the very act of participation may shift power relations in particular contexts or occasions. Participation implies a collective space and also presumes a certain equality between participants, with each person a partner in a shared world, "presupposing that one can play the same game as one's adversary."[4] There is always something potentially subversive, and unpredictable, in arrangements that imply this equality. The question before movements and activists in these participatory institutions today is not so much whether to engage with them at all (as more dismissive analyses might imply), but how to engage them strategically so as to leverage equality and inclusion to political ends.

NOTES

1. There is a very extensive literature on the social movements of the 1970s and 1980s in Brazil, which is impossible to review here (Boschi 1987; Cardoso 1988; Evers 1985; Telles 1987; Viola and Mainwaring 1987).

2. This draws on J. Alves (1998), esp. chap. 3. For the elevation of the MAB into a best practice, see http://www.ibam.org.br/urbanos/assunto3/blt5_1.htm.

3. There are other accounts of participatory experiments in Osasco in the state of São Paulo, Pelotas in Rio Grande do Sul, and Juiz de Fora in Minas Gerais. Today, as participatory experiments have become popular, there is some dispute as to who exactly invented the participatory budget.

4. Rancière ([2003] 2009, 78).

Chapter 2

CIVIL SOCIETY IN BRAZIL

From State Autonomy to Political Interdependency

LEONARDO AVRITZER

Civil society is a concept that was bound to the West until the beginning of the third wave of democratization (Cohen and Arato 1992; Keane 1988a). The concept of civil society emerged in the nineteenth century, around 1820 (Riedel 1984, 132), as a dualist concept capable of expressing two changes brought about by Western modernity: the differentiation between the family and the economic sphere caused by the abolition of bondage, and the differentiation between state and society caused by the systemic specialization of the modern state. In this context, social differentiation meant that "the state is not the state if it always merges with civil society and that the latter is not society when it is political society or the state" (Riedel 1984, 133). Thus, in its first formulation civil society is a dualist concept that expresses the beginning of a process of state and society differentiation in the West. The concept of civil society could not during the nineteenth century make its way out of the West because the social processes it expressed belonged exclusively to the West.[1]

The concept of civil society reemerged in the late twentieth-century political and social scene with two strong differences from its nineteenth-century meaning: it reappears involving a tripartite meaning in which civil society is differentiated from both the market and the state. Thus, differently from during the early nineteenth century, the market, understood as the realm of private economic activities, is also differentiated from civil society. Second, the concept of civil society reappears as a concept that seeks to explain social processes taking place in the West, the East, and Latin American societies (Arato 1981; Cohen and Arato 1992; Habermas 1995; Keane 1988a; Keane 1988b; Keane 1998). The tripartite meaning of the concept of civil society is linked to late twentieth-century differentiation between market and society. It has received different formulations in the literature. Cohen and Arato in their seminal work on civil society differentiated civil society from "the steering mechanisms that coordinate action in the economy (money) or in formally organized bureaucratically structured organizations (power)" (1992). They traced civil society to the institutional level of a lifeworld understood as a place for socialization, social interaction, and public activities. This is one of the roots of a tripartite model of civil society that may also be traced to other traditions of social thought, among them the differentiation between civil society, political society, and the state in Gramsci (Bobbio 1989; Oxhorn 1995). Those who advocated a Gramscian concept of civil society tried to focus more strongly on the idea of conflict and the idea of a struggle for the cultural hegemony within civil society (Fontana 2006). For them, the central element of Latin American civil societies should be the attempt to move beyond a functional conception of politics to concentrate on the disputes of hegemony in the realm of culture and in the geographical territory (Oxhorn 1995). There is still a third source for the reemergence of the concept of civil society that is a neo-Tocquevillian or neo-Durkheimian tradition that differentiated the realm of the state from the realm of voluntary associations. In this concept, civil society is an autonomous locus of producing social solidarity (Feinberg, Waisman, and Zamosc 2006; Shills 1990) that can be either traditional or modern.[2] In all three cases, civil society acquired the meaning of a concept whose revival went beyond nineteenth-century dualist models of state and society differentiation due to its independence from the market economy and due to the acknowledgment that the problem of social solidarity cannot find a satisfactory resolution within the private sphere.

Civil society emerged during Brazilian democratization as a concept linked to its new tripartite form. Civil society expressed the new tripartite conceptualization in its own way: it linked the emergence of the concept to the process of reconstitution of social ties by the Latin American poor (Alvarez, Dagnino, and Escobar 1998; Avritzer 1994, 1998; Oxhorn 1995) and middle-class sectors (Cheretski 2005; Stepan 1988; Weffort 1982) in a situation in which social actors were under the pressure of an authoritarian regime. Civil society was, thus, understood as being a concept capable of demarcating the newly emerging social actors from both the market, understood as the private economic interests associated with the authoritarian regime, and the authoritarian state. All Latin American authoritarian states with the exception of Mexico have pursued antisocietal forms of social organization through the intervention in trade unions and voluntary associations. Thus, the concept of civil society in Latin America emerged as a tripartite concept adapted to the forms of differentiation between market, state, and society that have consolidated in the region throughout the twentieth century.

Yet, one major caveat remained in the use of the concept of civil society as democratization took place in Brazil: the different forms of connection between civil society and the state (Dagnino 2002; Dagnino, Olvera, and Panfichi 2006a). There were no conceptual tools for understanding these new emerging situations. Some authors argued in the direction of a new corporatism in which civil society organization would play the role of new forms of societal organization to be integrated in the state structure (Reis 1995), whereas others wanted to stress the neopluralist dimension (Avritzer 1997). In all cases there was the necessity of theorizing the new democratic practices in which Brazilian civil society became involved and to figure out the ways in which civil society and the state interact.

Civil society theories during the late 1980s and early 1990s theorized the practices of civil society actors in terms of autonomy. Autonomy in that case was understood in a very broad sense as both organizational autonomy from the state,[3] as well as an independent sphere for state action (Avritzer 1994; Dagnino 1994; Sader 1988). The last dimension of autonomy proved itself very strong during authoritarianism but did not survive democratization. A second phase of both civil society action and analytical theory emerged in the mid-1990s and posed the issue of interdependency between civil society and the state. In the Brazilian case, interdependency was motivated by the association between civil society and democratic deepening (Dagnino, Olvera, and Panfichi 2006a). As Baiocchi argues in chapter 1 of this book, participation has had in Brazil a civil society origin linked to thousands of neighborhood associations and new movements claiming rights and services (Baiocchi, chapter 1). Civil society actors overcame a phase of demarcation of space with the state and started to interact with the state in policy councils (Tatagiba 2002; Tatagiba and Teixeira 2006) as well as in specific projects involving the implementation of public policies (Abers and Keck 2006; Avritzer 2008). In this chapter, I will describe the emergence of civil society in Brazil during the 1970s and analyze its main areas of action during its first phase. I will also analyze a second phase of state and society interaction showing that civil society is still semiautonomous in this second phase (Cornwall and Coelho 2007); that is to say, it interacts with the state, keeping its own organizational dynamics and/or its own process of decision making.

In both parts of my analysis, I will engage in a debate on the critique of the autonomy argument that is going on. Most of the authors who elaborated the idea of civil society in Brazil approached it in terms of autonomy (Avritzer 1994; Dagnino 1994; Navarro 1998; Weffort 1989). Most recently, these approaches have been sharply criticized by Peter Houtzager and Adrián Gurza Lavalle. The authors argued that

> the civil society perspective has a set of features that are shared by the literatures on civil society, deliberative democracy, and empowered participation. They ... bet heavily on, for analytic and normative reasons that are held in common to varying degrees, the rationalising and even emancipating potential of civil society. In broad strokes, the core of the civil society perspective is a normative dichotomous reading of the relations between state (authoritarian) and society (democratic); and, the conviction that authentic civil society actors are a democratising and rationalising force of public action because of their deliberative logic (vs. interest-based), decentralised nature and rootedness in the social life of local communities, and autonomy (for most people, from the spheres of the state, political parties, and interest groups politics). (Houtzager, Lavalle, and Acharya 2003)

In this sense, the authors deny the tripartite argument; they claim that civil society autonomy is a normative principle based on "authors' faith." They also argue that interest-based politics shows that autonomy does not exist. I will in both parts of this chapter engage with them, showing that the civil society perspective that proposed the autonomy argument is not a normative conception based on an article of faith but rather an empirical conception derived from civil society actors' real engagements in politics during the democratization process or, as the book's organizers posed in the introduction, "civil society appears in Latin America's oppositional discourse in the 70's and 80's as part ...

of the oppositional discourse of social movements." I will also show that the authors completely miss the complexities of Brazilian civil society and only analyze the movements that strengthen their arguments.[4] In the last part of this chapter I will propose a model for analyzing Brazilian civil society based on the "new move towards left and center left governments which advocate participatory democracy which has taken place in Brazil and other parts of Latin America" (Alvarez et al. 2014).

Civil Society in Brazil: Explaining the Emergence of the Concept and the Practice of Social Actors

The emergence of civil society in Brazil was a consequence of several processes: the anti-societal form assumed by authoritarianism in Brazil, which moved the poor population from the countryside to the cities and relocated the poor population within large Brazilian cities without providing minimal social services (Caldeira 2000; W. Santos 1987). Brazil passed through one of the fastest process of urbanization in history, being mainly a rural country in the 1940s and having more than 80 percent of its population living in cities by the end of the twentieth century (Santos 1987). In the process of moving from the countryside to the city, the Brazilian poor were stripped of all rights and settled in places with no social services. Cities such as São Paulo, Rio de Janeiro, Recife, and Belo Horizonte, among other capitals, sharply increased their population without having the capacity or the financial means to increase social services. The poor in Brazil passed through a process of deep deprivation of basic social services such as water, sewage, electricity, and transportation. The organization of the Brazilian poor to claim social services is one of the origins of Brazilian civil society.

A second reason for the emergence of civil society in Brazil was due to the technocratic characteristics of the process of economic modernization in Brazil, which transformed city planning, health, and education policies into technocratic issues (Escorel 2005). The Brazilian authoritarian regime assumed a technocratic view of urban development and public policies and tried to integrate middle-class actors in its top-down project of modernization. One of the important changes that took place in Brazil between 1964 and 1974, the first ten years of the authoritarian regime, was the increase in size and complexity of the Brazilian middle class. Both the state sector and the private sector increased their size during this period. However, middle-class actors reacted to this project and organized forms of collective action and associations to dispute these technocratic elements.

A third reason that led to the reorganization of Brazilian civil society was the opposition of liberal and middle-class sectors to the lack of rules and accountability in the political and civil processes, an opposition that transformed the Brazilian Bar Association (Ordem de Advogados do Brasil or OAB) into one of the main oppositional groups to authoritarianism. Although these characteristics had been present throughout the whole democratization period (1977 to 1988, when the new Constitution was enacted), they interacted with another factor that made civil society more or less autonomous vis-à-vis the state: democratic deepening that took place during and after the Constitution, making process and the way neoliberal reforms interacted with civil society actors responsibilities in public policies. As a result of this interaction, different patterns of relations between state and civil society emerged.

The key element for the organization of civil society in Brazil was the change in the position of the Catholic Church on the authoritarian regime and its involvement in the social organization of the poor population. The church was closely involved with the state in Brazil throughout the country's process of nation building (Bruneau 1974). From the mid-1950s on, in a few cities, particularly in the city of São Paulo, emerged new grassroots forms of organization linked to the Catholic Church: the Catholic Labor Action (Juventude Operária Católica, or JOC), Catholic University Action (Juventude Universitária Católica, or JUC), and Catholic Student Action (Juventude Estudantil Católica, or JEC) were all created in the early 1950s with the support of Cardinal Carlos Carmelo Motta and expressed the new way that the Catholic Church saw its engagement in Brazilian society, as a supporter of labor and student movements (Doimo 2004, 160). However, the Catholic Church was still deeply divided on the role it should play in Brazilian society during the 1950s and the 1960s, and important sectors of the Catholic Church in Rio de Janeiro and Minas Gerais gave popular support to actors who wanted the breakdown of democracy in Brazil. The so-called Marcha da Família com Deus pela Liberdade (Freedom March of the Family with God) was organized by church sectors in large Brazilian capitals (Dreifuss 1982). It was after the Medellín Council that the church as an institution involved itself with the organization of the Brazilian poor. In large Brazilian cities—such as São Paulo, Belo Horizonte, Recife, and Vitória—the church provided a "protective umbrella" for the organization of the poor. This would bring about the formation of many movements that would eventually lead to the health movement in the city (Lima et al. 2005), the labor pastoral that would be at the root of the new unionism (French 2006; Sader 1988), and the land pastoral that would contribute to the creation of the movement of landless peasants. Thus, the change in the position of the Catholic Church on its association with the state is at the root of the reorganization of Brazilian civil society (Casanova 1994).

Brazilian civil society emerged or reemerged during the so-called process of "liberalization" of Brazil that started during the mid-1970s (O'Donnell and Schmitter 1986, IV). Liberalization was a moment in which the Brazilian authoritarian regime released control over some prohibitions on voluntary associations' public meetings but not on the rules of political competition (Stepan 1989). Thus, students could reconstitute their movement; many professional categories such as architects, engineers, and lawyers started to meet again and to reorganize their associations; many trade unions started to be run by the opposition. It was as a result of this process that many forms of civil society organization emerged: (1) the organization of popular movements of the urban poor at the local level; (2) the organization of the *sanitarista* movement for a Unified Health System; (3) the movement for a National Urban Reform; (4) the organization of members of professional associations such as lawyers, doctors, and university professors, among others; (5) the development of many forms of organization in the Brazilian countryside including the emergence of the MST (Movimento dos Sem Terra) (Navarro 2002).

The process of democratization and organization of many forms of collective action that took place between 1974 and 1985 led to impressive changes in the country's pattern of association (Avritzer 1995, 2000, 2004; Baiocchi 2005; Gay 1994; Santos 1993). Brazilian democratization produced a marked increase in the propensity to create voluntary and independent forms of association. Renato Boschi (1987) has shown that more voluntary associations were created in Rio de Janeiro between 1978 and 1980 than during the entire previous democratic period. Wanderley Guilherme dos Santos (1993) showed a similar phenomenon for all categories of voluntary associations in the country's largest cities. It is worth calling attention to several aspects of this phenomenon: the total number of associations doubled in São Paulo in the 1970s and tripled in Belo Horizonte in the 1980s. The increase was lower in Rio de Janeiro than in the other two cities because, for political reasons, it already had the most voluntary associations. It is also important to note that there has been not only a quantitative increase in Brazilian associative life (in Belo Horizonte and São Paulo, the pace of increase in associations is twice the population growth in the same period), but also a qualitative change. Some forms of voluntary associations that were not very strong before the mid-1970s grew in number and influence: for instance, the number of neighborhood organizations increased from 71 to 534 in Belo Horizonte. In Porto Alegre between 1986 and 1990 the number of neighborhood associations rose more than 50 percent, from 240 to 380 (Baiocchi 2005). The increases in São Paulo and Rio de Janeiro were also very impressive: of the neighborhood associations in the two cities, 97.6 percent and 90.7 percent respectively were created after 1970. Other types of associations were also relatively new in all three cities: 92.5 percent of the health professionals' associations in São Paulo were created after 1970, as were 76.2 percent of the lawyers' associations in Rio de Janeiro (Santos 1993). In Belo Horizonte, all twenty-nine associations dealing with environmental, human rights, and ethnic issues were created during this period. Thus, it is possible in all four cities to speak of an impressive change in the pattern of association, a process that involved an increasing propensity to associate, a greater number of associations, new associations for claiming material benefits such as community improvement, and the emergence of associations dealing with postmaterial claims, such as environmental protection and human rights.

The changing pattern of association in Brazil supports both the density (Putnam 1993) and the equality (Cohen and Rogers 1995) arguments that have prevailed in the literature on the effects of voluntary associations on society as a whole. The rapid growth in the number of associations shows that voluntary associations are not simply linked to the country's process of historical formation, as Gabriel Almond and Sidney Verba and even Robert Putnam have claimed, but can change relatively quickly in response to political circumstances. In Brazil, the trigger for this change was an authoritarian experience in which the state intervened deeply into the everyday lives of the poor by removing slums from the central areas of Brazilian cities and encouraging a huge migration from the countryside to the cities, without providing adequate health, education, and infrastructure for the poor. The latter phenomenon shows also the egalitarian side of the process of formation of voluntary associations (Cohen and Rogers 1995, 43). Voluntary associations in Brazil grew in general. However, the ones that grew the most were those dealing with the insertion of the poor into politics. The poor organized themselves in Brazil in order to claim access to public goods that were unevenly distributed in Brazilian cities. Access to health, education, treated water, and sewage was very low in all regions of Brazil at the end of authoritarianism in Brazil (W. Santos 1987). Thus, the organization of the poor in voluntary associations created a new force that could influence the process of distribution of public goods.

The main characteristic of Brazilian civil society during this first period was the claim for autonomy from the state and political parties. Brazil's history from the 1930s to the 1980s saw strong state intervention in the societal organization (W. Santos 1979). During Brazil's democratization, the claim for autonomy had two major meanings:

(1) Organizational autonomy from the state. From labor to all other forms of organization of the poor, autonomy has been claimed by social actors in the period from 1977 to 1985. Autonomy can be understood in two different ways. Conceptually, it can be understood as "self-regulation, responsibility for own problems, and a non-conflictive partnerships with the state" as pointed out in the Baiocchi's chapter for this book. Empirically, it was understood in Brazil during the early 1980s as acting without asking authorization from the state and, at the same time, as ignoring the limits the state had placed against voluntary associations. This meant that new voluntary associations would arise and new forms of presenting claims in public to the state would become common practices. It was in this period that common practices that we may call a democratic repertoire of collective action by Brazilian voluntary associations emerged. Practices such as petitioning state authorities, demonstrating in front of public buildings, and organizing grassroots assemblies emerged in this period.

(2) Autonomy also meant trying to propose forms of administration of policies without the participation of the state. Thus, the health movement of São Paulo during the first half of the 1980s proposed a form of organization of health policies independently from the state. Still, during the VIII National Health Conference, there were groups proposing the self-organization of health care independently from the state (Avritzer 2008; Sader 1988). The movement for urban reform, in a similar fashion, proposed forms of local democracy independently from the state that would be able to veto state action related to urban policies (A. Silva 1991). Uampa (União da Associações de Moradores de Porto Alegre) in Porto Alegre during the late 1980s proposed decision making on budget issues based on a council of neighborhood associations. These are a few examples among a large number of cases. Thus, during the first phase of civil society organization, we can note two phenomena: the first one is the quantitative growth in the number of voluntary associations dealing with the organization of the poor and the participation of civil society actors in the implementation of public policies. The second phenomenon is the idea that civil society may deal with public policies independently from the state (Baiocchi 2014 and in this book). This was the conception of important movements such as the health movement and the urban reform movement. It is important that the critique by Houtzager and Lavalle on the idea of autonomy completely misses the Brazilian civil society debate in the moment of the country's democratization. Civil society autonomy was the result

of self-understanding on the part of civil society actors of their role during democratization rather than a normative idea introduced by intellectuals.

The concept of civil society autonomy was deeply reelaborated as Brazilian democratization evolved. There is a watershed between the claim for autonomy from the state in this first phase (1977–85) and the claim for autonomy during the second phase (1985 to today): the National Constituent Assembly. Civil society actors deeply engaged in the elaboration of social policy chapters during the National Constituent Assembly in Brazil. Thematic movements, such as the health movement and the National Movement for Urban Reform (MNRU, Movimento Nacional de Reforma Urbana), proposed parts of the 1988 Constitution's chapter on their areas and had a strong presence during the elaboration of the Constitution. After the approval of these chapters, that in a way resembled their proposals for political participation, they engaged in closer interaction with local governments. This triggered the transition to a new phase that I call democratic deepening. In the next section of this chapter, I will show how civil society actors in Brazil moved from a conception of autonomy, understood as the capacity to propose policies independently from the state, to another conception in which a conception of political interdependency was expressed. This move deeply redefined civil society action and generated a new concept of autonomy.

Civil Society and the State after the Constituent Assembly:
The Creation of Political Interdependency

The period between 1985 and 1988 marks a watershed in Brazilian politics. In 1985, President José Sarney called for a National Constituent Assembly (NCA, Nacional Constituent Assembleia). The Brazilian NCA allowed popular amendments and triggered a popular campaign to get signatures to many proposals linked to public policies. Some of the most important civil society movements, such as the health and the urban reform movements, joined this process in the same way that other important social actors such as the Central Labor Trade Union (CUT, Central Única dos Trabalhadores) or the MST also joined the campaign for popular amendments (Whitaker 1994). This was a first important moment of a process of democratic deepening that created participatory institutions in the areas of health, urban planning, environment, and social assistance. A popular amendment in the area of health was presented with a little less than 60,000 signatures (Rodriguez Neto et al. 2003). Its main elements were obliging the state to be the main health provider in Brazil, creating a unified national health care system without preconditions for access, decentralizing the provision of health care, and fostering broad popular participation in the elaboration and implementation of health services (Pereira 1996, 446). In spite of the late insertion of subcontracting to the private sector, the health care movement was very successful within the Constituent Assembly. The Constitution's Article 198 described health as an integrated system organized according to the following principles: (1) decentralization, (2) unified care with a focus on prevention, and (3) civil society's participation in policy deliberation. Yet, the Constitution required the elaboration of a health care statute to further specify the forms of participation required in article 198.

The elaboration of the Health Care Statute (Lei Orgânica da Saúde, LOS) took almost two years after the completion of the Constitution of 1988. The LOS was elaborated in Congress and sent for the approval of President Collor in 1990. Collor vetoed law 8.080, which sought to institute a unified health care system with broad political participation, singling out the articles on participation for veto (Rodrigues and Zauli 2002). Collor's veto created a stalemate with Congress, generating protests throughout Brazil. Law 8.142 in December of the same year solved the stalemate by regulating participation in the health care system through the establishment of two institutional figures: the health conferences and the health councils. According to the law, health councils "will be permanent deliberative institutions composed by representatives of the state, services providers and representatives of the population. They will act in the elaboration of strategies as well as in the control of the implementation of the health policies at each one of the levels of government" (Brasil 1990). In the aftermath of the approval of law 8.142, many Brazilian cities enacted local laws. They all forecasted the organization of health councils based on the parity between civil society and the state.

In a similar fashion, the MNRU also made a proposal of a popular amendment in the area of urban politics. The popular amendment on urban reform was presented to the National Constituent Assembly with 131,000 signatures and unleashed a lobbying battle with conservative real estate interests. The thematic Committee on Urban Issues and Transportation did not initially attract many powerful constituents since conservative sectors had more pressing short-term issues (Arturi 2001). Real estate interests inside the Constituent Assembly sought to transfer the final decision on urban issues to another arena outside the constitution-making process in order to avoid the automatic application of any new legislation (Saule 1995, 28). Most of the subcommittee's proposals on urban issues remained intact, but they were integrated with a requirement that cities should have "Master Plans,"[5] a proposal made by

Centrão, the informal organization that gathered conservative interests during the Constituent Assembly. Thus, Paragraph 1 of Article 182 of the Constitution of 1988 required both the participation of civil society organization in decision making on urban issues and a "city master plan approved by City Council as mandatory to all cities with more than 20,000 inhabitants" (Brasil 1988). All urban reform proposals were made dependent on fulfilling this clause. The consequence of the subordination of the urban reform agenda to master plans was what the Brazilian legal tradition calls a statute or an infra-constitutional process of specifying constitutional law. Thus, a thirteen-year battle followed since the proposal of the regulating legislation by Senador Pompeu de Sousa and its approval by the Brazilian Congress in December 2001. After the thirteen-year legal battle in Congress, the so-called Statute of the City was approved in 2001. The Statute of the City requires mandatory city master plans with public audiences in every Brazilian city with more than 20,000 inhabitants.[6] In these audiences the presence of civil society associations is required. Hundreds of Brazilian cities today have city master plans in which civil society and state actors interact closely.

At the same time that participation in the areas of health and city master plan unleashed an intense form of participation based on civil society associations, participatory budgeting was also on the rise. Olívio Dutra was elected mayor of Porto Alegre in 1988, and introduced participatory budgeting in the city. Participatory budgeting (PB) is a local participatory policy that responds to the plight of the poor in major Brazilian cities. It includes social actors, neighborhood association members, and common citizens in a process of negotiation and deliberation that takes place in two stages: a participatory stage, in which participation is direct, and a representative stage, in which participation takes place through the election of delegates and/or councilors. The PB in Porto Alegre from 1990 to 2004 involved two rounds of regional assemblies, one round of intermediary meetings, and the operation of a councilors' body called the PB council year-round. In these meetings, the population attends an assembly in each of the regions. In each of these assemblies the floor is open for about an hour, during which citizens express themselves about what has been taking place, about possible disagreement with the administration, and about what should be done in the region in the coming year. Participation in these meetings is crucial because they constitute the basis for participating in the remaining parts of the process. Participation in these meetings is individual, but individuals throughout the registration process are required to demonstrate membership in voluntary associations. In addition, the regions in Porto Alegre that have showed more willingness

TABLE 2.1. Affiliation with associations in São Paulo

	Total	Total Participants	Link with Association Formal	Link with Association Informal
BASE: Total sample	2403	447	166	281
	100%	19%	7%	12%
Participation in Associations	18.6	100	100	100
Religious	10	51	38	59
Civil	9	49	62	41
Nonparticipation	81			

Source: Avritzer 2004.

to participate through the process of implementation of participatory budgeting (1990–92) were the ones with the highest number of neighborhood associations (Wampler and Avritzer 2004). Again, we can see a strong interaction between membership in civil society organizations and the operation of a participatory process by the state. With the consolidation of participatory budgeting in Porto Alegre, many leaders of neighborhood associations would participate in the PB council.

Thus, we can note a strong change in the focus of participation from the mid-1980s to the mid-1990s. During the mid-1980s, Brazilian civil society was concerned with autonomy, democratization of public policies, and the establishment of forms of public control over the state. From the mid-1990s on, Brazilian civil society became concerned with the establishment of a broad form of public participation in most areas of public policy and with joining the state in the implementation of participatory forms of public deliberation. This has led to a change in the way in which autonomy vis-à-vis the state was conceived. In a survey on associated actors applied in São Paulo, these mixed characteristics of the participatory profile of participatory actors emerged. We asked 2,043 people randomly sampled throughout the city whether they participate in civil society. Table 2.1 above shows the results.

The above data show for São Paulo an interesting phenomenon to be analyzed. It shows a sharp division between the individuals who belong to voluntary associations in the city, with 59 percent of the participants belonging to religious associations and 41 percent belonging to civil associations. This autonomous logic is best expressed in the fixed number of participants in these associations throughout a long period of time. This core is stronger than the rest of all associations taken together. Additional data also show different behaviors: members of religious associations organize more independently from the state, whereas the civil group is the one who has joined public policies arrangements. Houtzager and Lavalle, in their eagerness to criticize the autonomy argument, miss the larger group which constitutes São Paulo civil society.[7] Empirically missing this group allows them to present the autonomy argument as ideological when, as a matter of fact, their research design only allows them to find the groups they are interested in discussing.

The key issue to be understood in the process of organizational transformation of Brazilian civil society is that civil society growth and political influence in Brazil did not follow an autonomous or a dependent logic,[8] but rather a mix between autonomy and dependency. The implementation of participation by two PT administrations and their later derailment by conservative administrations also led to contracting and expanding movements in São Paulo's civil society. The civil group in São Paulo's civil society is highly dependent on the implementation of participatory public policies by the city. The religious group has a more stable dynamic; thus, affiliation in religious associations did not change very much in between the different PT administrations. Data for São Paulo show that civil society associations have a core made up of religious forms of public participation that have an autonomous logic vis-à-vis state policies.[9]

However, as we take into account the group of more specialized civil society associations in charge of pressuring for the broadening of access to public policies, we see a different phenomenon going on. Within this group of associations, we see a decrease in the number of people joining voluntary associations in the year 2004. This decrease seems to be related to the changes in political society and in the partnership between state and civil society associations in these different areas of public policies. If we take the area of health or housing, which have been traditional movements in the city of São Paulo (Doimo 2004; Sader 1988), we see a sharp decrease in 2004 in relation to previous levels of organization and participation (see table 2.2). Not by chance, these have been areas in which previous administrations strongly invested in the partnership between state and civil society and in which joint actions between state and civil society have been derailed between 1993 and the year 2000 during conservative administrations. Thus, what we have in terms of civil society organization in the city of São Paulo is both a core of religious associations whose participation is strong and varies very little when there are changes in the political system and a second group of associations related to public policies in which participation varies according to the willingness of the state to establish or to derail forms of collaboration with CSOs (civil society organizations).

TABLE 2.2. Used to participate but no longer participates

Type of Association	Participates	Used to Participate but Is not a Member of any CSO
Neighborhood associations	2.0%	6%
Health associations	0.7%	2%
Housing movement	1.0%	3%
Religious associations	9.0%	8%

Source: Avritzer 2004.

In addition to that, it is important that forms of collaboration between civil society and the state vary a lot not only in São Paulo but in most Brazilian cities. In some cases interaction takes place at the level of deliberation and establishment of policy priorities, and in other cases it takes place at the level of implementation of a few policies on the ground. This involves the fact, approached by this volume's editors, that civil society plays a double role: "it represents and mis-represents, it politicizes and de-politicizes issues" (introduction). Thus, civil society in Brazil should be seen from this perspective: how it organizes itself in different ways and how it interacts with different public administrations. In the final section of this chapter, I will propose a model for understanding contemporary Brazilian civil society.

Between Autonomy and Political Dependency: A New Perspective on Brazilian Civil Society

Brazilian civil society is a new institution created by two processes: the reaction of popular sectors to the antidemocratic process of modernization of the country that sharply interfered with their daily lives, and a process of democratization that has made civil society associations strong players in the process of democratic deepening. During the 1990s, the democratic field further differentiated itself and different political projects became part of the civil society participatory drive (Dagnino, Olvera, and Panfichi 2006). One of the projects involved joining participatory institutions with the aim of being part of the process of political deliberation. The other involved being part of a large service sector created by most municipalities in Brazil and being in charge of *convenios:* the implementation of specific public policies. The two groups show radically different characteristics. Brazilian civil society is constituted by two strong groups—one group of religious associations that participate in self-helping activities and the other involving the organization of the urban poor for claiming public goods. These groups have a differentiated presence in Brazilian cities. In the city of São Paulo, the self-help group is important, particularly in its eastern district, and the self-help group is also strong in other cities such as Recife and Belo Horizonte. This group is less strong in Porto Alegre due to the higher influence of Left sectors in the formation of civil society in the city (Baiocchi 2005). It is impossible to underestimate the role of the Catholic Church in the formation of this group. Not by chance is it stronger in the cities where the Catholic Church pursued more progressive politics. This group is highly politicized, but it interacts less with the public administration than the public policy groups and keeps its conception of autonomous politics.

Brazilian civil society is also formed by a group of associations strongly connected with the state in the implementation of public policies. This group has deep links with the Left tradition in Brazil and stronger ties with the Workers' Party. This is the group whose participation drive varies according to whether the Workers' Party is in power. When the Workers' Party is in power, its associations expand in terms of members, showing a sort of expanding and contracting dynamic that is part of São Paulo's civil society behavior. The pattern of participation of this group has changed very much during the last ten years as participation became more technical and passed through a depoliticization process (Baiocchi 2014, 21).

The religious group is more stable, its members are more linked to the habits of the poor population, and geographically it is located outside the center of the city of São Paulo. The public policy group seems to be the one that is more strongly engaged in the democratization of state action. However, it is located overwhelmingly in the center and western districts of São Paulo, which are wealthier regions.[10] It also has a very strong presence in Belo Horizonte and Porto Alegre. This is a group that many times crosses the boundaries between politics and culture (Alvarez et al. 2014, 32).

It is impossible to understand Brazilian civil society without analyzing the two groups at the same time. Associations dealing with public policies are constituted most of the time by Left actors of middle-class ascendancy located in a few Brazilian cities (particularly in the case of the city of São Paulo). Taking civil society to be represented by this small group of associations dealing with public policies, as Houtzager and Lavalle do, amounts to ignoring the huge process of organization through which the Brazilian poor have been engaged during the last thirty years for the sake of reconstructing an old leftist argument on the party connections of civil society actors. It is better heuristically and politically to consider the broad array of actors and aims that constituted Brazilian civil society as a pluralistic institution. Brazilian civil society changed the pattern of association in the country. Brazil has made a difficult transition from a country with a strong tradition of privatism to a country with several political traditions, among them the tradition of independent civil society associations. If it is true that these associations interact with both the state and political parties, it is also true that they do it from the perspective of a pluralistic civil society that understands itself as being independent from political parties. It is precisely the independence of Brazilian civil society from political parties that allowed it to survive the political crises that have plagued Brazil during the last few years and keep its legitimacy among broad sectors of Brazilian society. These are associations and actors who are now engaging more selectively with the federal government, proposing policies at national conferences and many times joining public demonstrations for the improvement of the quality of public services in large Brazilian cities, such as the demonstrations of June 2013.

NOTES

1. Civil society was dualist in another sense, namely, in the demarcation between civil and uncivil (Ferguson, xx). In this second strand, it has been a form of exclusion of those not belonging to a so-called modern and individualistic society (see Alvarez et al., in the introduction to the book). Though I have written elsewhere on that dimension of civil society (Avritzer 2002), I will not treat it in depth in this chapter.

2. This is one of the ways of bridging a recent literature on indigenous movements and civil society. On the one hand, few among the recent indigenous movements have claimed a civil society inheritance (see Zamosc 2006, on the struggle for indigenous rights in Latin America). However, they claim the reconstruction of bonds of social solidarity that can be traced to civil society. This opens the room for one of the debates in the book on the relation between the insurrectionary Indian and the more moderated forms of claiming rights for the indigenous populations. (See Alvarez et al. 2014, 6, introduction to the book).

3. Brazil has had a model of corporatism introduced during the 1930s by Getúlio Vargas who governed the country from 1930 to 1945. In the Varguista model the state had the prerogative to intervene in trade unions and civil associations. The Ministry of Labor could remove by his discretion the president of trade unions. In addition to that, all civil associations in order to be able to act would have to be registered in notaries that obeyed state laws on the acceptable and nonacceptable form of organization (Weffort 1979). During the democratization process, the issue of civil society as well as trade union autonomy emerged strongly in the public space. Both civil society movements and the trade unionism claimed autonomy from the state (Keck 1989).

4. The empirical ground for all these findings is a limited empirical research carried out through a snowball method in the city of São Paulo. Houtzager and Lavalle interviewed 219 people in the city of São Paulo, all of them indicated by umbrella organizations as connected to politics, such as CUT (Central Labor Union). The problem with this method is that it overemphasized political associations and missed informal associations organized by the poor in São Paulo (see Avritzer 2004).

5. City Master Plans, or *planos diretores*, are not per se conservative devices though they have been considered conservative by the urban reform movement due to the way they emerged during the Constituent Assembly. Some Brazilian cities such as Porto Alegre have had city master plans since the late 1970s. The novelty introduced by the Constituent Assembly was the link between having a city master plan and being able to introduce the other devices approved by the Constitution in its urban chapter (see Avritzer 2008).

6. There is a very interesting case of cancellation of the city master plan of Salvador, Bahia, due to the violation of the public audience requirement during Imbassay's administration as mayor of Salvador. The city of Salvador called just one public audience during the preparation of its city master plan. The public audience was not broadly publicized and the Ministério Publico and the Brazilian public prosecutor asked for its cancellation, which was granted by a Salvador court (Avritzer 2008).

7. It is important to have in mind that due to severe methodological flaws, Houtzager and Lavalle miss this category. For Houtzager and Lavalle, "Ties to unions and religious organisations do not appear to affect civil society actors' propensity to participate" (see Houtzager, Gurza Lavalle, and Acharya 2003, 8). These authors used a snowball methodology to enter a universe that is very pluralist. All their entry points were related either to trade unions or to party-sponsored forms of actions. No wonder that they did not find the category that is the most expressive in terms of participation in the city of São Paulo, which is religious associations. In a survey on a statistical sample of the population, with 2,403 interviews, this emerged as the most important category (see Avritzer 2004).

8. Houtzager and Lavalle misunderstand the most important characteristics of this change in perspective by civil society actors. According to the authors, "The dichotomous reading of state-society relations, born in the struggles against various types of authoritarian rule in the second half of the 1970s and 1980s, has been central to the literature on civil society and has unfortunately been reinforced recently. . . . Although discussions of civil society have abandoned early oppositional interpretations of state and society in order to address a series of emerging themes—citizenship, new participatory spaces, local development, governance and accountability—the dichotomous interpretation of state-society relations has largely been reproduced, albeit in more subtle forms (Houtzager and Gurza Lavalle 2003). . . . The metaphor suggests autonomous agents who cross paths, discover certain overlapping interests and choose. To engage with each other through various institutional mechanisms." In contrast to the authors' argument, all the recent literature on civil society emphasizes the interconnections between civil society and the state. The reason is very simple: the full autonomy model was linked to a conception involving social actors and not to a preconceived normative conception as the authors claim (see Avritzer 2004; Dagnino 2002; and Dagnino, Olvera, and Panfichi 2006).

9. It is important to have in mind that most religious associations in Brazil are informal in the sense that they do not register themselves with the notary for the registration of voluntary associations. This also created important differences between religious and public policy associations (see Avritzer 2004).

10. Due to the division of the archdiocese of São Paulo by Pope John Paul II during the early 1980s and the later appointment of conservative bishops to the new archdioceses in the city, the southern region of São Paulo remained an underorganized region, with low numbers of associations and people affiliated to associations (see Doimo 2004).

Chapter 3

___

THE MAKING AND UNMAKING OF A
NEW DEMOCRATIC SPACE

ANDREA CORNWALL

This chapter reflects on the limits of the way in which citizen and civil society participation is framed in narratives of participatory governance, and the implications that this has for understanding the politics of institutionalized participation. It tells the tale of the making and unmaking of a new democratic space in a periurban municipality in the northeastern Brazilian state of Pernambuco, tracing the transformation of a vibrant site for citizen engagement into what Ranjita Mohanty (2007) has called an "empty space." It considers the options that open up when democratic spaces close down: from "strategic non-participation" (Cortez Ruiz 2004) to tactical reengagement via other people and other spaces. It begins by reflecting on contemporary narratives of civil society. It goes on to tell the story, in three installments, of the municipal health council, an institution that almost achieved the promise of its democratic design, but faltered in the process as a confluence of factors conspired to permit ambient cultures of politics to color, and contain it.

Unpacking "Civil Society"

"Citizen" participation is often conflated with the participation of "civil society." With this comes a normative narrative that pits the good guys against the bad guys: civil society, so the story goes, brings into the moribund, compromised, or plain ineffective workings of government vigor, commitment, local knowledge, and a concern with issues of equity and social justice. At the same time as concerns about accountability and representativeness are acknowledged, they make barely a dint in a persistently rosy view. There is much to commend in this narrative. It has produced and sustained a burgeoning population of nongovernmental organizations to whom the work of the state has been contracted (Edwards and Hulme 1997)—some of whom have come to supplant the state altogether. But the normative assumptions that constitute the basis of this narrative are wishful at best, and misguided at worst (Chandhoke 2003; Robins, Cornwall, and Von Lieres 2008). And they are profoundly unhelpful if we wish to understand the political complexities of the dynamics of participation in the new democratic spaces that have mushroomed in recent decades.

A significant critical literature unpacks the way civil society has been defined and explores the perverse effects of enthusiasm for "civil society participation." Sonia Alvarez (1999) shows how "NGO-ization" has neutralized and disfigured Latin American social movements. Evelina Dagnino (2005) analyzes what she terms the "perverse confluence" as the clamor of social movements to be heard and the outsourcing to the Third Sector of the neoliberalizing state converge on positing civil society as the panacea to the ills of contemporary governance. Islah Jad (2004) shows how, in the Palestinian context, the influx of donor funds for NGOs led to rifts within and the eventual weakening of the Palestinian women's movement—and the loss, at the grassroots, of political influence, as the void that was left was ably occupied by Hamas. Others highlight the dense linkages between civil society and the state, and the symbiotic relationship between them, undermining simplistic narratives that present an autonomous, and often oppositional, civil society (Houtzager 2003; Skocpol and Fiorina 1999).

In many countries, civil society organizations are deeply dependent on governments for financial support, compromising their autonomy. In small-town Brazil, the setting for the empirical case on which this chapter is based, there is much to lose in falling foul of government. It is not only the withdrawal of financial subsidies and other kinds of direct contributions that is at stake. It also involves contracts, jobs, and the other fruits of patronage. All this puts a brake on how oppositional civil society can actually afford to be. Add to this the webs of relationships, identifications, and allegiances thickened by shared party political affiliation, religious faith, and ethnic identification, and the result is a complex mesh of entanglements.

For all that the conceptual separation between the state, the market, and civil society served the development theorists of the 1990s, the global conjuncture is proving much more complex to categorize. As civil society, state, and market merge into each other, creating assemblages with increasingly blurred borders, it becomes impossible to disentangle these categories as bounded, distinct entities. "Civil society" becomes a residual category, composed only of what it is not. It belongs to a discourse in which fundamental issues of accountability and obligation are obscured in an ideologically driven focus away from government and toward some loose nexus of private sector, civic organizations, and society at large.

What we find in practice is a departure from this normatively driven discourse, and a lack of correspondence between the purported virtues of civil society and empirical evidence about actually existing civil society. Neera Chandhoke (2003) points out that one of the distinguishing features of the civil society discourse is precisely the tendency for the normative to prevail over the empirical. *The Conceits of Civil Society*, as the title of Chandhoke's book aptly puts it, are many; as she points out, civil society is only as civil as the society that gives rise to it. The normative conception of civil society is extended as a descriptive term for a diverse mass of institutions that include many which are neither civil nor particularly societal. As this chapter suggests, there are evident hazards in what amounts to willful disregard of the uncivil tendencies in civil society, not least that these organizations are no less prone to precisely the kind of ills—clientelism, corruption, and so on—that the promotion of civil society is supposed to "cure."

By reifying an imaginary realm in which people associate for the purposes of advancing the common good, the civil society narrative doesn't help us understand where and how *governments* can be effective or progressive. The presumption that it is civil society that is doing the "civilizing" leaves out the possibility that the relationship might work in the opposite direction: the very possibility that the impetus for democratization might come from within the state itself seems barely thinkable. Yet the state can be a driving force and vital source of support in democratizing citizen engagement, as well as in democratizing governance. The absence of political parties from the civil society narrative, as if politics lay in a completely separable domain, obscures the possibility of progressive governments that can transform the state as well as society.

By displacing party politics in this way, civil society becomes a pristine arena for the pursuit of the common good. Yet political party sympathies and affiliations are common among those who engage in public affairs. The cultures of politics and practices of political parties can have a huge impact on the public domain, occupying a major part of the political landscape. Leaving party politics out of the picture puts questions of ideology to one side. Yet it is precisely ideological questions that are the lifeblood of any debate about the common good, and with it the possibility of constructive disagreements about how our society should work that are constitutive of the political (Mouffe 2005).

To explore some of the issues raised here, I tell the story of a municipal health council in Cabo de Santo Agostinho, a municipality in the hinterlands of metropolitan Recife in the northeast of Brazil, with a population of around 140,000 and a mixed agricultural and industrial economic base. I describe how the municipal council was "conquered"—in the Brazilian sense of a triumphant gain, rather than colonization—and lost by civil society. By looking at a process of de-democratization, the dimming of democratic impulses and undoing of democratizing rules, in which civil society organizations were not only complicit but active agents, this chapter hopes to shed light on some of the complexities of civil society engagement in governance in practice and some of the fundamental questions of representation, power, and accountability that this narrative obscures. This chapter draws on research conducted over a period of visits of roughly three or four months apart over four years, repeat interviews with key protagonists, anthropological field notes, minutes of meetings, a failed survey of civil society organizations, participant observation in a dozen or so meetings of the *conselho* and analysis of the minutes, and later, the recordings of council meetings, over the period 2004–12.

Making Cabo's Conselho: 1994–2004

Modeled on radical experiments in São Paulo's East Zone during the dictatorship and given institutional shape by Brazil's "Citizens' Constitution" of 1988, a participatory governance system was put in place in Brazil in the 1990s. Sectoral participatory management committees were established at the three tiers of government—federal, state, and municipal—tasked with holding the executive branch of government to account for budgetary management and implementation of sectoral policy, *controle social* (literally "social control," social accountability). Over the course of the 1990s, *conselhos de saúde* (health councils) were put in place throughout the country, extending from the most distant municipalities in the Amazon (Shankland 2010) to the dense metropolitan areas of the south (Coelho 2008). They took a prescribed institutional form, composed of equal parts of "state" and "civil society." The state half was divided into two equal parts: commissioners and managers (*gestores*), and service providers, including health workers in the public health system and private providers. Composition of the "civil society" half of the council was initially left relatively open, with guidance suggesting a diversity of civil society stakeholders, serving as representatives of registered civil society organizations, not as individuals. A variety of means of selection, including elections—with electoral constituencies as narrow as the candidates themselves or as broad as participants at a public assembly—are used to decide who participates. Tenure is for two years, and *conselheiros* are not permitted more than two terms; as their presence is as representatives of a given organization, however, continued tenure can be easily secured by switching organizations.

Cabo's conselho was formally established in 1994 after the passage of the Municipal Basic Health Law. But it was not until 1998 that the institution began to gain functionality. Cabo's political history is distinguished by shifts of government between progressive reformers and conservative or populist administrations and a history of social mobilization and progressive social movements. The conselho was instituted on the eve of a Conservative (Partido do Frente Liberal) administration that did not care much for popular participation; it became a rubber-stamping mechanism filled with political appointees who would not make any trouble for the government. A popular front formed among civil society organizations of all kinds—from those associated with neighborhood associations and social movements to the progressive Catholic Church, unions, and other NGOs and civic associations. Together, they mobilized to insist that the municipal government honor its obligation to democratize the conselho and to hold a municipal health conference, an event that the government is constitutionally obliged to hold every two years to deliberate key priorities for municipal health policy and at which a similar parity of representation of "state" and "civil society" defines the composition of delegates.

When popular "postcommunist" (Partido Popular Socialista, or PPS) mayor, Elias Gomes, took over the municipal administration in 1998, he called in a veteran of the *movimento pela reforma sanitaria* (health reform movement, whose members are popularly known as *sanitaristas*) who set about reinvigorating the conselho, and putting systems and structures in place to guarantee its functionality. The fourth municipal health conference of 1998 marked the beginning of a new era. Hundreds gathered to debate priorities, hosted by an administration with a stated commitment to popular participation in their slogan "Cabo—aqui voce participa." The conference served to bring Cabo's civic organizations together to elect their choice of representatives. One of them was medic and feminist activist Silvia Cordeiro, veteran sanitarista and coordinator of Cabo's most prominent NGO, the Centro das Mulheres do Cabo (the Cabo Women's Center). As the new conselho moved to elect its chair, Silvia was chosen to lead the process of democratic renewal. For two successive terms, she led the conselho in intense debates and institutional reforms aimed at fulfilling its democratic promise. With evident relish, a senior government official of the era recalled the protracted arguments that would take place in conselho meetings: the lifeblood, he said, of democracy. Every government, he argued, needs to be kept on their toes; they should thrive on such challenges. Any government worth its salt, he went on, ought to be able to make itself open to question in this way: it is those who act as if they are beyond question who are dangerous for democracy.

Three provisions put in place during this period sought to ensure a sufficiently diverse representation of Cabo's civic organizations. The first was that the ten civil society representatives should come from different organizations than their ten substitutes, who would step in if the representatives could not be present for a meeting or were expelled from the council for persistent nonattendance. This effectively doubled the number of organizations represented on the conselho from ten to twenty, even if only the ten representatives had the right to vote. The second was that seats on the conselho were to be contested and allocated within particular categories. Half the seats were reserved for communities of place: neighborhood associations from the different regions of the municipality. Half were for communities of interest: social actors representing particular publics—such as women, disabled people—or interest groups, such as faith organizations. The third was that the election of user and worker representatives could only take place in the biannual *conferência* and that any changes to the regulations could only take place in the context of the conference.

The conferência of 2003 was one of the most successful and inclusive that the municipality had seen. Hundreds attended preconferences in the conselho's (then) four administrative areas, electing over 700 delegates to take priorities to the municipal level, where deliberations came up with 179 resolutions. The election of the new cohort of conselheiros at the conference resulted in an impressive diversity of representation. Half were women. User representatives' ages ranged from early twenties to mid- to late sixties. There were several black Brazilians, representing neighborhood associations as well as the black movement. There was a blind representative from the disabled people's movement. Representatives of the churches were from politicized organizations: the Movement of Progressive Evangelists (Protestant) and the Christian Workers' Movement (Catholic). Health worker representatives ranged across medical hierarchy, from a hospital-based doctor to community health agents.

For a third term running, the elected chair was a civil society representative: a retired public official, with no medical training and elementary education, hailing from one of the poorer barrios of the city. Many conselheiros were associated with or sympathetic to the Workers' Party; the majority of the most vocal members were card-carrying members. At that time, there was a faction of the Workers' Party who were broadly sympathetic to what the PPS was trying to do in terms of popular participation, which made for what one senior health manager described as "constructive co-operation" between those representing users and the state. In practice, this could take the form of pitched battles and tense standoffs within the conselho. Radical democracy demands no less; after all, as Chantal Mouffe (1999) observes, the consensus seeking that underpins some versions of deliberative democracy dims the passions that fire politics, with inevitable exclusions.

Senior health bureaucrats spoke of the need to deepen democracy in the municipality through creating spaces for disputes like these; they affirmed, in rhetoric at least, the value of having to account to society for what they were doing, even if at times conselho meetings became scenes of heated interrogation. The "Super-Secretaria" (chief secretary) for social policies in the PPS administration spoke fulsomely of the conselhos as "an opportunity for people to grow, to deepen democracy, to make debates—in this city, where we have such diversity" and as the "collective intelligence of society." For her, as for a number of the other senior managers in this administration, the principal problem was that civil society was not yet up to the task of making the most of these spaces: they pointed out that representatives often failed to consult those they claimed to represent, pursuing personal projects rather than the public good, and they spoke of a lack of understanding of what it meant to be a representative, of insufficient understanding of the health system and public finance, and of expectations of paternalism from the government. The solution was seen to be capacity development that would go beyond the kind of skills building and information about the health system that was currently on offer; in their radical democratic vision, there was a vital role for the progressive state to play in *civilizing* civil society.

For them, the conselho was a site in which conselheiros could learn democratic practices that they could take into engagement in other spaces. The conselho was, to them, less a site for the democratizing effects of civil society engagement than a "school for citizenship." Learning how to be more democratic in this arena could, they thought, help to inculcate and promulgate democratizing practices that could, in turn, civilize civil society organizations that were as much shaped by the ambient clientelist, paternalist, and authoritarian political culture characteristic of the region as other political spaces. But there was a permanent tension between the democratizing possibilities of this institution and the extent to which conduct within it was patterned by politics as usual. Silvia observed: "There's a culture of rights, a language of rights and demands in the *Conselho*. But there's also a culture of paternalism. What the population demands restricts what is possible, the idea of 'users' restricts to the users of services rather than a broader view of users as citizens. It is about favours versus rights; much of the time, it is still about favours."

The conselho of 2003–5 reproduced Cabo's diversity in microcosm; its representatives also represented a diversity of modes of representation. Some had been chosen by their organization. But others simply assumed this position because they were the organization's leaders. Few, I was told, passed anything back to the organization, nor sought opinions prior to meetings. Effectively, people said, they behaved like elected municipal government councilors (*vereadores*): speaking for those who elected them without any consultation with them. Some had simply found themselves an organization willing to host their candidature; at least one was a would-be vereador who switched organizations for each round of elections and treated the role of representative as an entry ticket to a space of power where he might be more easily noticed by the party-political masters, and some hoped that if they could prove their mettle here, they might get a job with government.

Others seemed to be on the conselho for very different reasons; several members appeared to show little interest in proceedings and remained silent—and occasionally asleep—in meetings. A further cry from vibrant civil society participation would be hard to imagine. There was, for example, the woman that people called the "silent nun." Her organization benefited from government contracts; her role on the conselho, it was surmised, was to raise her hand to vote with the government when required, to demonstrate her loyalty. There were those who liked to travel, especially to far-flung destinations like Brasília; one took pride in coming into the conselho office with a little plastic photo album full of pictures of her at meetings around the country, regaling the administrator with tales of the shopping opportunities these visits afforded.

In the run-up to the election of a new cohort of civil society and health worker representatives in 2005, changes in the internal regulations substantially undermined the diversity that the conselho had achieved and with it any semblance of independence from party politics and government. The unmaking of the fledgling democratic space established in the conselho was more swift and devastating than anyone could have anticipated.

A New Conselho, a New Administration: 2004–2007

The municipal election of 2004 brought an end to the two terms in office of the PPS. The mayor put up his son as his successor. Few in the municipality had ever heard of him. Elias Gomes Jr. was trounced at the ballot box. With the Workers' Party (Partido dos Trabalhadores, or PT) trading votes with Recife, the fate of the leftist conjuncture was sealed. The populist Center-Right Brazilian Workers' Party (Partido dos Trabalhadores Brasileira, or PTB) formed the majority municipal government, in alliance with the right-wing (Partido do Frente Liberal, or PFL), joined, after some internal dispute, by the PT.

I had seen in conselho meetings over the course of 2004, before the change of government, a spirited defense of the principles of controle social. The chairperson never let an opportunity to challenge the government pass him. He especially relished arguing with the municipal health secretary, who was permanently on the defensive. Representatives from the two most powerful NGOs in the municipality didn't hold their fire when debates became heated. Debates were almost always about the conduct of the government in relation to questions about public finance; there was little or no discussion of health policy. This is, in many respects, entirely consistent with the role of the conselho as an institution put in place to monitor the implementation of policy, rather than make it. But there was also a pervasive lack of interest in the content of health policy, with the long and detailed presentations given by visiting health system officials often being greeted with abject silence when it came to questions, or quickly brushed over in favor of lengthy debates on procedural matters that were more about the conduct of the conselho itself. But these were generally conversations between a relatively small number of people, who were principally health workers and civil society representatives who knew each other from the Workers' Party. Most of those representing civil society remained passive. Some spoke rarely, many never. They would file into the meeting room, take their seats, and sit through meetings that could last well over three hours and never even raise their hands.

The period between administrations saw the conselho meeting monthly, as usual, and taking charge of the situation: a particularly memorable meeting was one where no government representative was present, but in which the conselho continued to go about its business, approving minutes, debating a full agenda, reporting on activities and plans. The incumbent administration entered with the characteristic pitch of a new government, blaming the outgoing administration for corruption and inefficiency and promising the conselho something better—once they had straightened out what they said was a parlous state of affairs in the administration of health services in the municipality.

Two months into the new municipal administration, it was evident that they were not willing to fund the conference at which the new cohort of conselheiros were to be elected. The health conselho chair argued that he could not and would not extend anyone's mandate, including his own. It would be, he argued, illegal to do so and would set an antidemocratic precedent. Therefore, he proposed, an assembly should be held instead. After a fierce debate in the conselho—because to do so would breach regulations constructed foreseeing precisely this eventuality—the motion was passed.

The assembly was attended not by the diversity of Cabo's civil society organizations, but by the candidates themselves. Rather than having the seven hundred or so delegates elect new representatives, the candidates voted among themselves. Many were from small rural associations and had little or no previous experience of engagement with conselhos. They were, people told me, put up to it by those within the municipal government who wanted acquiescence from the conselho and were prepared to offer favors in exchange. Some eighty civil society organizations registered to contest for places. Thirty were found to lack the correct credentials: some existed only in name; others had no official papers of registration. A number were widely believed to be fronts for politicians.

In May 2005, the new conselho was sworn in. The chairperson was asked by the municipal administration to stay on for a further term; flattered, he accepted. Parity between women and men, achieved in the elections of 2003, was quickly lost: 80 percent of the health user representatives on the new conselho were male. Representation from the black or disabled movements reverted to zero. The younger members of the previous council were also gone; most were at least in their mid-thirties, with an average age around the mid-forties.

During 2005–7, there was still some semblance of the old council left in the deliberations in monthly meetings. Flames would be stoked by a passionate disagreement over issues of policy, and it would be just like old times. But increasingly the council came to represent a rubber-stamping apparatus; the government would come with PowerPoint presentations and people would sit dulled by the whole affair, not even bothering to ask questions. Part of the problem was that those with the experience of a conselho in which there was vigorous questioning of municipal government health policy had mostly left. In their place were those who had been recruited by contacts inside government, rather than those activists who had shopped around for an association to represent.

For those who interpreted their roles as requiring them to behave like elected councilors in the legislative chamber, there was as little semblance of the kind of engagement with their constituents as among those in the municipal legislature. For those who interpreted their roles in more descriptive terms, there was no perceived need to consult at all. And for those who were brought into the city in numbers to pad out the seats in the conselho, there was little sense, or so many of the older *conselheiros* told me, of what they were there for at all, let alone what or whom they should be representing. They remained entirely silent.

There were a couple of high points, where the energies of the old activists were galvanized. The municipal health conference of May 2006 was one such moment; it lifted spirits and affirmed all that these events can be so good for, as well as coming up with an agenda that reendorsed the progressive vision for publicly funded health services that constitutes all that is best about the Brazilian national health service. It was refreshing to see male community activists arguing with passion about how to best deliver services for cervical cancer screening. It was heartening to see the municipal state secretary deliver a ten-minute defense of why the municipal government wanted to focus its limited budget on amplifying preventive medicine—explaining, reasoning, justifying, rather than simply informing. And it was uplifting to have the conference motion passed with resounding force that deplored the municipal government for its lack of democracy in creating a separate table at which health managers were served their lunch.

But while the conference stimulated a temporary buzz, it was soon back to business as usual. Most of 2006 was spent in a protracted inquiry concerning the way the outgoing municipal administration presented their closing accounts. That there was nothing to be done about something that had happened didn't seem to come into it; the whole debacle took so much time and energy that the few who had been reenergized by the conference and had re-engaged began to drop out. By the end of term of the conselheiros of 2005–7, the council was a pale shell of its former self.

The Flagging Promise of Controle Social: 2007–2010

At its strongest, the conselho had lacked the independence to really live out the promise of controle social. Representatives of neighborhood associations were vulnerable to pressure from municipal government—as one put it at the time, "those who disagree may find they are the ones who have their *subvençoes* [regular subsistence funds given by the municipal government] cut." Some had the additional concern of alienating the health workers on whom their communities were dependent if they raised issues concerning the quality of care, attendance in clinics, or corruption. All of the NGOs represented on the conselho had contracts with the government for the provision of services. Under these circumstances, speaking out against the government could mean jeopardizing the survival of the organization itself, a risk few were willing to take.

It became evident in the conselho elections of 2007 that organizations that were once active in the council were no longer bothering to engage at all. The most vocal community leaders had long vacated the council. So had the vocal, and engaged, representatives of "progressive" Catholic and Evangelical (Anglican) church organizations. And even those who were not at all active, but who came to every meeting, had stopped turning up. The silent nun had gone back to her convent. The leaders of small neighborhood associations who would listen keenly but rarely speak were no longer there either. There were still some familiar faces. But the mood was very different.

I made a trip to Cabo in March 2007, shortly before the election of a new cohort of councilors. There was a lot of strategizing going on. The rules had changed again. Categories had been created within which people needed to contest for seats. And those who remained in any position to contest what was happening in the conselho had been slimmed down into one such category and forced to compete with each other for a seat. They had entered into an alliance to share power between them, half for each over the course of the two years. This had been rumbled by the ever-vigilant, but now former, chairman, who was making it a point of principle to take to Brasília an injunction against organizations sharing tenure in this way. But it wasn't all bad news. Fostered by a progressive left-wing state government and capacity development initiatives sponsored by the federal and state governments, there were new actors. A nascent association of sex workers had come to the council in early 2005 asking for help in establishing a base in the town; two years later, their leader was standing for election. An organization of pensioners had begun mobilizing for rights and was becoming active on the conselho. And a gay, lesbian, bi, and trans association had just been set up, and was seeking a means of representation in the conselho.

For those who could remember the heyday of the conselho, though, there was little optimism. One spoke of how lonely he now felt, looking around him and knowing that there was only one organization who would back him up when he began asking questions. Four years before he had spoken with a glow in his eyes of how the conselho was a space for growth and learning, of being patient and persistent, of the contribution the conselho was making to the realization of the promise of democracy in Brazil. "It's a long process," he had told me in 2004. "You need to be persistent or else you lose energy for it; it's something that helps you to grow, and it's something that's evolving, gestating." I had bumped into him leaving the municipal health conference in 2006, and he had said, "It's good to be here, to be heard, to name our desires, to be with each other here as civil society making our demands on the government. It gives us strength, the strength to be what civil society should be: we need to be the ones that hold them to account for doing these things, these things that are our desires."

Now, it seemed, he had lost that energy. 'The place is like a desert," he told me. He was pinning his last hopes on the federal training scheme that was about to be implemented; it could be, he said, that the problem is lack of knowledge, and this training course will teach people what they ought to be doing. And if that doesn't work? "If it doesn't work, well, we might as well shut the door."

A year earlier, Silvia and I had discussed what was happening to the conselho. She had emphasized how important it was not to give up hope. She had spoken of how vital it was to maintain a civil society presence in the conselhos—even if they had turned dysfunctional. "Os espaços conquistados não devem ser abandonados" [conquered spaces should not be abandoned], she had told me, mimicking the rhythm of "the people, united, will never be divided." Now she wasn't so sure. She spoke of the energy it took to engage in these institutions, of how her organization had to reconsider the time it was dedicating, weighing up what they were *not* able to do as a result. There were echoes here of Srilatha Batliwala and Deepa Dhanraj's (2004) observation that orchestrated participation can end up absorbing so much energy that women have no time to mobilize to address the bigger questions affecting their lives. But, Silvia argued, these times will pass. The issue for organizations like hers was to prepare for the return of a more democratic administration in the future. And there were some gains to be had from the current situation; thinking strategically had led her organization to reflect on its own positional power—and on how to use that power to open up spaces for others.

What of those who worked in the health system, especially those who had been with the conselho for years as health worker representatives and came along to meetings because they were committed to the conselho and what it stood for? When I had first met the health worker conselheiros, in 2004, I had been struck by their commitment. Over the years that followed, I had continued to be impressed: they rarely missed a meeting, and contributed as actively as they could under the constraints that they faced—especially lower-level health workers on insecure contracts, nervous about being seen to speak up against their employers. By 2007, they were no longer representatives. I sought them out. One after one they regaled me with stories of how dysfunctional the conselho had become, and how frustrated they felt about it. But all of them were fired with passion rather than deflated by despondency. Three of them swore that they were going to stand for election next time around: they weren't going to let all the hard work they and others had put into the conselho go down the tubes. For one, that passion came from a lifetime devoted to the vision of a Brazilian national health service that makes the right to health a reality. This was her lifeblood. She was not giving up on it. For another, service to her union and to the health workers she represented was uppermost in motivating her, along with an intense sense of irritation with what was happening politically, with the outsourcing of services to Third Sector organizations and shunting of burdens onto communities. She wasn't giving up either. For the third, it was not politics but a deep sense of moral duty to her patients that motivated her. She spoke of how the conselho allowed her to fulfill that duty, and how there was no way she was going to stop struggling for that.

Those to whose door the fate of the conselho might be brought were the health manager representatives on the council, the *gestores*. What did they have to say? They continued to underscore the importance of community participation, much as they had when I first interviewed them when the municipal government came into power in 2005. Their vision as public health officials had less to do with democracy than with improving service delivery and enlisting people in improving their well-being. Their brand of communitarianism meshed with the paternalistic populism of the current mayor and his promises to do the right thing for "his" Cabo because he knew what people there needed.

Changing Places

A central theme in the civil society narrative is that of the battle of civil society actors against the all-powerful, all-controlling state—a battle for democracy, rights, and justice. The civil society narrative leads us to the conclusion that the diminution of the democratic space of the conselho was the responsibility of the state. With a change of government to a Right-of-Center populist administration with a penchant for infrastructure, the political will to support popular participation had indeed vanished. Democracy was deadened with the return to paternalistic government, with its deployment of clientelism and authoritarianism to secure hegemony. As the populists co-opted civil society organizations, there was a corresponding demise of engagement in holding the state to account and in any sense of answerability among the public officials running the municipal administration.

This is certainly part of the story. But it is by no means all. First, the story also features actors who are much more ambiguously placed, such as public health officials who occupy senior positions in the executive and are committed to the democratizing reforms envisaged in the architecture of participatory governance. Within the state—some in positions that they acquired as a result of gaining visibility and connections as conselheiros—are also former civil society representatives on the conselho, who played an important part in the struggles for democratization that shaped its birth. Their political party colleagues remain in civil society, although most are now no longer involved in the conselho. These links and loyalties run far deeper than those associated with their positionalities on either side of the civil society-state divide.

The story is made yet more complex when the microdynamics of power are closely observed. The person with the greatest positional power, the municipal health secretary, arrived in post shortly after there had been a series of changes made to the internal regulations that had so severely reduced the conselho's inclusiveness; he had little idea of what existed before. Busy firefighting in a context where resources were ever more stretched, he did his best to attend meetings, but deferred to others to manage the conselho. This left considerable space for those who could claim the experience to do so, including people with personal and political projects to pursue. In effect, the conselho was captured not by "the state," but by some of the individuals who worked for the government. That so little challenge was mounted by civil society was because the most active and vocal either had their hands tied because of dependencies on the state, or had long since abandoned the conselho after tiring of wasting their time listening to unproductive wrangling about procedures rather than engaging in any debate of substance about health policy. Or, indeed, because they had found other ways to do business with the administration—like the civil society leader who said being on the conselho was useful because she got to know the key health officials in the administration, whose doors she could now knock on when she needed anything, rather than wasting time in the conselho meetings.

Ultimately, then, it was a combination of politics, projects, and personalities that led to the shrinkage of the democratic space of the council. Party politics polarized the council for a while, giving rise to disputes and animated disagreement but ultimately producing quiescence. The coalition that formed the current municipal administration captured the political loyalties of most of those within the conselho. And those who were not politically inclined had their own projects in any case. Some saw the conselho as a place in which to get noticed, and get closer to the government, a place that could launch them into a new career, or at least get them a job. Several had made that transition. Now, they returned to the council as representatives of the state, sometimes mimicking precisely the conduct on the part of government officers that they once so deplored.

The control of the council rested, by the end of 2007, with a health worker who had gradually gained considerable operational power under the leadership of a distracted health secretary. She had created a civil society organization through which to channel demands of a very specific kind: for more resources and recognition for a stigmatized disease. Those with the kind of vision of controle social that the architects of the system of participatory governance in Brazil had in mind had receded into the background, either giving up on the council or moving on to other things. Those who were left were, by and large, "ordinary people" with little history or connection to social mobilization, representing neither movements nor interest groups nor organizations. Having little to represent, they had little to say; the vast majority remained silent through the course of the meetings I observed. On top of all this, those health workers and managers who remained dedicated to the ideal of controle social were having to deal with far more pressing epidemiological and health systems issues—not least the serious challenge of finding doctors to staff rural primary care units—and the conselho was the least of their priorities. In such a setting, the colonization of the council by those who would pursue small-time politics, secure compliance or alienate dissenters, and procure career advancement was all too easy. There is much here to add empirical flesh to the arguments of Peter Houtzager (2003), Theda Skocpol and Morris Fiorina (1999), and others concerning the mutuality of civil society and government. There is also much food for thought about the naïveté of assuming that civil society participation is in itself any kind of democratizing influence on the governance institutions created as intermediary spaces between citizens and the state. In this example, it was civil society activists who "stole" the newly created democratic space that existed in the municipality, for reasons of politics, but also for personal reasons, who connected with their own careers and promoted of their client networks with figures inside the political administration. It was civil society who "sold" the institution that some of them had been instrumental in creating. And it was civil society organizations that stood by watching this happen, colluding, complying, and ultimately not contesting what was going on.

Yet, amid all these complications, the council carried on its daily work. As I observed in my field notes on a visit in 2007:

> In some ways, what I am hearing is the usual story—people who were once on the council complaining that things are not how they used to be. But when I enter the council office it's all very busy, there are plans to buy new computers, to digitize the archive and get organized for the training course. There's a quotidian doing that carries on irrespective of ructions and troubles and just about everything bar a municipal election, a getting on with things because there are always things to be getting on with. It's this very getting-on-with-things that comes to represent the council's institutionality—it's about that which becomes so regularized as to be part of the everyday.

I asked the conselheiros whom I had got to know over the years, people who maintained an investment in the conselho: well, is it now time to give up? And they said, unanimously, no, not yet—we need investment, we need people to be trained so they know what they are there for and what they should be doing, we need conselheiros who are not so closely linked with the government. The big question that everyone was stymied by was how to get there and whether indeed it would be at all possible within the limited democratic space of this current administration. Some believed that it was, that what was required is training and persistence. Some believed it would be better to withdraw, regroup, invest in other spaces outside those "invited spaces" (Cornwall 2002) that are now so under the grip of the administration, and build toward a return to a more progressive municipal government.

For all the best of intentions and for all the democratic designs that can be made in progressive times, unless a culture of participation has been created to bolster and support efforts to expand public engagement—one that can live beyond these efforts, after progressive government has gone—it is very hard to insulate participatory spaces such as Cabo's health council from the play of politics. These are after all *political* and not just management spaces. But, as Michel Foucault (1991) pointed out, spaces of power can also be spaces of resistance and transgression; and the configuration of power relations within participatory institutions where citizens come together with representatives of the state is constantly shifting, constantly being reconfigured. And those citizens bring cultures of participation from other spaces, notably from the spaces of collective mobilization, the vibrant social movements that have been so crucial a part of Brazil's democratization story—not just those from the *movimento sanitarista* who were such a vital motor of change in the health sector, but also the feminist movement, the black movement, the movement of people with disabilities, and movements for sexual rights and for environmental sustainability and economic justice, as well as the neighborhood social movements of the 1990s out of which so many local associations were born. *Their* political cultures also shape the cultures of engagement in institutionalized "invited spaces" such as the conselho, as terrains for contestation.

As long as those who have some degree of independence are able to exercise voice in these spaces—those in the health system with secure jobs, those from civil society who do not need to depend on the government's favors, and the ordinary citizens whom the civil society discourse tends to obscure—the optimism of activists who brought Cabo's conselho into being may not be misplaced. Around the corner there could indeed be the possibility that its democratic promise might be realized.

Postscript 2012

After a period in which health workers took control of the conselho, it became reenergized with a wave of training and investment in institution building, supported by federal-level initiatives and a progressive left-wing state government. On my last visit to Cabo, in 2012, I saw the makings of a renaissance in a now-matured conselho, with the return of some of the older and more experienced players, now the senior statesmen and women whose prodding of the government was done in a manner that delivers a gentle and lighthearted reminder that they know what's what. A black, wheelchair-bound representative of the disabled people's movement had been elected as chair. Analysis of the minutes for the intervening years shows a growing appreciation of the complexity of dealing with difficult health policy issues, and that out of the training and support has emerged an institutionality that includes inspection teams and subcommittees.

Chapter 4

___

UNCIVIL SUBJECTS, UNCIVIL WOMEN

Civic Participation, Ambivalence, and Political Subjectivity among
Grassroots Community Leaders in Porto Alegre, Brazil

BENJAMIN JUNGE

"Benjamin, we are participating in the construction of a more democratic society." Clovis Lopes spoke these words as he showed me around a low-income
district of Porto Alegre, the capital of Brazil's southernmost state, Rio Grande
do Sul. It was a warm mid-autumn afternoon in March 2002 and this seasoned
veteran of local grassroots politics, who also hosts a daily show on an evangelical radio station, had generously offered to show me some of the neighborhoods where he works. There was both delight and solemnity in Clovis's
manner of speaking: he savored his words and yet spoke carefully, as if out
of respect for what each one might signify. At the time, I was new to Porto
Alegre, just two months arrived from the United States and still looking for a
place to settle in for my fieldwork. Clovis's zeal was exciting to me and seemed

to reflect Porto Alegre's international reputation as a hotbed for participatory democracy and hope in a post-Seattle, neoliberal world. By 2002, that sentiment had reached fever pitch.

The Workers' Party (Partido dos Trabalhadores, or PT) had controlled Porto Alegre's city government for three consecutive terms, affording more than a dozen years for the PT to enact its vision of politics rooted in transparency, inversion of elite priorities, and decentralization of government power through direct citizen involvement. Among the PT's success stories was the Participatory Budget (*Orçamento Participativo*, or OP), a local initiative giving ordinary citizens a substantive voice in municipal planning and funding allocation. During the 1990s, the OP brought about massive infrastructural improvement in Porto Alegre's poorer neighborhoods, coupled with unprecedented rates of direct citizen participation.[1]

For two years in a row, Porto Alegre had hosted the World Social Forum (WSF), a mammoth international summit focused on grassroots alternatives to neoliberal globalization. This exposure cemented Porto Alegre's reputation as a setting where, as the forum's slogan goes, "Another World is Possible" and where that world is envisioned and implemented by "the people" rather than by government or corporations. Finally, 2002 was the year during which PT founder and ex-metalworker Luiz Inácio Lula da Silva campaigned in his fourth bid to Brazil's presidency. Unlike the previous attempts, during which his perceived radical posturing had been held against him, Lula was now the clear frontrunner. The PT's moment in national, regional, and municipal politics had arrived and Porto Alegre—the PT's stronghold—had played a key role in this process.

Back when I first met Clovis Lopes, he struck me as a poster child for this new form of citizenship, more or less fully interpellated as a participatory subject. Indeed, he seemed to recognize himself and his community within the discourses of Porto Alegre's new civic participation initiatives. Subsequent encounters with Clovis, however, brought me to perceive a much more complicated relationship between this individual and the discourses of citizenship circulating around his city. In other contexts, Clovis seemed more interested in salvation than citizenship ("first the human being, then the citizen"), or expressed indifference or outright cynicism about Porto Alegre's civic participation initiatives ("Citizenship is a bogus discourse [*papo furado*] . . . I don't want to hear about it anymore"). From the vantage point of Clovis's earlier declaration about "constructing a new society," these statements seemed to reflect contradictory or ambivalent political sentiments, and within the conceptual frameworks of the civic participation scholarship I had read, I found little analytic space to make sense of them. Did his seemingly contradictory statements indicate a less durable or defective form of citizenship, or a lack of authentic conviction?

As elements of political sentiment among grassroots community leaders, ambivalence, contradiction, and refusal have been underexamined in dominant, liberal scholarship on civic participation in Latin America since the 1990s. Much of this scholarship—including some of the most innovative and sophisticated work to date—has been informed by a set of normative assumptions, including a problematic narrative of progress (i.e., participation is inherently "good for democracy"); an overfocus on public, participatory spaces to the exclusion of nonpublic interactions and identities; and the attribution of much more coherency and durability to political subjectivity and identity than exists in the rough-and-tumble of raw experience.

The scholarly celebration of civic participation in the 1980s and 1990s coincided with a parallel celebration of on-the-ground social movement struggles, in which an active civil society was promoted as the sine qua non of the deepening of democracy across the region. The backdrop for the emphasis on civil society in the social movement sector was the concurrent consolidation of the neoliberal economic development paradigm characterized by privatization and trade deregulation. Indeed, the vision of citizen participation promoted within the development discourses of international agencies such as the World Bank and U.S. Agency for International Development (USAID) (glossed as the "Civil Society Agenda" by this volume's editors) was eerily confluent with social movement discourses (Dagnino 2003, 215).

In this chapter, I examine encounters with official civic participation discourse among a handful of grassroots community leaders from poor neighborhoods (*vilas*) from a Porto Alegre district called Beira Rio.[2] Focusing on the two initiatives most closely associated with Porto Alegre's reputation as a "leftist utopia," the World Social Forum and the Participatory Budget, I put two analytic vantage points into dialogue with each other to bring to light discursive contests between "civil" and "uncivil" forms of civic participation: on the one hand, the ideal participant envisioned in the official discourses of each initiative; on the other hand, "on the ground" reflections on participation by grassroots leaders, represented in ethnographic narratives constructed from interview transcripts and my own field notes. The time frame is early 2003, with Lula still in the honeymoon of his presidency and the PT's hold on Porto Alegre city politics mature, many would say, to the point of overripeness. I begin with additional critique of hegemonic social science approaches to studying civic participation and then outline an ethnographic methodology to address concerns raised. Next, I move through two ethnographic narratives (one of the World Social Forum, the other on the Participatory Budget), highlighting the ambivalence and refusal evident as community leaders encounter discourses of idealized civic participation. Finally, I discuss the implications of this approach for civic participation research in general and the Porto Alegre case in particular.

Dominant Approaches to the Study of Civic Participation: Critique and Corrective

Much social-science scholarship on Latin American social movements to date has been informed by a set of assumptions about the democratic character of civic participation, about the lines separating movement members from nonmembers, and about the formation of political subjectivity. At times echoing the neoliberal logics of World Bank/USAID discourses (glossed by Alvarez et al. as the "Civil Society Agenda," this volume), this body of scholarship reflects a set of prescriptive and normative assumptions about the contribution of civic participation initiatives in Latin America to political and economic transformation (i.e., redistribution of wealth, sustainable development, democratization of political institutions, etc.). For example, in assessing participatory initiatives in Brazil such as the municipal health councils and participatory budgets, scholars have tended to be idealistic, presuming that new forms of civic participation are "good for democracy" because of their focus on public, collective deliberation and opposition to clientelism and political opportunism. This conceptual orientation distracts scholarly attention from the possibility that new forms of civic participation constrain—rather than expand or deepen—democracy (that, for example, initiatives in participatory citizenship may depend on clientelistic, nontransparent modes of decision making as much as their nonparticipatory antecedents; cf. Auyero 2003a).

Second, civic participation scholarship has tended to understand the spaces and communities of participation as coherent, bounded entities "consisting of individuals committed to the goals of the collective" (Wolford 2006, 335). This presumption contradicts the fact that many individuals enter into (and exit) participation initiatives with ambivalence, with reluctance, and without explicitly political motivation. By privileging overtly public, deliberative spaces of participation, this body of work has tended to leave nonpublic, nonpolitical spheres of participants' lives more or less in the shadows.

The third shortcoming has been a problematic understanding of motivation and subjectivity, typically written from rational-choice or Marxist per-

spectives and assuming a clear motivation or intentionality behind an individual's entry into civic participation (Wolford 2006, 339). By likening civic
participation to a marketplace of ideas, this formulation in effect binds the
concept of agency to a liberal economic framework. With this assumption in
place, informants who state contradictory or "nonpolitical" reasons for participation are treated as lacking agency or fall out of the analysis altogether. Stemming from this deep emphasis on rational intentionality, previous studies have
also tended to attribute to political subjectivity undue coherence, durability,
and autonomy compared to other forms of self-awareness. Instead, processes
of civic identity formation are saturated in social logics and the ongoing reproduction of other forms of self-awareness (e.g., along the lines of gender, class,
ethnicity, sexual orientation, etc.).

To address these epistemological problems, three overlapping methodological moves are appropriate. First, attention needs to be given to ambivalence, contradiction, and refusal in the narratives of individuals involved in
civic participation initiatives (Abu-Lughod 1991, 137–62; Hart 2004, 97–98).
Next, a more nuanced approach is needed to analyze the senses of self as
experienced by social actors as they move in and out of participatory spaces.
Here, I conceptualize subjectivity to be constituted as individuals move in
and out of the subject positions of a range of discourses and social practices
(Merry 2003, 349; Moore 1994, 55). Such movement is often shaped by "concerns and ideas about the kind of person one would like to be and the sort of
person one would like to be seen to be by others" (Holloway 1984, 238).

Third, the inductive approach delineated above, which begins with ethnographically observed experience to generate theory subsequently, should be
put into dialogue with a more formal analysis of civic participation discourse.
In other words, the contours of ideal participation should be mapped out,
so as to understand clearly the subject positions to which individuals are
held. Against an uncritical reading of interpellation (Althusser 1972), however, I am interested in moments of felt ambivalence, reluctance, or refusal
at the prospect of being "taken up" by a discourse and the ethnographically
inferred feelings accompanying this reluctance. Risking a new spin on an old
term, I conceptualize this moment—when the social agent opts to engage or
disengage available ideological scripts—as a moment of "incivility": incivility
toward the discourse. In effect, I am reframing encounters with discourse in
performative terms to highlight the way people *both invest in and parody* the
democratic citizen subject.

The 2003 World Social Forum

BACKGROUND AND OFFICIAL DISCOURSES

The WSF of 2003 brought together a multitude of individuals, groups, and movements under the ideological banner of an emergent resistance movement to neoliberal globalization, understood to increase poverty, intolerance of social difference, and war, and to threaten justice, cultural autonomy, and the environment (Fisher and Ponniah 2003, 2). At the time, the primary neoliberal target was the Free Trade of the Americas Agreement (FTAA), which aimed to eliminate or reduce trade barriers among all countries in the Americas, excluding Cuba. The forum sees itself as a critical counterpart to the World Economic Forum, traditionally held in Davos, Switzerland: Porto Alegre's celebration of diversity, popular participation, and grassroots solidarity—in opposition to Davos's nondemocratic, unrepresentative, and intolerant composition of elitist, rich, white business- and states-men looking out for their own interests.

During the month of January 2003, ordinary Porto Alegrens could scarcely avoid the forum in the comings and goings of everyday life. Media coverage was extensive and sympathetic, and the city's major public spaces were virtually taken over. Against this backdrop, my analysis *begins* with an interest in how the residents of a city known for its distinctive array of leftist politics responded when a massive leftist event came to town. Within the forum, Porto Alegrens were repeatedly congratulated for their accomplishments such as the Participatory Budget. And yet, despite near universal awareness of the forum, most low-income Porto Alegrens did not attend—or even feel invited to— the forum. I begin by mapping out in broad strokes the images of citizenship promoted in official forum discourses, drawing principally from the WSF's Charter of Principles as refracted through local news coverage. It should be underscored that my approach looks at the WSF "from the outside in," rather than examining the internal experiences of participation and broader implications for global grassroots organizing.

The WSF's Charter of Principles hails a global citizen-subject who perceives the threat of neoliberalism and who sees herself as part of a global struggle to contemplate alternatives to the world neoliberalism has imposed. This struggle is advanced through reflexive thought, exchange of experiences, and democratic debate of ideas with other citizens and groups, and is structurally located within civil society, understood as the movement's natural home. In this configuration, civil society stands distant from government (a suspect neighbor since government and party politics are complicit in perpetuating the neoliberal order), and further yet from multinational corporations. Civil society is, moreover, heavily institutional in constitution—individuals without organizational affiliations are symbolically peripheral and illegible within official WSF discourses.

Within local media coverage, Porto Alegre's status as the WSF's host was heavily emphasized, with the city represented as modern, cosmopolitan, and fit to host the summit given its own demonstrated commitment to participatory democracy. This logic—Porto Alegre as the cutting edge in Brazilian leftist politics—was mapped onto a national and global scale: Brazil, under Lula, will lead the world in its struggle against neoliberalism. Newspaper coverage thus proudly conveyed a privileged role for Porto Alegrens and for Brazilians in the WSF process, with Lula as a central figure. Finally, the forum was represented as festive, fun, and part of a romantic revolutionary narrative.

THE WSF AS SEEN FROM THE PARTICIPATORY BUDGET

Three days before the WSF was to begin, I attended Beira Rio's final district-level Participatory Budgeting meeting in the annual cycle. Since the meeting has a full agenda, the forum comes up only twice, and both times by delegates who are also associated with a local NGO called Communities in Action. First to speak is Samuel, a military police officer and a local neighborhood association president: "Folks, we're putting out the word on these activities at the World Social Forum. First there's a march, Thursday at 5:00 PM, that's going to leave from Glênio Perez [downtown plaza], which is a global march for peace. Then, on the 27th, there's a march against ALCA [FTAA], Monday at six, leaving from the Gigantinho [Stadium]. And on the 26th of January, there's a thematic axis which is [called] 'political power, civil society, and democracy,' where some leaders [will be] . . . and I'll be helping them out."

As Samuel begins to speak, people in the room seem to be paying attention. The images he presents are both practical/organizational—there will, for example, be a large-scale march—and of the forum's ideological commitments (i.e., *for* peace and *against* ALCA) and thematic priorities (i.e., "political power, civil society, and democracy"). As is common in meeting talk, Samuel uses "we" in such a way as to the leave the pronoun's referent somewhat ambiguous. (He hasn't, after all, stated whom he is speaking for, and it isn't implicitly clear.) His speaking also asserts a claim to status—the status of one who is "in the know" about the forum's organizational details and ideological orientations. Samuel proceeds to provide more information on the satellite activity he is helping to organize:

We decided to invite all [district] leaders who want to participate, which we think is important, to have this discussion—political power, civil society, and democracy. And, an authority is going to come—we still don't know who it is, but it's a foreign authority that's gonna speak on this theme. It's also to show to the folks at the Forum, external folks, that our society participates and knows a little about politics, a little about democracy, and that here community matters are discussed. So, we'd like, whoever wants to participate, c'mon along, so that we can make some interventions and have a presence there.

Samuel's speaking here aspires to more than simply passing along information. Using a first-person pronoun ("we") to emphasize the importance of the activity's theme ("which we think is important"), Samuel validates the forum and, moreover, associates himself with an entity (presumably the activity's organizers) that has opinions about such lofty matters as "political power, civil society, and democracy." His mention of the presence of a "foreign authority" at the activity underscores the WSF's cosmopolitan character (and, by extension, that of those who participate in the activity). It also serves as a reminder that Porto Alegre's experiments in participatory democracy are of interest to the rest of the world. His enthusiasm for the WSF and his heavy reliance on the forum's own official lexicon underscore the extent to which he has taken up (at least for now) a subject position of official WSF discourse and is encouraging others to do the same.

Soon after Samuel's announcement, the meeting's facilitator, Cesar, who co-founded the NGO Communities in Action, adds the following: "Whoever might want to participate in the Forum […] and know about the program […] all you have to do is get [registered] as an observer there at the Gigantinho [Stadium] and we can go there. We have four workshops, one of them is gonna be the publishing of the book that was written last year, telling the story of our participation in the OP."

As in Samuel's announcement, Cesar's speech positions himself as someone "in the know." By the same token, he is clearly trying to make the forum seem accessible to the crowd in attendance (to dispel the perception of the forum as a closed, elitist gathering). When he starts describing the "four workshops," however, his speaking becomes vulnerable to more cynical readings. At no point does he mention the NGO Communities in Action by name—but it seems clear that this is the "we" to which Cesar is referring. For some present, this is unproblematic and even impressive. For others, his gestures toward inclusion are thinly veiled opportunism: a chance for self-promotion. Postmeeting and walking home, for example, two women, Thais and Sônia, both offered scathing commentaries. Thais, laughing incredulously, had asked me, "Could you believe he was promoting his NGO and that book? He just wants us to buy the book and show everyone his French girlfriend!" Upon hearing this, Sônia wondered aloud, "And for those that don't have their own NGO and a European girlfriend? What bullshit [*xarope*]!"

TALKING UP THE FORUM

I had been surprised and frankly disappointed at how little mention was made of the forum during the meeting. It seemed to me that part of the problem—and at the time I did think of it as a *problem*—was a set of mistaken perceptions of the forum: that it was unwelcoming to women and to individuals without NGO affiliations, and that it was a space of xarope rather than of legitimate sharing of experiences and strategizing. Following an embarrassingly reductionist logic, I reasoned that if people understood that these perceptions of the forum were ill founded, they would *naturally* want to participate. Here I was presuming both that local leaders would recognize the inherent resonance of their grassroots community work and the ideological commitments of the forum, and that they would *feel excited* at the prospect of interacting with social movement activists, NGO workers, and policymakers from around the world.

At the time, I was aware that my feelings and thinking were moving me toward a troubling prospect well known to anthropologists who take a personal interest in the causes and struggles they study: the possibility of knowingly and intentionally inserting myself into the scenes of my research, namely, by taking initiative to get the word out about the forum and to help make the event seem more accessible. With little time before the forum began, I resolved to take this step and, in the next couple of days, made efforts to inform people I thought would be interested. Only at the forum's website—inaccessible to the majority of *vila* residents—could the titles, places, and times of event activities be found. Thus, I went online and stayed up late downloading and organizing program information. Keeping in mind my core group of contacts, I jotted down information for activities related to initiatives in participatory democracy, to women and politics, and to a handful of other themes I imagined to be of interest. Then, I prepared an informal handout for each day of the forum, with activities, places, and times listed. Over the next couple of days, I was able to reach four of my closest community leader friends from around the district—Vera, Bethe, Thais, and Sônia—all women in their forties, all mothers, and all neighborhood association presidents. With each,

I sat down and went over the program, offering suggestions and explaining how the registration process works for nondelegates.

When I show up at Vera's house with program information for the forum, she is welcoming and excited, although somewhat intimidated by what seems a complex registration process and a confusing system of classifying forum activities (ranging from large-scale "lectures" to small-scale "workshops," as well as "panels," "seminars," and "testimonials"). I point out some activities I think she might enjoy and help her find information on workshops organized by the NGO with which Cesar and Samuel are associated. Vera has no *brigas* (arguments) with Cesar, she reminds me, so she feels free to attend events he's involved with. While we are talking, Vera's husband, Paulo, joins us in the living room, evidently just up from a nap. Vera explains that I'm helping her figure out the forum program, and quickly mentions the cultural program—a set of musical and theatrical events planned around the city during the week of the forum. "Jorge Ben Jor [a famous Brazilian pop singer] is going to play at the Sunset Amphitheatre!" Vera says to Paulo—and this gets his attention. Paulo and Vera both like the way the forum brings in interesting, different people from all over the world. It is *chique*—meaning, sophisticated and cosmopolitan. I leave the materials with Vera and Paulo and say I will swing by in a day or so to check in again.

When I arrive at her house, Bethe is welcoming and thanks me sincerely for helping out. She looks through the information and agrees that several of the sessions I've highlighted look interesting. I tell her Vera has suggested a group fieldtrip to attend a session together on Saturday. She says she'll look over the materials and think about it.

When I arrive at Thais's little house, it is a pleasant surprise to find Sônia there as well. Both women say they're interested in attending the forum. Thais, for her part, is interested in workshops on women and HIV. Herself HIV-positive, Thais says she doesn't get out enough and would love to come into contact with different kinds of people (*um povo diferente*). Sônia says, "It won't do to call Porto Alegre the paradise of Rio Grande do Sul!" and declares that she intends to attend one of Cesar's workshops, in which the Participatory Budget is being idealized. She'll come armed with photographs of the present-day reality of her vila to show. Sounding upbeat and more than a bit devious, she says she'll "mess things up" (*bagunçar*) and "scandalize" (*escandalizar*). Sônia's recourse to theatrics in her activism is well known: she once brought a giant dead rat to a public hearing, and it landed this illiterate mother of eight on the front page of the local newspaper (and got the government to speed up municipal trash removal).

When the forum begins a few days later, only Thais actually attends. Vera says she'd rather watch it on television (especially the street parades and musical shows); Bethe tells me on the phone, "Benjamin, I wish I could, but who's going to look after my kids?" (I don't take her statement at face value, as I know she could find someone to watch the kids.) When I swing by Thais's house to take the bus over to the forum with her, Sônia is there as well and tells me why she has changed her mind and will not be attending after all:

> Why am I not going to the Forum? Because I don't like the hypocrisy! I think it's hypocrisy: to bring a bunch of folks here and only show 'em the downtown neighborhoods. They gotta see the reality! I mean, the government, the mayor, he's gotta invite these people to take a walk in the vilas, in the poor neighborhoods of Porto Alegre. And he won't! What does he do? He sugarcoats the downtown area, cleans up the Gigantinho [stadium to be used by the Forum], using a team working 400 hours night and day to get it all spiffy. He oughta show the dirty side! The front of my blouse might be pretty but on the back there are 50 holes . . . Which am I gonna show you? I think this is ridiculous! And the Participatory Budget . . . our piece-of-shit experiment in participatory democracy! It used to work, well some of it did. I mean, we can't just say it never works . . . You have to see the good side of things . . . This democracy that people like Cesar preach, this citizenship that's there, it's a lie!

After blurting out this invective, Sônia gets up to go to the bathroom inside. Thais shakes her head and says, "Once Sônia's mind is made up, she won't listen to anyone. Anyway, she's just intimidated by all the smart people she'd have to deal with if she went to the Forum." Thais appears to have spoken too loudly, as Sônia emerges from the bathroom looking upset. "I need to get home and get lunch on the table," she says and leaves. Soon after, Thais and I take the bus across town to the forum and, after three mysteriously cancelled workshops, we finally attend a panel on homeless people in Porto Alegre. Afterward, we walk around a large cultural exhibition area and before too long, Thais heads downtown to run some errands.

DISCUSSIONS

The preceding ethnographic accounts point to the diversity in perceptions of the World Social Forum of 2003 and bring into relief the disconnect between the forum's internal discourses of participation and how "participation" was understood "from the outside" by grassroots community leaders. Accompanying my network of contacts as they became aware of the forum (and, in some cases, helping them to become aware of it), I have highlighted the range of interests and intentions people had regarding the forum and how they responded to representations of global citizenship, neoliberalism, and festive celebration pervading official discourses and local newspaper coverage. Largely absent from my ethnographic accounts have been overt references to the more utopian elements of official WSF discourse. Indeed, the forum's anthemic proposition that "another world is possible" was rarely taken up in an overt manner by my contacts. Even in Cesar's reflections on the NGO Communities in Action's work, the sense is of necessary improvements on the present world, rather than contemplation of a fundamentally different world. Sônia resents and resists any talk of alternative worlds, viewing such notions as indulgent distractions from the unsolved problems of the existing world. Sônia, like many, feels no sense of "global belonging" to a planetary society; she seems utterly uninterested in the ideals of translocal citizenship, solidarity, and resistance to neoliberalism. To Sônia, this is all smoke and mirrors—the illusion of a radical new politics she has come to perceive through her own cumulative disenchantments with politics in Porto Alegre. In her impassioned statements to Thais and me, there is a sense of resentment at being told to identify with the ideal citizen-subject of official WSF discourses.

Perceptions of the forum are often informed by a gendered understanding of "meeting space" as masculine in character. This understanding appeared repeatedly as my female informants distinguished between the formal program (e.g., workshops, plenaries, etc.) and "cultural" events such as the parades and music shows. In Sônia's diatribe, images of vice-mayors and forum delegates touring Porto Alegre's sanitized downtown neighborhood imply a tantalizing parallel between the hollowness of WSF citizenship and of the hollow promises of men. These gendered readings of the WSF strike me as ironic since they replicate the WSF's own critique of the World Economic Forum in Davos (namely, that Davos represents an overprivileged group of wealthy businessmen and government representatives). By the same token, perceptions of the participants and physical spaces of the WSF vary among my informants: whereas, for example, Thais, who is unmarried, finds the likelihood of encountering "different kinds of people" appealing, Vera's take on the forum is more ambivalent. She is, on the one hand, fascinated by the diversity of participants circulating through her city. On the other hand, she feels somewhat less comfortable entering into the forum's internal spaces of networking and deliberation, preferring in the end to watch the forum on television from the comfort of her living room. All other things being equal, the WSF public requires a caution from women not required of men. Married women, in particular, are likely to confront the possible interpretation of WSF participation as inappropriatcly "loose."

The Participatory Budget

BACKGROUND AND OFFICIAL DISCOURSES

Initiated soon after the Workers' Party took over the Porto Alegre city government in 1989, the OP refers to a decentralized network of volunteer community leaders' control over the city's capital investment budget, submitted each year to the mayor for approval. This occurs through two types of forums: district-level councils (one for each of Porto Alegre's sixteen districts), and thematic assemblies, which are aimed at long-term planning for the city as a whole.

Within official discourse, the normative OP participant is represented as the *cidadão ativo*, or "active citizen," whose concern for neighborhood, community, and city leads her to take initiative to bring about improvements in each of these spheres. For OP delegates, this means identifying the needs of one's own community and bringing them to the district council for deliberation. A core element of this active citizenship is *speaking*: putting internal thoughts into public speech and "speaking up" to demand funding. The OP citizen-subject speaks confidently, fearing neither government nor disagreement with fellow citizens. Alongside speaking (although with slightly less emphasis) is *listening*: listening to other people's priorities, questions, and suggestions, and considering them fairly. Active participation is represented as satisfying, enjoyable, and even festive. While the OP is represented as an "open" process, its official documents are disproportionately replete with images of women and working-class people.

The OP meeting I recount below took place a few months after the WSF of 2003 and involves two individuals already introduced: Thais (with whom I'd attended a forum event) and Cesar (the co-founder of the NGO Communities in Action and co-councilor for the Beira Rio OP forum). A longtime community activist and Beira Rio resident, Thais grew up in a downtown middle-class household, but for more than fifteen years has lived in a precarious vila where she has strung together part-time jobs to support her three daughters. Whereas Thais has identified as "poor" (*pobre*) for most of her adult life, Cesar has always seen himself as a member of the working class (*classe trabalhadora*).

After working as a telephone technician for twenty years, he fell on hard times in the early 1990s and relocated to a Beira Rio vila, where he owns a small but comfortable house.

BULLSHIT AND DEMOCRACY

I knew something was up when Thais tossed her half-smoked cigarette. She'd been hovering around the community center's front door since the meeting started, blowing her smoke outside but keeping a close eye on the discussion taking place inside. A city health official named Karen was giving updates on local health services and doing her best to explain delays in the construction of two neighborhood health posts secured through the OP. She seemed optimistic about the two projects, but reminded everyone that Beira Rio remains woefully underserved for primary care services.

Hearing this, the meeting's facilitator, Cesar, tells the thirty-some-odd delegates in attendance that this is a good reason for the forum to request a district health center—larger and more comprehensive in its services than the neighborhood-level health posts—as one of this year's top-priority demands. That's when Thais tosses the cigarette into the chilly autumn night. She's inside with her hand up before Cesar finishes his sentence. "Just one thing, Cesar!" she belts out, not waiting to be called upon. "Which lot are you both wanting to use [for this hospital]?" she asks, smoke from her last drag exiting her nostrils. Chitter-chatter around the room—a constant at these meetings— suddenly ceases, and all eyes turn to Thais and Cesar. Anyone who has been here before knows that Thais's question is rhetorical: She already knows that Cesar is referring to an empty, uncultivated 800-square-meter lot adjacent to the vila where she lives.

Cesar's opinion, shared by many, is that the field should be used for a district health center, a facility that would provide emergency care and other outpatient services to the entire district. Cesar has been promoting the idea for some time now, and it may now have enough support to be voted top priority at the end of this year's annual OP cycle, now just a few weeks away. Thais's disagreement with this plan is also well known: she believes the space should be used for a nursery school and to build houses for those residents of her vila whose dwellings are in the way of a cross-cutting street soon to be paved. Funding for both the nursery school and the houses was secured through the OP a couple years back, though without specification of where either should go. Many agree with Thais's oft-stated conviction that it should be for "the community" (she means her vila)—and not the OP council—to make this decision. People are aware, however, that Thais has a personal interest in the matter, as her own tiny dwelling sits in the space where the road is to be paved.

As Cesar begins to respond to Thais—"It's the area of..."—he remains calm and matter-of-fact. Since he faces her across a large hall, I can't tell if he is meeting her gaze or perhaps facing the crowd as a whole. "I just want to clarify a couple of things," Thais interrupts, "about the demand. Don't forget that you're demanding for that area of the nursery school that was approved this year. So now we're gonna start arguing [*brigando*] . . . nursery school or health post."

Ernesto, a fifty-something lawyer from the middle-class section of Beira Rio and longtime OP participant, now offers an opinion: "I think that these aren't incompatible positions . . . I think that it has to be both things." Several people nod, but Thais remains focused on Cesar. "The only demand [that was approved for my vila] is the nursery school," she exclaims.

Cesar fingers through the 2002 *Plano de Investimentos*, the official OP document containing the details of all approved *demandas* from the previous funding cycle. He reads verbatim, still evidently unbothered: "Listen up! Listen up! Let's be transparent here. OK, 'education' . . . hey, it's [under the funding category] 'education' . . . 'construction of a community nursery school of Vila Hipódromo for forty children, pending specification of the physical area to be used, and regularization of the unit's situation,' or, that is, not defined, it's pending."

"But the community of Vila Hipódromo already defined it," Thais retorts, now quite visibly irritated. Cesar remains cool. "That area was discussed before, and it was reserved for the health center." He's talking about a meeting last year, when without prior announcement a vote had been taken to determine the forum's position on the vacant lot. Two options had been debated—leaving the fate of the field in the hands of the adjacent vila (Thais's vila) or designating the space as principally for use as a health center—and Thais had been narrowly defeated. Cesar hadn't been at this meeting and makes this clear now by adding, "at least that's what I was told."

Thais is now livid. "It's because *you* wanted a health center in the first place and secondly the houses. I'm against this and still am and I'm gonna get the whole community in here."

"It was a decision here in the Forum," Cesar responds, now showing signs of annoyance.

Thais screams back: "It was not a decision of the Forum! It was *forced* here in the Forum. It was persuasion! You all didn't listen to the voice of the community that was here that time . . . It was manipulation! Manipulation! What bullshit this is!"

"You don't need to yell Thais, just a second. You don't need to yell, 'cause no one's yelling at you here." Cesar makes some overtures to move on to the next item on the agenda, perhaps as a way to divert attention from Thais or, in any case, calm things down. He starts listing off those individuals whose hands had been up when Thais began her outburst, but then abruptly yells out, "If you think this here is manipulation, you gotta go somewhere else, this here . . ." "Manipulation! Manipulation!" Thais yells back as she shakes her pointed finger at him. Cesar now makes no attempts to sound diplomatic and shouts out, "This here isn't manipulation! This here is democracy!"

Out front, postmeeting, several delegates remark on the evening's proceedings. I overhear Sara, for example, asking no one in particular, "I wonder what'll happen with that land?" Fernando, meanwhile, tells Sônia, "The district needs that space for a health center!" Sônia, in turn, responds tersely, "It's for Vila Hipódromo to decide, not us!" I also hear observations of a more personal sort. Everson, for example, exclaims to Patricia, "Wow, what a hot meeting tonight. I need to come more often!" to which Patricia responds, "Did you see? Cesar lost his cool!" Claudia, meanwhile, says to me, "Thais seemed really angry tonight. Things must be bad with her husband."

DISCUSSION

Is this heated quarrel consistent with forms of participation represented in official OP discourse? From one official vantage point, Cesar seems a model OP subject: he speaks rationally in terms of community needs and interests, adheres to procedure, and values room for multiple voices—including dissenting voices—to be heard. If his words can be taken at face value, Cesar understands the OP forum to enact "democracy" and to be the singular institutional entity through which district-level decision making should be pursued by community leadership. Thais, in contrast, appears abrasive, cynical, disruptive of procedure, and unaccepting of the district assembly's putative authority—all qualities that don't seem to fit with the cheerful participation imagery of official discourse. And yet, from another standpoint— also official—Thais is the *more authentic* participant: she speaks up, she demands, and she is intimidated neither by government representative nor grassroots political colleague.

I argue that Thais's performance not only represents an alternative vision of normative participation, but *opens up a pluralistic analytic vantage point toward official discourse.* Whereas Cesar appears as fully embracing and respecting official OP procedure, Thais's speech straddles (and morphs between) two relationships to official OP discourse: at times, she appears to work within it, appropriating terms and representational logics closely resembling official discourse (e.g., claims to representing her community, entitlement to speak up, following protocol). Elsewhere, however, she not only violates OP meeting procedure (e.g., speaking out of turn), but tries to discredit that very procedure as illegitimate. To be more precise, her discrediting gestures are directed at both the procedure *and* at Cesar specifically (though it is not always clear which is her target at any given point). As exemplified in statements such as "What bullshit this is!" Thais attempts to reveal Cesar's apparent adherence to procedure as subterfuge that he knowingly employs to conceal his own ambitions. Her speaking is overtly personal and immediate, as are her nonverbal cues (e.g., staring and pointing directly at Cesar when she addresses him). By moving between speech that appears to accept the OP's legitimacy and speech that aspires to reveal it as a sham, Thais troubles the notion of "transparency"—the idea that open discussion in accordance with a "democratic" protocol ensures honest and fair decision making. Her "incivility" toward the circumscribing logics of official discourse troubles the possibility of making sense of the meeting through any one interpretive frame.

Gender is also significant in shaping possible framings of the quarrel, as Thais and Cesar both carry themselves in ways that rub up against tacit understandings of gender-appropriate conduct. Thais, for example, speaks to Cesar in a way that violates a certain conservative view of female comportment in public spaces: she yells, she accuses, she threatens, and her mode of speaking carries a strong sense of entitlement. Cesar's diplomatic, "all-about-procedure" manner, meanwhile, could be seen as *passive*, since it requires him—at least for a time—to allow Thais to pounce on him (the OP is distinctive for placing women into a public space where they can yell at men, and placing men in one where they may be yelled at by women). Based on the postquarrel confabs I hear outside the building, it seems clear that at least some participants do consider Thais's behavior, at least for the moment, through stereotypes of intemperate and hysterical women. (While beyond the scope of this analysis, class dimensions to how the quarrel is made sense of should be acknowledged. Cesar's technical knowledge, not to mention his characteristic diplomacy and politeness [summed up in the term *educado*], carry a higher class status than Thais's "fiery" personality and impatience with technobureaucratic discourse.)

The possibility of a gendered interpretation of the quarrel is also shaped by how one views the OP assembly as a civic space. If, for example, one understands the meeting as an egalitarian field where people come together to deliberate interests, then Thais is easily perceived as unruly and Cesar's unwillingness (at least initially) to respond with similar belligerence a fitting way to manage the gender-inappropriate behavior of a misbehaved woman. If, however, one recognizes the meeting as an *unequal* playing field—in which men are accustomed to moving through public space with relative ease and to controlling the speech of women—then Thais's "speaking up"—her "display of passion" (Bailey 1983)—can be seen as a *democratizing* gesture: a way to make herself heard and thereby make possible the form of deliberation envisioned in official discourse. From this perspective, Thais is *claiming* her citizenship in a way not required of a man.

I see a powerful symbolism in the image of Thais tossing her cigarette and stepping inside to challenge Cesar, as her subsequent protestations disrupt the OP's official view of itself as a "pure" space of deliberation, separate from quotidian social experience. They also trouble the understanding that participants' actions in official spaces reflect simply the rational pursuit of individual interest. Instead, Thais illustrates the importance of viewing civic participation as performance and of retaining a healthy skepticism about the possibility of full discursive interpellation. To be sure, she finds value in performing the participatory subject, but she takes up this discourse selectively. She is skilled in performing the participatory citizen's entitlement to speak, criticize, and demand, even as she attempts to reveal some of the power dynamics of the field in which she speaks, critiques, and demands, such as the way it may be *compromised* due to Cesar's interventions. (Thais seems to be saying, "I will accept the rules of this game for now, but I reserve the right to reveal it as illegitimate later on.")

The multiple framings I have examined suggest that within participants' perceptions, there is an ongoing and inherent tension between singular and pluralistic modes of interpretation. Official readings are constantly subject to morphing into alternate readings (and vice versa): each has the potential to destabilize the other. This is perhaps reminiscent of a postmodernist politics, but for the fact that I do not conclude the impossibility of "consensus," "deliberation," "interest," and the like. Rather, I see these as practices that are sustained *as such* in the complex interaction between social actors predisposed to distinctive modes of perception and action, and a socioorganizational context in which multiple interpretive frames become manifest. In my reading, the quarrel's significance is not for its apparent questioning of whether a "democratic" process is being enacted, but rather for its performance of two views of grassroots participation—one that views participation in abstract, procedural terms, the other seeing it as inherently personal and driven by self-interest. In short, Thais reminds *delegates* that they are *people*; Cesar reminds *people* that they are *delegates*. This is not to align either individual with a distinctive philosophy of participation, but rather to show how the performances making up the quarrel beckon different relationships to official participation discourse.

Conclusions

In the preceding discussions, I have focused on the perceptions by female community leaders from one Porto Alegre district of the city's signature initiatives in civic participation. I have organized this analysis to open up an analytic space that contracted under the celebratory epistemologies of scholarly and activist understandings of civic participation initiatives in Latin America since the 1990s—space to consider ambivalence, contradiction, and refusal in grassroots political experience. Implicitly, I have tried to show how a methodology that places ethnography into dialogue with formal discourse analysis can shed new light on the fragmentedness of political subjectivity, on grassroots leaders' discomfort with (and incivility toward) the circumscribing logics of official discourses, and on the ways "becoming a citizen" is mutually imbricated with other forms of social reproduction. I have argued especially for the importance of the social lens of gender through which civic participation (both idealized and informal) is often interpreted. These insights, I argue, have too often been ignored in scholarship on the World Social Forum, on the Participatory Budget, and on left-organized civic participation initiatives in Latin America more generally.

Somewhat ironically, this analysis demonstrates that both in the center and at the periphery of civic participation initiatives, the civil society agenda elicits incivility in the form of acting outside of discursive and behavioral norms. In my view, however, ambivalence, contradiction, and refusal are part of citizenship and participatory democratic processes and therefore must be addressed to evaluate the possible contributions of these processes to promoting social justice and civic consciousness. With Thais's final impassioned statements in mind, we might say that, as a scholarly approach, the civil society agenda is (or should be) about both narrative *and* counternarrative— democracy *and* bullshit. Telling both stories together doesn't diminish the transformative potential of important initiatives such as the WSF and OP but, rather, shows a more real picture of how the forms of self-awareness incited in official discourse both endure and recede, and intersect with gendered and class subjectivities.

NOTES

1. For detailed studies of the Participatory Budget from a range of disciplinary perspectives, see Abers 2000, Baierle 1998, Baiocchi 2005a, Goldfrank 2003, Marquetti 2003, and Wampler 2007.

2. All people and locales below the level of municipal district are referred to using pseudonyms. This research was funded by the Wenner-Gren Foundation for Anthropological Research and the Fulbright Institute for International Education (IIE) program, and was approved by Emory University's Institutional Review Board.

Part II

MAPPING

MOVEMENT

FIELDS

Chapter 5

MAPPING THE FIELD OF AFRO-LATIN AMERICAN POLITICS

In and Out of the Civil Society Agenda

AGUSTÍN LAÓ-MONTES

The last week of February 2008, two conferences in U.S. universities discussed Afro-Latin Americans.[1] The counterpoint between a conference at Howard University titled "Times of Change and Opportunities for the Afro Colombian Population," organized by the Colombian embassy, and a conference "The African Diaspora in the Americas: Political and Cultural Resistance," at the University of Minnesota, exemplifies poles within the contested terrain of Black politics in the Americas. The contrast between the speakers and sponsors of the conferences at Howard and Minnesota represent two distinctive modes of racial politics that are associated with opposing social and political ideologies, cultural politics, and historic projects. The conference at Howard had speakers from the U.S. Agency for International Development (USAID) and U.S. Black neoliberal-politicians such as Gregory Meek, whereas the conference at Minnesota featured Jesus "Chucho" Garcia, a main leader of the network of Afro-Venezuelan organizations, as the keynote speaker. The same week Chucho Garcia published an article on the Internet critiquing the conference at Howard as an example of the complicity of "the Afro-Colombian Right" with global neoliberalism and the American imperial project. In the same vein, a U.S.-based coalition in solidarity with Afro-Colombian grassroots organizations denounced the conference as another example of a developing partnership between Black conservative elites in Colombia and the United States with the twin governments of George W. Bush and Álvaro Uribe. Likewise, an e-mail of the Proceso de Comunidades Negras, one of the largest organizations of the Black movement in Colombia, observed that what was named as the "Afro-Colombian week at Washington, DC," was "part of the enchantment that the Colombian government orchestrated to try to get the votes for the Free Trade Agreement." The title itself reveals an optimism about the current situation of Afro-Colombians from the viewpoint of an increasingly visible Black political class whose point of view sharply contrasts with the sad condition of millions of Afro-Colombians displaced by the armed conflict, and by the evidence from social research that shows that Afro-Colombians have among the worst indicators of social and economic inequality in the Americas (see Urrea-Giraldo and Viafara Lopez 2007; Urrea-Giraldo, Viafara Lopez, and Vivero Vigoya 2014).

The counterpoint between these conferences shows that in mapping Black politics in the Americas, one of the main contradictions is between Colombia and Venezuela. The Afro-Colombian elite is becoming a transnational showcase and imperial laboratory for a conservative neoliberal Pan-Africanism, while Afro-Venezuelan organizations are championing initiatives for articulating a hemispheric Black Left. Since 2006 Afro-Venezuelans organized four meetings under the name "Afro-Descendants for Revolutionary Transformations in Latin America." Even though there are close connections with the state given that there was government financing for both meetings, there is also a meaningful level of autonomy of the *two* Networks of Afro-Venezuelan Organizations and their leaders in relation to the Venezuelan state, as we shall see. In short, this contrast between the Afro-Colombian Black elite and the Afro-Venezuelan web of social movements is an important point of entry for a cartography of a complex and contested terrain of contemporary Afro-Latin American politics.

In this chapter, I will draw a general map of the field of Afro-Latin American politics that emerged at the moment in which neoliberal globalization took off in the region. The focus will be the significance of Black ethnic-racial politics, and on the heterogeneity of actors, discourses, perspectives, and ideologies, as well as on the complexities and contradictions in the field of Afro-Latin American politics in the context of a global crisis and the rise of resistances and governments of the so-called Pink Tide in the region.

Cartographies of Afro-Diasporic Movements

Black politics had always been heterogeneous, full of differences and debates between various political perspectives and ideologies that developed diverse ways of understanding the meanings of "race," racism, and antiracist struggles, as well as contending historical projects with their implications to forge alliances and foresee horizons (see Hanchard 2006; Laó-Montes 2007; Martin 2005b; Singh 2005). In the 1930s, there were substantive differences among the Pan-African leaders of the time. For instance, we identify three different views on Africa: first in Marcus Garvey's transnational Black nationalism, wherein Africa was the ultimate source of Black identity needed to be recast and modernized for of a sort of "Black empire," in contrast to W. E. B. DuBois's concept of Africa as a necessary referent in Black struggles for democracy and social justice, a project conceived as centered in the Americas; both different from C. L. R. James's understanding of African struggles for decolonization as a key moment in the larger project of socialist internationalism and particularly within the politics of the Fourth International. DuBois and James developed a tradition that Cedric Robinson calls "Black Marxism" (1997), which constitutes a challenge to both Western Marxism, with its tendency toward Eurocentrism and class reductionism, and to those dominant strands of Black nationalism that tend not to clearly see the links between racism and capitalism. Following a radical strand of Black feminism, I will add patriarchy and imperialism to such critique of capitalism and racism.

The Black Freedom Movement in the United States, one of the keystones of the tsunami of struggles that shook and transformed the world during the wave of antisystemic movements of the 1960s–1970s, was plural and had all sorts of internal differences. Most accounts tend to highlight distinctions between a southern-centered civil rights movement, whose climax is usually dated to the civil rights march of 1963 to Washington, DC, with the resulting approval of laws in 1964 and 1965, against racial discrimination and granting voting rights to Black citizens; and the Black power movement placed in cities of the north and west, traced to the rise of Malcolm X as premier leader of African American radicalism, to Stokely Carmichael's Black power slogan in

Student Nonviolent Coordinating Committee (SNCC) campaigns, and to the emergence of radical groups such as the Black Panthers in the late 1960s and early 1970s. The story is more complex and more details and nuances are beyond our scope here. But it is important to state that the differences between the reformist integrationism of the dominant tendency within the civil rights movement, and the revolutionary projects of transformation advocated by organizations such as the Revolutionary Action Movement and the League of Revolutionary Black Workers, reveal meaningful differences within the U.S. Black Freedom Movement of the 1960s–70s. This historical grounding is important for the analysis of Afro-Latin American politics that I will do in this chapter.

A second argument is that Black social movements go through waves or cycles situated in local, national, and global contexts. There is a relationship between the rise and fall of antisystemic movements in critical periods of crisis and restructuring in the world economy,[2] moments of emergence or decline of imperial hegemony, times of proliferation of war or relative peace, and times of rebellion or relative conformity. One of the historical dilemmas of strong cycles of protest is that their successes tend to create the conditions for subsequent periods of partial granting of demands and integration into state power with the consequence that movements tend to shed their antisystemic impulses.

The race cycles perspective articulates a comprehensive framework for a historical analysis of Black politics in the Americas in so far as it combines political-economic analysis and cultural interpretation, the interplay of national and transnational forces, the societal significance of critical conjunctures, and Black historical agency.[3] In this analytical schema racial formations are conceptualized as a complex field and a contested process marked by the "constantly unsettled meanings of race and their tension with other societal structures" (Sawyer 2006, 15). In the same vein, racial politics is understood as a structurally determined and historically contingent process, a contested terrain mediated by state formations, imperial statecraft, and the vast array of struggles that compose the everyday scenarios of power relations. The very concept of race cycles signifies a dynamic temporality in which a central scenario is the relationship between the racial state and Black movements as prime movers of the historical ebb and flow between moments of crisis and social unrest, and moments of equilibrium in dominance and hegemony.

These dynamics that characterize antisystemic movements and race cycles help to explain the changes in U.S. Black politics after the Black Freedom Movement of the 1960s–70s as well as the current conjuncture in Afro-Latin American politics, as we shall see. The passing of laws that extended the franchise catalyzed a considerable increase in elected position occupied by Blacks, while explicit state opposition to racism by means of laws and public policies against discrimination, and the increase in Black social mobility partly due to affirmative action policies, promoted improvements in education and employment. These are some of the achievements of the U.S. Black movements of the 1960s–70s. However, today class polarizations among Afro-North Americans are sharper than in the 1960s, while there is a weakening of grassroots organizations and Black Left currents even though they are reemerging especially in the South. At the same time there is a rise of Black conservatism, clearly evidenced in neoconservative figures such as Condoleezza Rice. The very same successes of the movement facilitated the integration of much of its political energies and civic activism within the structures of state and corporate power that are now advocating the racial ideology sociologists call "color-blind racism," an allegedly "post-racial society" (see Bonilla-Silva 2001; Alexander 1965), in which a new sort of racist regime combines political representation led by a Black professional-managerial class that emerged in the post–civil-rights era (e.g., governor of Massachusetts Deval Patrick) with an imperial multiculturalism championed by a Black president pushing wars in the Middle East and military bases in Colombia, paradoxically while there is an aggressive racist backlash against his presidency.

The Rise of Ethnic Movements and Racial Politics in Latin America

In contrast to the relative weakening of Black social movements and grassroots politics in the United States in the 1980s, in Latin America there was an effervescence of explicitly Black social movements, a change that we characterize as a shift of the main locus of Afro-American movements from north to south.

There is a long tradition of racial politics in Latin America. The Partido Independiente de Color in Cuba (1908–12) and the Frente Negra Brasileira (1930–37) are the principal examples of Black political parties that were first organized in the region. But, until the 1970s and 1980s most of Afro-Latin American political participation was in the main political parties (mostly liberal and Left groupings) and most grassroots efforts within multiethnic/racial labor unions, community and peasant organizations.

A constellation of social movements explicitly self-defined as Black (or Afro-descendant) began to emerge unevenly in Latin America and the Creole Caribbean in the late 1970s and early 1980s and began to bear fruits locally and regionally in the late 1980s and early 1990s. In my research, I found that many leaders of Black movements across the region used to be members of the Latin American Left and became disappointed with the racism and class reductionism of the white/mestizo Left. They consequently shifted gears in the context of the emergence of new social movements and the crisis of the Soviet bloc and socialist politics in general.

The following logical sequence of five factors can generally explain the emergence of Black movements in Latin America in the 1980s–90s:

1   The world-scale influence in political culture and Africana racial identity and consciousness of the movements for national liberation and Pan-Africanism in the African continent and the Caribbean of the third wave of decolonization in the 1960s along with the Black Freedom Movement in the United States during the same period.

2   The emergence of new social movements,[4] launching a plurality of claims including ethnic-racial, ecological, gender, sexual, identity, and territorial. This shift involved changes in the political culture, organizational forms, and modes of doing politics that facilitated the rise of social movements of Afro-descendants and Indigenous peoples who forged fields of ethnic-racial politics across the region.

3   The birth of new struggles and redefinition of old ones in the context of the establishment, maturation, and crisis of processes of neoliberal capitalist globalization. Here we highlight how transnational capital megaprojects of agribusiness and mining—that have been analyzed as "accumulation by dispossession" in zones with a high concentration of common lands such as the Colombian Pacific and Central American Caribbean—catalyzed the rise of struggles for territory, ecology, autonomy, and identity by Afro-descendants. In the urban frontier, neoliberal globalization exacerbated social inequalities and racial violence, phenomena that are crucial to understand the rise of Black urban social movements in cities such as Cali, Caracas, and Rio de Janeiro.

4   This world-historical context created the conditions of possibility for processes of globalization from below such as the formation of translocal webs of Afro-descendants and Indigenous ethnic-racial movements articulated at local, national, and transnational scales.

5   As a result of all of these historical developments, there was a turn in the forms of militancy and forms of collective action of Black activists as well as in the organizational level of Black communities. The result was a shift of Afro-Latin American political participation

away from Left and mainstream political parties to develop their own organizations that composed social movements as emerging fields of collective action. As suggested above, this was linked to the crisis of socially existing socialism as well as to racism and class reductionism in Left, social-democratic and liberal political parties.

In the late 1980s and early 1990s, Black and Indigenous movements in Latin America had been able to organize local grassroots organizations, articulate national webs of social movements in several countries, and weave transnational networks. In South America the leading Black organizations were in Brazil, Colombia, Ecuador, Uruguay, and Venezuela, while in Central America the leadership was from Costa Rica, Honduras, Panama, and Nicaragua.

Black and Indigenous movements had championed campaigns since the late 1980s to declare Latin American states as pluriethnic, multicultural, and plurinational by means of constitutional reforms, thus challenging white elite Creole discourses of mestizaje and whitening that had been founding ideologies of nationhood since the nineteenth century. This resulted in constitutional changes in Nicaragua, Colombia, Ecuador, Guatemala, Mexico, Venezuela, Bolivia, and Peru. An important landmark was the Campaign of 500 Years of Indigenous, Black, and Popular Resistance in 1992 against the celebration of 1492 as a "discovery." This campaign articulated and moved forward Black and Indigenous movements, following from the Indigenous uprising in Ecuador in 1990 and preparing the soil for the Zapatista uprising in Chiapas in 1994 that occurred in the context of the signing of the North American Free Trade Agreement. The mutual influence of Black and Indigenous movements that emerged together in that period place them with the emergence of new social movement politics (ecological, gender, sexual, cultural, ethnic) in Latin America and the world, changing political identities and cultures and the ways of doing politics.

By the 1990s there was an intense process of growth of organization and political participation in Afro-Latin America. Along with the so-called Washington Consensus, there was a rise of Black movements and organizations that led struggles against racism, and for cultural identity and recognition, ethnic education, land rights, economic justice, ecological integrity, ancestral knowledges, and political representation. Many Black organizations were born at the local level, then integrated into national networks of Afro-descendants that began to articulate transnationally by the middle of the decade. This process converged with the second moment of neoliberal globalization when, after the first period of savage capitalism with its tendency to reject any kind of regulation, there emerged a transnational regime of neoliberal governmentality in which capitalist exploitation matched with a multicultural discourse and advocacy of empowerment, participation, grassroots sustainable development by institutions of transnational capitalism, and neoliberal governments. Hence, the regional meetings that took place in Chile, Costa Rica, Dominican Republic, Ecuador, Honduras, Uruguay, and Venezuela were always inscribed by tensions about the influence of powerful metropolitan institutions such as the Inter-American Development Bank (IDB) and the World Bank, in Afro-Latin American agendas. What we call the agenda of civil society and its consequences for Black organization and politics were discussed and debated since the beginning. The tensions around NGO-ization and relations with states and transnational institutions were constitutive of the networks of Afro-Latin American movements and organization in the 1990s.

Several regional networks of Afro-Latin American organizations and leaders were organized by the end of the 1990s. The first was the Network of Afro-Latin American and Caribbean Women, organized in a conference at the Dominican Republic in 1992. It revealed an organizational pattern in which networks of Black women organized first and related to the fact that Afro-Latina women played an important role in bringing the question of race to the center of the feminist debate, including in the world conferences of women such as the meeting at Beijing in 1992.[5] The Black Organization of Central America was organized in Panama in 1994. The largest web of Black organizations in Latin America was named Strategic Alliance of Afro-descendants in a conference in Santiago de Chile in 2000 in preparation for the Third World Conference against Racism and Related Forms of Discrimination held in 2001 in Durban, South Africa.

The Road to Durban: The Patterning of a Field of Afro-Latin American Politics

The Strategic Alliance of Afro-descendants was the outcome of three intertwined processes: the regional articulation of Black movements and organizations, a call to organize toward the Durban conference against racism that facilitated several regional meetings, and North/South initiatives to organize Afro-Latin Americans sponsored by institutions such as the IDB and neoliberal geopolitical initiatives such as the Inter-American Dialogue. In spite of the heterogeneity and tensions that come with it, the glue that held the coalition together was the agenda against racism that was opened on the road to Durban.

The Durban process served as an organizational and educational space for the formation and consolidation of Afro-Latin American webs of social movements at the same time that it marked a political culture associated with the language and practices of the UN, states, and international NGOs. It was within this process of hemispheric organizing that the movement developed a collective leadership and a political identity. As put by Romero Rodríguez, a leader of Mundo Afro in Uruguay, in the meeting of 2000 at Santiago de Chile, "we entered as Blacks and came out as Afro-descendants," meaning that the movement coined the term "Afro-descendant" as an inclusive political identity of people of African descent of all colors, recognizing African ancestry and ties, and denouncing structural racism since slavery. The term was eventually adopted by the UN and all sorts of international organizations, thus becoming a staple of the civil society agenda.

A field of Afro-Latin American politics emerged with a variety of actors (state and societal), institutions, organizations, leaders, discourses and political cultures, and practices. The Afro-Latin American field of politics and political community configured in the road to Durban influenced the Declaration and Action Plan approved in the Third World Conference against Racism and changed the political-cultural profile of the region from the denial of racism to the recognition from all Latin American governments that it was a major problem to be solved.

After Durban: A Small Peaceful Cultural-Political Revolution?

After the Western boycott of the Durban meeting and its accord, led by the United States and Israel, the region of the world in which the Durban agenda against racism became more salient was Latin America. Afro-Latin American movements had previously obtained significant achievements such as the 1993 Law of Black Rights in Colombia, considered to be the most important piece of Afro-reparations in the Americas along with the land rights of Quilombolas in Brazil. The organized efforts and collective actions of the movements had captured the attention of the governments of the region to the extent that all of them signed the Durban accord.[6] After Durban, transnational institutions (e.g., World Bank, IDB), branches of the U.S. imperial state (USAID), and global NGOs used language against racism and financed Black organizations and leaders with a rhetoric of racial equality and empowerment. They took these actions in spite of ambivalence about the Durban agenda, which was considered too radical because of its call for reparations in light of the declaration of slavery as a crime against humanity and the structural racism that persisted. Indeed, Durban sampled the plurality of Black perspectives, including a long tradition that linked struggles against racism and colonialism, led at the conference by Afro-Latin American activists.

The changes promoted by Afro-Latin American activisms on the road to and after Durban can be characterized as a small peaceful political-cultural revolution,[7] insofar as there was a change of governmental discourse from denial to denunciation of racism along with advocacy for policies of racial equity with at least some impact in changing racist common sense. There is now a regional trend of state recognition of Black cultures and identities; in several countries, there are special legislations as well as governmental branches developing specific policies for Black populations. There also is an increase in elected and appointed officials of African descent together with the organization of a Black parliament in the region. There are programs of affirmative action developing in Brazil and Colombia, as well as observatories to document and legally challenge institutional and everyday racism. Governments throughout the region developed at local and national levels offices for Black affairs with explicit missions to promote racial equity. In Brazil there is a Secretariat for Racial Equality equivalent to a ministry, in Colombia there is a Presidential Advisory Office for Black Communities, in Venezuela a National Black Council, and in Ecuador a Corporation of Afro-Ecuatorian Development. However, the position of these government branches had been marginal with little political capital and small budgets, and therefore they had more symbolic value than impact on redistribution of wealth and power in favor of Black subaltern majorities.

In this process of construction of a field of Afro-Latin American politics the borders between actors located in states, transnational institutions, and movement organizations blurred. One Afro-Latin American officer of the World Bank told me in an interview that she is an activist of the Black movement from that institutional location, while an Afro-Caribbean officer of the IDB made a similar claim in a conference of the Global Afro-Latino and Caribbean Initiative (GALCI) in Argentina.

It seems that the very partial successes of the Afro-Latin American movements facilitated conditions for the emergence of Black elites (a political class and a professional managerial class), integration of Black activism into the state, and NGO-ization of some of its key leaders and organizations. But, the analysis should not be based on simple dichotomies such as state and civil society or conflate all forms of participation and engagements with states and/or relations with transnational actors under the rubric of co-optation.

We need a more nuanced analysis than opposing poles of co-optation to autonomy, normal to contentious, and oppositional to conformist politics to examine both the openings of spaces against racism and for ethnic-racial justice as well as the complexities of the current moment of Black politics in Latin America.

We need to analyze and evaluate the overall effects of the alliances and the funding with state institutions and transnational actors (that include some of the powerful representatives of transnational capital and the U.S. imperial state) in what for some sectors of the movement can be described as a shift from a politics of mobilization and grassroots alternatives to a politics of accommodation and integration into transnational networks of neoliberal governmentality. We need to ask key questions: Are we advancing in the struggles against racism and discrimination and, in this sense, moving forward in an overall agenda of social justice, or are we simply opening some spaces for social and political mobility that serve to reproduce the status quo in the name of racial equality? Are the policies and programs organized and advocated by governments, international NGOs, and some of our Afro-Latino organizations facilitating a process of decolonization of power or are many of them, rather, helping neoliberal projects of disciplining subjects and promoting conformed citizens? Are the majorities of Black subaltern subjects in Latin America improving their life conditions, political enfranchisement, and cultural recognition, or are the changes mostly cosmetic without much substantive change?

To begin answering these questions, we need to distinguish between different political formations and ideological perspectives within Black publics in Latin America. Within this general background we need to draw cartographies of Afro-American politics by identifying, differentiating, and defining the multiplicity of actors, practices, organizations, discourses, genres of action, and social-historical projects they articulate and enact. Hence, we differentiate between different kinds of actors and locations within the field of Afro-Latin American politics.

We define social movements as fields of action and communication, a constellation of collective actions (formal and informal) performed by a diverse group of actors (individual and collective) who maintain a relative autonomy from the political system (state and political parties), who engage in direct action to make claims of rights and needs as well as proposals for change, and who have a sustained character as well as pertinent effects in challenging the established order.[8] In light of this, the field of Black politics in Latin America is composed of three interwoven processes : (1) social movements,

(2) ethnic-racial state policies, (3) and the increasing importance of a diversity of transnational actors. Here I want to highlight multinational institutions, such as the UN and the Organization of American States; transnational capital, such the World Bank and IDB; branches of the U.S. metropolitan state, such as USAID and the U.S. Black Congressional Caucus; and NGOs, such as Global Rights. Concerning relations between national and local movements with transnational actors, and their effects of power, a revealing contrast can be the intentionality and impact of the Ford Foundation and USAID. For many years the Ford Foundation has been funding research on race relations and racism in Latin America and provided resources to movement organizations intended to promote policies of racial equality (e.g., affirmative action in Brazil) across the region. How and to what extent Ford funding contributed to racial equality and justice and if it had effects in demobilizing movements and making them part of the status quo are important research questions. On the other hand, USAID acts in conjunction with the State Department with the covert-yet-explicit imperial goals of promoting U.S.-style democracy in the region by developing diplomatic relations with Black elites associated with "friendly governments," assigning Black diplomats to work in Latin America, and giving scholarships and summer programs in Washington, DC, directed to Afro-Latin American youth leadership development.

Afro-Latin American Politics:
In and Out of the Agenda of Civil Society

The theoretical-research framework we developed in the *Interrogating the Civil Society Agenda* project is useful for this analysis. What we call "the civil society agenda" is a construct to characterize the current conjuncture in which both states and transnational actors advocate for "grassroots development," "participatory citizenship," "local empowerment," and "deliberative democracy" as goals and requirements for funding the nonstate sectors defined as "civil society." Scholars and activists characterize it as an appropriation and depoliticization of the language of social movements within the framework of neoliberal transnational governmentality with the intended effect of producing disciplined citizen-subjects, thus reproducing the status quo of neoliberal capitalist globalization. That analysis is accompanied with a critique of the NGO-ization of many social movements, which implies changes in organizational forms to be more bureaucratic and top-down, increased financial dependency linked to professionalization, and more reliance on lobbying and negotiations to the detriment of direct collective actions and confrontational politics. All of this corresponds to relative integration into national-states and powerful transnational institutions.

In our analysis of the agenda of civil society, one of the issues is which movements, actions, and actors are included and excluded from civil society. What are the requirements for "civility," and who are the others, and why, that fall under the rubric of "uncivil"? In the case of Black movements "uncivil" is a particularly loaded distinction given the long history of racist identification of Blackness and Afro-descendant cultures and behaviors as being uncivil and lacking civilization. Analogous to the favoring of what Charles Hale calls *el indio preferido* to signify the favoring by neoliberal institutions (states and transnational actors) of Indigenous leaders and organizations that do not challenge the established order (see Hale and Millamán 2006), I contend that the same institutions are favoring certain individuals and groupings we could similarly call *los negros escogidos* (chosen blacks). This should not overlook that there are leaders/organizations that bureaucratize and thus become employees or clients of states and international organizations, others that get some funding but are careful in maintaining organizational and political autonomy, and yet others who do not want much of a relationship with governmental institutions and transnational funding.

The Black leaders and organizations chosen for inclusion in the civil society agenda tend to be the ones with more public recognition whose leaders had gained national and international recognition, and got involved in governmental negotiations and electoral contests, as well as in representation of Afro-descendants in state branches. They also tend to get international funding for projects for economic development and racial equality. There have been some positive results in regard to some local economic development and in national/local programs against discrimination, but there has also been a partial bureaucratization and professionalization and the emergence of Black elites and political classes that tend to look out mostly for their own and divorce from the Black subaltern majorities that still suffer from severe conditions of social inequality and racism. These Black majorities, who largely remain outside of the official civil society and who in fact are still considered outside of the hegemonic domain of civility, often engage in collective actions and political activity that are still largely invisible in national and transnational public spheres. The struggles and interventions of these Black subaltern majorities are often contentious against the powers that be and the established order and represent a significant source of antisystemic activity when organized with more Black groupings and with other movements for economic, ethnic, cultural, gender, sexual, and ecological justice.

The political panorama becomes more complex if we introduce a contrast between antisystemic and prosystemic movements to distinguish between movements that intentionally or unintentionally challenge or help reproduce the modern/colonial capitalist world-system (see Arrighi et al 1997; Laó-Montes 2008a; Martin et al 2005a). Black social movements had always constituted a contested terrain, as in the distinction between assimilationist, autonomist, and separatist movements in U.S. Black political history. Insofar as Black social movements had historically been pillars in global politics of emancipation (including socialism, feminism, national liberation and revolutionary nationalism, radical Pan-Africanism, Black sexual politics against patriarchal and heteronormative oppressions, and land and ecological claims), there is a strong and enduring tradition of Black radical activism that has historically been a primary antisystemic force for democratization and liberation. On the other hand, the movements' capacity to challenge and provoke restructuring in global conditions and racial orders had the effect of transforming many key Black movements, along with some of their main actors and organizations, from formerly being counterhegemonic to becoming part of the hegemonic bloc. Winant argues there was a fundamental change in the post–World War II world racial order "from racial domination to racial hegemony."[9] This characterization is partly useful for understanding the period that has been named the "post–civil rights era" in the United States in which there has been a mainstreaming of Black politics into the dominant electoral arena (the bipartisan neoliberal pro-imperial terms of politics) along with the integration of most efforts of local organizing into state-client and quasi-state social service organizations and the relative marginalization of Black grassroots organizing and radical activism.

Black political histories of the United States can be of value for analyzing the current condition of Black politics in Latin America because of the mutual influences of movements of similar kinds in various world-historical conjunctures, but also because Latin American movements are arriving at a moment of relative success in some of their demands and their relative integration into state and transnational politics and policies.

Afro-Colombian Political Counterpoints

Colombia can be analyzed as a laboratory of the multiplicity of possibilities in Black politics and of the importance of ethnic-racial politics to larger contests over political economy, cultural politics, and geopolitics. A counterpoint between two national congresses of Afro-Colombian grassroots organizations

(May 2012 and August 2013) and the World Summit of African and Afro-descendant Majors and Dignitaries (September 2013) reveals the density of differences in the field of Black politics in Colombia and the region.

Both congresses of the grassroots were convened by social movement organizations such as Black Communities Process (PCN) and National Afro-Colombian Students Collective (CEUNA). A main goal was reviving a strong Afro-Colombian social movement, and for that purpose there was a process of local meetings across the country. The key issues addressed the main problems and aspirations of Black subaltern communities such as territory, ecology, peace with justice, and racism in the context of fighting against neoliberal globalization. The political language addressed questions of autonomy and self-government in the context of the twenty years of the Law of Black Rights of 1993, whose program of collective ownership of land is now undermined by forced displacement because of the combination of war and agribusiness based on palm oil, illegal coca plantations, and mining.

In contrast, the summit was opened with a speech by the president of Colombia, where he articulated recognition of the contributions of Afro-descendants to the past and present of the country with a clear denunciation of racism as a problem to be combatted with a defense of the Pacific Alliance as the path to development and the horizon of progress for all. The slogan of the summit, "Union, Progress, and Pride without Borders," enunciated the neoliberal ideology of Pan-African unity that guided the event. The summit consolidated leadership of the Afro-Colombian political elite at the national, regional, and global scale, at the same time that it was a space for discussion and debate of the large and heterogeneous Black political community of the country that very much participated and identified with such an important Pan-African event. It revealed convergences and contradictions in the Afro-Colombian political field.

The differences can be represented as contending politics of Black solidarity or clashing Pan-Africanisms. We can distinguish, on the one hand, a neoliberal Pan-Africanism that advocates for the neoliberal policies as a means for "progress and possibility," while the repression and killing of peasants, trade union members, and activists of Afro-descendants and Indigenous communities continues; from, on the other hand, a grounded grassroots Pan-Africanism that defends community self-government, ecological development, regional integration, and globalization from below. This counterpoint between the politics and ideology of social movement organizations (such as PCN and CEUNA) with that of the Afro-Colombian political elite calls for an analysis of the different ideologies of Afro-Latin American power and the distinct discourses and historical projects articulated by Afro-Latin American subjects and organizations. This is a task beyond the scope of this chapter that is an important element in my larger project of research.

Neoliberalism and/or Postneoliberalism? Implosion of Differences in the Field

One of the goals of the agenda traced in the Durban process is to establish a permanent forum for Afro-descendants in the United States that resembles a proposal by Malcolm X in the 1960s. The idea is to pursue a path similar to the Indigenous peoples who waited 110 years before obtaining the permanent forum. Following this road, Afro-Latin Americans championed proposals for the declaration by the UN of 2011 as the Year of Afro-descendants and 2013 as the beginning of the Decade of Afro-descendants as a step forward toward a permanent forum at the UN. But by 2011 the Strategic Alliance of Afro-descendants was divided, and the broad-based coalition formed in the context of Durban did not hold for several reasons. After Durban there was not a general goal that held together such a heterogeneous political community with a plurality of political perspectives, ideologies, and locations (class, gender, generation, place). The turning of many activists into government officers and of some grassroots organizations into NGOs implied some professionalization and bureaucratization of Afro-Latin American political action that fed competition among key actors while diminishing mass mobilizations and direct actions. Black transnational organizations in Latin America became fragmented in pieces, such as the Women's Network and ONECA, which themselves were contested terrains. Political and ideological differences exacerbated in 2011 when Celeo Álvarez, a Garifuna leader, made a call for organizing a world summit celebrating the international year of Afro-descendants in Honduras, a country which recently had had a military coup and where social movements were submitted to violent repression. Quickly, Afro-Latin American voices critiqued the move for a summit in Honduras, triggering a debate about the nature of Black politics that included a discussion over whether racial politics should be framed within or beyond Left-Right divides, raising key questions about democracy and about the relations between racial justice, social justice, and gender equity. This revived older discussions of contending historic projects focused on whether Afro-Latin Americans should advocate for representation and resources within neoliberal regimes or should instead engage in an antisystemic transformative politics.

The organizational outcome was the celebration of two large gatherings in 2011, the Fourth Encounter of Afro-descendants for Revolutionary Transformation in Latin America and the Caribbean held in Venezuela in June, and the so-called World Summit of Afro-descendants in Honduras in August. The summit in Honduras was sponsored by the top echelon of international funding—including USAID, IDB, and the World Bank—while the encounter in Venezuela was financed by the Venezuelan government. The summit advocated against racism, for racial equity and Black empowerment as an important component of neoliberal strategies for development and democracy, positioning President Obama as the great leader of the Black world. In contrast, the encounter was characterized by discourses against neoliberal capitalism and U.S. imperialism, and for the struggle against racism to be a pillar of the socialism of the twenty-first century in the tradition of Radical Pan-Africanism represented by figures such as Cabral, Fanon, and Lumumba. The two large events consolidated political and ideological divides in Afro-Latin America. The leaders of the Honduras summit became a permanent network that kept meeting in different places (Panama, Spain) to organize more events of the kind, while the Venezuelan encounter served as organizational template for the Regional Articulation of Afro-descendants of Latin America and the Caribbean that now have national chapters in Cuba and Ecuador and members throughout the region.

The present dynamics of Black politics in the Americas should be framed within the contested terrain of neoliberal globalization and the forms of state and economy associated with it, the geopolitical contest between the imperial designs of the United States and its allies against so-called progressive states that oppose it (especially Bolivia, Cuba, Ecuador, and Venezuela), as well as in relation to struggles over redefinition of nationhood and recognition, rights, and resources, that came with the increased politicization of Black and Indigenous peoples in the region. However, the historical scenario is far more complex than a divide between Left and Right corresponding to a distinction between dependent capitalist countries and progressive governments of the socialism of the twenty-first century or of the more social-democratic Pink Tide (e.g., Argentina and Brazil). As a regime of power instituted by capitalist modernity, racism had proven to transcend its origin in each of its three dimensions (structural, institutional, quotidian). Recently, Cuban President Raúl Castro declared that it is a shame that racism persists after fifty years of revolution. From another angle, Afro-Venezuelan activists are divided in two networks largely out of a debate about levels of autonomy from the Bolivarian government and about the extent to which the state is committed to racial justice. The eventual inclusion of constitutional clauses recognizing Afro-Venezuelans as a category, legislation against discrimination, and the creation of government officers and a national council were all products of political mobilization by Afro-Venezuelans. Indeed, the achievements both constitutional and in terms of policies against racism and for Black rights and representation (political and cultural) in Brazil, Ecuador, and Venezuela had been the product of collective actions (campaigns, marches, lobbying) of social movements of Afro-descendants.

Paradoxically, Colombia is now one of the countries with better laws condemning and criminalizing racism and is moving forward with policies of affirmative action; its government is only behind Brazil in advocating more explicitly for racial equity. Yet, at the same time many Afro-Colombians are displaced from their ancestral territories in the countryside to go live in the urban slums of the largest cities of the country and face fierce inequality and racism. The chosen Blacks (negros escogidos) of Colombia are now clients in the top echelons of government while the "radical" Blacks who participate in acts of resistance such as the peasant strike that was in place during the World Summit of African and Afro-descendant Majors of 2013, and those who challenge big capital (Colombian, U.S., Chinese, etc.), opposing large-scale mining, are put in jail and killed by paramilitaries.

The contradictions between constitutional discourse and concrete social relations are manifest in Ecuador, which has among the best laws in the world against racism and for reparative justice, recognizing Afro-Ecuadorians as a people as well as a Plurinational Plan against Racism and Discrimination but puts forth very little implementation. Instead of promoting mobilization of Afro-descendants to turn discourse into practice, subordinated integration into the state and orchestrated governmental efforts to suppress dissidence have been relatively successful in demobilizing Black activism. As a result of a rich process filled with local assemblies across the country, there was a National Congress of Afro-Ecuadorian Peoples in Guayaquil in September 2012, but after the congress there was no strong Black representation in the electoral process that ended in the general elections of November 2012, with the exception of a small Left coalition. In Brazil, after almost twenty years of meaningful representation in government, the conditions of social and racial inequality persist in spite of the emergence of an Afro-Brazilian middle stratum and political class. In short, there are contradictions in Afro-Latin American politics in neoliberal as well as in postneoliberal governments, which imply the need to analyze the relation between all forms of justice (class, gender, ethnic-racial, sexual, ecological) in all of these scenarios of power.

All of this poses big questions to Black politics and to Afro-American movements in particular. What is the historical project for the African diaspora, and what does this concretely mean in terms of the kind of policies of economic development, political democracy, and cultural politics that we are to articulate and enact? How is racial politics to articulate with class, gender, and sexual politics, and in search of which kind of project of freedom and equality? I will close by arguing that socioeconomic indicators from all sources reveal that Afro-Latin Americans suffer from the worst conditions of inequality, and in spite of the relative political and cultural achievements, the conditions of structural racism, cultural devalorization, and everyday racial violence and social marginalization characterize the life of many of our people.

NOTES

1. Afro-Latin Americans, Afro-Latinos, etc.

2. On antisystemic movements, see Arrighi, Hopkins, and Wallerstein (1997).

3. I take the concept of race cycles from political scientist Mark Sawyer and build from his analysis to start developing the frame I present here (see Sawyer 2005, 2007).

4. For a strong argument against a categorical divide between old and new social movements, see Alvarez, Dagnino, and Escobar (1998).

5. Afro-Brazilian feminists played a particularly important role in this process (see Alvarez 1998b).

6. In fact, the only two governments in the Americas who refused to sign the Durban agreement were Canada and the United States.

7. This is a paraphrase and reelaboration of Antonio Gramsci's concept of peaceful revolution.

8. This definition owes much to Sonia Alvarez's conceptualization of social movements as discursive fields of action (see Alvarez 2007).

9. See Winant (2001, 2004). Following Gramsci, he defines *hegemony* as integration of the opposition within the dominant order.

Chapter 6

SOCIAL MOVEMENT DEMANDS IN ARGENTINA
AND THE CONSTITUTION OF A "FEMINIST PEOPLE"

GRACIELA DI MARCO

The crisis in Argentina of 2001 marked a new transition, no longer from authoritarianism to democracy, as was the case after the military dictatorship, but one that would bring about change in democracy itself, with no role played by the armed forces. On December 19 and 20, 2001, popular calls of "que se vayan todos" [they all must go] and "no" to the state of siege launched an unprecedented process that sought new social and political relations, new collective subjects, and new forms of citizenship.[1] The political-institutional and economic breakdown made clear popular discontent with the party system and the delegative forms of democracy that had prevailed since the end of the dictatorship in 1983. It also enabled large sectors of civil society to question the consequences of the neoliberal economic model of the 1990s and its connections to the model implemented by the dictatorship.

In 1999, the Alliance for Work, Justice, and Education (Alianza por el Trabajo, la Justicia y la Educación) won the elections. The alliance, a coalition between the Radical Civic Union (Unión Cívica Radical, or UCR) and the Front for a Country in Solidarity (Frente País Solidario, or FREPASO), presented itself as an alternative to the neoliberal economic model implemented by the previous president, Carlos Menem. Events that unfolded in 2000, immediately after the alliance took office, led rapidly to institutional collapse; these included rising unemployment and poverty, increasingly unpopular structural adjustment programs, the resignation of the nation's vice president, Carlos Álvarez, along with many other FREPASO members, a weakened presidential figure opposed by his own party (UCR), and the active opposition of the Peronist or Justicialist Party. On December 20, after declaring a state of siege, President Fernando de la Rúa stepped down in response to pressures from protesters and mobilizations in what came to be known as the *argentinazo*, which left twenty dead in a single day as a result of police repression.[2]

The protests and mobilizations that culminated in the argentinazo had begun during the mid-1990s, in response to fiscal adjustment, market reforms, the restructuring of industry, and increased flexibilization of labor. Cities throughout the country experienced *puebladas*, small-town protests denouncing structural adjustment's negative effects on the public finances of the provinces. Around the same time, the Movement of Rural Women in Struggle (Movimiento de Mujeres Agropecuarias en Lucha, or MMAL) and the Peasant Movement from Santiago del Estero (Movimiento Campesino Santiagueño, or MOCASE) emerged. Other movements rose up to demand the clarification of crimes perpetrated by the police's repressive apparatus and to denounce corruption among politicians and civil servants. "Silent Marches" (Marchas del Silencio) called for shedding light on the 1990 crime against María Soledad Morales in Catamarca. The Coordinator against Institutional and Police Repression (Coordinadora contra la Represión Policial e Institucional, or CORREPI) and the Mothers in Pain (Madres del Dolor) began to organize in 1996 and 1997, respectively. Simultaneously, traditional unionism, which had allied with the government of President Carlos Menem to secure neoliberal reforms, was shaken after two new union confederations emerged, the Conference of Argentinian Workers (Congreso de Trabajadores de Argentina, or CTA) and the Movement of Argentinian Workers (Movimiento de Trabajadores Argentinos, or MTA).

The legacy of the human rights movements of the 1980s had formed a cultural substratum upon which many of the above-mentioned collective actions were built (Di Marco and Palomino 2003; Schuster and Pereyra 2001). The social movements that emerged after the mid-1990s placed demands on the public agenda that challenged neoliberal discourses. Necessarily conflictive, they incorporated fundamental rights and women's rights into a framework for building interdependencies among actors and organizations inscribed in a citizens' network with increasingly complex social and political identities (Schuster and Pereyra 2001). This process can be observed in the rise and configuration during the mid-1990s of the Movements of Unemployed Workers (Movimientos de Trabajadores Desocupados), also known as the picketers (*piqueteros*), the neighborhood Popular Assemblies (*Asambleas Populares*) in the aftermath of December 19 and 20, 2001, and the Recovered and Self-managed Companies (Empresas Recuperadas y Autogestionadas).

After 2001, various feminist, women's, and lesbian, gay, bisexual, transvestite, transexual, transgender, and intersexual (LGBTTTI) movements intensified their demands surrounding women's rights and sexual citizenship, requiring the articulation of many different actors and organizations of women and of mixed (men and women) membership. Diverse movements linked to citizens' socio-territorial-environmental demands also emerged, among them the horizontal assemblies against extractivist mining as well as peasant and indigenous movements (Delamata 2012; Giarracca and Mariotti 2012; Merlinsky 2008).

This quick overview of the diversity of social movements in Argentina during the last fifteen years offers a background for the main objective of this chapter, which is to analyze the moment of dislocation and antagonism following the crisis of 2001. New political articulations that arose at this moment led to the emergence of a people that we will call a "feminist people" (*el pueblo feminista*). Rancière claimed that "politics is the process of counting the part of those who have no part" (1996, 43). And who counts in democracy is contested, contingent, and undetermined.

A complex look at social movements reveals their heterogeneity, how they change through time, their construction of individual and collective identities, and their potential for political, social, and cultural transformations. For present purposes, we base our analysis on various movements made up of women and men, focusing especially on the Movements of Unemployed Workers (MTD), also called *picketers*, the Popular Assemblies (AP), and the Recovered and Self-managed Companies (ERA), from a perspective that analyzes their articulation with women's movements. I have selected these movements because, through their discourses and practices, they configured the "moment of the political" in Argentina since 2001, and most clearly contributed to the formation of a *popular feminism*, the basis upon which a pueblo feminista, "feminist people," could be articulated.

My focus is on the basic demands of these movements rather than on any particular organization, because these demands are what will constitute, or not, a collective identity. This will enable us to move through the discourses that arise so that we can establish a posteriori what kind of identity emerged, without having to demarcate the always-fluid borders between organizations and their discourses. What I am interested in observing is how these demands do or do not construct rights discourses and make possible the emergence of counterhegemonic identities (Laclau 2006, 7, 8).

Consequently, we distance ourselves from some perspectives on collective action, both the institutional and the *movimientista*, or movement-centered.[3] The former focuses on vertical dimensions of processes of political articulation, observing their contributions to institutional changes, especially those linked to the political system. From this position, it was difficult to acknowledge new leadership and identities, because the institutional approach minimizes the intensive learning experiences of popular movements, which heightened in the aftermath of December 19–20, 2001. This methodology missed the opportunity to examine what was happening in the formation of these new identities that, in the aftermath of 2001, unsettled the *civilized* conception of citizenship.[4] In short, the institutional discourse addressed the language and practice of political parties, labor unions, and NGOs, seeing these as channels and intermediaries of social demands.

The movement-centered approach, for its part, considers collective actions in epic tones and emphasizes horizontal articulations over vertical ones, which would enable movements to have a contestatory impact on the state or part of the state. Given our interests, we also call this approach "womanist" because it emphasizes the discourse and practices of women picketeers and women workers in some of the recovered factories, presenting them as the paradigms of women's protagonism in the struggle—though it rendered invisible the movements' complex gender relations, as well as those with the state.

Both approaches tend to overlook the complexity of the processes and relations that are the focus of our reflection. While the institutionalist approach was rooted in traditional analytical frameworks that minimize the possibilities that open up in new scenarios, the movement-centered or womanist approach remains immersed in the discourse that focuses on some women's epic achievements and lacks analytical nuance. Neither approach allows delving deeper into the challenges posed by both movement and institutionalization, which are linked to the political construction of a new hegemony. In understanding this process, the analysis of the existence or nonexistence of rights discourses formed in the making of demands is by no means less significant.

Our perspective is that *feminist politics must be understood not as a politics designed to pursue women's interests as women, but as the pursuit of feminist goals and aspirations within the context of a larger articulation of demands* (Mouffe 1999). As such, we consider the existence of many kinds of feminisms instead of defining a priori an appropriate feminist politics, paying attention to the articulation of feminist and other social movements' politics and their counterhegemonic possibilities. Consequently, we propose to foreground instead the process of building the "feminist people," a notion that refers to the chain of equivalences that allowed for the emergence of a people, exceeding the category women, while also acknowledging that women's movements were a nodal point for its constitution. The idea of a feminist people (*pueblo feminista*) confronts Argentina's deeply conservative and nationalist form of Catholicism, *Catolicismo Integral*, with demands for a deeper secularism and a more expansive democracy. To develop this argument, an overview of the struggles surrounding women's rights after the return to democracy (1983), as well as the formation of popular feminism, is in order.

We will analyze these struggles in the context of Catholic "integralism" (*integralismo católico*) in order to understand the church's institutional position vis-à-vis women's rights, emphasizing the peculiar form this has taken in Argentina. In so doing, we will discuss the domination the church exercises on state, society, and culture in most Latin American countries, as well as the particular characteristics of the Vatican's discourse and praxis adhered to by the leadership of the region's conservative Right. In Argentina, the Catholic discourse on sexuality is contested in a society that declares itself mostly Catholic, but wishes to practice freedom of conscience and expression free of dogma. This contestation has a name; we call it "feminisms."

The Movements

We will briefly discuss some characteristics of the Movements of Unemployed Workers (MTDs), the Popular Assemblies (APs), and the Recovered and Self-Managed Companies (ERAs), which, beyond their specific demands, experienced many different forms of articulation in the years that followed 2001.

The origin and development of the MTDs in Greater Buenos Aires (the area of the present analysis) took place in connection with an array of networks of governmental and nongovernmental organizations that had existed since the 1980s, including grassroots communitarian groups, NGOs, international donors, academic programs and university professors who worked in the field, and militant youth.[5] This heterogeneity of social actors resulted in the construction of diverse discourses: some of them were linked to international agencies, while others were closer to local political networks. These categories are not mutually exclusive; in fact, it has been possible to observe alliances, conflicts, and tensions between the different modalities (Auyero 2004; Di Marco 2011a, 2011b; Forni and Longo 2003).

The Movements of Unemployed Workers were not homogeneous, a fact that is the result of their origins and alliances: some of them emerged from political parties, others from labor unions, and yet others through independent organizing. Around 70 percent of all participants were women who worked managing communitarian projects and participated in the protests and campouts. However, except for a few studies carried out by feminist scholars (but only studying women), the literature considers the male figure of the picketers (piqueteros) as the universal subject, while women are considered only from a statistical point of view.

Picketer organizations were already political actors in the 1990s. They consolidated themselves through their struggle in the streets and, after the crisis of 2001, through the Plan for Unemployed Women and Men Heads of Households (Plan Jefes y Jefas de Hogar Desocupados, or PJJHD), the response to unemployment and poverty of the transitional government led by Eduardo Duhalde in 2002.[6] The implementation of this plan made possible an almost exponential growth of those organizations through monetary transfers obtained by PJJHD members. The MTDs became more visible compared to other social movements, such as the Popular Assemblies and the Recovered and Self-Managed Companies, because of their growth and main mode of action: road blockades.[7] The mobilizations sought primarily to obtain subsidies (*planes*) and food baskets (*bolsas de alimentos*), thus interpellating the state for the substantial realization of fundamental rights. The struggle to secure these rights would be the point of departure for the growth of the MTDs, which subsequently allowed them to insert themselves on the ground through community work, drawing on the political visibility that protests and campouts had earned them.

The Popular Assemblies originated in the city of Buenos Aires and other main urban centers of the country, in the context of the protests and demonstrations that led to the events of December 19 and 20, 2001. The APs were mostly made up of political and/or social militants and, to a lesser degree, of neighbors with no partisan affiliation. In terms of gender composition, they showed an almost equal proportion of men to women. Their discourses focused on horizontalism and criticism of the political system, at the same time making alternative proposals for deepening democracy (Di Marco and Palomino 2003). Among the APs' most salient characteristics was the appropriation of public space. Taking up the streets by protesting with pots and pans and then taking over the city's downtown during these two days inaugurated a form of assembly that continued with meetings at street corners or in neighborhood plazas. These assemblies developed a form of action that had no organizing center, but was composed of multiple effects and interconnections forming a network that allowed for the *autonomy* of each assembly and for a critical stance in regard to delegative democracy.

The Recovered and Self-Managed Companies emerged in the context of mobilization and politicization of the demonstrations and pots-and-pans protests (*cacerolazos*) that led to the aforementioned institutional crisis. Their slogan read: "occupy, resist, produce."[8] Men and women workers strategized the occupation and self-management of factories and companies as a way to keep their jobs. They built their demands around the politicization of immediate needs by going beyond the simple call for job security, claiming instead the expropriation of, and in some cases even the nationalization and workers' managerial control over, the companies. The emergence of labor cooperatives gave legitimacy to the experience of self-management and horizontalism, which had been central since the beginning of the occupations in one way or another. The ERAs redefined the traditional wage-based relationship between workers and employers; when workers constituted their cooperatives, they assumed the management of the companies, becoming their own bosses. Among these female and male workers, the most salient discourses were those of self-determination, the quest for autonomy, and the democratization of labor relations, thus weaving a new discourse altogether surrounding labor rights. The democratization of labor and property was the most important characteristic of the factories' occupation and self-management, beyond the ambiguities and contradictions that ensued within the heterogeneous productive units, along with rearrangements, changes, and ruptures, and the emergence of new organizations seeking to contain and support these proposals. The element of social change inherent in the democratization of labor and property—the political, economic, and cultural practices that politicize the economy and culture—make these self-managed factories and services into producers of concepts and of political tools (Di Marco 2010, 2011).

Demands for Job Security Only?

We women say: we do workshops, but we want condoms.

—MTDs, a woman

The emergence of movements of the unemployed and of workers of recovered companies coincided with high urban unemployment rates, unprecedented in the historical experience of the country. For this reason, the right to work with dignity (*trabajo digno*) appeared as the main demand shared by men and women, and it was also the unleashing force that drew actors to the movements.[9] In the daily practice of the movements, other demands also emerged, some of which resonated with diverse claims by other movements. Meanwhile, many MTDs survived thanks to the state's subsidies, and the ERAs managed to maintain their source of income—that is, their jobs—though not without fearless struggles.

Women demanded labor rights as well as sexual rights, and to make their claims, they set up committees within the movements to which they belonged. Their demands—which were related to rights to education, to sexual and reproductive health, to free birth control, and to legal abortion—all involved compliance with the two pillars of social rights in Argentinian society: free access to high-quality public systems of health and education. Women defended these key demands in their role as guarantors of their sons' and daughters' rights as well as their own. Consistent with the larger women's and feminist movements, women's activities in the new activist spaces sought the politicization of the private sphere. For example, they sought to make visible the forms of violence against women, as well as community-based ways to solve them, given the indifference and always-insufficient responses by the state's agencies and by many NGOs. Women demanded rights that had been confined to the private sphere historically: the right to live free from the violence exerted by men and the right to make decisions regarding their own bodies. These rights pertain to citizenship and constitute aspects of sexual citizenship.[10] Claims that referred to sexual practices, especially those that asserted rights to sexual pleasure and control over one's own body, have to do with sexual self-determination and bodily integrity. These latter two concepts posit relationships based on the absence of domination and of fear/rejection regarding unwanted pregnancies and the contracting of STDs. These concepts also include the rights to live free from harassment and violence, to access to birth control, and to abortion. They are demands for civil and social rights as well as a call for the creation of public policies that deal with, among other things, education and health, which are the foundation upon which many of these rights can be made concrete.

In the committees organized by the women, debates took place and continue to do so over the criminalization of abortion as a threat to health and a problem of inequality, since the middle- and upper-class sectors can safely access this service, while poor women cannot. Women were clear about the control that religious discourses had on their bodies and emotions, which in many occasions hampered an open discussion on this topic. The decriminalization of abortion did not seem back then to be a theme of sexual rights, which is not surprising. Feminists' strategy to achieve their demand consisted in locating the problem in the domain of health and inequality. Consequently, they demanded condoms because it was a resource that women themselves could distribute and use. They have linked this bold demand to one concerned with the minimal basket of basic goods for survival and have denounced scarcity in both respects. These demands would lead to the formation of "popular feminism" and laid the groundwork for its articulation with women from other movements as well as some men in the constitution of the "feminist people."

Affect and Naming: From Individual to Collective Identity

The meanings underlying a collective identity were constructed at a nodal moment; they took shape through coming out to the public sphere in piquetero protests, marches, and the occupation of bankrupt factories abandoned by their owners. What stands out in the collective construction of an "us" had a clear mark, namely, the taking over of the street. This "us" was allowed into the public sphere, that is, appeared in public (Arendt [1958] 2003, 239). While the MTDs demanded *work*, *dignity*, and *social change*, the ERAs called on people to *occupy*, *resist*, and *produce*. These discourses slowly built a collective identity, along with the work done in the territory of the neighborhoods, on the one hand, and the factory—itself a territory of relations—on the other. In the case of the MTDs, what was truly transgressive was to conquer the street, as was, in both cases, the ensuing articulation with the other movements.

Two central aspects of the construction of a discourse surrounding rights and identities should be underlined: first, the use of a proper name, and second, the dislocation of traditional identities among many working-class women. The name assumed by the movement produced a greater emotional charge in the name of the subject as such, rather than in the name of the leader.[11] As an effect of the name piqueteros, for example, the actors started naming themselves, and this naming was constitutive of their identity. In turn, such identity was endowed with affect, which made it possible for the name of a movement to become the *last name* of those men and women who discovered the collective struggle, as in "I am Juan, piquetero," or "I am Juana, from Factory X." It was recognition of an "us" qua people in struggle. This "us," which reinforces a sense of antagonism, necessarily defines an *other* (the management, the government, the system), on whom the demands are placed. Women built a female us within the larger collective identity, from which they made their specific demands. As we shall see, these demands were not confined to the particular, but sought instead to articulate with others.

Collective action had a transformative effect on women's and men's identities. Even so, this effect was more pronounced in the case of women, especially because of the new relations they established outside the private domain of the family and the dislocation of traditional feminine identities. These women were speaking about themselves—and not only about their children. They were women who enjoyed taking part in the protests, who decided to carry out security tasks in the course of those actions, who came home late or were gone for days for the first time in their lives, and/or who managed to create their own committees and activate the campaign for legal abortion. Those women were no longer the passive subjects of state or NGO assistance. This dislocation of working-class feminine identities led to the constitution of popular feminism. Many women also distanced themselves from their previous dependence on leaders, and they took full advantage of the capacity to self-organize (through their connections to women's and feminist movements), challenging male leadership. They also fought for more autonomous spaces and in some cases even directly confronted the male leadership. For women who had this experience of self-organization, collective action entailed a change in the discourse and practice of rights, mediated by their personal histories and identities and their own subjective temporalities.

The politicization of women's demands led to another discourse of politics, one that emerges when "the natural order of domination is interrupted by the institution of a part of those who have no part" (Rancière 1996, 24–25). This process lies at the base of the articulations that unleashed the emergence of popular feminism, powered by women's participation in various spaces of struggle and especially in the National Women's Encounters (Encuentros Nacionales de Mujeres, or ENMs). A group of Argentinian feminists had participated in the Third World Conference on Women in Nairobi (1985) and took the initiative to create these encounters, beginning in 1986. These are autonomous gatherings, which any woman may attend, that take place once a year in a province previously selected by the participants, who also set up an ad hoc committee for their organization. Participation has expanded from 2,000 women in the first encounter to 70,000 women in the last encounter, in Rosario, Province of Santa Fe, 2016.

Starting in 1997, women from the incipient MTDs and other organizations began to have a presence at the National Women's Encounters.[12] Simultaneously, they received increasing attention from the most reactionary sectors, as the church and provincial authorities started meddling with the encounters with the aim of hindering a debate about contraception, abortion, and the questioning of patriarchal conceptions of women and families. Leftist political parties linked to piquetera organizations also attempted to have an influence on ENM demands, hoping to focus on social and political struggles, but without recognizing women's struggles for their own rights.

In the Argentinian case, Catholic Integralism would be the key actor in the counteroffensive to women's rights. To understand these complex processes, we should stop for a moment to develop an analysis of the two antagonistic forces: Catholic Integralism, on the one hand, and feminist struggles for the legalization of abortion and the expansion of laicism, on the other.

The Hegemony of Catholic Integralism

In Argentina—as in most Latin American countries—the Vatican's positions shape public policies. Starting with the coups of the 1930s, the Catholic Church increasingly influenced every aspect of life. Since the 1930s, it has maintained an active presence in the state and civil society, and its ideology has also permeated culture, politics, and social organizations. The armed forces and the church became the actors in charge of driving forward the project to Catholicize and nationalize society: to make Catholicism entirely Argentinian and Argentina an integral part of Catholicism, in order to create a new national order (Mallimaci, Cucchetti, and Donatello 2006a, 2006b). This national Catholic order is thus understood as a totality. Indeed, Catholic Integralism is characterized by its identification of the "national" with the "Catholic," which explains why Catholicism had a presence in the state as well as in civil society. For this reason, Catholicism was much more than a religion to which the majority of the population adhered.[13]

The discourse on sexuality and the discourse on labor and workers were the two main axes that constituted the hegemony of Catholic Integralism.[14] Regarding the former, the Catholic insistence on sexuality as tied to procreation, on traditional maternity as the basis for a feminine identity, and on the negation of different ways of expressing sexuality are based on as well as reinforcing of patriarchy. This conservative position became increasingly apparent as it formed the basis for confronting women's demands regarding sexual citizenship (including the right to abortion, same-sex marriage [*matrimonio igualitario*], and the law on gender identity). It comes as no surprise that the church that calls itself the "Expert on Humanity" sees its hegemony displaced in a country where the majority of the population, even if it self-identifies as Catholic, increasingly proclaims a right to its "humanity" beyond religious scrutiny.[15] As a result of the joint struggles of the LGTTTBI movement in articulation with the feminist movement and the women's movement, two major laws were enacted: in 2010, the Law on Same-Sex Marriage and, in 2012, the Law on Gender Identity. On the other hand, the right to abortion continues to be a demand that cannot be fully incorporated institutionally.

Feminisms and the Abortion Question

Since Argentina's return to democracy in 1983, the abortion question has marked feminist struggles, with various strategies and results and without the support of other social forces. Only a few years into the democratic transition, some organizations proposed the creation of a commission exclusively dedicated to this demand. On March 8, 1988, several women's groups that played an important part in the National Women's Encounters founded the Commission for the Right to Abortion (Comisión por el Derecho al Aborto). Since that time, the cause has been taken up by several organizations and networks, including the Forum for Reproductive Rights (Foro por los Derechos Reproductivos, 1991); Women Self-Summoned to Decide in Freedom (Mujeres Autoconvocadas para Decidir en Libertad, MADEL, 1994); the Coordination for the Right to Abortion (Coordinadora por el Derecho al Aborto, 2002); the Assembly for the Right to Abortion (Asamblea por el Derecho al Aborto, 2003); and the National Consortium for Reproductive and Sexual Rights (Consorcio Nacional por los Derechos Reproductivos y Sexuales, CONDERS, 2003) (Di Marco 2010, 2011a, 2011b).

The ENM that took place in 2003 in Rosario (province of Santa Fe) marked a turning point in this process. Over 12,000 women participated in it, which prominently featured sexual rights, alongside economic demands and criticism of different kinds of violence that women endure. The use of green scarves to identify themselves as supporters of the legalization of abortion was inspired by the Mothers of the Plaza de Mayo's use of white scarves, which also points to an articulation with some sectors of the Mothers' movement. In the ENM of 2004, the main demands were the legalization of abortion and free access to this service, as well as access to birth control methods and the incorporation of sexual education in the educational system. In 2005, the National Campaign for the Right to Legal, Safe, and Free Abortions (Campaña Nacional por el Derecho al Aborto Legal, Seguro y Gratuito) was launched. Its slogan read: "Sexual education to decide, birth control not to have abortions, and legal abortion not to die." These demands referred to democratic principles of respect for women's human rights, equality, and social justice, and they were based on the recognition that poor women were the ones suffering and dying due to the practice of clandestine abortions. The presence of women from the social movements at the ENMs, along with the Catholic presence, which attempted to sabotage the event, were central factors that radicalized the proposal to legalize abortion. The right to abortion was one of the fundamental claims of working-class women alongside those related to violence against women and the demand for work with dignity.

Popular feminism emerged from these demands and from working-class women's practices during their struggles. These women connected with the feminist movement and other men's and women's organizations (social movements, unions, universities, legislators, and guilds), which joined the abortion campaign in increasing numbers, building a political identity that we have called the "feminist people" (Di Marco 2010, 2011a, 2011b). This identity defies traditionalist sectors by demanding a separation between sexuality and procreation. Such a demand worries traditionalist groups in a different way than same-sex marriage does, because marriage is a right granted to men and women alike and does not threaten the definition of life beginning from conception, a central point for those groups. Moreover, the legalization of abortion includes the challenge of an effective separation between church and state. Even if the Catholic Church actively opposed the demands for same-sex marriage, other forces were at play that led to its legal enactment: as gay-friendly tourist destinations arose, the country and its urban centers moved millions of dollars and as a result gave rise to what David Evans (1993) has called a market-based sexual citizenship.

From Popular Feminism to the Feminist People

When the discourse on demands around needs eludes hegemonic discourses concerning the private sphere and a market-based economy, it is possible for a moment of politicized runaway demands to open up (Fraser 1989, 169). On the other hand, if the institutional system is able to satisfy these demands, they get inscribed within a logic of difference and as such are isolated from a relationship of equivalence with other claims. These institutionalized demands are called democratic and distinguish themselves from popular demands, which attempt to create a new hegemony in which an articulation of a chain of equivalences can take place (Laclau 2005). Institutions and the discourse of experts responded to the demands regarding unemployment and poverty with social programs (conditional money transfers, subsidies to start up small businesses and, since 2009, the Universal per-Child Allocation [Asignación Universal por Hijo, AUH]).[16] Though claims for work and against the violence toward women address institutions and can be satisfied under the logics of difference, the demand for the legalization of abortion—as an "empty signifier" (Laclau 2005) of women's full-fledged citizenship, of laicism and pluralism—erects a boundary and transcends patriarchal discourses represented in the hegemony of Catholic Integralism. In the face of this hegemony, the articulation of demands from several women's movements and other social actors built a "feminist people," which is not the same as popular feminism. Nor is it the same as positing the category "women," even if its fundamental core is constituted by demands for women's full citizenship.

The "us the women," within the larger "us," articulated with other demands and with other actors. Through this articulation a "people" was born. For a theory of hegemony, this is a "potential historical actor," a construction that constitutes social agents; "it does not constitute an ideological expression, but a real relationship between social agents" (Laclau 2005, 96, 99, 151). The people is "the count of the unaccounted-for, the part of those who have no part" (Rancière 1996, 25).

The "legalization of abortion" is the empty signifier that articulates demands for laicism and pluralism vis-à-vis an archaic and a powerful Catholic Integralism. In this way, two antagonistic projects confront each other in a way that was unthinkable prior to 2001: one appears as a field of struggle and democratic possibilities on the offensive; the other, as a counteroffensive resisting the consolidation of new rights.

Contingent on heterogeneous elements, the articulation of feminist politics to other social movements combined an array of demands that attested to their multiplicity (among them piquetera women, female workers from recovered factories, female participants of popular assemblies, peasant women, indigenous women, and feminists). The process produced a chain of equivalences hegemonically represented in the legalization of abortion, which nevertheless did not reduce the pluralism of individual demands (such as the demands for work, land, indigenous rights, etc.). This chain of equivalences made possible a heterogeneous identity—that of women, with all the particularities within this category—and allowed for the discursive construction of the adversary—made up of forces that carried traditional and patriarchal values. What emerged was a political identity, a "people."[17] In Rancière's words, the *unaccounted-for* [women] [*las no contadas*] demand that they be fully integrated into the democratic *count* (1996, 43). What emerged was a demand that signified all demands. Women articulated themselves in the movement and with other social actors in the fight for the legalization of abortion, so that women could exercise their capacity to decide over their own bodies. In Argentina, this struggle links and condenses the fight for laicism, for plurality, and for citizenship.

Before the emergence of the above-mentioned movements, the particular nature of the demand for the legalization of abortion prevented it from connecting to other claims, such as labor demands or policies that dealt with violence against women, and it was considered contrary to the objectives of these other particular demands. The new historical moment of the early 2000s generated a relation of equivalence, which resulted in the emergence of the feminist people, articulating diverse struggles to expand women's rights and to consolidate a pluralistic democracy. Working-class feminism is a central component of the feminist people.

Day after day, the feminist people expands in the enthusiasm of the struggle, joined by new movements, organizations, and groups of men and women. Even the National Campaign for the Right to Legal Abortion is a movement of movements. With a contextualized strategy, new allies join in—not only women or feminists, but also universities, political parties, unions, and so on. In March 2001, the campaign proposed a law to decriminalize abortion with the support of 35 legislators, approximately 250 social organizations, and 16 national universities. The proposal aimed to give any woman the right to interrupt a pregnancy during the first twelve weeks. Well into the first decade of the century, with both social movements and the political scenario being reconfigured, the Darío Santillán Front (Frente Darío Santillán, or FDS) and the Juana Azurduy-Barrios de Pie Collective (Colectivo Juana Azurduy-Barrios de Pie) actively joined their simultaneous struggles for the legalization of abortion, same-sex marriage, and gender identity and participated in the campaign. An FDS-linked group, the Collective of Antipatriarchal Men, whose members describe themselves as "neither macho, nor Nazi" (*Ni machos ni fachos*), also belong to the feminist people, rallying under the banner of men for the right to a legal, safe, and free abortion (Di Marco 2011). Currently, many LGTTTBI identities seek inclusion in the feminist people, a fact that can be observed in the debate surrounding who constitutes the subject of feminism: whether heterosexual women must be the only subject in the struggle for a legal right to abortion, or if the subject must expand to include lesbians and trans subjects as protagonists. This synthesis accounts for a feminist people as a new identity that expands as new actors join in.

Conclusions

The crisis of 2001 and the ongoing grassroots protests changed Argentinian political life significantly. They also changed the relationships among demands for new rights regarding sexuality.

Uncivic, untamed identities took shape through the process carried out by social movements, even as there were contradictions. Many women especially resisted power involved in the policing of their bodies and emotions. These women's difference vis-à-vis established norms constitutes their identities as "politically incorrect." Activists know about institutions and the law, but they don't trust them; they want to push them beyond their limits or change them. To the eyes of an organized civil society and of politicians, there is something *savage* and *uncivic* in these "politically incorrect" discourses. Civil society and politicians respond with disdain to the movements' discourses and practices, which don't fit in the framework of "normal" politics, of what is institutionally allowed—"the permissible, authorized, tolerated forms of activism and participation" (introduction, this volume). For the movements, when there is tension between property and work, work prevails, and between law and life, life prevails, a life defined on its own terms and in its own economic, cultural, and relational context—as inscribed in a larger, more general political context. Particular attention should be given to the discourses and practices of women who initiated transformative processes regarding violence and the control of their bodies, through which they criticized institutions and laws that are supposed to guarantee their rights. Gender differences mark the transformations of individual identities. If gender differences had been subsumed under collective identities or if they had not been understood from a gender-based perspective, then the nuances would have gone unnoticed, preventing us from elaborating concepts such as popular feminism or the feminist people.

An articulation of working-class women and feminists was needed to define the counterhegemonic field that had been developing since 1997. Beginning with the historical circumstances of 2001, an articulation with other demands and identities took place. As many feminists admit, though they had made great achievements since the return to democracy, the emergence of working-class women's struggles was necessary to move the struggle forward and expand demands.

The legalization of abortion is an empty signifier in that this demand acquires a centrality exceeding its own meaning. The cathexis of this singular event (Laclau 2005, 153) condenses various claims for a fully secular state and rejects the influence of the Catholic Church on almost every aspect of the country's social, cultural, and political life, as well as the church's opposition to the full realization of women's rights and the disastrous role played by many of its representatives during the military dictatorship. For a culture and society such as Argentina's, this combination of claims for secularity and rejection of the church is counterhegemonic. In the unfolding struggle, we find a quest for complementarity between the horizontal dimension of these equivalences and their vertical absorption within the political system. In other words, an institutionalized influence on the state's powers is part of the strategy of the new grassroots identity. This strategy differs from what has been observed by Laclau (2005, 127, 130) with regard to the centrality of a leader's name giving cohesion to a group. In this case, we can't affirm that the name of a leader can represent a chain of equivalences, because the configuration of a "feminist people" is horizontal and does not have designated, but only situational, authority figures. The joint demands in this chain of equivalences favored the emergence of diverse, plural, and democratic collective identities, which were produced from multiple locations and particular identities. They found their condition of possibility in "popular feminism," which later became the site for encounters among feminists and women from the movements, with the National Women's Encounters as the nodal point. Such multiplicity has its raison d'être in the women's movements' horizontal and rhizomatic structure, with networks and articulations at the local and global level, and in cyberspace. Is this an obstacle for the constitution of a feminist people? We think not. On the contrary, these multiple connections indicate a potential for new counterhegemonic alternatives for a deepening of democracy.

NOTES

1. For a more thorough discussion, see Di Marco and Palomino 2003; Schuster and Pereyra 2001; and Seoane 2002.

2. His term was supposed to end in 2003. Faced with a vacuum of power, the Legislative Assembly replaced him in less than two weeks with Ramón Puerta, who was followed by

Adolfo Rodríguez Saá, by Eduardo Camaño, and finally by Eduardo Duhalde, all members of the Justicialist Party.

3. This discussion departs from the traditional aforementioned approaches on social movements, though it follows the discussions that emerged from them.

4. Similarly, Tapia alludes to a "savage politics" to refer to collective actions that questioned some forms of exploitation, domination, and discrimination (2009, 112).

5. They especially moved forward since the hyperinflation of 1989, with food programs, production for self-consumption or self-sufficiency, small businesses, work and service cooperatives, gardens, and communitarian bakeries. Taking over the land was also a tool used at the time. Some associations received economic assistance and support from the social programs financed by diverse international organizations. The participation of civil society was required for their implementation, justified in the climate at the time, characterized by the transfer of responsibilities from the state to society.

6. The PJJHD granted a sum of money to unemployed men and women from poor households who had children under the age of eighteen or disabled, or who had a pregnant partner. In exchange, the beneficiaries had to undergo training and do community service for their remuneration. Other activities carried out in exchange for money included completing the formal education cycle, undergoing professional training, or joining the workforce with a formal contract. In total, unemployed workers from the movements received approximately 10 percent of the 2 million dollars that had been granted for this plan.

7. For a discussion of the emergence of MTDs and their characteristics, see Delamata 2005; Di Marco 2011a, 2011b; Giarracca et al. 2001; Schuster and Pereyra 2001; Svampa and Pereyra 2003; Zibechi 2003.

8. In the present study, we consider these companies in the first few years of the 2000s as belonging to the second cycle, in order to differentiate them from those in the first cycle, constituted by the combination of experiences that appeared in the 1970s and 1990s. The recovered companies since 2004 are considered to belong to a third cycle.

9. This is the most common definition in Argentina. It resembles the International Labor Organization's category of "decent work."

10. This notion emphasizes the recognition of needs and sexual desires without linking them solely and exclusively to reproduction. It does not adhere to an essentialist notion of sexuality's objective. Because it is expansive, it contains reproductive rights (Richardson 1998; Di Marco 2012).

11. Laclau points out that the centrality of the leader's name resides in the affective investment as an empty signifier that represents the chain of equivalences (Laclau 2005, 127–30).

12. In 1997, there were at least 104 roadblocks organized by the MTDs in different Argentinian provinces. The objective was to make claims for new jobs, subsidies, and an increase in public spending on health, food, and education. Participants also petitioned for help from the national government in receiving delayed salary payment and preventing the loss of more jobs.

13. Most migrants (mostly Italian and Spanish) who arrived in the country between 1870 and 1929 and between 1948 and 1952 belonged to the Catholic faith.

14. This notion resides on a gender hierarchy where male providers receive a family salary to support their wives and children. According to the Argentinian Bishopric's Pastoral Letter

(2005) "work is a service to the community that grants you the right to eat in it." There is no mention of a possibility for workers to become the boss.

15. According to the results found in the study by the National Board of Scientific and Technical Researchers (CONICET) and four other national universities (2008), 76 percent of the population defines itself as Catholic, and 9 percent as evangelical, and 11.3 percent claims to be atheist, agnostic, or to follow another religion. Nonetheless, 63.9 percent of the population supports the right to abortion under certain circumstances, while 92.4 percent support sexual education in schools. This society, however, still adheres to a Catholic way of making sense of the world, as can be seen in the data from a poll by the Center for the Study of Society and the State (Centro de Estudios de Estado y Sociedad). If the decision to end a pregnancy rested merely on the woman's desire to do so, the percentage of support dropped drastically, compared to the support for women who are at risk of damaging their health or of losing their lives.

16. The AUH as a System for the Expansion of Social Security is a benefit that belongs to the children of unemployed workers who work in the informal market or who earn less than the minimum salary or a minimum living wage. It consists of a monthly payment of approximately 100 dollars for children under eighteen and 300 dollars for children with disabilities regardless of their age.

17. "Women" as a category constructed by patriarchy is *heterogeneous*. Heterogeneity is defined by its externality: "it is not a denied element that defines the identity. It is an external element that presupposes the absence of a common space" (Laclau 2005, 187).

Chapter 7

POLITICS BY OTHER MEANS
Resistance to Neoliberal Biopolitics

GRACIELA MONTEAGUDO

The Uruguay River flows lazily along the shores of Argentina and Uruguay, watering a generous brown and green landscape of soft hills that roll for miles on end. Upstream, the river comes to life in the Brazilian rainforest, where it is born at 5,900 feet above the sea. Downstream, its magnificent flow runs almost at ground level into the Atlantic. The river, after jumping high cliffs in Brazil, settles between Uruguay and Argentina, separating the two countries—countries that it used to unite. No one could blame the slow, sandy river for the separation. If anything, it seems that the blame would lie in the global and local forces that clashed in the region during the 1990s to create a new configuration of biopolitics in the Southern Cone.

Uruguay, a small country pressed by an economic and social crisis induced by neoliberal policies, planned for the installation of several multinational pulp mills on the shores of the Uruguay River, across the border from Gualeguaychú, Argentina. Alarmed by the knowledge of the environmental risks posed by this kind of industry, and after unsuccessfully petitioning both the Uruguayan and the Argentine governments, in the year 2005 the citizens of this town organized in the Asamblea Popular Ambiental de Gualeguaychú (Asamblea from now on) and decided to blockade the international bridge that connects Gualeguaychú with Uruguay. The Asamblea's action generated an international conflict involving both countries, as the bridge was permanently blockaded for four years.

Intrigued by the emergence of a horizontally organized movement concerned with the environment, one cold winter morning in 2008 I took a bus from Buenos Aires to Gualeguaychú. Before getting on the bus, I was introduced by activist friends to a psychology student in Buenos Aires, who put me in contact with a teacher involved with the Asamblea. I was well received by her middle-class family, who gave me a tour of the area. As I was sharing the popular green tea, *mate*, with some of the families involved in the struggle, I reflected on how the broad impact of neoliberal policies affected not only the poor and working class, but also middle-class people, who found their livelihoods threatened by the implementation of these policies.

On this Sunday morning, most of the people at the blockade were middle-class, white-skinned, employed homeowners, NGO activists, or organizers in social movements and political parties, several of them with university degrees. In spite of their apparent class status, these people had chosen to be on the barricades, stopping the few cars that attempted to cross, rather than with their families, enjoying Argentina's traditional Sunday midday meal. Their methods and their power structures were strikingly similar to those of the unemployed workers, the *piqueteros* of the mid-1990s and early 2000s. By the end of the 1990s, Argentine social movements featured a prefigurative tendency toward nonhierarchical organizing, the use of theater and art in their protests, a stronger presence of women in leadership positions, an emphasis on direct action, and a deep concern for their own territories.[1] However, while movements' power structures and tactics had changed, many of the activists present were or had been part of earlier, "old" social movements—key actors in democratizing the state during the transition from dictatorships to democratically elected governments (Alvarez 1998).

New to Gualeguaychú, I was nevertheless born and raised in Argentina. As a young woman in the 1980s I became deeply involved in organizing against the policies of the International Monetary Fund (IMF), and other international lending institutions, which many Argentines hold responsible for the destruction of their economy since 1976, when a military dictatorship took power. In 1994 I moved to the United States and became active in the anti-corporate globalization movement. Since then, I have done fieldwork with unemployed workers' organizations (Monteagudo 2007) and factories under workers' control (Monteagudo 2008). From 2007 to the present, I have worked with the United Assembly of Citizens (Unión de Asambleas Ciudadanas, or UAC), a horizontal coordinating body that hosts over 100 social movements and NGOs, which include the Asamblea Popular Ambiental de Gualeguaychú, and a number of organizations that resist open air mining and other corporate extractive practices in the Andes (http://asambleasciudadanas.org.ar/). The scope of this chapter, however, will only allow me to focus on the Asamblea and its struggle over the installation of a Finnish pulp mill across the river they share with Uruguay.

A genealogy of the contentious, creative, and diverse public interventions used by the Asamblea reveals a conception of politics as the continuation of war by other means (Foucault 2003, 15–19). In Argentina, both the deployment of policies favoring neoliberal globalization and resistance to them bear the signs of war: a war waged against the population, to which massive sectors of the population responded by strengthening preexisting social and political networks, as they created organizations that engaged in direct actions to challenge neoliberal policies. After years of frustrating traditional street protests, as the country plunged deeper and deeper into poverty, these social movements not only reorganized through nonhierarchical structures, but also introduced novel practices that pushed the boundaries of acceptable ways to manifest dissent. I think of these movements as constituting a field of "politics by other means." In this field, roadblocks, *escraches*,[2] and street theater were used when marches and rallies proved ineffective to reverse the disaster that followed the application of the structural adjustment policies of the International Monetary Fund (IMF).

To understand the emergence of this field, one must take a look at the history of the Argentine popular classes that emerged from the terror of the dictatorship (1976–83) with a different vision of the state. The state became, under the military juntas, a terror machine that destroyed dissenting citizens, creating a deeply ingrained distrust in its institutions that reached beyond the poor into the middle class—professionals, small farmers, teachers, small business owners, students, homemakers, journalists, intellectuals, and many others. As the IMF dictated the policies of the elected governments that followed, the distrust sedimented. This deepening of the population's negative view of democratic institutions was due not only to the catastrophic consequences of the adjustment, but also to the exponential increase in the level of state corruption at the executive, judicial, and legislative branches that accompanied it, in the form of bribes, favoritism, and illegal deals (O'Donnell 1997). As Neka, a *piquetera* (unemployed worker) in the south of Buenos Aires, explained, "We began to see the government as a manager for the IMF."[3] Not surprisingly, when the economy finally collapsed in 2001, the "Que se Vayan Todos" (Throw them all out) chant echoed in the streets of Argentina, giving voice to a deep disillusion in electoral politics and in the institutions of democracy.

While the role of the IMF contributed to a negative image of the institutions of democracy, the sidestreaming of feminisms (Alvarez et al. 2014) into popular organizing had a positive influence on the democratization of social movement power structures through the assembly movement (Di Marco, chapter 6 in this book; Schmukler 1995) and the nonhierarchical Encuentros Nacionales de Mujeres (National Meeting of Women).[4] Twenty-first-century Zapatismo (McCabe 2007; Vommaro 2003) and the World Social Forum were also influential in the visioning of alternatives to power, hierarchy, and politics as usual. Impacted by the fall of the Soviet Union, former Trotskyists, Communists, and Guevarists articulated a collective critique of their own past vanguardism while they participated in the popular assembly and unemployed worker movements.[5]

As neoliberalism weakened state institutions in the Global South and political parties and unions suffered a significant loss of legitimacy (Villalón 2008) due to their inefficacy in addressing the crises caused by neoliberalism, social movements that eschewed traditional politics sprung up in the Argentine public spheres by holding *piquetes* (roadblocks), sometimes for weeks on end, taking over and recovering abandoned factories, or meeting by the hundreds on street corners to discuss actions to confront the crisis. I argue that the appearance of these "uncivic" social movements is an unintended consequence of neoliberal policies and practices, which weakened democratic institutions in the Global South. They left in their trail not only impoverished and unemployed people, but also a population that had learned that the use of institutionalized democratic channels to solve dire social problems was ineffective. On December 19–20, 2001, thousands of people throughout Argentina spontaneously assembled on the streets to protest the result of decades of neoliberal politics. The rebellion signaled and raised awareness of the role of the IMF's structural adjustment policies in the economic and social crisis.

A vast array of untamed social movements, radical unions, progressive NGOs, and community organizations helped create the space where the biopolitics of neoliberalism came into question in Argentina, opening a path for the modified neoliberal economics of Néstor Kirchner's administration, which came to power in 2003, as part of the Pink Tide of moderate governments in the region.

Global, Ethnicized Extermination Technologies

During the 1990s, both Uruguay and Argentina went through a biopolitical project that completely transformed production and reproduction of life. The transfer of wealth of states to private multinational corporations, the lifting of restrictions on foreign imports, and the linking of local currencies to the dollar provoked social and economic disasters with long-lasting consequences on both sides of the river. A generation was left out of employment and education circuits, accounting for an increase in social violence, especially among the young, and creating spaces of exception—local enclaves in which transnational capital extracts labor in ethnicized ways (Ong 2006, 8). Polluting industries, such as the pulp mills, are moved to the Global South, where racist views of the population allow for their environment to be destroyed (Bullard 1993), while taking advantage of the high levels of unemployment and investment in education of some of the countries in the area.

The installation of the pulp mill impacted both Uruguay and Argentina, since the Uruguay River laps on the shores of both the Argentine town of Gualeguaychú and the town of Fray Bentos, in Uruguay, where the new Finnish pulp mill, Botnia, is now operating. But these towns' different development strategies meant that they were affected in different ways. The conflict that the installation brought on is crossed by a configuration of forces at play in the neoliberal era: a weakened state, international lending institutions such as the IMF and the World Bank, an impoverished population, and a wealthy, seemingly all-powerful, multinational corporation that produces cellulose paste to be converted into paper in Finland.

Pressed by the economic catastrophe that followed the implementation of IMF/World Bank economic recipes, Jorge Batlle, a conservative Uruguayan president, created a haven for international investments (Pakkasvirta 2008). In doing this, Batlle's government adopted domestic and international policies that were clearly "market driven truths" presented as "technical solutions" (Ong 2006). By lifting restrictions on foreign ownership of land, giving up the right of the state to impose taxes on foreign capital investments, and voiding restrictions on how much profit can be "exported" out of the country, the Uruguayan government limited its sovereignty and offered its highly educated, low-waged citizens and natural resources to foreign exploitation. In this way, global corporations are able to amass extraordinary profits, despite the fact that their practices have been known to pollute the environment. Indeed, the apparently "technical" nature of these policies obscures the fact that international investors' havens have been made possible by the fact that the Global South's popular classes were first beaten into submission by the repression of the 1970s and later assaulted by the brutality of structural adjustment, with the high unemployment rates and the widespread impoverishment that followed.

Fragmentation of Local Solidarities in the Global South

Although both Uruguay and Argentina suffered through the 1990s under the implementation of the IMF/World Bank plans, there were always tensions between them connected with the difference of size and power of their economies: Argentina's gross domestic product is fourteen times greater than that of Uruguay (https://www.cia.gov/library/publications/the-world -factbook/geos/ar.html). The citizens of Gualeguaychú envisioned the pulp mills in Uruguay as an imposition, not only by a European corporation, but also by the government and sectors of the population of a lesser country. Posters around the town showed a brave Argentine gaucho, on a horse, lassoing Botnia's phallic chimney, suggesting a male perspective on the issue of power over territory. Uruguayans violated international legislation—according to the Argentinian government—by failing to formally consult with Argentina over the installation of the pulp mill on their side of the river. To grasp the complex forces in the fracas over the pulp mills, it is necessary to understand how the 1990s impacted the lives of the citizens of Gualeguaychú. Argentina was not immune to neoliberalism in the 1990s and suffered devastating consequences, in a similar fashion to Uruguay. Until 1970 only 10 percent of the Argentine population was below the poverty line, according to the World Bank. By 2001, this figure had risen to 47 percent below the poverty line with unemployment at 20 percent, as the country plunged into an economic and social crisis of proportions never heard of before. The rural population, especially the small producers, were heavily in debt (Giarracca 2007). As Anibal, an older man connected with the Asamblea, said: "There was much suffering here during the 1990s. Many people were unemployed, many lost their lands, and many lost their homes."

The Argentine government, however, chose a different path from Uruguay's in the face of neoliberalism. By paying off the IMF debt, the Kirchner administration managed to create a set of hybrid economic policies, despite warnings by the IMF/World Bank. The emphasis on import substitution allowed for a partial rebirth of the defunct national industry. At the same time, an undervalued national currency secured high profits for agricultural exports, as the Andes were made widely available to global corporations for strip mining. For its part, Gualeguaychú managed to fit into this project, and devoted itself to the manufacture and production of exports such as transgenic soy,[6] honey, milk, beef, and blueberries, as well as to "green" tourism. By reorienting from domestic to international markets, from a resource extraction perspective, Gualeguaychú became part of a productive territory (Svampa 2008), rather than a nonproducing frontier (Tsing 2005). The local population did not have to open their territory to foreign corporations, because they were able to discipline and reinvent themselves by producing some of the specialized exports that became the basis of the Kirchner's administration economic model. The pulp mill installed across the river threatened this arrangement, since emissions from the plant were feared to pollute the river and consequently the land, affecting both agriculture and tourism. Having already been forced to make dramatic changes, this population was not willing to live through a new cycle of destruction of their livelihood. If Botnia, in fact, contaminated on a significant scale, as Mabel, a woman from the Asamblea said, "it would be like a cancer spreading through Gualeguaychú." She added: "After suffering through the 1990s, when the local economy all but collapsed, today, this socioeconomic model works for us. We will not allow for it to be destroyed." The Uruguayan and the Argentine economies' twists and turns in trying to adjust to and survive in a neoliberal world order increased the tensions and strained the relationship between these communities. Gualeguaychú responded by adopting a nonhierarchical, direct-action-based organization that resulted in the blockade of the international bridge.

Blockading Highways to Open New Paths

Argentina was once heralded as a laboratory for social change, and for good reason. While the population of Gualeguaychú opted for adjusting to neoliberal policies by redesigning their economy, producing mainly for export and offering services in the form of "green tourism," other sectors in rural and urban settings that were affected differently by neoliberal economic policies or who lacked the resources for these options, resorted to different strategies.

I argue that the direct actions of the unemployed and others during the 1990s and early 2000s changed the political-cultural processes of Argentina, influencing the citizens of Gualeguaychú who decided, in a nonhierarchical assembly, to blockade an international bridge. Although the primarily middle-class members of the Asamblea were offended when the media dubbed them piqueteros, as if they were the poor people who first took over the highways, it is undeniable that their way of organizing and their engagement in direct actions are consistent with the power structures and tactics of the working-class and low-income piqueteros.

Like the piqueteros, the Asamblea involved itself in peaceful, low-intensity warfare against Botnia, a wealthy, powerful, and savvy opponent. To counter the company's sophisticated media campaign geared to prove their use of safe technologies, the Asamblea resorted to a number of creative actions. These included permanently blockading the international bridge that connects Argentina with Uruguay, an escrache at the home of Botnia's manager, symbolic attacks on the pulp mill with "pirate" boats, and, as I will analyze later, even the deployment of half-naked female bodies in international arenas.

The Asamblea, however, was able to engage with the state from a position of power that the piqueteros lacked. As Gualeguaychú had adapted to a "cheap nature" export model, their claims over the environment worked well for the particular needs of the Kirchner administration. Kirchner met with members of the Asamblea in Buenos Aires. He declared that the struggle against the pulp mills was a "national cause," did not question the blockade of the bridge, and promised to take the issue to the Hague Tribunal to stop the construction of the pulp mill (http://www.pagina12.com.ar/diario/elpais/1-62891-2006-02-10.html). By saluting the struggle of Gualeguaychú as a "national cause," Kirchner was able to appear as the protector of the Argentine environment, though at the same time he was enabling the extraction of national mining resources by global corporations elsewhere in the country (Svampa 2008).

Making Gender at the Road Blockade

The nonhierarchical, horizontal organization of the Asamblea fosters wide popular participation as a way of socializing power. The broad scope of organizations in it helps to explain the contradictions in their gender balance. All are welcome to the decision-making meetings, and everybody can talk, make proposals, and vote under the coordination of a chair elected in assembly. All participants can literally make themselves heard by using a microphone in public meetings. The passing around of the microphone during the meetings was impressive as a sign of democratic procedures—so impressive that at first I missed the fact that though the microphone was openly shared, there were still power differentials in the voices that were heard. Women spoke less often than men and when they did, they were not listened to as attentively as men were.

Quiet in public, women had nevertheless a strong presence in the Asamblea. They were coordinating meetings, writing communiqués, bringing food to the shed by the blockade, and participating in the different actions. Women, therefore, were effective leaders with the capacity to generate and support spaces where people could express themselves. However, this leadership cohabited with an implicit—and at times explicit—notion that women were not listened to by the general public in the way that men were. The secretary of the Asamblea (a woman) was passing the microphone around, but Claudia, an unemployed woman with a long-term involvement in the movement, told me: "People listen more to men; that is why we let them talk in public." She had that experience herself in the Asamblea, where her voice was sometimes not heard, but whenever a man voiced her ideas people would listen to him and would vote in favor of what had originally been her proposal. "Si lo dice un tipo, le dan más bola" (if a man says it, they pay more attention),[7] she concluded.

I noticed that when men spoke, women would later approach them and hand them flyers, ask them to sign petitions, or fill out forms. The women had information and were organizing people away from the microphone. As it became obvious that women from different classes were more or less consciously implementing this quiet strategy, I asked one of them directly why she personally was taking less airtime than men in the organization were. A middle-class woman, Mirta, with two years as an activist in the movement, said: "I have only been learning about this issue for the past two years. It's best that those who speak in public are the ones that know more about this." "No me gusta decir boludeces" [I don't like to talk nonsense]. "But," I said, "many times the guys talk nonsense but do not seem to mind." "Oh yeah," she said, "You can write that!"

While there was room for women to hold leadership positions, they stepped back, self-erasing their public presence so that their message would go through. I saw women silently and quietly leading in almost every Argentine movement that I have researched. As they did so, they privileged their political vision over their own egos, at the same time that they allowed for the reinforcement of the already predominant male presence in the public spheres. As Catharine MacKinnon argues, masculinity defines humanity, as it relegates women to the "private, moral, valued, subjective," while men hold the values of the "public, ethical, factual, objective" (MacKinnon 1982). When social movements are represented in public almost exclusively by men, women are relegated to the sphere of the domestic, reinforcing the prevalent idea of masculinity as defining humanity—in public.

While power differentials within the Asamblea gatherings might not be evident at first, some of the organization's public appearances reflect clearly problematic engagements with gender. Perhaps the most notable example was at the European Union, Latin America and Caribbean Business Summit in Vienna, Austria, 2006, where the Asamblea did not hesitate to use a sexy, seminaked female body for the purpose of "advancing the cause." At the same time that a small statue of the Virgin Mary (a woman with a child who has never "known" a man) was prominently displayed among Argentine and Uruguayan flags at their booth, another woman, Evangelina Carrozo, queen of the local Carnival, was commissioned by the local chapter of Greenpeace in coordination with the Asamblea to disrupt the Vienna Summit. During this important meeting, Carrozo stripped off her fur coat and, clad only in her Carnival outfit, displayed a sign that read "NO PULP MILL POLLUTION," in front of the obviously amused heads of state. Though highly successful regarding publicity, Carrozo's appearance also directly reinforced gender stereotypes. The male heads of state present were dressed in serious suits, while Carrozo had to remove her clothing to call their attention. Since there is no inner core to gender, and since gender is constituted by a series of acts, it is our very acts that make gender (Butler 2004). Thus, the Asamblea strategy of relying on a woman's sexualized performance contributed to the fixation of traditional conceptions of femininity, in which women are identified with their bodies to the exclusion of their mental capacities. In contrast, women in positions of power in the Asamblea were performing leadership roles traditionally left to men, making new forms of gender, both for themselves and for the community. I analyze these contradictions as a result of internal disputes over the discursive aspects of their territory as proposals and ideas from different sectors came to clash within the Asamblea, producing a public persona in which women were at the same time seasoned, irreplaceable leaders and sexy subjects of cheap international publicity.

Protests and Performances

The Asamblea has been active not only in international arenas, such as the Vienna Summit, but also in the city of Buenos Aires. This ability of the Asamblea to mobilize beyond its own territory indexes its rhizomatic structure, a characteristic shared by many of the social movements active in the field of politics by other means (Monteagudo 2011). The Asamblea worked mostly with local organizations, or with the local chapters of those organizations. These included the Catholic Church; schoolteachers; elementary and high school students; the Universidad Nacional del Litoral; political parties such as the Union Cívica Radical and the Partido Justicialista (Peronists); guilds such as the ultraconservative Argentine Rural Society (Sociedad Rural Argentina, or SRA); and the Agrarian Federation (Federación Agraria, or FA); and NGOs and activist networks, such as the Madres de Plaza de Mayo (Mothers of the May Square) and the radical Ejército Alpargatista de Liberación Nacional (National Alpargatista Army of Liberation,[8] or Alpargatistas). Beyond their own territory, the Asamblea also had the support of members of the Lista Violeta, a teachers' union at the Facultad de Filosofía y Letras of the University of Buenos Aires (Universidad de Buenos Aires, or UBA), academics from different universities, and, most prominently, popular assemblies from different parts of the country. These preexisting networks constituted a condition for mobilization to occur (Melucci 1996, 291), as they effectively "made" the Asamblea through their participation in the meetings, outreach to their members to join in mobilizations, and material support to travel abroad to learn from the environmental predicament of other pulp mill towns.

The organizations' rhizomatic structure allowed them to spread their influence and actions into other geographic and political territories. In summer 2007, members of the Asamblea, with the support of leftist political parties and popular assemblies from Buenos Aires, set up two plastic pools in front of the Finnish embassy, one with clean water and the other one with dirty water, in allusion to what would happen to the Uruguay River if the pulp mills polluted its waters. Later, they boiled cabbages in huge pots in front of the embassy, as a material-aesthetic reminder of what the town of Gualeguaychú smells like when the wind blows the gas emissions of the pulp mill their way.

On several other occasions, the members of the Asamblea traveled five hours to Buenos Aires in an attempt to blockade the "upper-class" path to Uruguay, Buquebus, a fancy ferry that crosses the Río de la Plata to Uruguay. Although the Kirchner government had been supportive of their struggle as long as it was restricted to Gualeguaychú, it was made clear to the *asambleístas* that any attempt to stop the flow of upper- and middle-class tourists from Buenos Aires to Uruguay would be repressed. While the blockaded bridge allows for mostly local exchanges, Buquebus is used by the upper-middle urban classes of Uruguay and Argentina. As middle-class Argentines were upset about roadblocks by piqueteros in the city, Kirchner showed his strength by repressing an attempted blockade by a middle-class movement, while he continued to allow for the piqueteros' blockades, as part of a class that supported the Kirchner administration. Gualeguaychú was shocked when the TV screens showed the bloodied face of FA leader, Alfredo De Angelis, former Maoist, now turned farmer activist, as he was beat up and arrested by the navy police. De Angelis, credited with starting the roadblock by placing his tractor in the middle of the road, was a popular leader. Demanding his immediate release, in a matter of hours thousands of people blockaded Route 14 in Gualeguaychú, the Mercosur Highway, until De Angelis was freed.

While there were no dissonant voices when it came to freeing De Angelis, within the Asamblea there were always tensions and debates over how to engage the state, echoing somehow their contradictions over gender balance. In 2005, sectors of the Partido Justicialista in Gualeguaychú, for example, wanted an end to the blockade. As I was driven to the bridge for the first time, a former mayor of Gualeguaychú asked me for my "expert help" with "these people, who have constructed an identity around drinking mate by the bridge." His argument was not against the blockade, but rather about timing—the blockade was necessary at first; now more dialogue with the Argentine and Uruguayan governments might work better. Similarly, Greenpeace, which had coordinated many of the initial direct actions, had disagreements with the Asamblea starting in 2006 (http://edant.clarin.com/diario /2007/11/26/elpais/p-1549369.htm). While Greenpeace activists marched over the bridge in 2005, chaining themselves to Botnia's private bridge, as early as 2006 Greenpeace was criticizing the permanent blockade. By 2007, Greenpeace was openly calling for "clean" pulp mills and advocating the lifting of the blockade to engage in talks with Botnia and the Uruguayan and Argentine governments to allow for "clean" industries, while the Asamblea wanted Botnia to leave the area entirely. José, drinking mate by the side of the road, was certain that "if we lift the blockade, people will soon forget about our situation." At the same time, other neighbors without political or social movement affiliation mobilized the citizens of Gualeguaychú throughout the Kirchner presidency, appearing at almost every one of his public events with signs against the pulp mill. "We want him to have to say in public that he supports our cause," explained Ana, the working-class woman who organized the bus trips. The form and the timing for engaging the state seemed to be determined more by the opportunities that arose and the balance of forces within the Asamblea, rather than stemming from a preconceived notion of the role of the state.

Conclusion

Perceptions of the Asamblea's actions as uncivic need to be contextualized within the broader context of the incapacity of a weakened state to provide for its citizens. As Argentina plunged into previously unknown poverty, unemployment, and despair, social movements' roadblocks, occupation of buildings, and other direct action tactics created social consent for the implementation of politics by other means. These other means of making politics were credited with social successes such as the implementation of welfare plans for the unemployed. However, there is no denying that their particular form of protest normalized tactics that, when later taken up by right-wing movements, threatened the same social sectors of society that had introduced them in the mid-1990s: the unemployed.

In 2008 one of the cofounders of the Gualeguaychú Asamblea and leader of the FA, Alfredo De Angelis, led a massive, three-month-long farmer lock-out featuring road blockades that threatened the well-being of the population in the cities. Led by the SRA, rural producers rose up against an increase in taxes on agricultural exports destined to subsidize welfare plans (Fair Rzezak 2008). As the movement gained the support of vast sectors of the urban middle and upper classes, the government was defeated. While unemployed workers' early "uncivic" actions should be credited with pushing neoliberalism to a second, more inclusive stage (Cornia, Jolly, and Stewart 1987; Laurie and Bonnett 2002) embodied in the Kirchner administration, the success of the farmers' lock-out points us once again to the incapacity of the neoliberal state to support and protect its most disadvantaged classes. The struggle of the unemployed opened a discursive space that allowed for peaceful warfare (Graeber 2003) tactics in times when democratic institutions were not responding to traditional protests. It is nevertheless clear that once the boundaries of civic engagement were pushed, the rural landowners began to draw on a "toolkit" similar to that of left-leaning piqueteros—only this time they were protesting progressive taxation meant to support the poor and unemployed populations.[9] As modes of resistance are "never in a position of exteriority in relation to power" (Foucault 1990, 95), yesterday's successful popular tactics of resistance to the power of neoliberalism might create a scenario that hurts those same popular classes, further weakening democracy.

The Asamblea's permanent four-year-long blockade of the international bridge needs to be analyzed as resistance by mostly middle-class actors to ethnicized and localized neoliberal practices of dispossession (Harvey 2005), which threatened their ability to survive. While the Uruguayan government claimed to have no alternative but to offer its rivers, forests, and a highly educated population to a European corporation, the population of Gualeguay-chú, recovering—just as Uruguay—from the economic strictures of the 1990s, chose a different economic model, which rested on rejecting their territory's pulp mill pollution. After surviving the 1990s, Gualeguaychú's vision followed on the steps of Kirchner's modification of neoliberal biopolitics. In this model, while the Andes, as an "empty frontier," were and are still violated every day by polluting global industries, Gualeguaychú presented a productive territory for tourism and for export agriculture.

While the Asamblea's tactics resembled those of the piqueteros, their gender politics reflected the influence of the Encuentro Nacional de Mujeres and the sidestreaming of feminisms through the popular assembly movement in that women had leadership roles. However, as the Asamblea constituted a space that allowed for a multiplicity of social movements and groups with a variety of political positions—ranging from the SRA and the Catholic Church, to the Alpargatistas—the decision-making meetings of the Asamblea were spaces for the struggle over meanings and articulation of actions. Thus, at the same time that women held leadership roles, a woman's seminaked, sexualized body was deployed as a weapon of mass attention, while most women worked quietly behind the scenes, indexing the different tendencies and politics of the groups involved.

The women's silent work and the not-so-silent work of the men to protect the river proved fruitful. Out of the original plan for eleven pulp mills, only Botnia was completed and is still operating. In 2010, the Hague Tribunal reached a decision regarding this conflict. They established that both countries should closely monitor Botnia's emissions. At this point, the Argentine government forced the Asamblea to lift the blockade of the bridge, but the Asamblea remains vigilant and organized. Because of the Asamblea's struggle, there is dual-state supervision of the pulp mill's activities, following the Hague Tribunal guidelines. The Asamblea's nonhierarchical power structure and rhizomatic connections, its multiclass composition, its use of protest theater and art, and its engagement in peaceful warfare with women's incipient leadership, explains how its members were able to articulate vast sectors of the Argentine population and gain international attention for their cause. Drinking mate, I write these last lines in Massachusetts, and send my strength to the women who shared their mate with me, as we gazed over their sandy, lazy, beloved Uruguay River.[10]

NOTES

1. I follow Arturo Escobar's definition of "territory": "the fundamental and multidimensional space for the creation and re-creation of the social, economic, and cultural values and practices of the communities" (1998).

2. Following the official pardon by Carlos Menem in 1989 of all the military involved in state terrorism (1976–83), the children of the disappeared (Hijos por la Identidad y la Justicia contra el Olvido y el Silencio, or HIJOS) started organizing *escraches*. These mass mobilizations involved street theater and other peaceful tactics against military officers' private homes, in an effort to isolate these officers in their own barrios.

3. Translation is mine for this and for all the other ethnographic quotes.

4. The First Encuentro de Mujeres was in Buenos Aires in May 1986, with 960 women attending from all over the country. These days approximately 30,000 women discuss issues related to gender and feminisms, through horizontal connections and an emphasis on diversity. See http://encuentrodemujeres.com.ar/.

5. For details on these processes, see Monteagudo (2011).

6. Genetically modified soy requires the use of glyphosate, a chemical produced by Monsanto. The Asamblea remains quiet about the contamination brought by the use of this chemical because at the beginning, even the environmentalists involved decided that introducing the issue of the contaminant used to grow soy would divide Gualeguaychú (my interview with El Flaco, Alpargatista, 2014). Secondly, Asamblea members also explain that "comparing glyphosate with Botnia is like comparing a mild flu with cancer" (my interview with Mabel, teacher, 2007).

7. *Bola* is an Argentine slang for "attention."

8. *Alpargata* is traditional footwear of rural and poor sectors of the Argentine population.

9. I do not place rural landowners and their followers in the field of politics by other means, because their struggle was not against neoliberalism, but rather in support of neoliberal policies, as they rose up against state support for the most vulnerable.

10. While any mistakes are my responsibility, I am grateful for the help received in writing this article. Julie Hemment, Ann Ferguson, Millie Thayer, Sonia Alvarez, Vanesa "Yuli" Prieto, and Jeff Rubin provided great comments, suggestions and advice. I am also grateful to members of the Asamblea who spent their time talking with me about their relentless work to protect the river they so much love, especially Mabel and Luisina for their hospitality. I also thank the faculty and staff at the Center for Latin American, Latino and Caribbean Studies at UMass, Amherst, for generous support for my fieldwork in Gualeguaychú.

Chapter 8

———

THE "GRAY ZONE" BETWEEN MOVEMENTS AND MARKETS
Brazilian Feminists and the International Aid Chain

MILLIE THAYER

In the 1990s, I did ethnographic research with two women's organizations in northeast Brazil, both founded in 1980 as the authoritarian regime was beginning to come undone.[1] The Movement of Rural Women Workers (Movimento de Mulheres Trabalhadoras Rurais, or MMTR) had a large constituency of peasants and rural workers scattered across the semiarid sertão region; SOS Corpo was a nongovernmental feminist women's health organization located in Recife, a large city on the coast.[2] Over time, the two had developed a close working relationship. The NGO offered workshops and seminars to the rural women on sexuality, women's health, and the body, sharing feminist knowledge and pedagogies constructed in part through their creative engagement with movements in other regions of the world. Women from the sertão brought both access to their rural membership and local knowledge of organizing and working-class life. For many years, the two organizations collaborated on research projects and campaigns around women's issues.

As I spent time with each of them, however, I noticed a disturbing phenomenon: the subtle incursion into their relationship of practices more reminiscent of a competitive market than of feminist solidarity. At a meeting of the regional rural women's network in 1998, for example, members discovered that SOS had apparently taken a booklet on gender and rural women jointly produced with the MMTR and transformed it into their own exclusive product. Although the information on rural women had been deleted, the unilateral move provoked an outcry. "We can't manage to sell our own [booklet] and [then] those intellectuals go and make one and sell it!" said one woman bitterly.[3] "Our primer became an SOS text without consultation with the MMTR!" exclaimed another. A sense of betrayal hovered in the room. Although it was not clear whether the urban NGO was actually profiting from the sale of the pamphlet, the perception of the rural women was that institutional interests were taking precedence over long-standing political relationships based on trust and shared values. The class inequalities made the issue all the more sensitive: for the rural women, it appeared to be a case of middle- and upper-class urban privilege reasserting itself.

There were other signs of trouble as well. At this same meeting, members learned that the urban NGO was offering a costly five-day seminar to other activists on the topic of rural women, without having invited or informed the rural movement about the event. In this case, not only had the significance of their alliance been disregarded but, it seemed, their very life experiences had been stolen and converted into a commodity to be sold on the open market. As one woman put it, "They appropriated all of our production, the reality of the countryside." Their stories of suppressed sexuality and involuntary reproduction, of invisible labor and inaccessible citizenship, had suddenly acquired a new kind of symbolic value, which had simultaneously slipped from their hands.

In each of these cases, the MMTR challenged its urban counterpart over what it viewed as self-interested violations of the spirit of their alliance. Response from SOS Corpo was quick, discussions ensued, and ruptures were healed. In fact, theirs was among the most long-lasting and mutually respectful relationship between an NGO and a grassroots movement that I saw in many years of research.[4] Nevertheless, and perhaps even more urgently, these incidents and others that I observed raised troubling questions about the pressures on social movement relationships to take on calculative dimensions they may not have had in the past. What was the source of these pressures?

Where did these discourses and practices come from, and why did the late 1990s see them appear among feminist and other activists in Brazil?

Javier Auyero (2007) uses the term *gray zones* to describe the startling intersections he found between social movement activists and state actors in Argentina. In this chapter, I extend Auyero's conception of the gray zone to incorporate another set of murky relations: the encounters and engagements between movements and capitalist markets. In one sense, this is not a new phenomenon. Many movement organizations have made strategic decisions to enter a variety of kinds of markets—as a means of personal or institutional survival, a mode of disseminating critiques, or a method of demonstrating the viability of alternative social arrangements.[5] Microcredit programs, marketing campaigns, cooperatives, and collective enterprises all represent explicit and politically informed choices by social movement activists to try to turn markets to their own purposes. Whether their contributions to social change are judged positively or not, activist organizations have generally undertaken these strategies with their eyes open, after weighing the potential benefits and dangers to their values and long-term goals.

But here I am concerned with encounters that come from the other direction—not conscious decisions made by activists to enter markets, but stealthy incursions from commodifying discourses that threaten to restructure social movement practices and relationships, like the ones described above, uninvited. New kinds of calculative behavior and competition among allies, resurgent class divisions, the commodification of priceless goods, an emphasis on marketing at the expense of fundamental values, corporate-style organizational structures, and the elevation of quantitative outcomes over qualitative processes are among the troubling traces of the capitalist market that emerged in my fieldwork and have been noted elsewhere in the literature (Bob 2005; Cooley and Ron 2002; Incite! Women of Color against Violence 2007; Murdock 2008; Schild 1998).

My questions about this phenomenon revolve around the origins and mechanisms by which commodifying discourses invaded spaces often explicitly antagonistic to them. How is it that feminist movement organizations like those in Brazil, with roots in the Left and antineoliberal political commitments, at times found themselves—to their chagrin—reproducing what looked like entrepreneurial practices or relationships with one another? When and how did this begin, and what caused it to recur over time? Was it an inevitable outcome of a certain stage in a social movement cycle or, rather, the contingent reflection of a particular historical moment and form of global political economy?

Much of the literature answers the question of the origins of calculative behavior by pointing the finger at the way professionalization in the last two decades shifted the nature of activism, as well as its divisive effects on relations between middle-class feminists and working-class women (Alvarez 1999; Bickham Mendez 2005; Lebon 1996; Murdock 2008; Thayer 2001, 2010). But while the dynamics of "NGO-ization" may have been a proximate cause of these tensions, I argue that the emergence of market-based practices and discourses in social movement counterpublics, such as the one constructed around gender, must be situated more broadly in the shifting architecture of international aid regimes that span the space between Latin American movements and their financial sponsors.[6]

In particular, I argue, the period of the late 1990s, when the incident described earlier took place, was a key moment in which the relationships between market and movement were set in motion. During that time the aid regime came to take the form of segmented transnational relationships— what I call "shadow commodity chains"—that linked activists in grassroots organizations (GROs) in the Global South, their counterpart local NGOs, international funding agencies, states of the Global North, and their respective civil societies in relationships of discursive production, consumption, and exchange. Although analogous to the commodity chains first described by world-systems theorists Terrence Hopkins and Immanuel Wallerstein (1977), which connect producers or assemblers of manufactured goods in the Global South to distributors and consumers in the North, the goods traded along the alternative commodity chains described here were largely intangible. At each step in the chain, actors exchanged monetary contributions, or other forms of support, for discursive commodities, such as claims of success or working-class authenticity, which were then traded further "up" the chain, in the direction of the sources of economic capital. While commodity chains as conventionally understood are a constitutive element of the world economy, shadow aid chains played a fundamental role in what we might think of as the cultural economy of development—an arena in which narratives and representations surrounding the project of social "improvement," but also of social justice, were produced, exchanged, and consumed (Li 2007) (see figure 8.1).

Aid Architectures and Neoliberal Political Economies

The evolution of aid architectures that targeted social movements paralleled developments in the larger economic, political, and cultural context of the late twentieth and early twenty-first centuries. Private religious and philanthropic

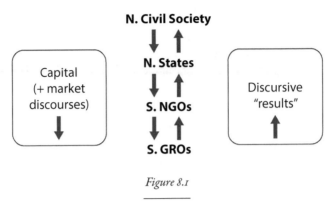

Figure 8.1

Shadow commodity chain.

agencies distributing humanitarian aid to the Global South initially emerged in tandem with colonial projects and then proliferated in response to the effects of World War I. However, the first aid regime aimed at supporting social change organizations did not take shape until the late 1960s into the 1970s in the wake of decolonization, as governments, churches, and the United Nations led a shift in aid from relief work to poverty-alleviation (Biekart 1999). In Latin America during this period, dictatorships ruled throughout most of the region including Brazil and, post-1973, a wide swath of nations faced economic crises linked to the international debt. The *solidarity aid regime* was constituted by nongovernmental donors in Western Europe and the United States who sought to sustain opposition forces and to support community-based organizing around survival issues from the high cost of living to the lack of local infrastructure. In the context of authoritarian rule, agencies sought to operate under the radar and to practice solidarity, rather than charity. The structure of aid was relatively informal and based on direct, trust-based relations between donors and grantees, with few requirements or onerous demands for accountability (Lebon 1998).

The late 1970s and early 1980s brought new political openings to Latin America, but also rising debt and draconian belt-tightening policies. By the mid-1980s, civil society struggles to reverse these policies or ameliorate their devastating effects, and the efforts of sympathetic nongovernmental donors in the Global North to support them, were beginning to produce a second, more complex, and increasingly structured aid regime—what I call the *shadow commodity chain*. As state aid programs retooled from supporting colonial policy to promoting "development" in the newly independent countries of Asia, Africa, and Latin America, officials began to view private aid agencies based in the North as offering more efficiency and better access to grassroots actors (Hulme and Edwards 1997b). State money poured in to nongovernmental donor agencies and, by the 1980s, their numbers had multiplied, and many were heavily dependent on government funds.[7] Over the next decade and a half, until the turn of the century, international funding underwrote the development of a "Third Sector" charged with filling the gaps left by the retreat of the state.

Hoping to push forward or take advantage of political openings in the region, in this second social movement-oriented regime, European and U.S.-based nongovernmental agencies funded not only service provision, but also the members of the multiple counterpublics that flourished during the 1980s and 1990s—the feminist, Afro-Latino, indigenous, LGBT, slum dweller, farmer, and other movements for the rights of marginalized, stigmatized, or exploited groups. Agencies—such as the Ford and MacArthur Foundations in the United States, Bread for the World in Germany, and Oxfam UK—provided sizeable amounts of funding to Brazilian feminists.[8] So too did the large donor institutions based in the Netherlands, which together provided a disproportionate amount of the aid that went to Latin American feminist and other movement organizations.[9] Feminist NGOs such as SOS Corpo came to depend to different degrees on the flows of funding that Dutch and other sources provided.

The goal of funding was, increasingly, not just to address particular social problems, but to construct an active civil society, capable of fostering and functioning effectively within the new democracies in the region. Part of this agenda involved the professionalizing of social movement actors, a process that led to internal specialization, rising demand for educational credentials among staff, and, often, a growing distance and/or greater tensions between NGOs and their working-class constituencies (Alvarez 1999; Bickham Mendez 2005; Lebon 1996; Murdock 2008; Thayer 2001, 2010).

By the 1990s, the relations between donors and social movement recipients had become more formalized and more strained. Newly minted advocacy-based NGOs in Latin America now often acted as intermediaries between grassroots movements and international development agencies. These professionalized movement organizations, in turn, answered to more insistent demands from the international agencies, who also found the purse strings held by their own state and private donors increasingly tightening, as the discourses and practices of the market spread through European and U.S. civil societies. It is in the context of the increasingly fraught aid regime of the mid-1980s to late 1990s that the shadow commodity chain was articulated and

TABLE 8.1. Aid regimes in Brazil

Solidarity Aid Regime	Shadow Commodity Chain	Diversified Local Funding Regimes
Late 1960s–1970s	Mid-1980s–2000	2000s–
Dictatorship / import substitution	Democratization / early neoliberalism	Pink Tide / late neoliberalism
Left-leaning European foundations, churches, voluntarism	International private funding agencies	The state, corporate philanthropy, feminist foundations, voluntarism

came to structure relationships between social movement organizations in the Global South and their Northern supporters.

In this chapter I focus on this seminal period for the construction of linkages between markets and movements. The next section examines the scholarly response to the development of international aid relations and the professionalization of social movements that it entailed. My own argument emerges in dialogue with the literature on commodity chains, finding both parallels and differences between the economic relationships theorized by Hopkins and Wallerstein and the cultural and political nature of the connections highlighted here. The body of the chapter then traces the shadow commodity chain whose links brought both calculative discourses and productive resources to feminist movements in the Global South, such as the ones I studied in Brazil. In the conclusion, I suggest that recent shifts in neoliberal formations over the last decade are being accompanied, at least in Latin America, by a third, much more nationally focused, configuration of *diversified local funding regimes* (see table 8.1).

Theorizing Aid Relations

Scholars of Latin American politics, many writing from the Left, responded with elation to the unleashing of civil societies as authoritarian regimes fell across the region in the 1970s and 1980s. Francisco Weffort's comment from the perspective of Brazil reflected the euphoria of the time: "We want a civil society. . . . [I]f it does not exist, we need to invent it" (1989, 349). But as activists moved from the clandestine struggle against dictatorships to participation in new democracies, they struggled with difficult choices about how and whether to take on the responsibilities of a retreating state for social welfare in highly unequal societies.

Scholarly analysis, meanwhile, grew increasingly critical of the role played by the proliferation of newly founded NGOs that were becoming the iconic face of civil society promoted by donors. Some, like James Petras (1997), argued that the NGO-ization of social movements in Latin America embodied "neoliberalism from below," the velvet glove on the iron hand of free trade and structural adjustment. Others critiqued the imposition of Western forms of knowledge and identities and the depoliticizing effects of development's "anti-politics machine" (Escobar 1995; Ferguson 1994). And many interrogated the status of alleged North-South "partnerships" and their effects on the autonomy and critical character of Latin American social movements.[10]

Each of these critiques gave us tools to understand the perils of aid relationships for those committed to making transformative social change. Institutionalization, co-optation, and discursive absorption continue to represent real dangers facing social movement activists in the contemporary world (Alvarez 1998). But too often descriptions of the processes that can lead to these outcomes had the conspiratorial feel and foregone conclusions of some versions of power elite theory: money always seemed to produce its desired ideological outcomes. The implicit assumption was that when funding is present, activists will abandon their principles, target constituencies will take on—unmodified—the identities they have been assigned, and dominant discourses and the minutiae of technical remedies will definitively disable critical faculties and make political challenges not only impossible but "unimaginable," in Dylan Rodríguez's words (2007, 27).

Feminist work, much of it grounded in recent case studies in a wide range of settings, offers a far more nuanced picture of funding relationships (Alvarez 1999; Bagic 2006; Bickham Mendez 2005; Ewig 1999; Ford-Smith 1997; Hemment 2007; Incite! Women of Color against Violence 2007; Lang 1997; Lebon 1996, 1998; Murdock 2008; Nagar and Sangtin Writers 2006; Silliman 1999; Sperling, Ferree, and Risman 2001; Thayer 2001, 2010). These studies depict feminist NGOs not as victims caught in a global funding web, but as agents making strategic choices within the constraints of difficult circumstances. The power may still be unequal, as Valerie Sperling and her coauthors (2001) point out, but the contestation evident in these studies belies simple narratives of subjection and co-optation.

Rosalind Petchesky, citing Pheng Cheah's analysis of human rights discourse, comments that "there is no pure and innocent place to be" (2003, 24). Movements always operate within discursive fields of power relations—these are the shifting grounds on which they do their work.[11] Effective strategies require an understanding of the structure of the particular circumstances with and in which movements contend. I suggest that the field of power confronted by Brazilian feminists in the 1990s took the form of the segmented series of relationships that stretched from the Brazilian *bairros* and backlands to the middle-class core of its cities and then on to Europe and the United States, linking Southern grassroots organizations and advocacy NGOs, Northern nongovernmental donor organizations, states, and civil societies.

In many ways, the aid chain was reminiscent of the commodity chains theorized by world-systems theorists. Capital in the form of aid money traveled down the chain and was exchanged for products at each of a series of intermediary sites. But, as Priti Ramamurthy (2004) also finds in her study of images of Indian cotton producers in the Land's End catalogue, the commodities being traded for cash were discursive, rather than "real." What was produced and exchanged at each site were not physical goods, but symbolic products: claims of representativity, assertions of authenticity, and narratives of success. Through their participation in the chain, actors were linked not to the world market as Hopkins and Wallerstein understood it, in its narrow economic dimension, but to *discourses* of the market as generated by global capital and transmitted by the development industry.

The sometimes troubled relations between the rural women's movement and the urban NGO feminists of SOS Corpo, described at the beginning of the chapter, constituted the first link in the shadow commodity chain that joined Brazilian women's movements with their distant donors in the late 1990s. In what follows, I will trace the chain as it moves North through two further sets of links: first, the relation between SOS and its international donor agencies; and second, the relation between one particular set of Northern donor agencies—those in the Netherlands—and the Dutch state. I will then, briefly, suggest some elements in the relation during this period between the Dutch state and its own "donors"—civil society and political parties. At each stage, I will argue, the material resources that moved "down" the chain were embedded in particular discourses and practices of the market that recipients were forced to engage. But engagement was not equivalent to passive incorporation. Actors "lower" on the chain enjoyed an intangible form of leverage— the symbolic capital that they themselves produced and that they exchanged for material resources at every site along the chain. The last section in the body of the chapter illustrates some of the actors' struggles to negotiate or refuse market-based meanings. I conclude with a glimpse of the new aid regime that has begun to reconfigure the shadow commodity chain in more recent years, leading social movement participants to turn from international aid to relationships with states and other, increasingly local, actors.

SOS Corpo and the Donor Agencies

The NGO described above, SOS Corpo, began as a small collective of urban middle- and upper-class women who met to talk about sexuality and practice gynecological self-help exams together in the late 1970s. Its members had been influenced by *Our Bodies, Ourselves*, the women's health manual published in Boston in 1969, as well as by feminist health movements in France, where some had been exiled during the dictatorship (Boston Women's Health Course Collective). These movements claimed as a means of empowerment for women the bodily knowledge that had been monopolized by the medical establishment. But the Brazilian founders of SOS had their roots in the Left movements against dictatorship and faced a different social and political context than did feminists in the United States and Europe. As a result, their attention soon shifted across class boundaries to the peripheral bairros of Recife and, later, the rural interior, where they did outreach and popular education about women's health and sexuality.

By 1997, the organization had evolved from collective to professionalized NGO with a $500,000 budget, 80 percent of it from international donor agencies. Its projects had multiplied, and its members' voices were beginning to be heard in the institutions of the state, as well as in the bairros and the sertão. Over time, the NGO's practices shifted as it responded to the urgent demands of defending women's rights to health on a broader scale. The organization increasingly concerned itself with achieving visibility, maximizing impact, and positioning itself vis-à-vis other NGOs. Instead of holding workshops in the bairros, the organization redefined itself as a kind of think tank that would produce knowledge, train decision makers, and foment national and international debate. And, as a consequence, its relationship to working-class women in grassroots movements became more distant than it had once been.

These political choices were made in the context of changes in the nature of the international aid regime. The explosion of new NGOs in Brazil in the 1980s meant increased competition among them for donor dollars in the 1990s, giving funding agencies greater leverage to make demands on grantees. Agencies increasingly took a "strategic" approach, providing sizeable grants with multiyear commitments to only a few chosen recipients. And, as material resources flowed downward through the aid chain from Europe and the United States to places such as Recife in Brazil, they were accompanied by a series of market-oriented meanings embedded in agency requirements and funding criteria.

The first of these discourses claimed that *healthy competition* would strengthen some (market) actors and weed out the weak or deficient. The assertion was materialized in quantitative indicators that often fostered comparisons and intensified preexisting rivalries among potential grantees in a way that was less evident when the forms of evaluation were more holistic. Second, the agencies' demand for *efficiency and calculable results* required NGOs to deemphasize time-consuming efforts to raise consciousness and involve working-class women in project design and evaluation, in favor of activities that produced measurable outcomes, such as numbers of workshops held or quantity of documents produced.

Third, the discourse of *self-reliance and sustainability* was reflected in the way SOS and other NGOs were forced to peddle their wares in order to acquire matching funds: videos, publications, workshops, and consulting time all became commodities to be sold to the state as well as to other social movement organizations. The SOS conference and booklet that provoked so much anger among the rural women may have been a case in point. As a result, groups that once were simply feminist allies now also became, respectively, vendors and clients, with the attendant tensions that this implied. Finally, the power of the discourse of *accountability* surfaced in the way staff found themselves spending more and more time justifying their work to ensure the continued flow of funding. They complained that endless cycles of report writing and the frequent evaluator visits interfered with their ability to do the organizing and education work the organization was founded to do. In the version of the term they were encountering, the lines of accountability ran upward to the agencies, rather than downward to groups such as the MMTR.[12]

Clearly there were multiple influences on the strategy and structure of NGOs such as SOS, but I argue that the relation with international funding agencies was a key site for the production and dissemination of market discourses to women's movements in northeast Brazil. The following section uses the case of aid agencies in the Netherlands, among the most significant sources of funds for Latin American feminists in the 1990s and early 2000s, to describe what was happening at the next set of relationships on the shadow chain: how these meanings and practices were produced within the agencies and disseminated to NGO "partners" in the Global South including SOS.

Donor Agencies—the State

The aid industry and its relationship to states varied to some degree across Europe in terms of policies and the onset or intensification of neoliberal political pressures on aid policy. The Netherlands, with its strong welfare state and historical commitment to aid to the postcolonial world, took longer to show the effects of neoliberal discourse on aid relations than did other countries, but by the beginning of the 2000s they were definitively on display. The Netherlands was home to a number of private, nonprofit donor agencies with a long history of supporting feminist organizations such as SOS Corpo around the world. The outsourcing of development aid by the state through a system called "co-financing" led to a situation where the aid budget was literally divided between the four largest agencies in the Netherlands—CEBEMO, ICCO, NOVIB, and HIVOS.[13] In 1993, the share of income received by these donor institutions from state sources ranged from 71 percent to 98 percent, making them highly vulnerable to shifts in the prevailing political climate.[14]

Indeed, the Netherlands experienced a political zigzag beginning in the early 1980s from neoliberal reforms precipitated by economic crisis, to prosperity and more progressive policies in the latter half of the 1990s and into the new century. However, in 2002 the discursive universe swerved right once more with the emergence of an ultraconservative, anti-immigrant political party. Although the party's leader, Pim Fortuyn, was assassinated and the party itself lost support because of its internal conflicts, the right-wing coalition government elected in 2003 launched renewed welfare reform, privatization of health care, and stricter immigration policies. My research there a few years later illustrated the significant effect of the neoliberalized political climate on aid policies and relations between donor agencies and their counterparts in the so-called developing world.[15] This was the period when the shadow commodity chain, already entrenched elsewhere, reached its full expression in the Netherlands.

In 2003, the Dutch state tightened the purse strings to the cofinancing agencies. Rather than guarantee funds to the four largest agencies, the ministry created a competitive bidding process, receiving applications from more than 100 donor institutions in the next round of allocations in 2006.[16] Simultaneously, new market-oriented requirements were imposed. In their proposals for government funding, agencies were asked to list not only broad objectives, but also the specific, quantitatively expressed outcomes they expected to receive at the level not only of their immediate grantees, but also of the grantees' target groups, for each of the succeeding four years. For example, the agency would have had to ask SOS to project not only the results they as an organization would produce in this time, but also the outcomes of the work of their rural counterparts in the MMTR, among others. In a final move, the government required the agencies who received their funds to raise at least 25 percent of their budget from private—corporate or individual—donors.

Whether or not the earlier cofinancing system was an ideal one, these changes clearly represented a move toward an aid regime structured around market-based discourses and practices. Ironically, the discursive packaging for the new policies was quite similar to the one being disseminated to feminist NGOs in Brazil by these self-same agencies, with similarly problematic outcomes.

Just as feminists in Brazil were expected to vie with one another on the aid market, the Dutch state sought to promote ostensibly *healthy competition* among donor agencies. While this was billed as a means of democratizing the aid process, my interviewees reported that the outcome was a climate of rivalry and mutual suspicion among nongovernmental donor institutions, in which those who once collaborated now hesitated to share new ideas that might give them an edge in the next round of funding applications. As in the case of their Brazilian NGO grantees, donor agencies were asked to become more *self-reliant and self-sustaining.* This led them to resort to increased efforts to tap individual donors. Direct mail campaigns not only sharpened competition for scarce donations but, interviewees confessed, led to an effort to simplify the message and to "brand" themselves, just as SOS and other Southern NGOs were being forced to do to attract donor agency funding. It also encouraged the commodification of their "product," the deserving Latin American (or Asian or African) poor, often in the form of dramatic visual depictions of the victims of poverty. Positioning the donor institutions as the salvation of the "Third World" poor was at odds with the political critiques of development held by many of their staff members, as well as their self-conception as allies, rather than as rescuers.

The new discourse of *accountability* took material form in the demands for applications and reports that were often hundreds of pages long, full of statistics, pie charts, and glossy photos. Just as for their Brazilian "partners," preparing these documents required an enormous investment of staff time from Dutch agencies. The process also signaled a new kind of relationship to the state, which brought with it the potential of political censorship. Indeed, one organization had had its hands slapped by the government when it funded a protest of immigrant deportation. The implicit threat was that those who didn't follow the party line would not receive funding. Finally, the discourse of *results,* which required agency staff to specify the ultimate outputs of their aid in the hands of grantees and their "targets," had similar effects in the North as it did in the South: aid staff were forced to reduce social change goals to measureable units, at the risk of emphasizing visible events or tangible products over harder-to-see, but more long-lasting, qualitative transformations. Ultimately, the agencies passed the pressures from the Dutch state for quantifiable outcomes on "down" the chain to their grantees, along with the discourses of accountability, self-reliance, and healthy competition. The new "results-oriented" market discourses coming not only from the Netherlands, but from donors in other countries as well, led to the kind of conflicts between NGO grantees and their own working-class allies described at the beginning of this chapter.

The State—Political and Civil Society

The final step in the chain, which I will just mention briefly here, was the relationship between Northern states and a public sphere in which a variety of economic and political actors—transnational corporations, multilateral institutions, right-wing political parties—actively circulated and promoted the discourses that we have seen being expressed at other sites along the aid chain. In the Netherlands in particular, public anxieties about the decline of what had been one of the strongest welfare states in the world and about growing immigration were channeled by these forces either toward vindictive xenophobia, or toward narrowly defined "efficient" and "effective" charitable solutions to poverty and oppression in the postcolonial world. The state—and the development agencies it financed—were called to account by a taxpaying public increasingly concerned about its own future and impatient with the apparent incapacity of Dutch development aid in the face of ever-expanding global poverty.[17]

Struggles along the Shadow Commodity Chain

The origins of market-based discourses in the shadow commodity chain are difficult to pinpoint; what is clear is that the pressures they exerted for particular forms of results and accountability, of self-reliance and competition, were felt—and then reproduced and passed on—by actors at every site along the chain. The process posed significant dangers for relations among the diverse and widely scattered members of the feminist counterpublic.

This could be read as a story of invulnerable discursive power—but the shadow chain was structured around a series of exchanges, and the flows of meanings moved in more than one direction. At each site along the chain, cash was exchanged for "results"—discursive evidence or at least promises of development and gendered social change. Images of successful cooperatives, well-attended meetings, and productive campaigns—backed by the involvement of authentic working-class women—were the currencies initially traded for financial and other kinds of support by social movements at the least economically advantaged end of the chain. These discursive commodities were then redeployed by the recipient, whether Brazilian feminist NGO, Dutch cofinancing agency, or the Dutch state, to satisfy its own "investors" further up the chain.

The exchanges along the shadow chain threatened to commodify local identities and resources and to produce friction among allies, as we saw earlier. However, the outcomes were not foreordained: capital did not always triumph, nor did the market always have its way. The structure of the shadow chain was such that those with more economic capital and political power depended for their own survival and growth on the images of successful development generated by subaltern actors. The reciprocal nature of exchanges offered two kinds of power to less economically advantaged actors. On the one hand, they gained a certain amount of instrumental leverage to advance their immediate interests—whether winning or extending a grant, bargaining for more reasonable timelines, or reworking evaluation criteria.[18] But apparently disempowered actors also drew on another kind of symbolic power, one which worked through values and meanings shared to different degrees across the chain. Running parallel to the currencies of "results" described above, but in reverse direction, were moral and political discourses of transnational feminist solidarity, downward accountability, and alternatives to global capitalism which constituted the oppositional political space contained in the feminist counterpublic (see figure 8.2).

These forms of moral capital made possible a series of cooperative challenges to the discourses of the market by rural Brazilian women, feminist NGOs, and donor agency staff.[19] Struggles were sometimes undertaken at one site along the chain, but in other cases stretched across sites and involved collusion among a variety of actors. At one end of the chain, grassroots organizations such as the MMTR staked a claim to independence, invoking their legitimacy, as representatives of a large constituency of working-class women, to define the nature of their own projects and the criteria used to evaluate their success. In venues including a public meeting organized by SOS Corpo that I observed, rural activists called out paternalistic donor practices, which they viewed as reflecting a "colonizing mentality." They also resisted the discourse of *results* by making an invitation to donors to visit the sertão—the rural interior—to show them the conditions that they faced and the absurdities of some of the agencies' demands.

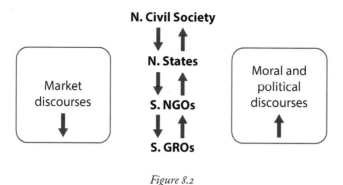

Figure 8.2

Parallel discursive flows.

Further up the shadow chain, Latin American feminist NGOs formed national and transnational networks to both negotiate and collaborate with their distant funding sources, thereby insisting on downward, rather than upward *accountability*. One such effort, in which SOS played a coordinating role, was La Red Entre Mujeres (the Network among Women). The network, which included Dutch agency NOVIB staff and grantees working from feminist or gender-sensitive perspectives, became a vehicle for promoting feminist perspectives on development and for advocating for changes in inequitable funding relationships. There were also attempts to challenge the discourse of *competition* by collectivizing the process of fundraising, sharing contacts, and strategizing with other feminist organizations. For example, the non-profit Association for Women in Development (AWID), based in Mexico and Canada, launched a research project "Where's the Money for Women's Rights?" Among other activities, the organization held a conference in Mexico that drew 300 representatives from women's organizations around the world to learn about different sources and discuss the how-to, as well as the ethics and politics of, fundraising.

Higher on the chain, funding agency representatives made transnational alliances with their grantees to lobby Northern states and multilateral institutions around development policies. Staff members of Dutch cofinancing agencies argued that doling out aid was not enough when European trade policies served to perpetuate global inequalities. In effect, they demanded greater *self-reliance* from European states, rather than from the poor in the Global South, who have too long borne the economic burdens of the North. One last approach has been the creation of new women's funds, including

Fundo Elas in Brazil, Semillas in Mexico, and the Fondo Centroamericano de Mujeres in Nicaragua, which raise funds locally and provide seed money for women's and feminist projects. Among their innovations have been alternative forms of evaluation that involve grantees and recognize qualitative as well as quantitative "results."[20] In all of these ways, feminists and fellow travelers both challenged the sources of commodification and defended the values that sustained their counterpublic.

Conclusion/Postscript

This chapter has explored the first shadowy encounters between movements and markets, through the lens of women's and feminist movements in Brazil and their donors in the Netherlands. Gray zones are, by nature, contested sites where divergent discourses and practices encounter one another. The shadow commodity chain was such a space, one that facilitated the passage of neoliberal meanings, but also created openings for critical discourses and practices that embodied hopes for a different kind of future. Actors in different locations used their leverage to improve their standing vis-à-vis others, but, like SOS Corpo and the MMTR, they also collaborated to contest the very nature of the shadow commodity chain and the inequalities on which it was premised.

I have argued that to understand the dynamics of such gray zones requires attention to the structure of larger international aid regimes in which social movements encounter markets. The shadow commodity chain emerged in the mid-1980s, after the demise of early solidarity-based aid relations. By the end of the century, funding relations in Latin America had begun to shift, and yet another, more locally oriented, aid regime was emerging.

The new panorama coincided with a modified form of neoliberalism, an ostensibly kinder, gentler form in which states were resuscitated to mitigate the worst excesses of the market.[21] It was also the era of the Pink Tide, which swept Center-Left governments to power across Latin America, beginning with the election of Hugo Chávez in Venezuela in 1999. The Brazilian Workers' Party (Partido dos Trabalhadores, or PT) governments of the last decade, like others around the region, had roots in and links to social movements, including feminism, and promoted gender- and race-sensitive policies. At the same time, at least until 2011, Brazil experienced significant economic growth, based in large part on the social investments of the PT government, and a segment of the population moved from poverty into the lower middle class.

International funding agencies, already under pressure from states and publics at home to produce results in the war against world poverty—or address more local problems—seized the moment. Arguing that the region's more democratic profile and improving economic indicators made their aid less necessary than it might once have been, the donor agencies that had sustained feminist NGOs and played such a key role in the shadow commodity chain, began to disinvest from Latin America, cutting back drastically on donations or pulling up stakes altogether.[22] Some claimed they were heading for needier regions, such as Sub-Saharan Africa. At first it was just a trickle, but by the mid-2000s, the outflow had reached flood stage, with contracts often broken in midstream and grantees left scrambling to find funds to cover rent, salaries, and project expenses. For many, who had become dependent on international funding, it was a bleak time.

Into the breach stepped the state.[23] In Brazil, government institutions, from municipal health departments to the federal Ministry of Agricultural Development, subcontracted social movement and other NGOs to implement their social and educational programs. Unlike the earlier period, when international agencies funded social movements to press their claims while governments relied on less politicized NGOs, now even advocacy-based organizations were drawn into service to the state, on the grounds of their shared political goals. Beyond the opportunities for government contracts, there were consultancies with state entities for those with feminist expertise, and competitive new grant opportunities from the national Women's Secretariat, as well as from state-owned industries, such as the oil company, Petrobras, and the Banco do Brasil.

In the 2000s the segmented transnational chain of exchanges that prevailed in earlier decades was broken down and reconstituted as a complex web of predominantly local aid relationships in which different kinds of bargains were struck than those made in past decades. For Brazilian feminists, relying on government funding raised age-old questions about autonomy and institutionalization. Becoming a subcontractor for the state, even a progressive one, ran the risk of circumscribing the political imagination and undermining the capacity to push the limits of conventional gender relations.

The transformed architecture of funding also engaged activists once again with the discourses of the market first encountered on the shadow commodity chain. As the agencies departed, they lectured their former beneficiaries about the importance of "walking with their own legs"—becoming *competitive* and *self-reliant* through means that included branding themselves and marketing their feminist commodities. Vying for state contracts required just that, as well as the ability to produce often highly specified *results* that fulfilled the objectives of the state. While greater numbers of women attended at clinics, or more students exposed to sex education were surely laudable objectives, they had only an indirect relation to the kind of critical feminist politics that many organizations held dear. Finally, the self-reliance acclaimed in this third social movement regime went hand in hand with proliferating *accountabilities* to an array of paymasters, each with their own set of specific requirements.

The diversified aid regime expanded the gray zone, drawing movements into collaborative and contentious relations with the state, while their struggles with neoliberal discourses remained ongoing. With Brazil's economy now shrinking, and the Right reemerging with a vengeance, these struggles will most certainly intensify. For feminists, navigating on this uncertain terrain will require analyzing the discursive cross-currents of the contemporary aid regime and the points of leverage it offers for the pursuit of transgressive political dreams.

NOTES

My deepest gratitude goes to the feminists and fellow travelers, in Brazil and the Netherlands, who generously shared their wisdom with me. Thanks also go to Geske Dijkstra, Julia Elyachar, Rachel Schurman, and anonymous reviewers of this volume for their invaluable insights, and to my coeditors for the thoughtful feedback and provocative discussions. Finally, I am grateful to the Bureau of Educational and Cultural Affairs of the U.S. Department of State, which awarded me a Fulbright Fellowship to Brazil in 2010, and the UMass, Amherst, Office of Research Affairs and the School of Social and Behavioral Sciences, which supported my research in the Netherlands.

1. This research was published in Thayer 2001 and 2010. The current chapter relies on the field and archival research conducted in a series of trips of varying lengths to Brazil from the mid-1990s to the mid-2000s, as well as on interviews and ethnography carried out in a yearlong stay in 2010–11 and during a shorter trip in 2013. I also conducted interviews in the Netherlands with donor agency staff in 2005 and 2006.

2. The MMTR's name is translated in some sources, including Thayer 2001 and 2010, as "Rural Women Workers' Movement."

3. It was not immediately clear why the MMTR could not sell the pamphlet—it may have been because the grant that covered its production stipulated that it should be distributed free of charge, or because the rural organization lacked the distribution networks available to the NGO. In any case, the speaker linked the complaint about their restrictions to resentments about SOS's use of the original text. These and other quotes were translated from the Portuguese by the author.

4. Indeed, when I returned seven years later, in 2005, the two organizations were engaged in a collaborative, participatory research project together.

5. In this chapter, I am concerned with capitalist markets though—as authors including Elyachar (2005) and Gibson-Graham (2006) have pointed out—markets may take a variety of forms, not all of which share the same kind of commodifying orientation.

6. The term *counterpublics*, first articulated by Felski (1989) and elaborated by Fraser (1997) and others, refers to oppositional political spaces organized around issues in contention, such as gender, race, or religion. See Thayer (2010) for a discussion of the concept of transnational feminist counterpublics and the different kinds of relationships that constitute them.

7. According to Kees Biekart, citing Organisation for Economic Co-operation and Development (OECD) figures, total aid income for private aid agencies rose from $860 million in 1970 to $4 billion in 1989. In 1970, official aid represented 1.5 percent of the total, while by 1980 it was over 40 percent (1999, 68). These averages hide the variation from one country or agency to another. In some cases, by the early 1990s dependence on official aid reached as high as 98 percent (see the useful chart in Biekart 1999, 61).

8. By 2003, almost 79 percent of the members of the Brazilian Association for Non-Governmental Organizations (Associação Brasileira de Organizações Não Governmentais, ABONG), responding to a survey, reported that they received some percentage of support from "international cooperation and solidarity" (private, European, and U.S. aid agencies). For 57.7 percent of respondent organizations, more than 60 percent of their income came from these sources. Although a thematic breakdown of the NGOs represented in the survey is not available, in 1998, 56.2 percent of ABONG's affiliates worked on projects related to gender relations, women, and/or reproductive rights, and it is likely that their income sources followed the general pattern (ABONG 1998, 2010).

9. In 2003, for example, the Netherlands gave the most Overseas Development Aid (ODA) to NGOs in absolute terms ($697 million) of any other donor nation (cited in Clark et al. 2006). The commitment of Dutch Christian Democratic governments to development cooperation in Latin America dates from the 1960s and 1970s during the period of dictatorships.

10. See Hulme and Edwards (1997a) for a sampling of these authors.

11. For a similar approach, see also Pearce (2010).

12. For further discussion of the discourse of accountability, see Thayer (2014).

13. These were the four largest Dutch aid agencies. Two were religiously inspired—ICCO (Protestant); and CEBEMO, later renamed Bilance and then CORDAID (Catholic). Two were secular (NOVIB and HIVOS). A fifth, Plan Nederland, was focused exclusively on projects related to children.

14. The percentages of state income received by each agency in that year were: ICCO, 71 percent; CEBEMO, 90 percent; HIVOS, 96 percent; and NOVIB, 98 percent (Biekart 1999, 61).

15. Bebbington (2005) describes the effects of this trend on Dutch funding relations with Peruvian NGOs.

16. Agencies focused on specific themes, such as the environment, human rights, gender, etc., which had previously received funds from thematic entities within the Ministry of Foreign Affairs, were also required to participate in the same competition.

17. This clamor only increased with the 2008 financial crisis in the North and the shrinking of agency endowments. In 2012, a survey conducted in the Netherlands found that 80 percent of the Dutch public favored decreasing overseas development aid. In 2013, the Dutch aid budget was cut by nearly 20 percent—1 billion Euros (cited in Arutyunova and Clark 2013, 21).

18. This set of instrumental moves was analogous to the maneuvering for advantage by firms envisioned by recent versions of commodity chain theory (Gereffi and Korzeniewicz 1994; see also Bair 2005).

19. Elsewhere I have described these challenges as taking the form of reverse "translations," efforts not only to refuse unwanted discourses, but to convey an alternate set of meanings (Thayer 2014).

20. See, for example, Criquillion (2007).

21. This stage has been variously described as "neoliberal multiculturalism," "rollout neo-liberalism," and "inclusive liberalism," among other labels (Hale 2002; Peck and Tickell 2002; Porter and Craig 2004).

22. This process took a bit longer in the Netherlands, where the state had had a long-standing commitment to spending 0.8% of GDP on development aid. But in 2013, the Dutch government made a decision to cut overseas aid budgets below this historic level, promising continued decreases in the future.

23. Although the state's participation was the most significant, it was accompanied by several other actors: a few donor agencies, including the Ford Foundation, hung on, providing a more limited roster of grants to feminist NGOs than in the past, and there was some much reduced bilateral aid and funding from multilateral institutions, such as the European Community and UN Women/ONU Mulheres. Finally, a small but growing corporate philanthropy movement was emerging, though the amounts provided by these donors to women's organizations were still minor and available only to noncontroversial projects aligned with company marketing concerns.

Part III

THE NEXUS

OF CIVIC AND

UNCIVIC POLITICS

Chapter 9

"THIS IS NO LONGER A DEMOCRACY . . ."

Thoughts on the Local Referendums on Mining on Peru's Northern Frontier

RAPHAEL HOETMER

During my next term of office, I will respect the will of the rural people of Ayavaca and
I will not allow any mining company to rule over the Ayavaca people.
—Alan García Pérez

Politics is the art of preventing people from taking part in
affairs which properly concern them.
—Paul Valéry

I arrived in Ayavaca's sports stadium at eight o'clock in the morning as a member of an observation mission for a local referendum on mining activity in the region,[1] Sunday, September 16, 2007. When I got there, hundreds of peasants, women and men, were already waiting at the stadium entrance. They had been arriving in this town in the northern Peruvian Andes since the previous day. Dozens of them slept in the main square—after many hours of travel by truck, horse, or mule, or on foot—from distant hamlets and communities in the region. Only their ponchos protected them from the penetrating cold.

The town councils of Ayavaca, Pacaipampa, and Carmen de la Frontera had organized the referendum.[2] Its purpose was to assess the opinion of their citizens regarding the future of the enormous, high-value mineral and metal reserves in the region, which had drawn the attention of several transnational companies. As early as 2003, the Chinese-British company Majaz had been engaged in exploratory activities for a mining project in the territories of peasant communities in Yanta (in the province of Ayavaca) and Segunda y Cajas (in the province of Huancabamba).[3] Majaz never managed to get the communities' appropriate permission to carry out its plans. During more recent years, peasants had on numerous occasions expressed their opposition to the mining project.

The Peruvian government rejected the referendum aggressively even before it took place, even though it constituted an obviously peaceful and highly institutionalized practice, was organized by the local town councils (state actors) allied with different actors in civil society, and would not result in a binding decision, as the referendum "only" sought to consult the local population's opinion regarding the mining project.

Despite the lack of collaboration of the state's specialized institutions, the referendum took place with considerable efficiency. The impressive images of self-organization and of people's engagement and enthusiasm gave me the feeling that a deep and really democratic practice was taking place. This referendum on the Northern Frontier of Peru therefore invites us to critically reflect on the multiple and complex relationships between what the editors of this volume call "the Civil Society Agenda" and "Uncivic Political Activism."

In this chapter, I argue that, beyond their mere existence and formal organization, democracy, development, territory, sovereignty, and citizenship are all the result of complex dynamics between social, state, and private actors, which include both confrontation and negotiation and which are produced at various geopolitical scales. At the same time, these dynamics define the reality of imaginary and formal citizenship; give form to the (re)organization of our territory, state, and development; and can pave the way for a deepening of democracy, as well as for authoritarian tendencies.

Chronicle of a Conflict: Precedents and Results of the Referendum

The conflict on the Northern Frontier of Peru is part of a wider scenario wherein the expansion of mining and of conflicts between companies and communities has grown and spread throughout the country.[4] The neoliberal and proextractivist reforms first implemented in a structural adjustment program by then president Alberto Fujimori (now in jail) were consolidated following the return to electoral democracy, during the presidencies of Alejandro Toledo, Alan García Pérez, and Ollanta Humala. As a result of this, mining concessions showed spectacular growth from 2.26 million hectares in 1991 to 26 million by 2013. These governments created legal and political conditions that enabled the incorporation of an increasing number of geographical spaces and aspects of society into transnational financial, productive, and commercial networks (De Echave, Hoetmer, and Palacios Panéz 2009; Hoetmer et al. 2013; Pinto 2009). Through these policies, the major Peruvian political and economic actors (in association with global political and private actors) sought to reconstitute and reterritorialize the Peruvian state, economy, and society, confirming its historical integration in the global economy as a primary exporter of its natural resources.

Due to the social, environmental, and cultural consequences of the expansion of extractivist activities over recent years, so-called socioenvironmental conflicts have, according to the national ombudsman (Defensoría del Pueblo), become the main category of social struggle in the country, thus converting mining into the most conflicted economic sector in Peru.[5] A wide array of motivations and demands sparked the mining conflicts. These ranged from claims for a greater share in the distribution of profits and compensation for environmental damage, to resistance to the exploitation of potentiality affected populations by the mining companies. Generally speaking, the struggle between the mining companies and the communities over the control and management of the common goods and the ways in which these are integrated into the local, national, and global economies are the central axes of conflict. Therefore I prefer to speak of "eco-territorial conflicts" (Hoetmer 2013), as this reflects more accurately that these conflicts actually express disputes between different collective projects for local society.

The mining conflict in the Peruvian North finds its origins in the discovery in 1994 of copper and molybdenum reserves at the so-called Henry's Hill. The Río Blanco Copper S.A. mining company is the present license holder of the project. The company itself belongs to Monterrico Metals, which in turn belongs to the Chinese consortium Zijin. The project consists of eight concessions that cover an area of almost 6,500 hectares. Nonetheless, there are various indications that the project is part of a plan to establish a broader mining district (Bebbington 2007), which even includes territories on the Ecuadorian side of the border.[6]

The social polarization and conflict surrounding the Río Blanco project followed the January 22, 2003, presentation of the mining company's petition to the Ministry of Energy and Mining (MinEM) for approval of a study of the project's environmental impact. This study was a requirement for the exploration of the zone, and it was approved on November 28, 2003. Meanwhile, the communities of Segunda y Cajas (on May 2003) and Yanta (on January 10, 2004) unanimously decided, in a community assembly, to reject mining activity on their territories. After the first protests in 2003, thousands of peasants (*comuneros*) walked for many days to the mining project zone in April 2004 and July 2005, in response to continuing explorations. They were faced with a ferocious state repression that caused the death of two peasants, Remberto Herrera Racho in 2004 and Melanio García Gonzales in 2005. The repression also left dozens of people wounded and resulted in the illegal detention and torture of thirty-two protesters by the mining company's security staff, apparently in complicity with federal agents.[7]

The first protest against the mining settlement caused the conflict to "explode" (Diez 2009). In this process, a climate of confrontation simultaneously intensified and expanded as spaces for dialogue and agreement were created. The Front for the Sustainable Development of the Peruvian Northern Border (Frente para el Desarrollo Sostenible en la Frontera Norte del Perú, FDSFNP), which had been established in September 2005 by several actors critical of the project, emerged as the main actor in this process. It included a coalition of communities, social organizations, and religious groups, as well as the town councils of Piura and other potentially affected zones in the neighboring department of Cajamarca (in the provinces of San Ignacio and Jaén), and was supported by environmentalist and human rights NGOs.

Meanwhile, the Office of the Ombudsman—the entity in charge of overseeing the state as guarantor of the people's rights—concluded in a report of November 14, 2006, that the Majaz Company did not have the required permits for its use of the relevant land. The "Majaz Affair" was included in a hearing at the People's Permanent Court, Vienna, 2006, among many other human rights violations of transnational companies, and the case even reached the parliament of the United Kingdom.[8]

In the face of growing national and international attention to the case, the company began to apply a new strategy. It orchestrated a media campaign that included public apologies for the confrontations with the communities, accompanied by significant efforts to promote parallel organizations in the affected mining area and systematic slandering and harassment of the people opposing the project. In the first months of 2007, the Zijin Consortium, partially financed by the Chinese government, became Monterrico Metals' main owner, while the protests against the mining project continued.

In this context, the FDSFNP decided to summon a referendum in an attempt to look for a solution to the conflict. The initiative had been inspired by the Referendum on Mining, carried out in Tambogrande in 2002 (also in the department of Piura), which had caused the mining company Manhattan to withdraw from the district, after 98 percent of voters rejected the project. Following the formal petition filed by the Yanta's community assembly, the district town councils of Pacaipampa and Carmen de la Frontera, as well as the provincial town council of Ayavaca, called a referendum, using national and international legal references to legally support their bylaws.

Despite the countercampaign organized by both the federal government and the company, the referendum took place in the three areas. The only participation on the part of the state was the deployment of a large number of police officers to the area, but it was the peasant patrols (*rondas campesinas*) that really guaranteed the security of the referendum.[9] The result was overwhelming. Despite the big investment intended to discourage community participation, almost 60 percent of the population turned out to vote (table 9.1). Among those voters, almost 95 percent said *no* to mining. Almost all the national press (including the major conservative newspaper *El Comercio*) interpreted this result as a significant defeat for the federal government. The week following the referendum, the government invited communities to a new round-table dialogue, while simultaneously announcing twenty mining projects of national interest, including that of Majaz.

Table 9.1 shows that voters chose the *no* by 95 percent in all three areas. The level of participation varied from 50 to over 70 percent in each of these. The line for "effective votes" only accounts for the voters who chose either *yes* or *no* to the question "Do you agree with mining activities in your district?"

Interpreting the Conflict: The Fight over Territory, Democracy, and the Environment

A superficial but common reading of this and other mining conflicts in the public debate might suggest that the conflict in Ayavaca is mainly due to opposed perceptions of the environmental impact and economic results of the mining project on behalf of different actors and the local population. On that reading, the conflict could be overcome through dialogue and scientific research that would analyze and clarify the project's "real impact." On the one side, the company and representatives from the federal government present the Río Blanco project as "modern mining," based on a policy of social responsibility that would benefit local communities, while having a minimal impact on the environment. The opposition, on the contrary, considers these claims as extremely dubious, a belief in part fueled by the history of mining in the country.[10]

TABLE 9.1. Referendum results

	Yes	%	No	%	Blank	%	Null	%	Votes	Voters	Part
Ayavaca	176	1.98%	8294	93.47%	159	1.79%	244	2.75%	8873	17714	50.09%
Carmen de la Frontera	73	2.39%	2825	92.53%	48	1.57%	107	3.50%	3053	5152	59.26%
Pacaipampa	36	0.59%	5914	97.09%	32	0.53%	109	1.79%	6091	8522	71.47%
Total	239	1.33%	17033	94.78%	239	1.33%	460	2.56%	17971	31388	57.25%
Effective Votes		1.38%		98.62%					17272		

Source: www.consultavecinal.org/computo.htm, accessed September 30, 2007. See https://www.servindi.org/actualidad/2584, and http://guajo.com/2007/09/listos-los-resultados-de-la-consulta-vecinal/.

Even if, without a doubt, there are different perceptions surrounding these conflicts, there are at least three fundamental arguments that go beyond this explanation of conflict, sustaining a more fundamental opposition to the mining project in this case. As we can read in the words of Magdiel Carrión Pintado, former president of the Provincial Federation of Peasant Communities in Ayavaca (Federación Provincial de Comunidades Campesinas de Ayavaca): "Our communities have our own developmental model, based on agriculture, ecotourism, and our social organization. We have the same rights as citizens of Lima or anywhere else in the country. We want our communities' decisions to be respected. This is how it goes in a democracy, and besides, both Peruvian and international law grant us the right to decide over our future and over the future of our territory."

Carrión insists on the fact that the mining company entered and remained illegally in the territory of peasant communities of Yanta and Segunda y Cajas. First, even if the Peruvian Constitution establishes that the national government makes the decisions about the use of common goods, it also establishes that there must be a previous agreement to use the territories belonging to peasant and indigenous communities. To achieve this, the approval is required of two-thirds of the peasants in attendance at the community assembly (the highest political level of community proceedings). The ombudsman's report explains that, in the mining company's petition to the MinEM, it presented documents on exploration of the mining zone that failed to comply with these requirements.

Second, people who oppose the project insist on their right to make decisions regarding their own future. They argue that this element is central to a true *democracy*. They specifically propose that peasant communities, local town councils, and the region in general have already decided on their own development strategy, and that these cannot be subordinated to decisions made by the federal government. For various interviewees, the denial of these rights confirms a common belief in Peru that there exist two levels of citizenship with highly differentiated access to rights. The peasant communities also claim a special situation, based on international law regarding indigenous peoples, because their right to choose their own development model is key to the protection of their territory and identity.

The central government, however, considers it has the right to make all decisions regarding the use of common goods because these are part of a national development strategy that trumps local and regional rights. This leads to the third basic cause of the conflict. The arguments against mining express other "languages of assessment" (*lenguajes de valoración*) (Martínez Alier 2002) that dispute the notion of development. For the company and for the federal government, the space defined for the project should be "assessed" according to its insertion in the global market, while FDSFNP members consider that the value of a regional ecology resides in itself. The mining project would operate in a unique, fragile, ecological area consisting of cloud forests and tundra ecosystems. Defending the environment, especially defending water, are therefore central elements in the argument against the project. Moreover, many people in the region consider mountains and lakes as living beings endowed with special powers, and that they ought to be respected as such. The communities' leaders insist that agriculture is a more sustainable, democratic, and economically inclusive activity than mining, as the latter depends on a highly specialized labor force and on the concentration of profits in the hands of a handful of foreigners. Finally, they state that both activities are incompatible, as mining has an enormous negative impact on water's quantity and quality available for agriculture.

The conflict concerning the Río Blanco project therefore reveals a "territorial tension" (Porto Gonçalves 2001) between two complex networks of actors, both with different conceptions of development, democracy, and territory. While the federal government and the company, in alliance with some settlers in the region, consider land an economic resource, for the locals it is a space that sustains social relations, economic practices, and cultural traditions, all of which give meaning to the life of people in the area. Provoked by profound outrage among peasants against the abuses of the federal government and the company, local identity and the opposition to the mining development model have mutually strengthened one another during the conflict.

The network of actors opposing the mining project includes state officials, town councils, communities, peasant patrols, environmental and human rights NGOs, urban and activist collectives, producers' organizations, the National Confederation of Peruvian Communities Affected by Mining (Confederación Nacional de Comunidades del Perú Afectadas por la Minería, or CONACAMI), journalists, and the media, as well as international organizations and networks. The heterogeneity of the actors involved evidently generates discussions, tensions, and continuous negotiations over the strategies, common goals, and the meaning of the struggle, all of which allows for a constant and complex remaking of a collective identity (Melucci 1996). Simultaneously, it enables the opposition to act, using different strategies at different scales or geopolitical spaces—such as in the communities, the legal system, the international sphere, and mass media—without requiring acceptance of a hierarchical and highly centralist management. Moreover, many of the actors involved in the opposition came with the experience of the Tambogrande case, thus bringing with them a series of lessons and already-established relations of value to the FDSFNP (Bebbington 2013).

Apart from such complementarities among the different actors, their struggle is basically upheld by three key elements. First, the community organizations (and the peasant patrols in particular) are the principal groups exercising social and territorial control in the highlands of Piura. Second, the diversity of actors constituted the FDSFNP as the body recognized by all groups opposing the Río Blanco project for strategic discussions, for dealing with internal conflicts, and for the articulation of the resistance on different scales and by different actors. Finally, the dialogue and dialectic between these actors allowed for working out a perspective, proposals, and practices of alternatives to extractivist development in the region.

Producing the Referendum:
(Im)possibility, (Il)legality, and (Il)legitimacy

By organizing the referendum, the FDSFNP hoped to open a high-profile media and political campaign that would channel and diffuse the generalized violence and confrontations, the two main expressions of the conflict at that point. As such, it sought to generate a landmark that would change the correlation of forces, as well as the public image and political debate on the issue.[11] The opposing side (FDSFNP) assumed that the referendum was going to be a powerful argument for negotiations over the future of the region. This is because the participants foresaw that the federal government was not going to recognize it as part of a direct institutional solution. Consequently, the logic of polarization and confrontation that sustained the conflict was consolidated after the referendum was announced, though partly by other means and through other logics. Now, the different actors involved did everything in their power to create the (im)possibility, (il)legality, and (il)legitimacy of the referendum in various legal, media, political, and social spaces.

The referendum's organizers had to decide whether it would take place at a community level (according to the International Labor Organization Convention 169) or at the town council level. A community referendum would depart from recognition of the communities' right to decide over their territory according to customs and traditions (*usos y costumbres*), and it would be limited to the two communities directly involved. A neighborhood referendum (i.e., a referendum at the town council level), on the other hand, would depart from recognition of the local town council authority to plan its local economy and to consult with the population to that end. The second option would expand electoral participation to all citizens under its particular jurisdiction. The issue was resolved by leaving aside debates over communitarian autonomy and the structure of the Peruvian state and by recognizing that the neighborhood referendum would have a greater impact and legitimacy on society than the community version. On the one hand, this implied that more people would express themselves about the mining project and the process would enable a broader relation, with more urban and national actors working toward a referendum. On the other hand, this position assumed that if the town councils organized the referendum, it would make it more legitimate in the eyes of the general Peruvian public than if it had been organized by the communities.

The referendum's organizers insisted on its technically impeccable organization, for which purpose they put together an electoral committee, a technical office, and an ethical and observers' committee that included national personalities as well as national and international observers. They also created an electoral webpage, worked with regional and town electoral rolls from 2006, and facilitated broad media coverage. They had previously carried out training workshops and information campaigns, and had engaged the media, institutions, and national politicians who agreed with the right of local populations to hold a referendum.

For its part, the federal government and the mining company put together a discrediting campaign against the referendum's organizers. Journalists, analysts, government supporters, ministers, and economists accused the peasants of being ignorant, antimodern, allied with Chileans (the main copper producer in the world), terrorists, and communists.[12] And Prime Minister Jorge del Castillo continued insisting on the illegality of the referendum despite declarations to the contrary from the Office of the Ombudsman and the Department of Justice's Commission on Human Rights. The National Office of Electoral Processes declined the invitation to facilitate the technical elements in the referendum process, the Regional Board of Education denied organizers the possibility to use educational centers to carry out the referendum, and the National Electoral Commission rejected the validity of the referendum and (unsuccessfully) denounced the participating mayors and members of the technical team as usurping their functions. Meanwhile, the Majaz company offered $80 million to communities for the use of their lands (paid during their occupation of the region), money that was rejected on the grounds that neither health nor environment were for sale. In the days leading up to the referendum, the government suddenly invited the region's actors to a new dialogue, insisting that the consultation would not solve the conflict.

(Economic) Citizenship, (Un)Civil Society, and the Exertion of Force

Even if clearly the referendum is a very "civilized" action that was called for by a local government, this did not guarantee its recognition as a valid mechanism for citizen participation, nor as a mechanism for self-determination for the local population. Meanwhile, the mining company enjoys the benefits of an "economic citizenship" (Sassen 1996) guaranteed by neoliberal interests and legal-political frameworks that privilege the rights of transnational corporations over those of people and communities. Both local population rights and the institutionality of the state appear in this process as social relations whose particular materialization depends on the exertion of power by different, often conflicting, public, private, and social actors. Consequently, an analysis of the conflict allows par excellence for critical reflection on the multiple and complex relations between a "Civil Society Agenda" and "Uncivic Activism," which the editors refer to in their introduction to this volume.

A first reflection refers to the heterogeneous composition of the networks of actors supportive of the mining project. Evidently, the Peruvian state is not homogeneous in its interests nor in its relations with local populations and, therefore, it has not acted in a uniform way. The local town council integrated what we might call the "critical block" of opposition to the mining interests, while independent interventions from the Office of the Ombudsman and the Department of Justice's Human Rights Commission provided arguments for the critical block's position. In the process, this evidently "civilized" quality can also be found in the rise of new rights and notions of development, which allow for an expansion of a citizenship discourse and practice in Peru. Beyond the right to hold a referendum and to decide on the developmental model for local populations lies the recognition of the intrinsic value of nature, which suggests an emerging environmental citizenship.

A second point is that the diversity of actors critical of mining activity in the Northern Peruvian Frontier allowed the development of multiple strategies and actions at different geopolitical scales. These include legal action, media campaigns, international lobbying, participation in spaces for dialogue, and the organization of the referendum, as well as protests, detention of mining company staff, roadblocks, the burning of materials distributed by the mining company, and other contentious action. The understanding of the strategies used by these actors to determine their own destiny therefore requires the analysis of the relationships and dynamics in between "a proliferation of civil participation," and the "more anti-establishment, less 'civilized' collective actions" within complex processes shaped by negotiations among a variety of social actors embedded in their own histories, repertoires, and discourses. The examples described in the major studies of mining in Peru suggest that direct action and the willingness to use force continue to be necessary for local populations to get their voices heard and influence local territorial development, either to negotiate local conditions for mining or to reject extractive projects (Bebbington 2007; De Echave, Hoetmer, and Palacios Panéz 2009; Hoetmer et al. 2013). The exertion of force has been a central component in the strategies and in the popular collective imagination in Peru, because it has historically forced the central state to recognize or respect certain rights or demands.

A third core element of the analysis posits that, in this scenario, the kind of responses that social organizations critical of mining must face do not depend on the actions undertaken. Organizers of the referendum as well as of the street protests have been threatened, criminalized in the media, attacked by national politicians, and accused of terrorism. Rather, these responses result from a combination of their structural inclusion in Peruvian society and their critical position against the economic model promoted by the country's elites. On the one hand, the unfinished historical process of building a sovereign national state in Peru has taken place through the production of "large numbers of poor, marginalized or ethnic others as outsiders, people who are not yet ready to become citizens or included in the true political-cultural community" (Blom Hansen and Stepputat 2005:36). During the era of neoliberal capitalism, the "noncitizen" populations opposing this project—or the opposition from second-class citizens as contemplated in the national Peruvian imagination—depend on a heavy cultural, legal, and political media projection of these populations as savages, premodern, and antidevelopment. They are portrayed as incapable of deciding their future and of participating in the decision-making process concerning local and national social development. They do not feature as an integral part of Peruvian civil society.

This discursive production of the mining opponents as external to Peruvian civil society, democracy, and citizenship becomes a justification for the persistence of the mining project in the region, for its coercive nature, and for uncontrolled violence against its opponents. It is clear that the incorporation of these new territories into the transnational productive and business networks requires disciplining the "uncivilized" population in order to contribute to the "modernization" and "civilizing" of the country and its people.

Finally, this historical production of certain populations as external to citizenship also generated a relative autonomy from the Peruvian state, as peasant communities administrate justice, maintain an internal political organization of their own, and actively exercise the control of their territory. Therefore, the "territorial tension" also implies a tension of sovereignties, between the central state and local populations and their political structures. Contrary to the cases of "civil participation through the so-called 'Third Sector' and governmental programs" here there are no preestablished rights. Rather, we find a battlefield in which citizenship, sovereignty, and democracy themselves are a matter of negotiation (Chatterjee 2007). In fact, when peasant men and women reclaim their rights, they speak as much about their recognition by the state as about their right for recognition beyond the state: "Let us solve our own problems." Political action not only creates or materializes rights, but it puts limits on state or corporate intervention in the communities.

All of this shows that the superficial identification of some actors as "civil" and others as "uncivic" or even as uncivilized hinders a more complex and historical comprehension of democracy's precariousness, its partiality, and low intensity, and of the excessive violence in our societies. The mining conflict around the Río Blanco project clearly shows that the government, in association with the mining company, exerts the most intense and planned violence. Simultaneously, in the context of this conflict, tensions and conflicts arise in overall social relations, deepening structural violence at the base of Peruvian society. For example, the conflict itself encourages coercive practices within communities to maintain their internal unity. For that purpose, they have incorporated in their statutes that any collaboration with the mining company can even be punished by expulsion from the community.

The Impact of the Referendum and the Continuation of the Conflict

In this context of struggles over the re-creation of ways of life and of sovereignty at the Northern Frontier, the immediate impact of the referendum was significant. For several weeks the Majaz case was one of the main topics in the political and media agenda in the country and even drew international attention. After the referendum, the government and the company found themselves, for a while, on the defensive, creating conditions for a new round of dialogue. The main impact and results of the process, however, reside at another level.

The process of organization and execution of the referendum strengthened the institutions upon which it was based. The FDSFNDP managed to establish itself as the single place for the expression, discussion, and political representation of the opposing side, while the prominence of the peasant patrols as the main social force behind the referendum's success allowed for a greater legitimacy within the local population and even in the media for the organization.

The successful execution of the referendum created a collective identity for opponents of Majaz, forcing the more silent actors—such as town councils, urban organizations, and the church—to get more publicly involved in the struggle. Moreover, organizations and institutions that were previously unknown or that remained distant had to collaborate during the referendum process. Their efforts also raised the consciousness of the local population. Thus, beyond all political, cultural, and even personal differences, the commitment to "make everyone respect the referendum" has now become a central element in local politics.

It is interesting to note that the referendum has different meanings for the different actors involved. On the one hand, for NGO representatives, the referendum is a matter of citizenship participation that could translate into an institutionalized mechanism for dealing with the process of approving (or denying) extractivist mining. On the other hand, they saw it as a media strategy (both in this conflict and in the broader struggle for a democratic governance of extractivist industries) that could put national and international pressure on the Peruvian state and the mining company to respect the rights of local populations.

For the town councils, the referendum was a means for recovering their capacity to define a development model against the federal state and to generate de facto decentralization. At the same time, it allowed them to maintain legitimacy among the local population, particularly the peasants. For the CONACAMI, the referendum was a first step toward the establishment and formalization of a community right to fully decide about their territories, and, in this way, create the basis for a plurinational state. Finally, the community leaders affirm that the final decision over their territories should rest with the communities, but they are aware that this requires pressure on the government until it yields. In this sense, they assume that the referendum serves as a kind of translation of an already-made decision at the community level to the rules and languages of liberal democracy, so that it can be understood by the company, the federal government, and the public in general.

Although the referendum represents an important moment in changing the correlation of forces in the conflict and has imposed an indefinite delay on the project, it did not manage to completely cancel it. In the months following the referendum, a new dialogue went into crisis. The communities of Yanta and Segunda y Cajas filed a complaint against the usurpation of their land rights. And President Alan García himself explicitly referred to the project in an article in *El Comercio*, insisting that the population's rejection was irrational (García 2007). Facing government insistence on continuing with the project, the communities organized a protest in the form of a "sacrificial march" to the departmental capital, Piura. The massive march ended after six days. Over 10,000 people walked the streets of Piura, demanding respect for the referendum results.

In following years, the conflict went through various moments of tension and violence, including a violent irruption at the Río Blanco facility, November 2009 (for which culprits have yet to be found). This attack killed three people: two guards, Luis Gómez Vílchez and José Severino Zapata, and the mining camp manager, Eduardo Ramirez. As the investigation unfolded, two peasant leaders, Castro Cástulo Correa Huayama and Vicente Romero Ramírez, fell victim to police violence during a raid on the Cajas Canchaque community. The ombudsperson, Beatriz Merino, stated that they had been shot in the back.[13]

While the conflict was in a relatively calm phase, the communities and the NGO CooperAcción inaugurated the economic and ecological zoning processes in Huancabamba and Ayabaca. This was to establish a general framework for the future use of land in the province. For its part, the Peruvian state returned the "Study on Environmental Impact" to the mining company, with comments and remarks. Also, key leaders in the process won the election for provincial mayor in Huancabamba (i.e., Wilson Ibañez), and one became president of the CONACAMI (Magdiel Carrión).

Despite language critical of mining activities during Ollanta Humala's electoral campaign, his presidential election provided an opportunity for the mining sector to go ahead with projects that had been delayed for a decade. These included the Río Blanco project. There are various indications in the company communications, as well as in its intensified presence in the region, to believe that it is creating conditions to execute the project. Although the FDSFNP does not have the power and dyamic it had a few years ago, it keeps going and has restated its critique of the project. The growth of informal mining in the provinces of Ayabaca and Huancabamba, at the hands of local settlers, has become a factor complicating the conflict in the region.

Another area in which the impact of this process at the Northern Frontier is at best ambivalent lies in the implementation of institutional innovations regulating mining activities. For NGOs in particular, this was one of their main objectives. The subsequent initiatives regarding the Territorial Zoning Code, and particularly the Law on Free and Informed Prior Consultation, might find its precedents in the Piura conflicts (Bebbington 2013), but their implementation has been at best contradictory and very much below the expectations of social organizations. Also, the peasant patrols and peasant communities continue to be excluded from the right to be consulted by the Peruvian government.

Also, part of the current (2012–14) tendency toward a greater capacity to generate political proposals in the wider scenario of ecoterritorial conflicts is indebted to links and interactions between the Northern Frontier and other regions. One example of this is the case of the resistance to the Conga project in the department of Cajamarca. It is evident, however, that despite this increased intensity in the conflicts, a change of norms in relation to extractivist activities continues to be very limited in Peru.

Final Considerations: What Is at Stake?

I have argued that the conflict caused by the illegal presence of the Majaz mining company in the communitarian lands of Yanta and Segunda y Cajas expresses dynamics of (re)negotiation of the impacts and limitations of different sovereignties in the contemporary world.

On the one hand, the conflict concerning the Majaz company is a continuation of a long historical process of negotiation between marginalized populations and the local and national elites, over the territorial, political, and economic organization of the region and the country. In these conflicts, the federal government appears as a strategic actor. Its position in the conflicts between communities and local powers (formerly landholders, currently mining companies) can change if social and political forces in the community are strong enough (Damonte 2007; Starn 1999). In this sense, the FDSFNP's demand that the state assume its role as guarantor of their rights and facilitator for a resolution of the conflict follows a historical pattern. It is evident that in this negotiation-based relationship, the possibility of exerting force has always played an important role.

On the other hand, the various processes commonly known as globalization have generated a new geography of power (Sassen 1996, 29–30). Here political sovereignty is shared in transnational networks that emerge from supranational institutions, stock markets, the media, other transnational actors, and the national states. Given that most of these networks do not follow democratic principles, the capacity for self-determination by democratic political means is conditioned by economic and social policies. This does not necessarily imply a weakening of the state. Rather, the state has been transformed and integrated into wider networks and configurations of power at a global level, playing a crucial role in facilitating and defending the current economic model.

More than the absence of the state, the Majaz case shows a very selective presence that seeks to reinforce the company as a new source of sovereignty in the region, above that of town councils or communities. It is not, therefore, surprising that the attempt to create a new normative framework on communitarian territories, in order to foster their commodification, came along with a repressive system supporting it that seeks to criminalize dissidence. This was started by the authoritarian government of Alberto Fujimori and consolidated under the democratic governments of the last decade.

Both processes—the creation of a normative framework favorable to extractivist activity and corporate sovereignty, and the implementation of a repressive system supporting it—seek to rebuild the region's territories, their subjects, and their imaginaries according to an understanding of life, a notion of the state, and a development model at the service of a capitalist market, of a Eurocentric rationality, and of the nation-state—all key components to what Aníbal Quijano (2000a) calls the "coloniality of power." Community capacity to resist these processes relies on inhabitants' existence at the periphery of Peruvian state sovereignty and of the capitalist market. Since the abolition of hacienda land tenure in the 1970s, communities have learned to live simultaneously with the state and the market and without them.[14] The continuity of community justice, the peasant patrols, and the community assembly as the highest political authority are some examples of this relative autonomy that has transformed communities into locally sovereign forces with a certain capacity for negotiation with other local sources of authority.

It is in these cases of confrontation and negotiation that democracy, the development model, sovereignty, and the territories are reconfigured. As such, the opposition to the Río Blanco project actually creates localized negotiation on the restructuring of a local, Peruvian, and global society. For this purpose, networks of actors have been built who act at various geopolitical scales and in various spaces of the social system using multiple strategies. The organization of the referendum can be seen as a mechanism for citizenship participation that creates an impact on the conflict and prefigures possible institutional innovation, seeking to democratize the governance of natural resources. In this sense, it is a mechanism that integrates broader strategies that combine "the civil society agenda" with "antiestablishment collective action."

Thus, the community organizations do not seek to destroy the state or the market (Damonte 2007), but rather to negotiate ways in which they will be inserted within them, and the limits to this integration. First, local populations struggle with the current democratic government, demanding another form of democracy based on the respect of their rights and their participation in matters that concern them. Second, communities seek to negotiate the terms of their insertion in the market, globalization, and so-called modernization. Throughout the process, they pose other economic principles, based on their desire for a developmental model consistent with their identity and culture. Either way, a negotiation of the limits of autonomy and of national sovereignty is at play. The communities want to "solve their problems on their own" in order to continue reproducing the community way of life, but also want the support of the state to achieve a developmental model based on agriculture and ecotourism.

The radical nature of the struggle, then, does not reside in the kind of actions undertaken, nor on some ideological basis (as suggested by the adjectives applied to them by mining supporters, such as violent, terrorist, communist, or anticapitalist).[15] Rather, their radicalism resides in their insistence that it is possible to organize life, the economy, the state, and politics in a way that differs from the hegemonic developmentalism. The discursive production of the opponents to mining as uncivilized, opposed to development, and unpatriotic departs precisely from the neocolonial equivalence between capitalism, development, progress, civilization, and patriotism—the bases upon which economic elites, the company and national government seek to produce disciplined subjects and territories to incorporate into a commodified and fragmented society. The question if our democracy is still a democracy, posed through a song by peasant women in Cajamarca and Puno, states that such a disciplinary project eliminates real democracy, even if formal democratic procedures remain in place. On the other side, the FDSFNP and the community resistance—with all their internal contradictions and limitations—contribute to a debate over possible paths for a deeper democracy, for the reorganization of the territory and of the state, and for an economy and culture based on the diversities that compose our societies.

Acknowledgments

I am grateful to the peasants of Ayavaca y Yanta, and especially to Magdiel Carrión and Mario Tabra, for their hospitality and openness. I also wanted to thank all the interviewees and especially José De Echave, Luis Vittor, Vladimir Pinto, Jorge Tacuri, Mario Palacios, Lieven Pype, Diego Saavedra, and Mar Daza for the significant ideas they shared with me. I also want to thank Peter Waterman for his help with editing the English version of the text.

NOTES

Epigraph 1: Before election as the new president of Peru, Alan García Pérez gave a speech in Ayavaca, 2006, in which he not only promised to respect the will of the people of Ayavaca, but also stressed the risks associated with industrial mining and the dubious transnational investments. It is available at https://www.youtube.com/watch?v=dRNr_PlYAGM.

Epigraph 2: I heard this sentence several times from women in Ayacucho and Cajamarca at different moments of the conflicts related to mining in recent years.

1. I represented the Network Institute for Global Democratization. The town councils involved in the process had invited a team including people from Ecuador, Chile, Bolivia, Canada, the United States, Spain, Germany, and Switzerland.

2. In the article I use the more common English term *referendum*, though the literal translation of the Spanish term *Consulta vecinal* would be "Neighbor consultation." In any case, the referendum was a nonbinding consultation of the local citizens to make known their opinion on mining activities in their districts.

3. In the period following the referendum, the company changed its name to Río Blanco Copper S.A.

4. For a more detailed account on the development of the case, see *La resistencia* (Hoetmer 2010), or the semestral reports of the Observatory of Mining Conflicts.

5. The department for the prevention of social conflicts and governability publishes a monthly report on the state of social conflict in Peru, which is accessible here: www.defensoria.gob.pe /conflictos-sociales/home.php.

6. Zijin Mining has twenty-seven other mining concessions under its subsidiary mining company, Compañía Minera Mayari, right next to the Río Blanco project. The company's thirty-five concessions extend over 28,263 hectares of land. In January 2009, the Peruvian NGO CooperAcción also published a report in which it detailed the existence of mining concessions belonging to Zijin on both sides of the border.

7. In early 2009, this public denunciation was supported by publication of photos showing peasants being tied up, beaten, and wearing plastic bags over their heads, and security agents proudly displaying the underwear they had taken off a woman in the group.

8. At this moment, Monterrico Metals was still mostly British. After this meeting, an independent scientific mission was organized by the British Peru Support Group. This was intended to establish the nature of the project, the intensity of the conflict, and the claims made on both sides. It was carried out between September 30 and October 5, 2006 (Bebbington 2007).

9. The so-called peasant patrols are a crucial social organization within peasant communities in northern Peru. They emerged at the end of the 1970s in response to the Peruvian state's incapacity (and/or lack of will) to stop the rise of cattle rustling in the region. The peasants began to keep a collective eye on their lands. During the next two decades, they assumed more community responsibilities, including a partial administration of justice. Currently, the patrols have gained increased political prominence in defense of community identities and traditions in northern Peru (Starn 1999). The defense of territory and of common goods has become a central axis of their activity (Hoetmer 2013b).

10. The scientific mission organized by Peru Support Group declared in its report that "in fact, it is difficult, and one could even say impossible, for the mining sector to point to any locality in Peru where the expansion of mining has resulted in a significative human development for the local population" (Bebbington 2007, 7). Several leaders affirmed in their interviews that knowledge of the cases in Cajamarca and Cerro de Pasco contributed to their increased opposition to the mining project.

11. The notion of the referendum as a landmark in the conflict was pointed out to me by Luis Vittor and José De Echave.

12. The references to "terrorism" and "communism" belong to a Peruvian government discursive strategy that began in the 1990s and that attempts to identify social organizations, NGOs, and progressive intellectuals with a violent policy of internal war. Mario Palacios, CONACAMI ex-president, commented on the subject in an interview: "It's ironic. There come the good communists to invest in mining and here we have the bad communists that want to prevent it."

13. See the *La República* interview on the case with Beatriz Merino, ombudsman at the time: http://larepublica.pe/16-12-2009/comuneros-les-disparon-por-la-espalda. Maria Elena Castillo, December 16, 2009, *La Republica*, Lima, accessible at: www.larepublica.pe/archive/all/larepublica/20091216/1/node/238788/total/01.

14. Aníbal Quijano proposed this idea at the Indigenous Continent Summit in Puno. Neither the state nor the market have been able to resolve community problems, which have always implied a need for the communities to self-organize according to other principles.

15. I am not claiming with this that ideology plays no role in the conflict. There are discourses and politicized leaders that have fueled the positions of the FDSFNP and the communities. These, however, cannot be considered the basis of the struggle, nor is the FDSFNP controlled by a particular political party or tendency.

Chapter 10

FROM AFRO-COLOMBIANS TO AFRO-DESCENDANTS

The Trajectory of Black Social Movements
in Colombia, 1990–2010

KIRAN ASHER

This chapter traces the dynamics of Afro-Colombian social movements from the late 1980s to 2008. A critical focus on this trajectory reveals that the outcomes of black organizing are contradictory and contingent on many different factors. Afro-Colombians have gained remarkable national and global visibility partly because of Colombia's official multiculturalism, and of Law 70 of 1993, which grants ethnic, territorial, and socioeconomic rights to black communities. This visibility is also the result of the efforts of groups such as the Process of the Black Communities (Proceso de Comunidades Negras, or PCN) who demand "identity, territory, and autonomy," that is, recognition beyond legislative rights. Afro-Colombians and their struggles also occupy center stage because a large percentage of Colombia's black population lives in the Pacific lowlands or Chocó region, which is considered one of the world's "biodiversity hotspots" and is the target of large-scale natural resource-based economic development. Since the late 1990s, black communities have been caught in the crossfire of the accelerated armed conflict in the region and are specific targets of violence, death, and displacement. Thus, even as several tenets of Law 70 are implemented, Afro-Colombians face homelessness, an exacerbation in existing inequalities, and renewed forms of social exclusion.

Afro-Colombians are not unique. As contributors to this volume illustrate, various subaltern groups in Latin America are subject to what Comaroff and Comaroff (2001, 8) call the "experiential contradictions of neoliberal capitalism" and the "uneasy fusion of enfranchisement and exclusion." There is by now an extensive literature on how factory workers, peasants, women, urban squatters, and ethnic groups in Latin America arose in protests against the state and forces of late capitalism of the 1980s and beyond (Escobar and Alvarez 1992; Jelin 1990; Redclift 1988). These "new social movements" participated in creating and expanding democratic spaces across the continent. Following the end of military regimes and debt crises of the 1980s, many Latin American nations from Mexico to Chile adopted political and economic reforms. A "trademarked" democracy came to Latin America (and indeed other parts of the world). By this I mean that it is a "liberal" variant of democracy, emphasizing electoral participation, legislative rights, and official multiculturalism. It also arrived hand in hand with neoliberal economic reforms, which called for trade liberalization and a greater role of the private sector including civil society organizations. These last were considered important not only to strengthen the economy but also to deepen democratization.

Many previous social movements in Latin America became incorporated into, or developed links to, this civil society. However, neither democratization nor the civil society agenda have been unmitigated successes in terms of ameliorating (socioeconomic) inequalities or addressing (political and cultural) exclusions. That is, the results of this participation or engagement with the state have been decidedly mixed, even where left-leaning and proindigenous regimes have come to power. As discussed at length in the introductory chapter of this volume, the "Civil Society Agenda" has institutionalized and rendered technical the demands of radical groups, and thus depoliticized social struggles. This depoliticized civil society agenda is seen as part of the apparatus to entrench neoliberal capital and state power. Or as an editorial in *Crítica y Emancipación*, the Latin American Journal of Social Sciences, notes, "all cats are grey at night, as civil society now included everything, at the cost of blurring the social nature of each one of its components" (Crítica y Emancipación Editorial Board 2008, 16).

Others invoke this very multiplicity, to contend that civil society understood variously as the Third Sector, NGOs, social movements, and cultural actors enables the rearticulation of the relations between democratic practices and neoliberal economic policies. While remaining attentive to the gains of the last few decades, I concur with the claims in the introductory chapter that we need to reassess the proposition that civil participation in formal institutions of power and politics will lead to stronger democracy and democratic practices.

I contribute to this reassessment by drawing on my long-term research on Afro-Colombian movements (Asher 2009) to critically examine their strategies and achievements. While black resistance and organizing in Colombia have a long history from colonial times to the present, the lead-up to, and adoption of a new, Constitution in 1991 opened new spaces for black organizing. The Constitution of Colombia of 1991 is an ambitious political charter that aims to expand democratic participation, strengthen civil society, decentralize the political administration, and promote economic growth and development. It also includes Article 7, which recognizes and protects the ethnic and cultural diversity of the nation. But this purported multiculturalism hides widespread ambivalence toward black ethnic and land rights. Under the new Constitution, indigenous groups were granted greater administrative, financial, and territorial autonomy. Rights for black communities were outlined in the brief and ambiguously worded *Artículo Transitorio 55* (AT 55, Transitory Article 55), which stipulates collective land titles for riverine black communities in the Pacific. AT 55 was ratified two years later as Law 70. The passing of Law 70 in 1993 notwithstanding, the recognition of black rights made little immediate difference in state policies and practices. It did however help draw attention to the official invisibility regarding black identity, demography, and culture.

While some black groups strove to take advantage of the new political and economic opening in the country, PCN leaders saw the changes at the turn of the century as an opportunity to organize a broad-based "autonomous" black movement. In the post–Law 70 period, they attempted to rally diverse black groups around their identity as "Afro-Colombians," and to formulate proposals for a collective "ethnic territory" in the Pacific region. They asserted that diverse black and indigenous communities could come together in this ethnic territory, administer it autonomously, and negotiate their own culturally appropriate and ecologically sustainable visions of development.

Arturo Escobar (1995, 2008) sees the PCN's efforts as a form of "cultural politics" (Alvarez, Dagnino, and Escobar 1998b, 7) that offer real possibilities of an alternative modernity or development. Peter Wade (1995) also reflects on the "cultural politics of blackness," but unlike Escobar he views the state as an important interlocutor and controller of black mobilization (350). He also sees the new political conjunctures as playing a constitutive role in shaping new black identities (353). Escobar's and Wade's reflections redirected my own observations of post–Law 70 black struggles. I noticed that the cultural legislation in Colombia has double-edged effects on its ethnic population (Dover and Rappaport 1996; Gros 1991). On the one hand, ethnic and territorial rights are premised on the ability of these communities to prove that they are "ethnically different" from the rest of the population. On the other, the state attempts to incorporate them as citizens and members of civil society in a nation-state that had recently proclaimed itself multicultural. Indeed, as Charles Hale (2002) argues, such "neoliberal multiculturalism" depends on a certain minimal recognition of cultural rights while rejecting the more radical demands of ethnic groups.

How this neoliberal cultural politics reshapes racial politics and policy in Latin America, and how it functions for Afro-descendant versus indigenous groups in Latin America have received much critical attention in the past decades. Here I specifically direct analytical attention to how Afro-Colombian cultural politics unfold in relation to political economic conjunctures. The impetus to understand ethnocultural strategies within the context of *coyuntura* of the Pacific came from black activists. *Coyuntura* (rather than the more awkward English "conjuncture") is a difficult notion to explain satisfactorily. Its literal translation as "articulation" warns against misunderstanding it solely as economic "structures" that determine or constrain action. Stuart Hall's (1986, 6) discussion of Antonio Gramsci's relevance for the study of race and ethnicity highlights how Gramsci makes important contributions to understanding social struggles by reading Marx nondeterministically and from his peripheral or southernist perspective. In his remarks on "the State and Civil Society," Gramsci grapples with the complex and nuanced relationship between economic forces and "culture," noting that state power is constituted at least in part through civil society, though without entirely satisfactory conceptualizing of state or civil society ([1971] 1995, 207). But the importance of "conjunctural analysis" is revealed precisely in this difficulty in finding a definitive way of understanding the relationship between these two closely intertwined entities. Gramsci thus pushes us to be nonreductive, and to analyze the specific conjunctures within which social and cultural movements working toward radical change interrelate with economic and political forces (Laclau and Mouffe 1985).

Gramsci's insights (and my engagement with postcolonial feminist scholarship) then steer me clear of binary explanations of power and resistance and implicitly shape my long-term observations and analysis of Afro-Colombian social movements. In what follows, I focus on three periods of black organizing over the past two decades in a heuristic schematic that is further developed elsewhere.[1] First, from the constitutional reform process of the late 1980s to the passing of Law 70 in 1993; second, in the 1990s, when attempts to implement Law 70, and go beyond it to assert "Identity, Territory, and Autonomy" coincided with large-scale economic development and conservation initiatives in the Pacific lowlands; and third, from the turn of the century onward following the massive displacement of black communities from the Pacific, and the internationalization of their struggles. My aim is to foreground the particular conjunctures of economic and geopolitical forces within which Afro-Colombian movements contest state power, but also constitute it through their claims for cultural and territorial rights. I conclude by reflecting on how the contradictions and contingencies of ethnic struggles are a caution as much against romanticizing resistance as against reducing social struggles to structural effects.

Black Organizing from 1980s–1993:
Becoming Afro-Colombian

After Brazil, Colombia has the largest black population in Latin America. But it was only at the end of the twentieth century that both countries conferred specific rights to their black populations, or indeed recognized blacks as a distinct group within the nation. Why this is so is linked to a number of factors—histories of nationalism, the perception of blacks and blackness within prevailing ideologies of "race" and culture, and the structures and dynamics of political economy—and how these function in each context. In Colombia, the dynamics of color, culture, and class played out differently for indians and blacks.[2] While indigenous communities were historically viewed as culturally distinct and their special rights recognized, or at least legally articulated, blacks were "invisible" in official registers. Both peoples have been marginalized in socioeconomic and political terms, and they have organized to redress their situations since colonial times.

Before the 1980s, most black organizations or movements in modern Colombia were local or regional in orientation. These organizations reflected the differences among black communities—of class, occupation, political ideology, regional location, and local histories.[3] For example, in the 1970s and 1980s urban blacks formed study and research groups such as the Movimiento Nacional Cimarrón which focused on problems of racial discrimination and economic marginalization. In rural areas, Cimarrón's discourse of international black solidarity and universal human rights had little resonance. Black peasants were more likely to be engaged in struggles for land, or organized around specific work and social activities. Under the aegis of early state-sponsored development programs, black peasants and rural women also formed user groups to help with subsistence production, and cooperatives to market regional products (Rojas 1996). In the late 1980s, when commercial logging concessions threatened their livelihoods, one peasant group, the United Peasant Association of the Atrato River (Asociación Campesina Integral de Río Atrato, or ACIA), along with the regional organization of Emberá indians (OREWA), organized to fight them. Such struggles laid the groundwork for taking black demands to the national stage during the 1980s.

During the constitutional reform process, black leaders and activists sought to organize disparate black communities with heterogeneous interests into national-level coalitions. In the department of the Chocó, the state with a majority black population, the Organization of People's Neighborhoods and Black Communities of the Chocó (Organización de Barrios Populares y Comunidades Negras de Chocó, or OBAPO) mobilized shanty dwellers in the capital, Quibdó, and in several coastal communities. Among rural, riverine communities, peasant associations such as ACIA expanded their reach, and new river-based associations were formed. In the southwestern Pacific departments of Valle del Cauca, Cauca, and Nariño, a group of students and intellectuals (many with prior links to Cimarrón) focused on bringing together peasants, artisanal fisherfolks, loggers, and miners from rural areas. Several activists from the Atlantic coast and Bogotá joined this core group from the southwest Pacific, and collectively called themselves the PCN. It was during this time that the term "Afro-Colombian" came into circulation to stress the African descent of black communities and their connections to the Colombian nation-state. Despite disagreements over nomenclature and definitions, during my fieldwork in the 1990s, the terms *black communities* and *Afro-Colombians* were most often heard and used interchangeably, as I do in this chapter.

These groups and movements provided the nucleus around which Afro-Colombians organized in unprecedented numbers. Even black politicians linked to the two main political parties (Liberal and Conservative) joined them to participate in workshops and seminars to discuss Afro-Colombian needs and interests. At the local, municipal, and regional levels, various NGOs and the Catholic Church, with its important presence in the region, played key roles in organizing communities. Black women were a visible and crucial part of these mobilizations.

But this black coalition was divided regarding the parameters and proposal for black rights in the new Constitution. On the one hand, there were those who wanted to formulate black demands in terms of antidiscrimination and equal opportunity (both economic and political). On the other hand, there were those who wanted to formulate black rights in terms of the needs and realities of rural black communities living in the Pacific region—an area where 90 percent of the population was black. The latter proposal was spearheaded by the PCN. While mobilizing in the Pacific littoral, PCN members became inspired by the everyday realities and quotidian practices among rural communities. Rather than thinking of black rights largely in terms of racial equality or economic development, the PCN began to envision an Afro-Colombian ethnocultural movement based on the right to be different from the rest of Colombian society and to validate black identity. The ACIA's struggles against logging concessions, and the focus on the Pacific as a resource frontier and a locus of environmental conservation, also influenced the PCN to think about protecting the future of black communities by staking a claim over the Pacific as a biethnic territory.

Like the black struggle, Colombia's constitutional reform endeavor in the 1980s was neither its first, nor was it smooth. But in response to internally induced changes and forces of regional and global geopolitics (promoting economic reforms and democratization yet again), the process went ahead, and a new Constitution was ratified on July 4, 1991. Its principal focus is the creation of a "modern" state, ready to play a significant role in national, regional, and global affairs. This is reflected in the Constitution's liberal-democratic language and its emphasis on rights, whether political, economic, social, or environmental. A key mechanism specified to assure access to these rights is political participation along the legislative, executive, and judicial axes of state power.

In contrast to the expansion of democratic legislative spaces, the 1991 Constitution's economic reforms were in keeping with earlier state policies and the prevalent neoliberal agenda. The new policies centered on restructuring the national economy to make it more competitive in regional and international markets. That is, "structural adjustment" reforms were appearing in Colombia as elsewhere and ushering in what Colombians call the *apertura económica* (economic opening). With as-yet-undeveloped natural resource assets (including oil and gas deposits), regions such as the Amazon and the

Pacific (with the additional advantage of having proximity to the economically powerful countries of the Asia-Pacific Rim) had important potential for economic growth. At the same time, these areas emerged in the spotlight of a new era of environmental politics.

Ethnic and cultural issues and the rights of minority groups were not a crucial part of the constitutional reform agenda initially. But the presence of indigenous representatives in the Constituent Assembly, national debates in favor of multiculturalism, and such international agreements as the International Labor Organization's Accord 169, which demanded the recognition of ethnic and cultural rights of peoples within nations led to the inclusion of Article 7 in the new Constitution. The juxtaposition of environmental, economic, and ethnic issues played an important role in the articulation of black rights in Colombia's Constitution of 1991. Prior to the constitutional reform process, black demands were rarely couched in terms of the recognition of their cultural difference. But in the early 1990s, Afro-Colombians (like other aboriginals in Latin America and beyond) made alliances with environmentalists, who saw rural, grassroots communities as "stewards of nature" and advocated their participation in sustainable development and environmental conservation efforts.

But the appeal to indigeneity, multiculturalism, and environmentalism worked differently for indigenous and black groups. Under the Constitution of 1991, indigenous groups were promised expanded control over their communal lands, and administrative autonomy in judicial decisions, finances, and development policy. Blacks went into the constitutional reform process in an ethnic double-bind: discriminated against or exoticized because of their "racial difference" but not considered sufficiently distinct from Colombia's *mestizo* (mixed race) population as indians to merit special legal status. This ambivalence was reflected in Transitory Article 55 (AT 55), which restricts black rights to collective land titles for riverine black communities in the Pacific.

Between 1991 and 1993, black activists and leaders worked to turn AT 55 into a law of substance. But beyond agreeing that the mandates of AT 55 needed to be expanded to recognize and include the rights of diverse black communities, not just those along the Pacific rivers, the black coalition remained divided. These divisions paralleled earlier ones. On the one side were those who saw a law for black communities primarily as a means for obtaining extended political participation and equality within established institutions, and on the other were PCN activists who wanted to redefine the terms of democracy and development from an "ethnocultural" perspective with the Pacific region as the territorial fulcrum. Grueso, Rosero, and Escobar (1998,

200) note that the PCN wanted to emphasize the importance of "maintaining social control of territory and natural resources as a precondition for survival, re-creation, and strengthening of culture." But government officials, black politicians affiliated with Colombia's two main political parties, and several members of the special commission charged with drafting a law for black communities were ambivalent or actively hostile to the PCN's proposition. Despite these difficulties, Law 70 was passed in 1993 after two years of negotiations and official foot-dragging.

The new law managed to expand the focus of AT 55 considerably, but black communities were not, as the PCN proposed, granted autonomous control over the Pacific region. Law 70's eight chapters and sixty-eight articles focus on three main issues: ethnic and cultural rights, collective land ownership, and socioeconomic development. Law 70 does expand the terms of AT 55 to recognize the rights of all Afro-Colombians, but in restricted terms. These rights are modeled on the perceived realities of black communities of the Pacific and emphasize collective property titles for groups living in rural areas and engaged in subsistence production.

Still the passing of Law 70 was a significant victory for Afro-Colombians. However, it did not unite Afro-Colombians under a single organizational umbrella. The unstable black coalition split apart further. Black politicians and Chocoan groups focused their efforts (to varying degrees) on gaining entry into traditional state politics and political institutions. The PCN continued to emphasize the importance of "identity, territory, autonomy" for black communities. That is, post–Law 70 black social movements were fraught with tensions and deeply intertwined with the political economic dynamics of development in the Pacific region.

Afro-Colombians Organizing in the 1990s:
"Identity, Territory, and Autonomy"

Black organizations proliferated across the country in the 1990s. They included cultural groups; new collectives organized around logging, mining, and other productive activities; myriad community councils; and women's groups. While some of these groups had origins in earlier organizations, a considerable number emerged during the black mobilization process that led to AT 55 and Law 70. These organizations had small memberships, limited mandates, and few independent funds. Many were linked rather loosely to one or more of the three broad factions outlined above (black politicians, Chocoan groups, or the PCN coalition).

A significant number of Afro-Colombians already lived in Colombia's Andean cities. Since the 1970s, there had been a steady stream of migrants from the coast to urban centers. After Law 70 was passed, there was a resurgence of youth and squatter groups in these areas. Cimarrón also continued to be active in urban universities and periurban areas. However, in the 1990s the principal locus of black organizing was the Pacific lowlands. This was not only because 90 percent of the region's inhabitants are Afro-Colombian, but also because many of Law 70's terms coincided or clashed with other state plans for the region.

The four coastal departments that span the Colombian Pacific Littoral— Chocó, Valle del Cauca, Cauca, and Nariño—compose a large part of the Chocó biogeographic region. The Chocó region extends 1,300 kilometers from the southern tip of Panama to the northern tip of Ecuador and is rich in natural resources (timber, precious metals, fisheries, etc.). A global biodiversity "hot spot," the region is home to a variety of ecosystems (coral reefs, mangroves, rock and sandy beaches, coastal forests, high- and lowland tropical moist forests), and myriad plant and animal species, many endemic.[4] Despite this resource richness, the Pacific was considered poor and marginal in economic development terms.

In a country with a complex geography where regions are physically and politically disconnected from each other, the Chocó was long relegated to the periphery of post–World War II national development. With the arrival of neoliberal globalization in the late 1980s, however, state officials and development experts held that it was strategically and economically imperative to modernize hitherto "isolated" regional economies (such as in the Pacific and Amazon areas), and to integrate their "backward" inhabitants with the rest of the country. Even as the parameters of black rights were being debated, state planners were engaged in talks with multilateral donors such as the World Bank to fund a large-scale economic modernization initiative. Called *Plan Pacífico*, its explicit aim was to develop the region's natural resources and stimulate economic growth.

The biodiverse Chocó was also fast becoming a key target of national and international environmental conservation efforts. In 1992, the Colombian government launched a five-year biodiversity conservation program called Proyecto BioPacífico. With a mandate to devise mechanisms for the protection and sustainable use of regional biodiversity, Proyecto BioPacífico became linked to the economic aims of Plan Pacífico. As awareness of these programs spread, indigenous and Afro-Colombian groups drew on new global discourses of "rights-based development" and "community-based conservation" and began to pressure the state to make good on its promises to recognize their rights. In response to such pressure, the collective titling of ethnic lands, local participation, and the preservation of traditional knowledge of natural resource management became subsidiary goals of economic development and environmental conservation programs.

But the state, NGOs, and Afro-Colombian activists had very different understandings of the region's political economy and what local participation and inclusion implied. For a large number of state and development entities, the path to a better future for all Colombians, including black communities, lay in political and economic modernization. And recognizing Afro-Colombian ethnic rights meant incorporating them as resource stewards into its development and conservation practices: this was the purpose, as much as the product, of land titling. For the PCN and to some extent Chocoan groups, ethnic recognition implied more than property rights and participation in Plan Pacífico and Proyecto BioPacífico. Rather, these activists wished to shape the region's economic, ecological, and territorial dynamics according to their conceptions of the links between culture, ethnicity, and territory. The PCN, especially, mistrusted the state and its intentions, and took an anti-institutional stance vis-à-vis Afro-Colombian struggles. In January 1994, in an interview with Arturo Escobar, PCN leaders noted: "The state wants to close the door and leave the window half open so that not many people can pass through, nor much air. . . . For the state, Law 70 is a way of giving legal rights to the blacks, of institutionalizing their problems and concerns. This political opening is 'a cushion of air' for the economic opening. So if the problems are institutionalized they can be managed" (OCN 1996, 247).

Within this context, PCN activists noted:

The black communities of Colombia need *espacios propios*—rights over our territory—but also spaces where we can consolidate our positions. We have differences within, we have a different position than *Cimarrón*, . . . or the politicians. Our purpose is to form and to strengthen the process of organization so that the very same communities generate processes of resistance or alternative visions to confront what is being imposed on them by the state.

We aspire to construct a new society, where we all fit with all our differences, where no one is excluded or marginalized or segregated, where there is mutual respect for differences. We are not against the concrete demands of water, electricity, health care, transport. But we had to take a position—respond to a series of concrete petitions or work to open up spaces from which we can formulate our politics. We chose the latter (OCN 1996, 252).

Obtaining espacios propios—conceptualized variously as autonomous physical territory, political space, and ethnic homeland—was central to the PCN's understanding of ethnic rights. Drawing on the terms of Law 70, the PCN aimed to organize a black social movement according to the politico-organizational principles of "identity, territory, and autonomy" they outlined in 1993 at one of the first national conferences of black communities held in Puerto Tejada. The PCN's key goals were:

- to organize a broad, grassroots-based black social movement based on diverse Afro-Colombian identities and interests,
- to envision a political strategy that would enable organized black communities to make autonomous decisions regarding their livelihoods,
- to develop culturally appropriate, ecologically sustainable models of economic development,
- to establish autonomous territorial control over the Pacific.

In Gramscian terms, the PCN seemed to want to engage in the "war of position" and the "war of manoeuvre" simultaneously. Leaders from the PCN knew that the former was a protracted struggle across different fronts, and that Law 70 was not a sufficiently definitive victory in the war of manoeuvre. But like the terms of Law 70, the PCN's goals were lacking in specifics and ambitious in scope.

In the short term, the PCN did not succeed in putting forth a concrete culturally appropriate alternative to mainstream economic models. However, attention to black cultural practices and concerns did become part of Plan Pacífico and Proyecto BioPacífico, thanks to the mobilizing efforts of the PCN and other groups. Youth groups such as Juventud 500 in Buenaventura, cultural groups such as Ecos del Pacífico in Tumaco, community groups such as Fundación Atarraya in Guapi, and numerous women's groups in all four states were among the local organizations that gained new momentum in the 1990s. Working in conjunction with the PCN but also with the state and NGOs, these groups developed ideas of black identity and cultural politics in interesting and creative ways. Across the Pacific, riverine communities also began organizing, and the first collective land titles were handed out in the Atrato region in 1997. But even as these achievements gained increasing visibility overseas and inspired other Afro-descendant struggles, the dynamics in Colombia were changing.

The Constitution of 1991 marked the dawn of a new hope of democratic politics for Colombians, and especially for Afro-Colombians. The end of the decade seemed to signal the twilight of this hope, as the country plunged into yet another political and economic crisis. Corruption was one of many elements responsible. Another was the rapid spread of drug traffickers and of guerilla and paramilitary forces as the latent low-intensity conflict emerged fully into the foreground. After a brief and abortive attempt at peace talks with insurgents, the official response became one of stepping up the military offensive (against guerrillas and drug traffickers) and economic opening—a policy maintained to this day.

Black and indigenous communities in the Pacific became increasingly caught in this crossfire, or became specific targets of violence, death, and displacement. By 2005, an estimated 2 million Afro-Colombians had been involuntarily displaced from their homes.[5] With the acceleration of armed violence and the targeted killing of leaders and activists, local communities could not exert control over their lands even when they had managed to obtain collective titles. As black communities literally and figurative "lost ground" in the region, the tenor of black movements began changing.

Black Organizing in the New Millennium: From Afro-Colombians to Afro-Desplazados and Afro-Descendants

At the turn of the twenty-first century, the prevailing political and economic strategies in Colombia were framed by efforts to counter narcotics and terrorism. Key among them was the U.S.-funded Plan Colombia, which started as an antidrug campaign but soon expanded into an armed offensive against guerrillas. However, both the antinarcotic and anti-insurgency tactics were ineffective against their targets. Rather, they fueled conflicts between drug traffickers, guerrillas, paramilitary forces, and the Colombian Army in order to gain military and economic control over the region. Military operations stepped up sharply under President Álvaro Uribe's terms and did little to achieve the goals of "peace and security" (or what he called *seguridad democrática*, or "democratic security"). Under Uribe, the environmental and ethnic gains of the previous decade in the Pacific also eroded. Forests and natural ecosystems, as well as cultivated food crops, became the "collateral damage" of the nonselective chemical herbicides used to eradicate drugs. Areas cleared of natural vegetation and coca are quickly replaced with more coca, or taken over for illegal mining and agroindustrial projects. Key among the latter are the high-profit, export-oriented plantations of African oil palms, which destroy ecosystems and subsistence crops. Black and indigenous communities remain at the center of this vortex, facing death and forced displacement.

In the context of these changes, both the loci and foci of black movements expanded on multiple fronts. In the Pacific, the PCN and Chocoan groups continued to engage in the strategic struggle for long-term ethnic and territorial rights. But from the end of the 1990s, there was a new urgency—the immediate needs of rural peoples whose lives and livelihoods were destroyed by aerial fumigants, and other aspects of the wars on terror and drugs. Many rural peoples ended up in regional towns in the Pacific as *afro-desplazados* (displaced Afro-Colombians) where they lacked housing and basic services. To address these urgent tasks, local black organizations such as community councils and women's groups began working in conjunction with various state and international humanitarian assistance and relief services agencies. Black activists also made alliances with NGOs involved in recording human rights violations, and accompanying communities to prevent displacement, or enable their return.[6]

With increasing U.S. involvement and funding for the problematic Plan Colombia, and the entrenchment of free-trade neoliberalism, black movements also rallied international support for their struggles, making connections with solidarity groups, Washington think tanks, and development NGOs. Also proliferating were links with U.S. politicians, especially the Congressional Black Caucus. Representatives of these entities visit Colombia regularly and work in various ways to keep Afro-Colombian issues on the U.S. policy agenda. Instrumental in fostering these links were activists who regularly traveled abroad, such as Grueso and Rosero; politicians such as Piedad Córdoba; and displaced Afro-Colombians living in exile in the United States. Among the latter are Luis Gilberto Murillo (former governor of the department of Chocó) and Marino Córdoba (an activist from Chocó). Like many activists, Córdoba left the Pacific in 1996 after receiving death threats. In 1999, with PCN members and others, he established the Association of Displaced Afro-Colombians (Asociación Nacional de Afrocolombianos Desplazados, AFRODES), an organization dedicated to addressing the needs of displaced Afro-Colombians. In 2002, continuing threats forced Córdoba to leave Colombia, but he continued AFRODES activities from the United States. The struggle for black rights began to be couched as much in terms of "human rights" as in ethnocultural terms. The call for the latter also began reformulation as stressing the right of black communities to return to their homes and collective lands to live a life of dignity and peace. This change in the discourses and foci of black movements was reflected in the change in the PCN's slogan from "Identity, Territory, and Autonomy" to "Identity, Territory, Dignity, and *Life*."

As the number of black communities displaced by violence took on alarming proportions, the black sectors described in the first part of this chapter (Cimarrón, the PCN, Chocoan groups, and black politicians) formed coalitions across their differences. They also joined forces with or renewed alliances with other sectors (including traditional political parties) and social groups in Colombia. During a visit to Colombia in 2004, PCN activists including Carlos Rosero confirmed what I was observing—that the PCN's position with respect to formal or institutional politics had begun to change. Black movements were engaging more actively in electoral politics as they felt it more imperative than ever to draw and keep political attention on the struggles, rights, and needs of their peoples. In August 2007, Rosero told me that Afro-descendant groups were pursuing these goals through alliances with other progressive political forces, including the Polo Democrático, a new, independent left-wing political party.

Black struggles in Colombia also internationalized in various ways. Afro-Colombian leaders were key participants in the United Nations World Conference against Racism held in Durban in 2001, where they connected with other black groups in Latin America and beyond. It was during the Durban process that the terms *Afro-Latino* and *Afro-descendant* gained currency in the Afro-Colombian movements. Also at this time there was resurgence in activism against racial discrimination, for socioeconomic and political equality, and reparations for indignities suffered in the distant past as in more recent times (Mosquera Rosero-Labbé and Barcelos 2007).

Black struggles in Colombia continue at multiple fronts, but black organizations and movements remain split and splintered over how to engage the state and economic reforms. While PCN and other grassroots movements are more open to electoral strategies and public policies than before, they remain skeptical about the possibility of bringing about progressive social change through mainstream political channels and legislative means. This skepticism is especially justified in light of the mixed success for black communities through Law 70. Law 70 has indeed brought many gains for black groups. The most tangible success appears in collective land titling statistics, though these vary. Based on data from the Colombian Institute of Rural Development (Instituto Colombiano de Desarrollo Rural, or INCODER) data, a United Nations Development Programme report estimates that between 1996 and May 2010, 162 collective titles over 5,215,977 hectares were processed in the Pacific (PNUD 2012). In addition to collective land titles and reserved seats for black delegates in the Chamber of Representatives, special entities such as the Afro-Colombian Subdivision in the Office of Ethnic Affairs specifically address black concerns. National research institutes, such as the Colombian Institute of Anthropology and History, began funding research on Afro-Colombian themes. Wade (2004) cites evidence to show that Law 70 also spurred legislation to include Afro-Colombian history and culture in the national curriculum, and to award special grants for black students to attend universities. There are several cases of black communities in the Andes and the Caribbean drawing on Law 70 to articulate their concerns and demands.

Black representatives are part of several government ministries (Rural Development, Environment, Education, etc.) and regional development corporations. However, as activists note, Afro-Colombians who are elected to official posts or appointed to government posts usually do not represent the poor black base of either rural or urban areas. That such gains are not without contradictions is also evident from the "land grabbing" by private and illegal groups often with the help of extralegal means. The lands thus acquired are then used for African oil palm cultivation or mining. New laws under the Uribe presidency and the "green multiculturalism" associated with oil palm cultivation give short shrift to environmental and social goals and promote free trade and entrepreneurship (Cardenas 2012).

As in the previous decade, then, despite progressive public policies including laws for the restitution of victims of violence and displacement, *Afro-descendientes* in Colombia face a grim reality. According to data from the National Planning Department and the University of Los Andes' Observatory of Racial Discrimination, 76 percent of Afro-descendant people live in extreme poverty, 42 percent are unemployed, and only 2 percent go on to attend a university. Activists, journalists, and human rights observers note that displaced Afro-Colombians are regularly denied services, despite the substantial institutions created expressly to guarantee the rights of displaced citizens. In sum, the new strategies and configurations of black social movements are no less heterogeneous, contradictory, or intertwined with state- and market-led changes than those that emerged at the beginning of the Law 70 process.

Conclusion

In the Pacific region (as elsewhere), democratic changes unfolded simultaneously with a new phase of economic globalization, which advocated a greater role for the private sector and civil society. These changes neither brought the disappearance of the state nor the victory of social struggles through their inclusion as civil society. Autonomy as a goal, however, was at the very least problematic. Black communities could not simultaneously divorce themselves from state, NGOs, and development interests *and* negotiate with them over the region's future. The result was rather an explosion of movements contesting state power while simultaneously seeking state recognition. As one AFRODES activist said to me in 2007, Afro-Colombian movements were now a recognized part of "Colombian civil society." Black communities linked their demands for ethnic and territorial rights to the latest phase of capital intrusion and state formation in the Pacific, which had acquired "environmentally sustainable" and "culturally sensitive" hues.

While never merely struggling for inclusion, black communities were neither outside the discourses of development nor content to remain on its margins. Rather, they were constituted as subjects of prevailing development and ethnocultural discourses even as they attempted to disrupt them. For example, despite their anti-institutional stance PCN leaders utilized, even in the early phases of their organizing, prevailing discourses of participation and new constitutional guarantees of citizenship rights to demand that the state recognize the tripartite Afro-Colombian claim of "identity, autonomy, territory." Activists of the PCN did not seek formal political posts, but did work in various capacities with state institutions involved in addressing Law 70 and with other development entities. Indeed such engagement increased in the new millennium and without it the PCN would have risked de facto exclusion from important ongoing discussions affecting their present and future.

The shaping of black movements and identities by political economic forces was hardly a one-way street. True, issues of environmental sustainability and the ethnic promise that Van Cott (2000) envisioned in the Constitution were virtually absent from the initial drafts of Plan Pacífico. But state and economic planners faced immediate pressure to address social, cultural, and environmental demands. Such pressure came not only from ethnic movements and the language of the Constitution and Law 70, but also from NGOs and state entities, some of which were staffed by women and men genuinely committed to environmental and social justice.

In 1992, the World Bank approved a loan to fund a resource management project under Plan Pacífico with the condition that the titling of ethnic lands and preservation of traditional resource-use knowledge be included as components. Subsequently, a small percentage of the project's funding and a great deal of bank attention were dedicated to titling ethnic, including black, lands. Such an expansion of the project was in part a result of the intervention by the PCN, other ethnic groups, and NGOs during project negotiations. Similar interventions during discussions to implement the first phase of Proyecto BioPacífico and other conservation activities also led to the inclusion of ethnic concerns in environmental projects. But a celebration of these advances as the development industry's sensitivity to cultural and environmental issues, or even as an unconditional victory for ethnic groups, would be naive. The collective titling of ethnic land was in keeping with neoliberal aims of clarifying property rights to reduce conflicts over resources and facilitate private-sector growth. Involving black and indigenous communities in resource management and biodiversity conservation was another attempt to address concerns over "local participation" and "environmental sustainability" while helping to integrate these heretofore marginalized populations into the market. While clarifying property rights has not reduced land conflicts, private-sector growth and market integration rather than culturally appropriate development became the dominant economic paradigms by 2010.

To see such developments merely as the co-optation of black struggles would be equally uncritical however. In the past decades, several Afro–Latin American groups have taken advantage of the broad interest in "Afro-descendant" communities to seek support from multilateral development banks for their land rights and other democratic guarantees promised under the new constitutional reforms (Thorne 2001). One need not be an apologist for globalization to note that far from being uniformly homogenizing, the effects of the "civil society agenda" are contradictory and circumscribed by local politics and culture.

Near the end of the twentieth century, ethnic rights and traditional knowledge (along with sustainable resource use and biodiversity conservation) became key idioms through which modernity and democracy began to be asserted and understood in the Colombian Pacific and many other places in the "Third World." Such expressions of democracy had another seemingly paradoxical effect: at a moment when neoliberal globalization measures and the emphasis on private-sector-led economic growth called for a decrease in the role of the state, these expressions played a major role in helping the Colombian state gain legitimacy and constitute itself. The restructuring of the national territory, of which collective land titling became a subset, was also aimed at creating a governable nation-state (Asher and Ojeda 2009; Ng'weno 2007).

During the mid-1990s, many state and subsidiary agencies appeared in a region where they heretofore had little presence or influence in order to promote development, environmental conservation, and the recognition of ethnic and territorial rights. Such state legitimacy was partial and weak at best, as the increasing presence of drug traffickers, paramilitary, guerrillas, and other extralegal armed groups in the Pacific in the last decade bears tragic testimony. Nor could legal recognition guarantee the realization of rights: even as the first collective land titles were handed out in 1997, black groups began to be displaced from the Pacific in vast numbers because of the dramatic escalation of violent conflict. Since then and after 2010, black struggles were increasingly framed in terms of demands for peace.

The reality of the Pacific and the black movements was very different by the end of the first decade of the twenty-first century. The bleak state of affairs in the Pacific can be seen as a failure of black struggles against state modernization and neoliberal globalization. But such a conclusion only emerges from and reinforces a false binary—that Afro-Colombians in particular, and local groups in the Third World in general, are completely separate from the state. Their social movement struggles are not simply outside the civil society agenda, but rather emerge from their relations to it. These are complex, contradictory, and contingent ways in which the state and civil society structure each other with specific conjunctures of political economic changes.

NOTES

1. For ethnographic details that substantiate my observations, see my monograph (2009) and other excellent studies on recent Afro-Colombian movements.

2. I use the term "indian" because anthropological and postcolonial work in the past decade has shown that "Indian" identity is as multiple and mobile as other cultural categories such as "black" and "mestizo."

3. In addition to a substantial representation in the Colombian metropolises (Bogotá, Medellín, and Cali), there are six regions of important black presence in Colombia: the Atlantic/Caribbean coast, the Magdalena river valley, the Cauca and Patía river valleys in the Andean region, the San Andrés and Providencia archipelagos (where English predominates), and the rural riparian zones of the Pacific Littoral.

4. In 1993, the 8 million hectares of the Colombian Chocó (6.2 percent of the country) encompassed 5.5 million hectares of forests, of which 3.5 million are considered pristine or without major interventions. Two and a half million hectares of this area were in eight national parks, and one million hectares were in seventeen indigenous *resguardos*. The rest was considered *tierras baldías*, or empty lands, belonging to the state, even though they were inhabited by a significant percentage of Afro-Colombian communities.

5. Figures on the total numbers of internally displaced persons (IDPs) differ, with the Colombian government's figures lower than those of major human rights groups. The Consultancy on Human Rights and Displacement (Consultoría para los Derechos Humanos y Desplazamiento, or CODHES), one of the most respected and authoritative nongovernmental sources on IDPs in Colombia, estimates that between 1995 and 2005, 3 million people

were forced to flee their homes because of violence related to armed struggles or disputes over territory and resources. According to the International Committee of the Red Cross, despite the supposed demobilization of paramilitary groups in 2005, internal displacement figures remain on the rise: from 45,000 in 2005 to 67,000 in 2006 and an estimated 72,000 in 2007. IDPs tend to belong disproportionately to minority groups, with Afro-Colombians accounting for around 33 percent of the 412,500 persons displaced during 2002.

6. Among the most notable being the UN's High Commission for Refugees, Doctors Without Borders, Amnesty International, Project Counseling Services (from Sweden), Peace Brigades International, the American Friends Service Committee, and the Washington Office on Latin America (WOLA). A host of other organizations also maintain a presence in Colombia.

Chapter 11

IN THE STREETS AND IN THE INSTITUTIONS

Movements-in-Democracy and the
Rural Women's Movement in Rio Grande Do Sul

JEFFREY W. RUBIN

This chapter explores the ideas and practices of a social movement that acts simultaneously through uncivic contention in the streets and civil-society-based participation in government. Brazilian activists would describe this as acting in the streets and in the institutions. By highlighting this duality of social movement practice, I call attention to a new way of being a movement in a democratic regime, which I call movement-in-democracy.[1] I illustrate what it means to be a movement-in-democracy, why this is difficult to achieve, and what might make the construction of movements-in-democracy more likely.

This possibility of combining civil and uncivic activism can be discerned on the ground in the case I examine, the Movement of Rural Women Workers (Movimento de Mulheres Trabalhadoras Rurais, or MMTR) in the southern

Brazilian state of Rio Grande do Sul, even though it has not taken shape in enduring form there. Aspects of movement-in-democracy occurred at various moments in the history of the MMTR, tangible enough to elicit comment and discussion among activists, and between activists and me, over the course of fifteen years. Based on the history and experiences of the MMTR from 1985 to 2012, I offer conclusions about this mix between the civil and uncivil, including propositions about how to contain difference within movements and deepen progressive reform in democracies.[2]

By movement-in-democracy, I mean a movement from within which people can participate in institutions and institutional practices—elections, government agencies and commissions, labor union confederations, participatory budgeting—and *also* mobilize, protest, disrupt, and create new programs and practices outside of formal and mainstream institutions, through demonstrations, land occupations, marches, and other forms of performance or civil disobedience. That is, movements that can develop and maintain, more or less simultaneously, capacities to press for reform and change from within and without, with civil and uncivil tactics, and that see this duality as a valid and perhaps important way of being *one* movement. In my discussion of this combination, I go beyond one of the main conclusions of this book—that successful social movements over the past decade combine civil and uncivil forms of activism—to suggest that such combinations are particularly suited to promoting progressive reform in democracies. I suggest that by containing, in one movement or movement field, forms of activism that more often overflow the borders of movements, activists might more effectively challenge inequalities and exclusion. Indeed, the capacity of a movement to hold difference, or of a counterpublic to establish forms of horizontal communication and strategizing, affects not only its own mobilizations, but the capacity of the ordinary, day-to-day activities of democracy to sustain effervescence and creativity.

Where a Movement-in-Democracy Almost Happened

In the mid-1980s, a group of rural women activists separated from a vibrant and growing set of male-led social movements that refused to take gender seriously to form the MMTR and address gender and class concerns simultaneously.[3] The MMTR achieved spectacular successes in securing economic and political rights for rural women—including pensions and maternity leaves—and in challenging gender relations within families. But by the end of its second decade, the rural women's movement had fragmented over deep disagreements concerning whether to do politics in the streets or the institutions, whether to prioritize democracy or hierarchy inside the movement, and where to place gender in relation to economic transformation in a radical political agenda.

Much of this process of organizing as an autonomous movement and then splitting into a variety of initiatives—including but not limited to the movement itself, with its headquarters in the provincial city of Passo Fundo—was shaped and galvanized by the presence of two powerful forces in Rio Grande do Sul, the Liberation Theology Church and the Movement of Landless Rural Workers (Movimento de Trabalhadores Rurais Sem Terra, or MST). Initially, the church was the actor that politicized young people and brought them into social movements in the final years of the dictatorship (Doimo 1995; van der Schaaf 2001), and activist priests and nuns in the region continue today to speak for radical economic transformation, as well as for subjecthood on an individual level and pluralism within movements. At the same time, however, the church counseled and exemplified a process of consensus building guided by hierarchy.

The MST originated in Rio Grande do Sul in alliance with the Liberation Theology Church and in its early years functioned through incipient forms of democratic deliberation. In the course of the 1980s, however, the MST embraced a Leninist approach to political strategy and practice, even as democratic procedures were being established and deepened in Brazilian institutions and in other social movements. By and large, over the course of the period under discussion here, decisions in the MST were made by a central group of male leaders, with endorsement of MST strategies and programs required of members and participation in government and labor unions eschewed.[4] Thus in rural Rio Grande do Sul, the church and MST, which had provided early training grounds for MMTR leaders, did not provide the language, tools, or cultural knowledge for the kind of argumentative dialogue essential for the rough and tumble of internal democracy.[5]

Today there are women's movement activists in multiple locations carrying out varying forms of activism. These multiple forms of action occur in the streets in protest demonstrations and direct action, such as occupying corporate laboratories and destroying genetically modified crops; within institutions such as labor unions, political parties, and city government; in alternative women's pharmacies in rural towns and in local workshops that address a range of progressive topics; and in individualized, market-based projects such as the sale of Herbalife, a nutrition supplement marketed out of Los Angeles. While in a general sense all of these efforts fit loosely under the umbrella of "rural women's movement," and more than one can be carried out simultaneously by the same person or group, the practitioners of these different approaches do not communicate directly about them or strategize together on issues of gender or economics. In contrast, I suggest that movements or counterpublics that manage to combine civil and uncivic practices—simultaneously animating democracies from within and challenging them from without—stand a better chance of bringing about enduring reform.

The Context of Rural Brazil

Fighting for reform in Brazil means challenging harsh realities. Brazil has been a democracy since 1985 and boasts the seventh largest economy in the world,[6] but these achievements have not translated into inclusion or decent standards of living for vast numbers of Brazilians. Today, despite reductions of poverty and inequality under Workers' Party governments since 2002, Brazil is one of the most unequal countries in the world. Its shantytowns, ringing ultramodern cities such as São Paulo and Rio de Janeiro, have come to symbolize the desperate and enduring poverty of Latin America that recent democratic governments have been struggling, with limited success, to ameliorate. Brazil is an agricultural powerhouse—among the largest exporters of soy, oranges, coffee, sugar, and beef in the world—but many of the women in Rio Grande do Sul, descendants of the poor European immigrants who came to Brazil's south, grow and prepare most of their own food and have to struggle to send their children to the doctor and pay basic school fees. They face poverty, unemployment, and the threat of losing their land. In a country where the rule of law is uneven at best, those who fight for change in the countryside face police hostility and paramilitary violence.

The crisis that threatens small farmers in Rio Grande do Sul today began with the rural development policies of Brazil's military dictatorship.[7] One of the tools that farmers have used to fight back, the rural unions, dates from the same period (Houtzager 1998; Navarro 2010; Picolotto 2009). In the 1970s, surveying an unproductive countryside and a hemisphere marked by rural rebellions and guerrilla warfare, Brazil's military decided to promote large-scale, corporate agriculture and finally to incorporate rural workers, including small farmers, into a union structure. New agricultural policies offered landowners in Rio Grande do Sul credit and cheap inputs for large-scale production of wheat and soy, rather than the more diversified set of products that had long been the mainstay of farming in the state and included the foods people consumed at home. The union component of the military's rural development program provided men who worked in the countryside with limited but significant economic benefits, such as small pensions and access to health care, through a national union closely allied with the government.

The development model pursued by the military, based on mechanized production on vast tracts of land, laid the groundwork for the agricultural bonanza that has driven Brazil's economic growth in the 2000s. It also threatened the livelihoods of small farmers, who still today hold 43.8 percent of the land in the state of Rio Grande do Sul and account for 57 percent of its agricultural production (Schneider and Niederle 2010, 384). These small farmers became dependent on credit to buy seeds, fertilizer, and machinery. They no longer produced the food they and their neighbors consumed, and they saw the land around them bought up by large landowners and corporations.

The children of many small farmers left the countryside, often for a life of poverty in urban shantytowns, which expanded exponentially during this period. Some of the farmers, however, along with increasing numbers of their children, learned to make use of the union structure to fight back. With the backing of priests and nuns schooled in liberation theology, they fielded progressive slates in union elections and gradually, in the course of the 1980s and after, won key positions and initiated local struggles for credit, health care, land, and new approaches to agriculture.

As military dictatorship gave way to elections and then to the process of writing a new Brazilian Constitution, the young people who began their activism in the unions went beyond where their fathers were willing to go. Faced with vast inequality in landholdings and plans to destroy whole communities by constructing a network of dams, so as to advance yet further the agenda of large-scale modernization, the young activists formed new, more radical movements to defend the small farmers and landless people of the countryside. At the same time, nuns in the rural communities of Rio Grande do Sul pressed women to insist on their rights and to participate in the unions. Speaking with farm women, the nuns brought the authority of local experience to their claims on behalf of women's rights (van der Schaaf 2001). They also brought religious legitimation and blessing to what otherwise seemed so daring as to be impermissible—insisting on the rights and participation of women in rural society.

It was in this context that the views of some young women, who refused to accept the limits faced by their mothers, fused with the historical moment. Because of the work of the nuns and priests, as well as the keen sense of injustice the young women themselves were feeling, the debates and union battles coursing through the countryside prompted many women, young and older alike, to leave their houses and make claims for themselves and their families in public places, such as union halls and churches. As a result of the conflicts this engendered, the rural women's movement was about ordinary speech as much as formal rights. If they could win the legal designation of "rural worker," women who toiled long hours alongside their husbands on family farms would themselves gain access to social security, paid maternity leave, and health care. And if they participated in unions and became leaders, they could play a role in shaping rural development policies, finding economic alternatives for small farmers, and breaking the isolation and silence that characterized the lives of women on family farms.

The History of the MMTR

Women in rural Rio Grande do Sul first organized autonomously in 1985, forming local women's associations, called Mulheres da Roça, or Farm Women, in a number of small towns in the northern region of the state. The women of Mulheres da Roça constituted themselves as a statewide organization, the Movement of Rural Women Workers (MMTR)[8] in 1989, soon after Brazil's new Constitution recognized women involved in agriculture as "rural workers" and accorded them the same social security pensions, maternity leaves, and health care benefits guaranteed to male agricultural workers and to male and female workers in Brazil's cities. In choosing the name MMTR, the women underscored their role as rural workers, connecting their convictions about class inequality and workers' rights to their commitment to gender equality and women's rights. Linking hundreds of neighborhood groups in small towns across the state to regional and statewide networks, the rural women's movement in Rio Grande do Sul mobilized between 5,000 and 15,000 women in any given period, reaching many more through family and friendship ties (van der Schaaf 2001, 154–57; Stephen 1997, 219).[9] The MMTR also established close relations with rural women's movements in Brazil's other southern states, with which they coordinated campaigns that focused on national legislation in Brasília.

The early national campaigns, in the years following the formation of the Mulheres da Roça, focused on influencing the Constituyente, the network of public organizing and debate in Brasília that was charged with producing the new Constitution. But as soon as the Constitution guaranteed economic rights to rural women, it became clear that securing these rights in practice would take a whole other battle, one that would come to form the core of the MMTR's organizing efforts through the first half of the 1990s and gain it the commitment and loyalty of tens of thousands of rural women. Constitutional rights to pensions and maternity leave, it turned out, required enabling legislation, which in turn required that bureaucracies establish procedures to carry out the laws and then actually implement them.

In response to the disconnect between what the Constitution said and what occurred on the ground, women in the MMTR in Rio Grande do Sul joined with women in rural women's movements nationwide to collect signatures, form "caravans" that converged on the national capital, lead demonstration after demonstration, take over buildings, and occupy the floors of state legislature. They learned to do these new and disruptive acts as they went along, borrowing tactics from other social movements and improvising new ones. To succeed, they had to convince rural women who rarely ventured out in public to follow them and risk police violence and arrest in so doing. Leaders of the MMTR also lobbied key legislators, a strategy they honed in the campaign to overturn a presidential veto on maternity rights, and learned to do politics "inside the institutions" among elected officials, as well as in the streets. Thus their strategies combined civil and uncivic actions from the get-go.

It wasn't only the prospect of economic rights, or even gaining a voice in their own families, that drew women into the women's movement, however. It was also what they did together at meetings, which included singing and pageantry, crafts projects, and self-help exercises, along with attending lectures about Brazilian economics and politics and discussions of their experiences at home and in their communities. The meetings were a destination for which women left the house and a deeply collective antidote to isolation. Meetings created a "counterpublic" where alternatives to real-world silencing and exclusion were put into words and enacted, so that images of a different future could then be brought home, along with crafts projects and self-help strategies.[10]

The MMTR was always about both economics and gender, but the economic part was more clear cut, more acceptable to men, and, in the end, easier to secure. Over the course of two decades, it proved much harder to get men to share the housework than to gain economic rights through mobilizations and protests in the streets, and the new households women envisioned in the early years of the movement were painfully slow in materializing. At the same time, women in the MMTR recall how frank discussion of women's bodies and women's roles in the household transformed their lives. In place of silence and uncertainty about matters such as menstruation and birth control, they gained information for themselves that they could impart to their daughters. And rather than accept farm labor and unending housework as their fate, women could now say that since men shared the food and tracked mud onto the floor, they should do dishes and sweep, as well. This resulted in real, if uneven, changes within families, with sons and husbands taking on more housework and women framing marriage as partnership and taking on new roles inside and outside the home. At the same time, the women grappled with the unexpected tenacity of men's conventional roles and of violence in their households (Rubin and Sokoloff-Rubin 2013, 102–6).

Achieving democracy in the women's movement proved to be a similarly uncertain process. What did it mean to be a democratic movement, and was that important? Early on, the MMTR organized itself in four tiers—small groups in tiny communities, then gradually larger groups at the municipal, regional, and state levels. In the early years of effervescent discussion and mobilization, when the Mulheres da Roça was fighting to have rural women's economic rights written into the Constitution and the MMTR campaigned tirelessly to turn those rights into reality, democracy seemed to mean discussion. It was embodied in the constant interaction among the movement's various levels, with ideas and suggestions transferred back and forth between local women and regional and state assemblies and leaders. Later, however, when social security pensions and maternity leave had been secured, yet gender equality seemed ever harder to achieve and globalization brought new economic threats, what it meant to make decisions democratically became much less clear. At the same time, the successes of the MST and its burgeoning alliance with the international peasant movement Vía Campesina offered an attractive model for the effectiveness of national alliances, centralized decision making, and a unified political analysis.[11]

Securing economic rights for women came to be the founding achievement of the rural women's movement, one that gained it legitimacy and won enduring loyalty on the part of rural women of all ages. It was also a goal about which everyone, including men, could agree. In contrast, the path ahead was less clear. In the course of their transition from daring teenagers to committed political activists, partners, and mothers—a transition that coincided with the deepening of Brazil's democracy, which their activism helped to bring about—women's movement leaders disagreed about the strategies and goals of the MMTR and made different personal choices. Once a tight-knit core group, alternately facing police repression and attending each other's weddings and the baptisms of their children, they chose different paths for pursuing women's equality.

Four Pathways of Activism

1. By the mid-2000s, the women's movement leaders at the *sede*, or headquarters, in Passo Fundo had united with rural women's movements in other states to form a national movement, the Movement of Peasant Women (Movimento de Mulheres Camponesas, or MMC). The national movement emphasizes the struggle for a new agricultural model, based on sustainable farming practices and egalitarian local economies. Women's rights and violence against women appear at the bottom of their long lists of objectives, though they continue to be a women's movement and provide meeting places for women at demonstrations, in the pharmacies, and in the classrooms of movement schools. The Passo Fundo sede functions not only as the headquarters of the state women's movement, but as the national office for the MMC as well. The women in the sede, who explicitly rejected the path for working "within the institutions" and expelled women who took up that option, run a national women's movement, linked to the largest national and international movements of rural people in the world, fighting for radical change in the countryside. These groups sponsored the invasion of the agricultural giant Aracruz and the destruction of its laboratory of genetically altered crops in 2007, and they form part of the international coalition making headway on a new UN convention on peasant rights.

2. For other MMTR leaders, in contrast, women's issues have become part of a new set of Civil Society Agenda approaches in local governments, institutions, and universities. Vera Fracasso has been developing this vision of government together with her husband, Celso, for two decades, since she left the MMTR to focus on the farmer's union in Sananduva and eventually become its first woman president. From 1994 to 2002, Celso headed a Left-of-Center coalition government in Sananduva. As mayor, along with his team from the Workers' Party, he began to articulate and put into practice policies on health, education, and rural economic development that they believed would bring economic growth and greater equality to the struggling town. But the leftist coalition was voted out of office, and Vera began to develop a progressive vision of her own that she hoped could again win elections and govern.

Like many couples in which the wives have been women's movement leaders, Vera and Celso have been forging new ways of balancing home and work in their marriage. There is nothing easy about this, and as Vera indicated in conversations over the years, she does not know precisely what equality means or where the possibility of reshaping gender roles will lead. Vera believes that men and women are different, but that such differences are not fixed, and she is sure that women should have a voice in all aspects of their lives. Vera knows that who does the dishes is neither the central issue in gaining rights and voice for women nor irrelevant to that effort, and it is surprisingly difficult to change.

Elenice Pastore, now a professor at the university in Passo Fundo, studies issues directly related to women, believing that women's movement activists should focus fully on such issues, rather than directing their energies to the struggle for a new agricultural development model, which other movements can pursue. To address her commitment to improving women's lives, Elenice designed a research project on the incidence of domestic violence in rural households, a phenomenon that everyone agreed was widespread, but about which there were no data and little action.

3. The women's pharmacies established by the MMTR constitute a third form of activism, bringing together women who have otherwise taken different directions, but seek counsel and remedies in the alternative spaces created by the project. In the pharmacies, collectives of local women produce and dispense herbal remedies, while also offering a space for discussion. Within five years of their initiation in 2001, the pharmacy collectives had received equipment through a grant from the state government, run training sessions for women from multiple towns, sent members for training in massage therapy, and established cooperative stores. At the pharmacy *encontros*, or training sessions, women discussed issues of class and gender and their interaction, from the impact of the pharmaceutical industry on rural women's mental health to the effects of consumerism on rural families and the dynamics of sexual relations in marriage. In these meetings, members of the MMC, the national women's movement, mingle with women who have rejected that organization's move to militancy and centralization, identifying locally with the MMTR and its banner and refusing to adopt the new national name, with its unfamiliar use of the word *camponesa*, or peasant. Leaders who stayed local and joined the government or the unions in their towns, pursuing Civil Society Agenda approaches there, also support the pharmacies, recognizing their role in addressing day-to-day needs and connecting those needs to strategies for change in gender roles and local economies. When the collective of women who ran the pharmacy in the small town of Ibiraiaras took over the local organic farmers' market there, they refashioned the store into an outlet for produce, crafts, baked goods, and herbal remedies that also functioned as a gathering place, looking right out over Ibiraiaras's central plaza, for rural women and town dwellers alike.

4. Activists in the women's movement also pursue activities further afield from the movement's original goals, while continuing their activism. During a research trip in 2007, Marilda, a rising leader of the local women's movement, invited my daughter and me to dinner, along with two couples we knew, ostensibly to discuss gender roles in families. After driving several kilometers on winding, unlit dirt roads, we pulled up to the modest, three-room house, constructed through a government-sponsored housing initiative for rural families, where we twice before had conducted interviews with Marilda and her extended family. We were greeted by the mixture of hesitation and warmth with which many rural families received us and each other.

Marilda's formal welcome, however, caught us off guard. "We're happy to offer you," she said brightly from the corner of her tiny living room, alongside the TV, to the assembled guests, "um novo coquetel," a new cocktail. Then she introduced us to Herbalife, and we watched a DVD, produced in Los Angeles, about the globally marketed nutrition supplement. The DVD was accompanied by tall glasses of Herbalife shakes, along with a smooth sales talk, replete with charts and photographs, delivered by Marilda's sister and brother-in-law, who had long worked as activists for a progressive, Church-based NGO in the region and for leftist municipal governments.

Now the sister-in-law and her husband sold Herbalife in what seemed a classic combination of Mary Kay and pyramid scheme. A healthy modern life, they urged their friends, could be achieved by substituting the Herbalife liquid drink for breakfast and dinner. They emphasized that chubby children like their daughter—as well as overweight adults, as the husband had been—would become thin and self-confident with the nutrition supplement, while busy working moms saved time in the kitchen. This approach to feeding a family seemed particularly out of place in a farming region characterized by readily available fresh produce, where most families had limited funds for commercial purchases. The Herbalife team urged one of the men present, adrift since his father's death and uncertain about how he and his wife would support their family, to buy an Herbalife kit and begin selling its products, while there was still a wide-open market for the product in their town.

Women's movement activists today thus pursue at least four different forms of activism: *uncivic mobilizations in the streets*, as in the invasion of the land and laboratories of the Aracruz corporation and destruction of its experiments with genetically altered crops; *Civil Society Agenda participation in the institutions*, generally in alliance with the leftist Workers' Party, as evidenced by Vera and Celso's activities in municipal government and the rural farmers union in Sananduva, as well as the MMC's participation in the international campaign for a UN convention on peasant rights; *progressive civil society activism*, such as workshops and programs focused on socioeconomic, health, and gender issues, along with the network of alternative women's pharmacies; and *nonprogressive, individualizing initiatives* such as the marketing of Herbalife.

Movements-in-Democracy

How are we to understand the multiple directions taken by rural women activists? Partly, these multiple women's initiatives reflect the fragmentation of social movements that often occurs in democracies. This results from arguments and splits long familiar on the political Left as well as the diverse opportunities that liberal democracy provides for participation, employment, and policy making. Such differentiation has been characterized positively as webs (Alvarez and Dagnino 1995) or as associative networks (Chalmers et al. 1997), though criticized by those who see such fragmentation, along with participation in government programs and institutions, as contributing to the global implementation of neoliberalism (Schild 1998). From a mainstream perspective on democratization, this panorama of activities—illegal destruction of corporate property, work in a union or municipal government, establishment of alternative pharmacies, and the marketing of products such as Herbalife—constitutes not only a predictable outcome, but a positive contribution to democracy, through the development of social capital in a diverse civil society. In this view, the panorama of activist paths in Rio Grande do Sul gives evidence of considerable associational energy, with even Herbalife a sign of the robustness of civil society, despite its tension with women's movement goals.

In contrast to this positive view, I want to highlight the fragmentation of the MMTR—the splitting or dispersion of social movements between the streets and the institutions, the uncivic and the civil—as a *risk* of democratic government, indeed the way in which democratic government can effectively turn mobilization and activism into governability and governmentality (Alvarez, chapter 16 in this volume). By this I refer not only to the ways in which the Civil Society Agenda incorporates and domesticates participation, as has been demonstrated in several of the chapters in this book, but to the process by which social movements themselves, for reasons both internal and external, fail to contain difference and sustain themselves, in democracies, as ongoing, horizontal, and multifaceted forces for change.

To envision an alternative to such fragmentation, I point to something else, something that can clearly be glimpsed here—and of which women activists themselves spoke repeatedly—but that did not fully take shape in this instance. That is what I'm calling movement-in-democracy, referring to empirical phenomena in the MMTR's history, as well as to a normative idea that took shape in discussions with MMTR activists. What I mean by this term is allowing enough diversity within a movement—enough subjecthood, pluralism, and voice—to maintain a broad and energized movement whose members can work simultaneously within and outside the institutions, in civil and uncivic ways, and in so doing bring ongoing energy and force to democratic politics. I am highlighting the possibility of containing all of the forms of activism that rural women in Rio Grande do Sul have undertaken, from destruction of corporate property to running municipal health departments, in one movement, or in some kind of integrated cluster of movements and initiatives.

Many of the MMTR activists, together with those who have advised or allied with them, reflected on moments at which such a goal might have been realized, questioning and lamenting the inability of the movement itself to hold difference, to maintain itself as a broad movement. This is a matter of great nostalgia, of efforts to fight back against fragmentation, of self-criticism of actions taken in the past, and of new visions for the future. Key women's movement leaders have said they "don't know why [they] didn't fight back" against those who wanted the movement to take one particular path and that they should have waged this battle. Sentiments of this sort emerged in women's thinking and in their conversations with me years after the *afastamentos*, the moments when they were purged from the women's movement. "Why can't we have one movement, with some women supporting the unions and others supporting the MST?" one activist asked in 2002, at a moment when conversations were under way on the subject of reclaiming the movement for its original, and broader, constituency.

"Perhaps we should have had more flexibility" a prominent ex-leader, Gessi Bônes, told me several years after she had made choices that were rejected by the leadership of the movement. "I am a militant of the rural women's movement," Gessi said, "even though now I am not in the leadership, and I'm working in a municipal government that emphasizes popular participation." Despite her clear claim, however, leaders in the women's movement headquarters in Passo Fundo explained firmly that Gessi, whom they regarded fondly and whose leadership skills they valued, was in their view no longer a militant in the movement. "It's about what's fundamental," they told me, "the character of the movement"; the leaders in the movement headquarters were willing to lose key activists so that the MMTR could join with a larger, more radical movement and maintain a single analysis and strategy.

Without the ability to hold activist commitments together in a new way, democratic modernity in Latin America may be characterized by enormous "uncivil" mobilizations, such as the MMTR's destruction of genetically altered crops in 2007 or the mass street demonstrations in 2013, *and* the proliferation of market-based and individualist strategies for social change, such as Herbalife, as occurred among some MMTR activists, or Pentecostal promotion of entrepreneurship. In addition to fostering antisystemic activism at the expense of forms of transformative progressive reform within the system, this polarization means that progressive institutional and civil society initiatives—such as women's participation in municipal government, workshops on gender and on economic concerns, and alternative pharmacies—come to lack the animation and pressure that derive from involvement in social movements. That is, without the animating force of social movements, democratic processes themselves may become sustainers of the status quo rather than focal points for conflict, deliberation, and progressive change. Thus the capacity of a movement to hold difference, or of a counterpublic to establish forms of horizontal communication and strategizing, affects the capacity of the ordinary, day-to-day activities of democracy to sustain effervescence and creativity. Deep democracy, in a country or a movement, needs both unruly actions and formal procedures.

But what does it mean to be a movement-in-democracy? It is my argument in this chapter, based on my research on the MMTR and my dialogues with its activists and leaders, that being a movement-in-democracy means two things: it means acting in the streets and in the institutions simultaneously; and it means holding and allowing difference within the movement. For the rural women's movement, being a movement-in-democracy means developing the capacities of selfhood, speech, and mobilization that the MMTR forged over two decades and then going one step further: holding together that multiplicity in one movement, even if it doesn't seem to fit together. Or, if different groups spin off from the original organization, then movement-in-democracy means keeping them in active dialogue one with the other, openly and without hierarchy, forging complementary strategies. Such a movement-in-democracy might combine aspects of the horizontalism, multiplicity, and open-endedness of anarchist mobilizations with a more movementlike coherence, engagement with states, and explicit and at-times reformist goals.

Key women's movement founders regret not fighting back, not staying in the MMTR, with its rough-and-tumble, even harsh and mean-spirited politics. They didn't know how to do this at the time or even think of doing it. The activism they learned from the church meant consensus—reaching agreement through discussion—not fighting hard and outmaneuvering your opponents while adhering to agreed-upon democratic procedures. The activism they learned in the MST meant discerning one effective strategy and enforcing adherence to that path (Wolford 2010).

In contrast, what would make holding diverse beliefs and commitments, civil and uncivic, in one movement more possible? My research on the MMTR and other Brazilian social movements suggests several contextual and strategic factors that might have promoted greater holding of diversity in the past, in terms of both voice and practice, and might do so in the future, particularly if they are incorporated into ongoing social movement theory and practice. These involve recognizing and grappling with (1) the intractability of oppressive social conditions and forces; (2) the ambiguity and contradiction in social movements; (3) the importance of internally democratic procedures; (4) the dynamics of movement fields and counterpublics; (5) the centrality of emotion and affect in sustaining activism; and (6) the organizational and communication innovations of "post-Tahrir" mass movements, such as Occupy, the Spanish and Greek Indignados, and the Chilean student movement. All of these factors have been discussed by MMTR activists in partial ways over the trajectory of the movement and addressed in creative ways by scholars and activists over the last decade (Graeber 2013; Sitrin 2012).

Social movements almost by definition confront intractable issues. For example, it is extraordinarily hard to change gender relations and challenge government-promoted, corporate agricultural models. Beyond some partial successes, most of the time these sorts of things don't change, though they also *do* change, at times incrementally and at times dramatically. Women's movement activists reflected repeatedly, first with surprise and then with resignation, on the unexpected tenacity of conventional gender relations in their families and communities and the difficulty of promoting organic agriculture among both farmers and consumers. Workshops on gender relations, they observed, had changed little in two decades (Rubin and Sokoloff-Rubin 2013, chs. 8, 11). Dealing with this absence or slowness of change is something social movements and the people in them do all the time, but it is rarely acknowledged or theorized.

Social movements have messy internal dynamics, deeply ambiguous and contradictory, on both sides of the civil-uncivic divide. And both sides of this divide tend to write out internal conflicts and messiness as they explain and strategize social movement activism. Activists from the MMTR spoke only in private conversations, and then with difficulty, of disagreements and conflicts in the movement. Recognizing and theorizing the contributions of ambiguity and contradiction—the bedrock of movement daily life—to mobilizational force could expand pluralism and subjecthood within movements and enable movements to combine uncivic and civil practices more flexibly over time (Rubin 1998).

The MMTR developed in tandem with a host of mobilizations and experiments in Brazilian grassroots and national politics. In the 1980s and 1990s, the Workers' Party pioneered the use of democratic procedures and internal primaries to combat factionalism and promote deliberation and transparency, breaking with traditions of centralization and hierarchy characteristic of Latin American leftist parties. The much-heralded process of participatory budgeting, which Workers' Party (Partido dos Trabalhadores, or PT) leaders pioneered in the capital city, Porto Alegre, to empower the residents of poor *vilas*, came to the countryside as a set of procedures for municipal government. Because they were seen as a means of participation in the institutions, however, many rural social movements did not consider one of the key lessons of internal primaries and participatory budgeting alike: the remarkable capacity of a set of procedures to promote democratic deliberation (Baiocchi 2005a), despite or even because of the personal, gendered, and religious dynamics of ostensibly neutral and secular participation (Junge 2012, 2014).

Through many kinds of meetings and activities over the course of its first two decades, the MMTR fashioned a counterpublic of women, of a range of ages and backgrounds, who questioned and took on the work of challenging their government, communities, and families. Michael Warner, in his work on movements involving gender and sexuality, emphasizes the pain and fear of bringing the "private" to public spaces, of coming out of the closet (2005). Seen in this light, meetings and mobilizations must continually combat and rearticulate such emotions as pain and shame, which are not dispensed with in a single moment or in a straightforward process of consciousness raising or solidarity. Meetings and mobilizations also develop and rely on particular affective states that enable and sustain activism, such as enchantment (Bennett 2001; Rubin and Sokoloff-Rubin 2013) and reworkings of melancholy and disappointment (Flatley 2008; Kim 2008). Activists of the MMTR acknowledged the value of this affective dimension of social movement practice as an aspect of subjecthood, the sense of self and agency the movement sought to develop among rural women. At the same time, it was little theorized as a constitutive element of enduring activism.

234 · Jeffrey W. Rubin

Active awareness of this affective dimension of movement politics contributed to the emphasis on procedure, prefigurative politics, and transnational networking in post-2010 movements such as Occupy Wall Street and the Spanish Indignados (Movimiento 15M), which offer tools for containing difference that were not readily available in the past (Milkman et al. 2013; Sitrin 2012). The earliest activist experiences of women in Rio Grande do Sul occurred through the Catholic Church and the MST, both of which fostered subjecthood and hierarchy simultaneously. In contrast, the international diffusion of anarchist and horizontalist approaches, from anticorporate globalization movements of the 1990s and Argentine protests of 2001 to Occupy in 2011 and Brazilian street protests of 2013, provides both ideals and tools for new and explicitly democratic internal procedures, as well as for valuing the prefigurative dimension of social movement activity, in which practices and emotions created within the movement itself are seen to anticipate broader social change.

The daily experiences of women in the MMTR, at meetings and marches and in their families, bear out these insights concerning intractability, ambiguity, internal democracy, counterpublics, affect, and horizontalism, all of which have woven through the experiences and discussions of activists over the past two decades. Both sides of the civil-uncivil divide, within the MMTR and other movements, have tended to write out ambiguities and contradictions as they explain and strategize social movement activism (Rubin 2004, 1998). In many Brazilian social movements, discussion of voice and democracy took a backseat in recent decades to strategizing for mobilization and confrontation with the state. Bringing in and acknowledging these subjective, multiple, and at times painful social movement experiences—apparent in the day-to-day experiences of activists—may contribute to expanding pluralism and subjecthood within movements and enabling movements to combine uncivil and civil practices more flexibly. Bringing these experiences into common discussion and awareness—in scholarly analysis, political strategizing, and movement practice—would make coherence more possible in movements, coherence not in the sense of seamlessness, but as horizontal forms of holding together. In this sense, coherence acts in constant tension with, and takes advantage of, the "overflow" characteristic of social movements in the twenty-first century (see the conclusion, in this volume).

To reject either the streets or the institutions is to silence speech, to close speech down even as you open it up.[12] In contrast, the opening up of speech, through deromanticization and recognition of complexity—of pathways of change and of the internal dynamics of movements—may foster more flexible forms of social movement activism, more horizontality of authority and decision making, more combining of civil and uncivil strategies within single movements—and as a result, more radical reform in democracies.

NOTES

1. The concept of movement-in-democracy, which grows out of the experiences of a Brazilian social movement formed in the 1980s (and broadly representative of social movements of that time), overlaps and can be in productive dialogue with horizontalist and anarchist approaches to mobilization such as those that developed in Argentina in 2001–2 and in the "post-Tahrir" movements and mobilizations in Latin America and elsewhere since 2008, such as Occupy Wall Street, the Spanish and Greek Indignados, and the Chilean student movement. The movement-in-democracy approach that I propose in this chapter, discussed in greater detail in the final section, places more emphasis on bounded movements with explicit and at times reformist goals than the post-Tahrir mobilizations, drawing on recent work on movement fields (Alvarez, chapter 16 this volume) and counterpublics (introduction and Thayer, chapter 8, this volume). At the same time, in contrast to much social movement research and activism in Latin America, the concept of movement-in-democracy emphasizes holding a diversity of strategies within one movement or movement field, and it embraces the internal democracy, holding of difference, networking, and prefigurative politics characteristic of horizontalist movements.

2. The MMTR of Rio Grande do Sul joined with other rural women's movements in Brazil's south and northeast to become the Movimento de Mulheres Camponesas in 2003. The process of unification and name change was linked to the loss of the movement-in-democracy characteristics I describe in this chapter. Many of the activists in Rio Grande do Sul rejected the new name and continued to call themselves members of the MMTR.

3. These male-led movements included an antidam movement (Movimento Nacional de Atingidos por Barragens, MAB), a land reform movement (MST), and the progressive wing of the rural labor movement (Confederação Nacional dos Trabalhadores na Agricultura, or CONTAG). For more on these movements, see Navarro (1996). For the MMTR's theorization of class and gender, see Paludo and Daron (2001).

4. While there is general agreement on the radical and anti-institutional political position of the MST (and its modifications in practice), there is considerable controversy concerning the internal practices of the movement and the extent to which it might be considered democratic, in terms of voice, accountability, and dissent. For a strong critique of the MST, including its internal practices, see Navarro (2010). For the most ethnographically detailed and politically balanced work on the MST, see Wolford (2010).

5. In contrast, training for argumentative dialogue and democratic procedures occurred through the actions of the Workers' Party as it developed participatory budgeting in the neighborhoods of Porto Alegre, the state capital.

6. Brazil's economy is ranked between seventh and eighth in the world, depending on source and standard of measurement.

7. For an outline of the economy of Rio Grande do Sul and how it has changed since the 1970s, see Navarro 1996; Schneider and Niederle 2010; van der Schaaf 2001, 82–97.

8. For book-length treatments of the MMTR, including analysis of its formation, trajectory, achievements, and internal dynamics, see Rubin and Sokoloff-Rubin 2013; van der Schaaf 2001.

9. Accurate data on statewide MMTR membership is difficult to obtain, and these numbers are approximate.

10. My thinking about the work that movements do, including the kinds of publics they produce and the way they weave visions of the future into the present, has been shaped by Warner (2005) and Koselleck (2004).

11. For background on Vía Campesina, see Borras (2008).

12. I thank Ivone Bonês for her observation that "as soon as you open up speech, you also close it down," in her discussion of the silence surrounding lesbianism in the spaces of discussion fostered by the MMTR (Rubin and Sokoloff-Rubin 2013, 159).

Chapter 12

REFOUNDING THE POLITICAL

The Struggle for Provincialization in Santa Elena, Ecuador

AMALIA PALLARES

Latin America has recently witnessed new forms of collective action that involve novel collaborations between civil society and political actors at the local level, the participatory budget in Porto Alegre being one of the most notable examples. Less attention has been paid to other modes of civil/political society collaborations that have recently developed in Andean countries that have established refoundational regimes. Refoundational regimes of the Left—experienced in Venezuela, Bolivia, and Ecuador—involve the early establishment of an assembly to create a new Constitution that fundamentally alters the rules and institutions of governance as well as a specific style of politics characterized by distinct political ideologies, strategies, and identities. One characteristic of refoundational regimes is a rearticulation of political society that combines the tactics, strategies, and logics of social movements with the administrative and participatory practices of local governance in a quest for change. Like traditional social movements, coalition members share a common goal, develop common strategies, and combine contentious and non-contentious tactics. Unlike most social movements, they are often led by local public officials and in some instances sponsored by powerful national politicians. Ironically, it is a style of antipolitics that melds the work of politicians and social movements, challenging the usual state-society opposition.

This chapter analyzes a local example of refoundational politics, focusing on the struggle of inhabitants of the Santa Elena region to become a separate province in the context of intense opposition from the province of Guayas. I will explore how the Santa Elena case exemplifies this trend of combining political and civil society in order to achieve a greater level of political self-determination. I will analyze the factors that help explain this new mode of organizing and, finally, reflect on how the case of Santa Elena challenges us to think in new ways about the relationship between civil and political society, and between civil society and uncivic contention.

Background: Santa Elena

The Santa Elena Peninsula is located in Ecuador's southwestern coast. Until November 2007 it was part of Guayas Province, dominated by Guayaquil, a large city of 3.3 million. Consisting of three cantons—Santa Elena, Libertad, and Salinas—that total approximately 300,000 people, Santa Elena was administered by the Provincial Council of Guayas, consisting of twelve *consejeros*, or council people, and a president. With one notable exception, most of the council representatives were from Guayaquil, and rarely were representatives from areas outside of the city elected to the council. Among the main grievances raised by Santa Elena inhabitants were their systematic exclusion from the council and very limited access to resources. The major exceptions were projects that facilitated travel and tourism of Guayaquil's inhabitants, *guayaquileños*, to the peninsula. Additionally, Santa Elenienses complained of Guayaquil centralism, as every important administrative transaction forced them to travel to the city, where they often felt mistreated or disregarded in public offices.

While the idea of separating from Guayas and becoming a province had circulated for more than a decade, the campaign for provincialization was not initiated until March 2003, when a group of educators, businessmen, and public officials created a commission that called for a popular assembly that would in turn create a pro-provincialization committee. During the following two and a half years members of this initial committee held lectures, information sessions, and meetings with several members of civil society—including neighborhood organizations, university students, fishermen co-ops, and *comuneros*—aiming to both educate people about the project and motivate them to support it. In December 2005 a popular assembly was held to address the topic. Approximately 3,000 people attended, including 387 delegates from different sectors of civil society representing over 200 organizations. A provincialization committee was created, and its members were elected. The mayor of the city of Libertad, Patricio Cisneros, was elected president; the mayor of Santa Elena, Dionicio Gonzabay, was elected first vice-president; and the mayor of Salinas, Vinicio Yagual, was elected second vice-president.

By January 2006 the committee had collected 68,000 signatures of support. It presented these signatures and a proposal of provincialization to the Alfredo Palacios administration. In June it submitted a formal proposal to President Palacios to be debated in Congress in August. When *peninsulares* learned that the issue would not be debated because the government had apparently "lost" the proposal, they staged their first strike in the village of Villingota on July 7 and 8. As the 2006 presidential election heated up, the committee asked both candidates for the second round of elections to visit Santa Elena and make a commitment to provincialization. Candidate Álvaro Noboa never committed. In October, candidate Rafael Correa went to Santa Elena and stated that even though he did not believe that provincialization was the solution, he would follow the sovereign will of the people. He signed a statement confirming his commitment.

After Correa won the election he sent a decree to Congress in March 2007 petitioning for provincialization, but the measure did not receive the necessary votes. Despite the committee's lobbying work with several congressional representatives, many who had committed their vote ultimately voted against the proposal. The antiprovincialization forces were significant, including Guayas elites, the Social Christian Party, most of the Institutional Renewal Party of Social Action (Partido renovador institucional acción Nacional), several members of the Patriotic Society (Sociedad Patriótica, or SP), and the Transit Commission of Guayas, bolstered by elites who had economic interests in the peninsula. When the measure failed to pass, rumors that votes had been bought and sold in a context of intense opposition from Guayas Province incited passions on both sides of this issue. With simultaneous mobilization and advocacy work, proponents got the Congress to agree to reconsider the issue in October.

In October, when the Congress failed to consider the matter even though it was scheduled, there was public outrage among the masses of Santa Elenienses who were outside of Congress as well as those in the peninsula. After Salinas mayor Yagual gave the order, 30,000 people staged a second strike in Villingota between October 11 and 13. The crowd combined the rank and file of *comunas* (communes), workers' organizations and cooperatives, and *juntas cívicas* (civic organizations), as well as unaffiliated supporters and youth. Transportation workers closed a bridge, stopping all traffic traveling from Guayaquil to the peninsula for a holiday, and fishermen cooperatives stopped all fishing and commercial activity. On Saturday, October 13, the central government ordered the national police to surround Santa Elena and stop people from going to Villingota; the people, however, overcame the police. The following day Santa Elenienses suspended the strike in order to send more than 8,000 of the people in Villingota to surround the Congress in Quito. Congress was finally pressured to pick up the discussion of the proposal, and on October 16 the law was approved with seventy-four votes in favor and twenty-six against. On November 7, 2007, Santa Elena formally became the twenty-fourth province of Ecuador. It's important to note that protest was not the only factor that led to approval; between June and October the Correa administration had deposed fifty congressional representatives who refused to support a referendum for a new Constitution. The congressional representatives' replacements were far more amenable to a referendum and other policies favored by the president and far more likely to produce a positive vote for provincialization.

New Modes of Politics

The provincialization process illustrates a couple of new modal patterns of doing politics in Ecuador. First, as seen above, the pressure for change combined uncivil politics with the potential to produce actions that are *no permitidos* (not allowed) conducted by "masses," and the "civil" interventions of public officials and civil society organizations. This is a combined mode of politics that surfaced first in national mobilizations such as the presidential removals of 1997, 2000, and 2005, characterized by massive mobilization combined with the leadership of social movement and civil society leaders, as well as politicians and institutional actors. In this combined mode, those representing the civil or *lo permitido* serve to legitimize and often speak on behalf of the mass mobilization, while the potential threat of the mass mobilization's incivility is mitigated by leadership participation and approval, becoming *casi permitido* (almost allowed) in the process. This combination has become a more prevalent mode of local politics in the current refoundational regime.

Second, as I discuss further below, the provincialization process embodies the growing importance of the politics of place, in this case specifically a spatialization of class and ethnic identity that challenged existing regional cleavages. The politicization of ethnicity by the indigenous movement since the 1980s, and the more recent repoliticization of class in the Correa regime, have at times coincided with regional cleavages and at others reinvented them to reinforce existing distinctions or create new ones. In the case of Santa Elena, class and ethnic politics played a key role in a respatialization of traditional constructions of Ecuador's regions as highland, lowland, and coastal by proposing the separation of Santa Elena from Guayas and thus challenging the dominant notion of a unified, homogeneous coast purportedly represented by Guayaquil.

Rethinking the Social and Political

The partnership between civil and political society has at least three main features worth analyzing: the prominent role played by the three cantons' mayors in what was viewed primarily as a societal struggle, the use of administrative and participatory governance strategies that gave it contemporary and global legitimacy, and the strategic use of protest as pressure when all else failed. Taken together, these strategies suggest a shift in modal patterns of doing politics that blur the distinction between civil and uncivil as well as the one between political and civil society, as both civil society and political actors engage in civil and uncivil politics.

The melding started early. While most popular assemblies elect members of civil society as their top leadership, in Santa Elena assembly participants voted for the mayors of the three cantons—Libertad, Salinas, and Santa Elena—for the presidency and vice-presidencies of the provincialization council. Interviewees cited important reasons why the mayors had to lead the council.[1] While the universities (particularly the University of the Santa Elena Peninsula [Universidad de la Península de Santa Elena, UPSE]) and their faculty had provided the initial energy, mayors provided access to the resources, contacts, and professionals that were necessary to get the process going. Additionally, Patricio Cisneros and Dionicio Gonzabay had long trajectories in politics and were well-liked and widely supported. Cisneros, for example, was in his third term as mayor of La Libertad and had a reputation for meeting directly with people of all class and ethnic backgrounds. The three mayors also had strong ties to labor organizations and comunas in their respective cantons and proved able to mobilize them in subsequent months. Additionally, due to the absence of business elite sponsorship or significant transnational NGOs in the region, Santa Elenienses did not have any alternative resources that they could count on to further their efforts. Many interviewees who were members of the council explained that despite their years of work in local government or in the university, they did not know how to get the information and specialized maps necessary for the formal provincialization proposal the central government required. The mayors' ability to request special permissions and favors, from military personnel and other central government officials, allowed them to access highly restricted information. Additionally, they invested public resources in architects and administrative personnel on the municipal payroll to work on the project. Council member Fausto Fajardo recalls: "Well, we wanted the presence of the mayors for their logistical support, their economic support, their power to convene, because the work with the state was going to be easier because they represented the cities" (June 2009 interview). Some respondents questioned the narrative that people in the assembly had clamored for the mayors (a few claimed the election was carefully planned in an effort to wrest control of the process from members of the UPSE). However, in retrospect practically all of them, including UPSE members interviewed, sustained that mayoral leadership gave their cause more legitimacy. For the mayors, the massive support for this initiative was understood as both an opportunity to further local development and an obligation to their constituents. Dionicio Gonzabay claimed that massive popular support led Mayors Cisneros and Yagual (initially reluctant) to join the cause: "They changed their mind in the moment when we did the first motorized caravan and all the people of the peninsula took to the streets and showed their allegiance in an extraordinary way. Politically they were interested in this voluntary, spontaneous allegiance, so they had no other choice but to join."

Another reason the mayors were elected as leaders of the council was to pressure the mayors affiliated with the Partido Social Cristiano (which was publicly opposed to provincialization) to choose sides on the matter. Gonzabay, of the Partido Roldosista Ecuatoriano, explained that he opted for a vice-president role and pushed Cisneros, of the PSC, to be president so that Cisneros would have to seriously rethink his affiliation with the PSC. Eventually, Cisneros and Yagual did disaffiliate from the party before the party moved to expel them.

Initially, there seems to be a contradiction between the leadership role of the mayors and their claim that they are merely executing the popular will.

However, instead of viewing this as a false modesty of the mayors, or an instrumental performance designed to mask mayoral interests, this contradiction needs to be understood as a constitutive aspect of this hybrid committee that was trying to carve out a space of internal cooperation in a broader context of *antipolítica*, or aversion to politics as usual. The committee was working with local and national state institutions but also against the status quo. It sought to be associated with collective engagement and not with electoral competition, the main way in which "politics" is defined. Despite wanting mayoral leadership, most council members were concerned about appearing to be seeking political advantage for the mayors. Representations of the process as belonging to *el pueblo*, and as the product of civil society forces, were key to its public legitimacy, as illustrated by specific strategies that emphasized narratives of public ownership of a cause that was not open to appropriation by the mayors. For example, one strategy used was to prohibit members of the council from running for office. Three council members resigned from their candidacies during this period. The mayors were considered exceptions because they had already been elected.

Fausto Fajardo explained: "And this committee proposed as a first condition to not politicize, knowing that the project is political." This statement points to the logic underlying the council's work. The internal suspension of the political for the common good leveled the playing field internally—no one, civil society actor or politician, could be involved in this for their own political benefit. This gave the council the moral authority to then engage in a very contentious and explicitly political struggle that directly intersected with existing regional partisan and ideological conflicts.

The Importance of the Civil

Another key feature of the provincialization campaign was its reliance on claims of administrative competence and participatory methodology to demonstrate its preparedness for self-governance. Many Guayas elites claimed that Santa Elena was not only financially incapable of becoming a province, but administratively incapable as its citizens lacked the experience needed to progress independently. Without Guayaquil's guidance, they claimed, a Santa Elena province was doomed to failure.

As a region that has traditionally been viewed as poor, rural, and undeveloped, Santa Elena had to demonstrate its administrative capacity, competence, and ability to govern itself.

In this context, the campaign for provincialization itself became a model that would demonstrate Santa Elenienses' capacity to implement a plan successfully. Several videos produced locally and widely distributed showed the number and skills of professionals involved in putting together the plan, the technical competence and civility of the process, the high levels of the communications and exchanges with national and other local politicians, and the ability of local professionals to develop visionary plans for the effective use of these resources. Fishermen representative Eduardo Macías reflects on the importance of this campaign for proving provincialization opponents wrong: "For all these things we had to fight with these monsters, because they were political and economic power. We had to seek technical people to engage in a struggle of professionals. We had to get to Congress with a solid foundation and knowledge" (June 2009 interview).

A second feature that had to be proved was the capacity to organize and plan in a participatory framework. A crucial instrument here was the widely attended participatory assembly held in 2006, where the council was created. The use of participatory methodologies supported by donor foundations and NGOs has become a new barometer used to ascertain the legitimacy of local governance in much of Latin America. In Ecuador the past decade has witnessed a proliferation of different efforts to apply participatory methodologies, with varying levels of effectiveness (Cameron 2009). At the very minimum, scores of municipalities have implemented participatory development plans that invited civil society actors to come together to envision the future of their cities. Hence, local governments are increasingly relying on the implementation of participatory methodologies as a way to claim democratic governance and acquire legitimacy, regardless of whether they are in effect participatory. In the case of Santa Elena, the participatory methodology was not continuous or all-encompassing. The assembly was a space where certain political and civic actors were included in some instances, but others were not. However, after provincialization, no participatory spaces were maintained. The claim of participation had apparently already served its legitimizing purpose.

Another novel form of participation was the collection of signatures from people who supported provincialization. In refoundational regimes the referendum has become a crucial conduit to change. According to Catherine Conaghan and Carlos De la Torre (2008), the Correa administration exemplifies the plebiscitary presidency, a mode of government that constantly relies on the monitoring and promotion of popular support, leading the president to be in a permanent campaign to maintain a positive public opinion. The collection of signatures in Santa Elena followed this national referendum model. Eligible voters were invited to sign at booths throughout the three cantons. Because there is no law that stipulates what the creation of a province requires, the collection of signatures was not legally necessary. But it was a step that provincialization proponents believed would bolster their case to others, help persuade the Congress, and document their struggle. The 68,000 signatures collected were impressive, since they constituted 75 percent of the people eligible to vote, providing the symbolic mandate that local leaders felt was necessary to move forward.

The demonstration of administrative capacity on the one hand and the very public, if limited, use of participatory methodology and the referendum were efforts at becoming civil in two senses of the word: "civil" *as* civilized, that is, modernized, knowledgeable, and able to engage in contemporary forms of administration and governance; and "civil" *as* engaged, as groups of united citizens participating autonomously in a democratic, political process. Both of these "civil modes" provided the provincialization with a form of civic "worthiness" and granted legitimacy to the provincialization process while buttressing the politics of refoundation, in which the polity seeks a better fit between policy and popular aspirations.

The Work of the Noncivil

In contrast to the civil efforts, the popular protest that was also part of the provincialization process straddled the border between civil and uncivil, or that which is allowed and that which is not, leading to outcomes of varied desirability for provincialization supporters. While essential as an expression of popular unrest and for the final push for provincialization, it also at times appeared to work against the image of civility that Santa Elenienses had created.

As previously stated, the campaign relied on protest, such as marches, massive mobilizations to Quito, and most important, two major strikes in which a bridge to the region located in the village of Villingota was blocked, impeding all touristic and commercial activity. Both strikes happened in instances when Santa Elenienses felt disrespected, lied to, or ignored and believed that protest was the only option available. The second strike lasted three days and was very intense, with repeated confrontations between the crowd and police, leaving some Santa Elenienses wounded. These protests were purposeful; none of them, much less the controversial last strike, were the product of spontaneous reactions that countered or undermined councils' less contentious strategies, but were planned with the mayors' knowledge and initiative. One anonymous informant who worked with Vinicio Yagual recalls Yagual's call to strike: "I was called at 12:30 AM by my *compañeros* who told me 'wake up, wake up, we are going to war. . . . the mayor has decided to close the peninsula. . . . When the compañeros expressed bewilderment, Vinicio said, there is nothing else left to do but to close the peninsula'" (July 2009 interview).

This merging of political authority and popular resistance confused the public authorities, who did not make distinctions between protestors and politicians. Barrio co-op leader Alfredo Tandazo recalls the crowd's reaction to police aggression against Mayor Dionicio Gonzabay: "The police break the picket line and target some people, among them the mayor of Santa Elena . . . and the mayor is hurt . . . and Santa Elena responds. It was a marvelous moment. There was no political color . . . and the people started making the police back down . . . people gained force and the police could not enter Santa Elena" (May 2009 interview).

For Santa Elenienses this strike was widely credited for pressuring Congress to reconsider the issue at a point when congressional representatives kept stalling the discussion. Former Libertad Mayor Patricio Cisneros recalls: "The strike was the trigger, the culminating action that made this process happen. In the next congressional meeting the same thing [being ignored] would have happened if we had not pressured" (April 2009 interview).

Fishermen co-op member Eduardo Macías also stated the unequivocal importance of the protests: "And we pressured with the marches because they are the only language in the world. Marches are what sensitize human beings. They are what lead to yes or no" (June 2009 interview).

However, this sensitization can work in different directions. The same marches that granted the provincialization movement its legitimacy also upset its image of civility. During the strike in Villingota one of the participants passed the Guayaquil flag through his rear end, an incident that inflamed Guayaquil elites once the video went viral. It was used as evidence that Santa Elena protesters were "uncivilized savages" willing to desecrate the flag in the worst way imaginable. Many Santa Elenienses who had worked so hard to establish their reputation for having a civic approach attempted to disassociate from this image and even repudiate it. Local water co-op leader "Ricardo" was one of several of my interviewees who distanced themselves from it: "I did not participate in that protest. We stayed here, but as a citizen of civil society we can say that it was extremely wrong. An investigation will determine how this happened, because there must be something behind it, these youth were pushed to do this."

For Ricardo the act was incongruent, and therefore planned by some external force. The investigation that was being conducted at the time of the interview (with no tangible results) was an attempt to clear the provincialization campaign from any uncivil wrongdoing. In speaking as a citizen of civil society, Ricardo is drawing a distinction between civil society and this particular group of protesters.

However, others describe the incident differently. "Lucia," president of her local parish council, describes the moment as an act of anger, and does not disassociate from it, but rather links it to a broader "we," to the response of a community that felt scorned: "I see that incident as an act of anger. For those from Guayas to lose such a distinctive territory with the Route of the Sun, to lose it . . . the campaign they did was to not come to the peninsula. And they would leave signs on the road saying 'visit Playas.' [Another beach community in Guayas]. We knew that people with their money could go wherever they wanted. I think that what happened with the flag was a moment of anger" (July 2009 interview).

For Lucia, those uncivil acts are not foreign but an extreme mirror, the exacerbation of the most difficult conditions faced by Santa Elenienses; they are also "we" and are acknowledged as part of the struggle. For others like Ricardo, however, the action was detrimental to the cause. Because uncivil acts are the boundary of the civil and thus help to define the civil, any actions that straddle this boundary become sites of contestation not only between movement members and their opponents, but within the movement itself.

This contestation happens because despite the blurring of lines between the civil and the uncivil in political performances, massive acts of resistance can never be perfectly managed or coordinated by political or civil society elites. And perhaps in this spontaneity lies uncivil resistance's greatest power: its ability to increase polarization. The flag incident, for example, first confirmed the fears and accusations of the opposition. The long-standing claims from Guayas's elites that Santa Elenienses were ignorant, uneducated, incapable of self-governance are crystallized in the desecration of the flag, which they considered an act of savages. Next, the opposition's intense reaction deepened the existing polarization, exacerbating tensions, furthering the social and political distance between factions. This led to more recalcitrance among the opposition, enabling supporters such as Lucia to justify their claims against those who used the incident to further attack and devalue them. Further, for those who were not in either of the opposing camps, the intense exacerbation of conflict moved the debate from the intellectual to the sentient, demonstrating the inability of the territorial units to work together again, and the inevitability of provincialization as a conduit to peace.

Lacking much economic and political capital and confronted by some of the most economically well off families and institutions in Ecuador, provincialization activists relied on a broad range of strategies that were not without contradictions. The roles traditionally played by civil society and political actors were also stretched and at times conflated, making it very difficult to use concepts such as co-optation or appropriation to characterize this partnership. While the reasons they relied on such different strategies seem obvious from their statements, they are not necessarily inevitable or commonsensical. Rather, they challenge deeply embedded views about the state-society divide, the distinction between political and social movements, and the distance between political elites and their constituents.

However, in addition to a new mode of politics, the provincialization process was also informed by a new content of politics that emphasized class-based and spatial/territorial dimensions that politicized social differences in new ways and facilitated new allegiances to the national regime. In this next section I argue that underlying processes in Ecuadorian politics and society help to explain how Santa Elenienses made common sense of this struggle. I will focus on two dimensions: the contemporary spatialization of class and ethnicity, and the role of region in national refoundation politics.

The Spatialization of Class and Ethnicity

The provincialization movement is informed by region-based class differences and power inequalities that mark poorer places and municipalities as inferior when compared to richer and more developed regions such as the metro areas of Guayaquil, Quito, and Manta. Following global models of economic pole development, Guayaquil and Manta have undergone an urban revitalization in the past fifteen years that has beautified these cities and dramatically improved their touristic infrastructure, confirming other coastal cities' perception of being left behind. Guayaquil is specifically faulted for dominating the allocation of resources in Guayas as projects that benefited Guayaquil tourists were privileged over projects that would benefit Santa Elena's economic and social development.

Telmo Herrería commented: "The peninsula was seen by guayaquileños and by the Guayas province only in tourist season. In tourist season we were fumigated and our roads were fixed. But once the season was over, not anymore.

They forgot about us, like we were the backyard of the *señores guayaquileños*" (April 2009 interview).

Further, while Guayas Province has historically called for administrative autonomy, denouncing Quito-based centralism, Santa Elena and citizens of other coastal cities complained instead of bicentralism (Quito's and Guayaquil's dominance) and, within the coast, of a Guayaquil centralism that has severely limited Santa Elenienses' development opportunities. This claim unsettled a long-standing historical divide supported by Guayaquil elites that posited a Quito-centric model that siphoned most resources to Quito to the exclusion of Guayaquil and the rest of the coast.

By contrast, Santa Elena was deconstructing the coast, as it represented itself as a poorer region, ill-treated and seeking redress from what is considered rampant structural injustice. Administrative separation was thus understood not merely as a conduit to improved governance or economic development, but as an act of social justice and democratization that could counter patterns of exploitation and restore economic and political rights to Santa Elenienses. In this view space and class overlapped, as the effect of class differences among Santa Elenienses in the campaign was sometimes acknowledged, but considered less significant in relation to the larger class difference between Guayaquil elites and Santa Elena dwellers. One interviewee claimed that this oppression from Guayaquil had been able to unite all Santa Elenienses, of all races and classes, to fight for provincialization. According to Alfredo Tandazo: "[in the provincialization] there was everybody, with every surname [indigenous origin and not], everybody, all mixed in. There were no classes, whites, blacks, more *cholos* [of coastal origin], less *cholos*. Fat, skinny, the doctor, the shoeshine man, the fisherman, the teacher, we all united in a civic embrace" (May 2009 interview).

There is some basis to the claim that class differences among Santa Elenienses are less stark than the ones between Guayaquil elites and most of their constituents. Most of the Santa Elena economic elites owned middle-sized to small businesses, as the wealthiest business owners are actually investors from Guayaquil. All of the mayors were the children of laborers—two of them had fathers who had worked in oil exploration for the British in the canton of Ancón. The national police force's "mistake" in physically handling Mayor Gonzabay further illustrates the racial indistinguishability between the mayors and the majority of protesters. Additionally, several council members and economic elites distinguished themselves from others as having had more access to education, but still self-identified as cholos.

Moreover, while differences among Santa Elenienses were minimized, class differences among the Guayaquileños were underscored to show that the opposition to provincialization did not come from all of Guayaquil, but only from the elites. Jimmy Pinoargote explained: "We made a survey in the newspaper *Expreso*, and learned that Guayas was not against us, . . . the ads [against us] that Guayas published were signed by the Chamber of Commerce, economic institutions, the economic power of Guayas and not the people" (July 2009 interview).

Hence, Santa Elenienses relied on this distinction between poor and elite guayaquileños to challenge the notion of a homogeneous Guayas threatened by provincialization efforts to one of class conflict that both distanced Santa Elena from Guayas elites and grouped the Santa Elena and Guayas poor as having a shared social location.

Further, while a discourse of cross-class unity *within* the peninsula was dominant in descriptions of the provincialization movement, a discourse of racial distinctiveness *between* the peninsula and Guayas became more prominent as a justification for the separation. The *cholo peninsular* is a cultural and racial identity that has been proudly assumed by many Santa Elenienses in recent decades, as descendants of coastal indigenous communities reclaimed their ethnic heritage, and sought rights to their communal lands (Alvarez Litben 2001). The Ecuadorian indigenous movement's politicization of indigeneity has influenced the nascent political struggles and identifications of other groups (blacks and *montubios*) as well as cholos. However, in distinction from indigenous ethnic identities, cholos are what Roger Brubaker (2006) might call softer identities, characterized by boundaries that are more porous, with stronger and weaker modes of self-identification. While the cholos *comuneros* (members of legally recognized communes, *comunas*) have their own organizations and agendas, it is not uncommon for non-comuneros from the region to assume the cholo identity as well. Some of them are even able to join comunas if they are voted in.

While porous, membership in a comuna does depend on having roots in the peninsula, allowing the cholo identification to be one that can be as rooted in a sense of origin or place as it is in a perceived racial commonality; interviewees' discussion of self-determination and distinction from non-peninsulares was often tied to a cholo identity. Alfredo Tandazo, for example, discussed the underestimation of the capacity of the cholo and the need to have peninsulares own their own destiny: "We should not have to send for administrators outside the peninsula . . . who do not belong to Santa Elena. Because they do not know the value of the peninsular cholo, that cholo hardened by the warm hug of our shores" (May 2009 interview).

Jessica Falconí also spoke of the connection between cholo identity and place: "They [Guayaquileños] viewed this as if we were taking something away from them when this territory belongs to the comuneros. This territory belongs to the peninsular cholo, not to the people of Guayaquil. People from Guayaquil have made their houses here because it is a pretty area, but this area belongs to the cholo from here" (July 2009 interview). In sum, Santa Elenienses politicized space in new ways by deconstructing and challenging traditional regional demarcations and creating a new regional identity based on racial and class difference. They did this while simultaneously emphasizing their class similarities with the majority of Guayaquil's inhabitants. This challenge to the image of a homogeneous coast through the emphasis of class difference can be directly linked to the work of the refoundational presidency in confronting the regional stronghold of the PSC and traditional Guayas elites. Undermining the region through the politicization of class and ethnicity was a way for the Correa presidency to also confront his strongest political opposition.

Region and Refoundation in National Politics

It is difficult to imagine that Santa Elena's provincialization would have been possible in another political moment. A moment of refoundational politics provided Santa Elenienses with the political opportunity to push and succeed in a campaign that had eluded the Santo Domingo de los Colorados (Pichincha Province) provincialization campaign for forty years.

For some scholars the uprisings against old regimes and the creation of leftist populist refoundational regimes embody a wave of antipolítica sentiment that involves a severe decline in the public opinion of elected officials and political institutions (Conaghan and De la Torre 2008). In Ecuador, as in other countries in the region with a similar backdrop of two decades of structural adjustment policies, antipolítica became a reaction against the usual politicians and anything that appeared to be part of traditional political parties, practices, and institutions. Political candidates who have opposed standing presidents have gained status and legitimacy for their oppositional acts (former president Lucio Gutiérrez and current president Rafael Correa are obvious examples). Moreover, politicians with a history of partisan affiliation have reinvented themselves as representatives of new "movements" that are linked to their individual candidacies.

In this context, political reform seemed too timid a response: political refoundation became the preferential option, involving presidential removals, a constituent assembly that redesigns institutional frameworks and formulates new policies, and the rise of new political actors or reinvention of old ones. Rafael Correa won the presidency on the basis that he would hold a constituent assembly and refound the state in the same way that Hugo Chávez and Evo Morales had done in Venezuela and Bolivia respectively.

In 2007, as oppositional traditional parties with large representation in Congress were in battle with the Correa administration over the possibility of a referendum for the new constituent assembly, the president used his emergency powers to challenge the legitimacy of the standing Congress and the constitutional tribunal (Conaghan and De la Torre 2008). As mentioned earlier, when PSC and PRIAN congressional members seemed unmovable, Correa deposed sixty Congress members and then deposed members of the constitutional tribunal that refused to affirm his decision. The *suplentes*, or replacements, people from the deposed members' parties who had been elected as substitutes, got with the program immediately and were far less likely to oppose Correa. This directly benefited Santa Elena's struggle, since Congress voted to hold a referendum for the constituent assembly as well as to provincialize Santa Elena.

After the congressional stand-off, the battle with the PSC continued in Guayas. While PSC is a national party, its regional stronghold is in Guayas and some pockets of other coastal provinces. A conservative right-wing party with a neoliberal orientation unable to win a presidential election since the Sixto Durán Ballén administration, PSC has retrenched to its regional base in Guayas. Historically, it has had a large contingent of congressional representatives and dominated the Guayas Provincial Council and the Guayaquil municipal administration. For more than a decade, it had counted on sizeable corporate elite support, and had an important presence in most important local public and social institutions and foundations, ranging from the autonomous Guayas Transit Commission to the Junta Cívica de Guayaquil.[2]

Correa aimed to curtail the autonomous power of Guayas (and hence PSC power) by redesigning municipal structures so that more revenue would go through the central government instead of directly through Guayas, and removing some of the duties of the Comisión de Tránsito de Guayas. Support for the provincialization of Santa Elena (about 18 percent of the population of Guayas) was interpreted by PSC and many Guayas elites as a way for Correa to punish and undermine Guayas and to gain more electoral support in the coast. If not necessarily evident at first, the Guayas elite's vehement reaction to this administrative split did ultimately become an opportunity for Correa to counter PSC dominance.

Conclusion

This chapter has analyzed a provincialization movement that involved new political modes and contests that blur distinctions between the social and the political, and the civil and the uncivil, and enable novel linkages between extant political identities and strategies. In the case of Santa Elena, the civil society effort underscored the growing importance of civil society as an alternative to political society in the quest for broader political and social change. What appeared to be primarily a local struggle over territorial administration was about much more: class conflict, ethnic empowerment, local self-governance, and the PSC-Correa opposition. The complex scenario of forces at play in a refoundational context enabled Santa Elena to tap into a number of different debates, challenge a regionally dominant party, garner strong presidential support, and ultimately achieve its objective of provincialization.

The case of Santa Elena lies at the intersection of the civil and the uncivil, since neither of these approaches would have been able to achieve singlehandedly the immediate goal of provincialization. The institutionalization of the campaign and the direct relationship with local and national politicians was critical, but so was the disruption of mass protest and the possibility of more. However, seven years after provincialization, asking the larger question from this book's introduction of how this intersection might transform society or deepen democracy, provides no easy answers in terms of effects on development, electoral change, and broader political transformation.

Today, regardless of their political stripe, most would agree that Santa Elena did achieve meaningful provincial autonomy, but has yet to achieve its larger goal of economic and social development. Santa Elenienses now have their own local and national representatives and public offices, as well as a significantly expanded budget for local infrastructure and maintenance projects. The national government has also invested significantly in the province, especially in a network of local roads, and a few focused economic projects. This investment makes it difficult to discern between benefits from provincialization alone and benefits that stemmed from the Correa administration's focus on the province. For example, interviewees often claimed national investments as benefits of provincialization, though they were outside of the purview of provincial government. However, even the most positive of interviewees who are not government officials agreed that provincewide touristic and agricultural development projects have yet to be developed. Explanations for why this is the case range from the lack of local administrative experience to conflict among elites with different visions. In sum, provincialization is understood as a founding of autonomy and therefore a beginning of new possibilities, but not necessarily a guarantee that major development goals will come to fruition.

On the electoral front, ironically, none of the three mayors that headed the council were reelected after provincialization. While Patricio Cisneros, former mayor of Libertad went on to win the elections (held in April 2009) as the new president of the Provincial Council, Dionicio Gonzabay (Santa Elena) and Vinicio Yagual (Salinas) both lost their mayoral bids. While Yagual was predicted to lose due to a decline in the popularity of his administration (for reasons unrelated to provincialization), Gonzabay's outcome was a surprise when he lost in a very close race to Otto Vera, a candidate from the president's party Movimiento País (now Country Alliance [Alianza País, AP]). The AP also scored the Libertad mayoral position, with Marco Chango as the winning candidate. In the National Assembly elections of 2009, two of the three representatives elected were from the AP. In the National Assembly elections of 2012, two of the three candidates elected to the National Assembly belonged to the AP. Undoubtedly, Correa's party was rewarded for supporting provincialization, benefiting candidates who played little or no role in provincialization and whose selection was designated from above.

However, two caveats are in order. Affiliation with Movimiento País is not a panacea. It did not rescue Vinicio Yagual (the only one of the three mayors to join the AP) from defeat, nor did it prevent the incumbent and AP candidate Ana Triviño from losing the council president position to Cisneros in 2009. Second, while the AP dominates, it has not completely monopolized power, as opponents with strong personal support have successfully run in opposing parties. The best example of this is Patricio Cisneros, who was elected as the president of the Santa Elena Council as a member of the national party, the Municipalist Party (Partido Municipalista, or PM). Additionally, former assembly member Jimmy Pinoargote was elected as a PM member in the National Assembly election of 2009. However, the PM lost national strength in subsequent years, and in the National Assembly elections of 2012, Cisneros's nephew Daniel Cisneros ran and won under a new party that the older Cisneros founded: Peninsular Creyendo en Nuestra Gente. However, the two other spots were taken by the AP. Hence, AP domination since provincialization means there is an existing but limited space for opposition parties that are headed by very popular individual politicians,. Moreover, the AP has learned from its losses (nonreelection of many AP politicians) and created an alliance with the party of the previously independent Patricio Cisneros and his nephew Daniel for the elections of 2013. In a national context in which many AP candidates for mayor lost, Patricio was reelected president of the council and Daniel became mayor of Salinas. Independence from the government was still possible, as Dionicio Gonzabay was able to regain the Santa Elena mayor position under an alternate party, the Creo Creating Opportunities Movement (Movimiento Creo, Creando Oportunidades, or CREO). Of the three original mayors of the provincialization assembly, Cisneros and Gonzabay have sustained and heightened their power, while the government has learned the limits of nominating candidates who do not have long-standing local support.

Finally, what were the transformative political effects of provincialization beyond elections? Did this intersection of the civil and the uncivil lead to a deepening of democracy? This Santa Elena struggle had national ramifications, as it bolstered the decline of the PSC, provided a stronghold for the president's party in a region where it sorely needed support, and profoundly unsettled a century-old scheme that had framed a highlands-coast and Guayaquil-Quito divide as a central social opposition. Perhaps local refoundations are not only becoming main sites of political struggles, but producers of new political possibilities and imaginaries.

The Santa Elena process marks a significant departure from more traditional elite politics. In a context of antipolítica, politicians seem to require the legitimacy of civil society and popular protest to attain political change. This blurring of the political and social can also lead to the crossing over to that which is uncivil, leading to more unstable and contestable meanings than the political elites would prefer. Perhaps this is most evident in the increased politicization of the cholo ethnic identity after provincialization. Having won provincial autonomy, local comunas (which vary greatly in degree of internal democracy themselves) have reinforced this notion that Santa Elena is for the cholos, and this has become articulated in local development projects, renewing conflicts with non-cholos over land, touristic projects, and state resources. While the province appeared unified during the provincialization campaign, race and class differences have become more pronounced since, as comunas—reinvigorated after experiencing the potential benefits of popular pressure—seek specific resources in their towns, challenging local economic elites in the process. In these conflicts, AP representatives and officials have favored comunas' demands on multiple occasions though not all parties involved view these decisions as the most civil, democratic, or environmentally sound. Moreover, in terms of more access to state resources, more attention to local road and infrastructure projects, and integration into some social and cultural development activities, local communities have benefited from provincialization and feel that local leaders are more responsive to their needs.

However, the political elite's strong guidance of the civil society process and ultimate lack of a broader participatory process after the provincialization campaign points to significant limitations to more societal leadership in provincewide developments. The hierarchies that were evident in the provincialization campaign have not been significantly challenged. The cross-class and cross-sector coalitions that were created for provincialization have not been sustained. Moreover, national AP hierarchies have overlaid local hierarchies, leading to the rise of new elected elites who were selected from above and have no connection with provincialization efforts nor the coalitions created in that period. (The recent Cisneros election being a key exception.) Civil society's hierarchies have impeded a broader post-provincialization participatory process, and civil society's close links to political society and dependence on presidential support for development gains lead one to question its autonomy and sustainability outside of the electoral/institutional context.

NOTES

1. Interviews were conducted between February and July 2009. Research assistant Diana Falconí conducted interviews between February and June and transcribed all the interviews. The translator conducted interviews in July 2009 and conducted field research in July and August of 2009 and July of 2013. All the translations are the author's.

2. After 2009 a split in leadership led Mayor Jaime Nebot of the PSC to create a separate party called Madera de Guerrero.

Part IV

MOVEMENTS,

REGIMES, AND

REFOUNDATIONS

Chapter 13

THE COUNTERPOINT BETWEEN CONTENTIOUS AND CIVIC COLLECTIVE ACTION IN VENEZUELA'S RECENT DEMOCRACY

MARGARITA LÓPEZ MAYA AND LUIS E. LANDER

In Venezuela, social and political actors have recently begun to use contentious collective action as their primary tool in the quest for their interests and aspirations. Contentious action, what we also call "uncivic" activism, has been the most visible method and has played a key role in the deep transformations experienced since the end of the twentieth century, particularly following the Caracazo of 1989. The institutional decay, and the crumbling of political parties and of the political system established after 1958, turned the contentious collective action (CCA) into the most available and/or efficient form of sociopolitical struggle. Although today Venezuela is totally polarized, actors from both sides of the political divide have equally used contentious or civic collective action, reflecting the tendency discussed in the introduction to this book.

We explore here the ways in which actions confront and complement each other in a counterpoint between these two modalities of collective action, and review their results from the mid-1980s until 2012. After reviewing the available information, we can distinguish three stages.

The first took place from the mid-1980s until the first presidential term of Hugo Chávez in 1999. During this time, poorly organized working-class sectors were the main protagonists of CCAs. Their interests had been increasingly excluded from institutional spaces for mediation and representation. Through this type of action, these sectors contributed to the creation of a climate of instability and ungovernability that occasioned the outbreak of a struggle for hegemony, a struggle for a qualitative change in the power relations in society.[1] For their part, during this period, middle-class-centered organizations promoted political reforms that would decrease the political parties' power and introduce instead mechanisms for direct democracy. Thus, they also contributed to unleashing the struggle for a change of hegemony.

This dynamic resulted in Chávez's victory in 1998 and his alliance with sociopolitical forces known as the Patriotic Pole (Polo Patriótico, or PP). This victory opened up a second stage that lasted from 1999 until 2006, when Chávez's first presidential term ended. During this time, many actors continued to resort to CCAs, but the government opened up spaces for civic actions, mainly among the working-class sectors. A political polarization neatly emerged as expressed in the collective actions of different groups. At one pole, the middle and upper classes were mainly identified as oppositional to the government, and now called themselves a "civil society." In contrast, the working-class sectors carried out street actions primarily to defend the government from their adversaries while practicing civic actions in the spaces that the government opened up for the co-management of public policies.

The third stage corresponds to Chávez's second term, between 2007 and 2012. As is well known, this was when the government promoted the idea of "Twenty-First Century Socialism" (*socialismo del siglo XXI*), replacing the vision of participatory democracy so central to Chavez's first term. The CCAs that took place at this time were mainly motivated by socioeconomic demands, and occurred in a context of [slightly] less social and political polarization than during his first term. The CCAs motivated by civil and political rights fluctuated in number according to the political circumstances, but the polarization persisted. At this time the government continued supporting working-class civic actions while seeking to weaken the organizational autonomy and diversity of these sectors, thus favoring the Communal Councils (CC) and the communes within the conception of a "Communal State." The government resolved to put all social organizations at the service of its "revolution."

Stage 1: Predominance of Contentious Collective Actions

The last decade and a half of the twentieth century was characterized by the vitality of popular urban street uprisings.[2] This phenomenon highlighted the launching of a "politics of the streets," namely, of a more direct and immediate kind of relation and negotiation of power among diverse social actors. We identify this kind of relation with its various modalities as CCAs. According to the human rights NGO Provea, during the nine years between October 1989 and September 1998, there were an average of approximately two protests per day, with most intensity during the 1993–95 political crisis and in 1998, immediately after Chávez took power (table 13.1).[3] Provea's data do not include the tens of strikes organized by public servants, a common form of contentious action during these years.

Following Sidney Tarrow (1989), in previous works we distinguished three types of CCAs: "conventional," "confrontational," and "violent." The conventional CCAs are types of routine actions that are frequently legal and, when they fail to be, they do not produce a feeling of fear or apprehension among the participants or among nonparticipants. Before the Caracazo, social protests in Venezuela were mostly conventional. Afterward, confrontational and

TABLE 13.1. Total of peaceful demonstrations, Provea 1989–1998

Years	Protests in Total	Daily Average
From October 1989 to September 1990	675	1.8
From October 1990 to September 1991	124	0.3
From October 1991 to September 1992	654	1.8
From October 1992 to September 1993	1,047	2.9
From October 1993 to September 1994	1,099	3.0
From October 1994 to September 1995	581	1.6
From October 1995 to September 1996	534	1.5
From October 1996 to September 1997	550	1.5
From October 1997 to September 1998	385	1.1
Total	5,649	1.7

Source: Provea, *Human Rights Situation: Yearly Report* (corresponding years).

violent protests gained an increased visibility.[4] Confrontational protests are characterized by their capacity to generate surprise, tension, and the adversaries' feeling of being threatened or in danger, although they never reach the use of violence (Lander et al. 1999). Many times they corresponded to illegal types of protest, such as street closures, takeovers of public institutions, illegal strikes, and public gatherings and marches that had not been previously announced to the authorities. Sometimes, an action such as public nudity or the unleashing of blue rats against the authorities, to mention just a few of the student protest modalities during these years, can turn a protest from conventional into confrontational and make it more efficient as a means to disseminate a message and reach participants' objectives (tables 13.2 and 13.3).

Violent protests are the ones that because of their nature or their results produce damages to property and/or bodily injuries. They reached almost a third of all protests covered between 1989 and 1998 by the newspaper *El Nacional*, compared to the previous years, when this kind did not even reach a tenth of all recorded protests (table 13.3). Violent protest peaked

TABLE 13.2. Protest visibility in Venezuela according to kind:
News clips from *El Nacional*, 1985–1998

Year	Marches	Roadblocks	Takeover and Invasions	Disturbances	Burnings	Lootings
1985	12	1	16	6	3	0
1986	10	2	8	4	1	0
1987	21	3	2	27	16	6
1988	13	5	6	16	4	3
1989	24	13	18	39	11	26
1990	22	4	4	29	7	7
1991	11	3	3	29	16	4
1992	10	12	10	44	18	10
1993	21	13	10	50	26	16
1994	25	30	21	61	29	13
1995	27	15	14	42	18	9
1996	28	29	17	69	25	16
1997	21	18	7	21	12	1
1998	23	20	1	18	0	0
Total	268	168	137	455	186	111

Source: Database El Bravo Pueblo (BDEPB 2007).

TABLE 13.3. Popular protest visibility according to type:
Clips from *El Nacional*, 1985–1998

Year	Conventional	Confrontational	Violent	Total
1985	206	41	15	262
1986	51	16	3	70
1987	36	15	32	83
1988	70	17	16	103
1989	75	85	53	213
1990	39	54	30	123
1991	8	36	31	75
1992	13	56	64	133
1993	52	64	58	174
1994	49	65	73	187
1995	64	62	63	189
1996	53	122	98	273
1997	81	44	50	175
1998	77	67	22	166

Source: Database El Bravo Pueblo (BDEPB 2007).

during the political crisis between 1992 and 1994, and until 1996, with a notable tendency to decrease toward the end of Rafael Caldera's presidency.

The type and kind of CCAs that became widespread during these years were closely related to efforts to delegitimize labor and trade unions and political organizations that took place during the economic crisis and the establishment of neoliberal programs.

The Venezuelan political system constructed since 1958 had consolidated thanks to a series of pacts between parties, unions, and other key actors—all of which had established mechanisms for mediation and representation based on a bipartisan system. Thanks to their access to the income generated by the Petro-State, the political parties Democratic Action (Acción Democrática, AD), and COPEI had woven a large network of patronage, which permeated labor and trade union life and any form of civic organization, limiting their autonomy. The fiscal and socioeconomic crisis entailed the weakening and delegitimizing of political parties, which resulted in the collapse of the entire institutional scaffolding and induced the decline of the channels of communication between civil society and the state (Roberts 2001). The institutional vacuum stimulated the CCAs and the emergence of new actors. These new actors included some who had previously maintained a low profile, some entirely new actors, and some who broke free from partisan influence.

Their scant levels of organization and meager resources contributed to their mobilizing characteristics, emphasizing actions that were the most efficient and drew on the fewest resources. These included closing the capital's streets to all traffic, taking over public buildings, chaining protesters to the ground, and burning tires. These strategies are relatively easy and cheap to organize among people who lack money, contacts, and networks to organize conventional protests, and can have an impact on the media and on political leaders. Violent actions can also be explained in some cases by the relative isolation of some actors. Through these actions, they sought to make claims against the state directly and without mediation.

The emergent actors had diverse origins and interests. Most were poor and/or had a limited access to spaces where decisions were being made. Their organizing had various degrees of strength and consolidation. Street peddlers, for example, were very active and increased in number as they lost their jobs. Retirees and pensioners, mostly from the public sector, survived on pensions that dropped to ridiculous amounts when paired with inflation. People living in poor and middle-class neighborhoods increasingly needed basic services such as water, shelter, or personal safety. Taxi drivers joined in, overwhelmed by the insecurity on public roads and by the rising costs of vehicular parts, as did the unemployed. High school students protested against the diminishing budget allotted to education and the deterioration of school buildings and of the quality of teaching. Students stood out because of their long experience with street struggles and their political vocation, both of which served to guide and mobilize other sectors.

These sectors became the most important part of civil society at the dawn of the twenty-first century. Households living in poverty increased from 38.88 percent in 1986 to 48.3 percent in 1997. Rates of extreme poverty increased from 17.6 percent to 27.6 percent (IESA 2000). The organizations representing diverse sectors of the poor eroded the governability of the country through their disruptive actions. Beginning in the 1990s, the unemployed, public employees, and informal workers, among others, became through their protests the most important actors in a struggle for hegemony, which sought to build a new and inclusive sociopolitical project.[5]

This proposal slowly took the shape of an "agenda of the poor" (López Maya and Lander 2001), later taken up by political actors such as La Causa R or the Fifth Republic Movement (Movimiento Quinta República, or MVR). At first, these actors had little weight in the political party system. Their demands included the recovery of socioeconomic rights, such as the right to a living wage, housing, health, and public education. After their civil and political rights had been postponed, among them the right to peaceful protest without fear of repression or the right to hold transparent elections, they began to find some answers in the management of local and regional governments. Emergent actors, some of them from the Left, had access to these governments precisely amidst the crisis of dominant parties and a wave of political reforms geared toward decentralization and electoral rights. In 1989, regional and local authorities secured their right to hold direct elections for the first time. The first elected leftist governments in some town councils and states began to implement novel modalities for the direct participation of communities in public governance. In this manner, they sought to make governments more inclusive, democratic, and efficient in their delivery of social services. They also experimented with citizen assemblies, participatory budgets, roundtables on water management, social consortia for the physical rehabilitation of working-class neighborhoods, among other approaches (Harnecker 1993a and 1993b). Also, other local governments, such as the governorship of the Capital District under the party Convergencia Nacional, elaborated bylaws that prohibited the use of weapons against peaceful protests, which marked the beginning of decriminalization of protest in the country (López Maya 2003).

This dynamic coexisted alongside civic actions executed by organized middle-class actors, who preferred to make claims in institutional spaces such as the Presidential Commission for the Reform of the State (Comisión Presidencial de Reforma del Estado, or COPRE). They pressured the state for greater democratization of the political system by means of decentralizing the state and its administration, a "one-person-one-vote" electoral model (incorporating features of a uninominal voting system instead of the traditional lists of candidates chosen by the parties), and the recognition of rights such as gender equality, the respect for environmental equilibrium, and the quality of life in residential areas (Gómez Calcaño 1987; Gómez Calcaño and López Maya 1990).

These civic actions contributed to the approval of legal instruments that promoted administrative decentralization and the opening up of spaces for direct citizens' participation in local government. Its highlights included the Organic Law on Town Council Governance (Ley Orgánica de Régimen Municipal, 1989), which separated town councils from national elections, created the figure of a mayor elected by direct and secret vote, and incorporated the referendum; the Law for Direct, Universal, and Secret Election of Governors (Ley de Elección Directa, Popular y Secreta de Gobernadores, 1989), which removed the National Executive Branch's right to designate regional authorities; and the Organic Law for Elections and Political Participation (Ley Orgánica del Sufragio y la Participación Política, 1998), which traded an electoral system of closed party lists for a mixed system in which half of the members were nominally chosen while the other half were selected by a proportional distribution among political parties' lists and electoral groups (Gómez Calcaño and López Maya 1990). The struggle of the women's movement achieved the Law on Violence against Women and the Family (Ley sobre la Violencia contra la Mujer y la Familia, 1998).

This stage was characterized by the strategies used by emergent actors from the working and middle classes as well as from the new political parties. New parties rejected traditional political parties because they were considered obstacles to a larger democratization of the state. These were times when neoliberalism exerted a strong influence through transnational information technology companies and through international financial agencies. As in other countries in Latin America, an antipolitical culture developed in Venezuela, one that *romanticized* the new social movements and civil society as better actors than political parties for the deepening of democracy.

Stage 2: "Empowering and Participatory Democracy"

The Bolivarian Movement that Chávez led in his electoral campaign of 1998 was one among many new actors that had emerged during a societal crisis that featured a struggle for hegemony. By 1998, it was basically an electoral movement composed of a heterogeneous and contradictory ensemble of social sectors and sociopolitical actors. This included, for example, soldiers of low and middle ranks who had been conspiring against the established political order with the Bolivarian Revolutionary Movement 200 (Movimiento Bolivariano Revolucionario 200, or MBR 200).[6] It also included celebrities and organizations from an ideologically diverse and fragmented Left that had participated in the armed struggle during the 1960s only to be defeated by a series of democratic governments. These organizations each had their own interpretations of the defeat of the armed struggle, and thus, different positions vis-à-vis the regime after 1958. Finally, a multitude of diverse working-class organizations joined the movement, enchanted by the retired Lieutenant-Colonel Chávez's charismatic leadership and discourse.

Chávez's presidency opened up a structure of opportunities for the concretizing of proposals that had been developing for a long time and now coalesced as a new sociopolitical project. The Constituent Assembly of 1999 was the vehicle by which a variety of emergent actors promoted deep changes to the state's articulating principles and structures as they had been established by the Constitution of 1961 and its derivative legal framework. A new Constitution passed and was approved in a referendum held in December 1999. The name of the country changed from Republic of Venezuela to Bolivarian Republic of Venezuela, which was refounded by substituting a representative democracy with a "participatory and empowering [protagonistic]" one.

During Chávez's first term, the CCAs and civic actions continued developing with unusual force among all actors, but with different motivations as compared to the previous stage. The working-class sector, which mostly supported a change of hegemonic model, used more forms of collective civic action and combined them with contentious actions. The former allowed them to participate in open, government-created modalities for co-management or management of public policies aimed at defending their socioeconomic rights. Through this process, they increasingly received resources and exerted influence on the government. They resorted to contentious actions mainly to defend the process of change against the attacks of actors from the opposition.

Society in this stage was deeply polarized, both socially and politically. The middle and upper classes, excluded from institutional spaces where they previously had operated, preferred CCAs to protest against the government. Some actions became extreme, even reaching insurrectional levels, such as in the coup of 2002 and the oil strike of 2002–3. The end of this stage saw their capacity to summon society diminished and their influence on its development weakened.

Polarization and Insurgency
in Contentious Collective Actions

During this stage, CCAs constituted the main form of political confrontation. Their use spiked between 1999 and 2004, when deep institutional changes took place and the polarization reached extreme levels. Unlike in the previous stage, both political factions used CCAs in the pursuit of their interests and projects.

Since the elections of 1998, this political polarization had divided the society in two factions that repeatedly expressed themselves in each electoral process. From the presidential election of 1998 through the presidential recall referendum of 2004 and Chávez's reelection of 2006, electoral processes displayed a ratio of approximately 60 percent of citizens supporting the government and 40 percent opposing it. The prominent role of these two factions' CCAs can be explained by both sides' continued mistrust and/or rejection of

TABLE 13.4. Peaceful and violent actions, 1998–2007

Years	Protest Actions	Daily Average	Peaceful		Violent	
				%		%
98–99	855	2.34	805	94.15	50	5.85
99–00	1,414	3.87	1,263	89.32	151	10.68
00–01	1,312	3.59	1,169	89.10	143	10.90
01–02	1,262	3.46	1,141	90.41	121	9.59
02–03	1,543	4.23	1,243	80.56	300	19.44
03–04	1,255	3.44	1,037	82.63	218	17.37
04–05	1,534	4.20	1,417	92.37	117	7.63
05–06	1,383	3.79	1,280	92.55	103	7.45
06–07	1,576	4.32	1,521	96.51	55	3.49
Total	12,134	3.69	10,876	89.63	1258	10.37

Source: Provea's annual reports and my own calculations.

political parties and of the previous political system. This rejection made it hard to develop institutional spaces for mediation and representation and left no choice but to engage in an antipolitical culture that most emergent actors shared, whether they belonged to the government side or to the opposition. In these adverse conditions for conducting politics, factors of power and social actors such as the private media, corporate organizations, leaders from the Catholic Church, unions, neighborhood and professional associations, and autonomous grassroots organizations, as well as others created by the government itself from within (e.g., Bolivarian circles and electoral battle units), came together to substitute for political parties. All these actors took their politics to the streets. These new conditions for deinstitutionalization further weakened a state characterized by institutional debility in the past, a combination that fostered a sustained growth of CCAs as political tools.

The CCAs grew in number and in proportion compared to the previous stage. The daily average increased from 1.77 to 3.70 (table 13.4). In nine years the press reported over 12,000 protests in absolute numbers.

Between 1999 and 2004, when the presidential recall referendum placed Chávez as the victor, CCAs registered high rates of violence, at times even reaching the double digits. This tendency reached its climax between 2002 and 2003 (table 13.4), only to abruptly decline in the following years. Violence can mainly be explained by its voluntary use on the part of polarized actors who were engaged in a political confrontation. While in the past violent protest was mainly an actor's response to the repression and criminalization of peaceful protests, in this new stage, on the contrary, there was an institutional recognition of the right to protest in public and without fear of arms. Thus, repression lost its relevance as a cause of violence (López Maya 2005 and table 13.5).

The increase in violence was closely related to the rise of politically motivated protests.[7] Between 2001 and 2004 there was a spike in the percentage of politically motivated protests, many of which were called to either support or oppose the government. They even surpassed a third of the total protests, and they coincided with the years with most violence (tables 13.5 and 13.6).

During these years, the middle and upper classes competed with the working class and the student movement over control of the streets. This phenomenon began at the end of 2001 as a reaction to the changes in land, fishing, and hydrocarbon rights, sensitive subjects that the state approached by announcing its Enabling Law (Ley Habilitante). That same year, on December 10, these actors organized a successful civic strike that secured the unification of many organizations that had previously been dispersed, but that shared an adverse relationship to the government. This moment led to a feverish pace of marches that lasted all through 2002 and until Febru-

TABLE 13.5. Repressed peaceful protests, 1990–2007

Years	Peaceful Protests	Repressed	One In
90–91	124	46	3
91–92	654	113	6
92–93	1,047	157	7
93–94	1,099	133	8
94–95	581	55	11
95–96	534	50	11
96–97	550	43	12
97–98	385	49	8
98–99	805	33	24
99–00	1,263	54	23
00–01	1,169	42	28
01–02	1,141	41	28
02–03	1,243	35	36
03–04	1,037	31	33
04–05	1,417	18	79
05–06	1,280	58	22
06–07	1,521	98	16

Source: Provea's annual reports and my own calculations.

TABLE 13.6. Kinds of rights demanded, 1995–2007

Years	Protest Actions	Socioeconomic and Cultural Rights		Civil and Political Rights	
		Actions	%	Actions	%
94–95	591	458	77.5	133	22.5
95–96	628	583	92.8	45	7.2
96–97	632	590	93.4	42	6.6
97–98	422	374	88.6	48	11.4
98–99	855	797	93.2	58	6.8
99–00	1,414	1,271	89.9	143	10.1
00–01	1,312	1,180	89.9	132	10.1
01–02	1,262	882	69.9	380	30.1
02–03	1,543	840	54.4	703	45.6
03–04	1,255	719	57.3	536	42.7
04–05	1,534	1,209	78.8	325	21.2
05–06	1,383	1,039	75.1	344	24.9
06–07	1,576	1,088	69.0	488	31.0

Source: Provea's annual reports and my own calculations.

ary 2003, when the general strike failed and the oil industry collapsed. Among the most common CCAs used by the opposition were the pots-and-pans protests (*cacerolazos*), which called on actors to stand up against the government during the oil strike. They stood out for their tenacity, frequency, and efficacy to create a climate of tension. The cacerolazos summoned people every night for a period of over two months, and they took place mostly in residential areas where these social classes lived. Meanwhile, during the months following the coup (May–December 2002), for each march by the opposition there was a countermarch by government supporters. The oppositions sought to keep the government in check with the frequency of its collective actions. The coup of April 2002 was followed by the general strike in the oil industry in 2002–3 and ended with violent street actions that preceded the presidential recall referendum known as the *guarimbas* (López Maya 2006b). This period culminated with Chávez's victory at the polls as evidenced in the results of the Presidential Recall Referendum of 2004. After that, all the opposition's organizational attempts weakened, opening up the possibility of returning to more institutional paths to overcome the political crisis. The Presidential Recall Referendum was a civic strategy of collective action, supported by the Organization of American States (OAS) and the Carter Center.

Civic Collective Actions: Participatory Innovations

This period also saw the development of new forms of civic action promoted by the government. The "participatory and empowering" democracy of the Constitution of 1999 made its citizens "protagonists" by consecrating their right to participation in a "direct, semi-direct, and indirect" way, not only through the vote, but also through the formation, execution, and control of public management (Exposición de Motivos 1999). The participatory approach of the *new* democracy differed from the Constitution of 1961 in that even if it maintained forms of representative democracy, it transformed participation into the key practice to redress the unequal power relations that existed in Venezuelan society (Article 62). In an official document entitled "General Guidelines for the Economic and Social Development of the Nation 2001–2007" (*En las Líneas Generales del Desarrollo Económico y Social de la Nación 2001–2007*), it was claimed that participation fostered self-development, instilled coresponsibility, and promoted the citizens' "protagonism" (LGDESN 2001).

The roundtables on water technology (*mesas técnicas de agua*, or MTA) are an example of the new institutional spaces. Public water companies sponsored the roundtables so that organized communities could manage the utility service for drinking and waste (gray) water. The successful experience was replicated to deal with problems related to the distribution of gas and electricity (roundtables on gas and energy technology), so that this modality became more widely used though with a lesser impact than the water roundtables had had.

In seeking to address the long-unresolved issue of land tenure in working-class neighborhoods, in 2002 the presidency issued Decree 1,666, which promoted the creation of Urban Land Committees (*comités de tierra urbana*, or CTUs). The goal was to organize communities so that they could conduct a land registry in their neighborhoods with the government's support. This registry was a necessary prerequisite for the formal granting of legal titles to individual or collective properties. According to this decree, the CTUs were also directed to conduct a census of families and reconstruct the history of the corresponding neighborhoods with the help of their inhabitants, with the goal of strengthening communal ties. The government explicitly sought to increase the social cohesion of communities as part of their empowerment, but also as a means to change the values of a political culture rooted in the tradition of paternalism and cronyism. These were the objectives delineated in the General Guidelines. During this period, a transition to a socialist society had not yet been set forth. The proposal instead was to build a deeper democracy through the democratization of property and the means of production. The Law of Lands of 2001 promoted the creation of rural land committees (*comités de tierra rural*, or CTR), proposing similar objectives for farmland.

Organizational demands on communities had important social objectives. This was the case of the Barrio Adentro I neighborhood Mission (*Misión Barrio Adentro I*), which promoted health committees to support the delivery of services and ease the living conditions for the community doctor; members of the committee would accompany him or her in providing preventive health services. The Housing Department (Ministerio de Vivienda y Hábitat) encouraged self-managed organizations so that the community would be responsible for administering several improvement projects for the physical rehabilitation of their neighborhoods. In exchange, they received the support of the government's institutions and technicians. At the end of this stage, CC were created, which were later institutionalized through the Law of Communal Councils (Ley de Consejos Comunales) of 2006.

The government stimulated civic actions using diverse tools to foster the democratization of economic activities. Initially, cooperatives were strongly promoted through a combination of state financing and public policies designed to incentivize them. Although the cooperative movement in Venezuela has a long history, this impulse translated into unprecedented growth (Provea 2007). In the countryside, agrarian cooperatives known as *fundos zamoranos* and a system of self-organized rural associations (Sistema de Asociaciones Rurales Auto-Organizadas, or SARAO) were created. Later, both in the countryside and in the cities, the nuclei of endogenous development (*núcleos de desarrollo endógeno*, or NDE) were created with the idea of launching a developmental process guided by this participatory principle (Parker 2007; Vila 2003).

These participatory innovations included community assemblies as the foundation of the decision-making process. The government sought to foster these dynamics at the base as a means to educate citizens in the exercise of direct democracy. The process generated important working-class organizational activity that enabled civic collective action to manage and solve community problems. It created the conditions to empower people, although with limitations. On the one hand, the microlocal assemblies did not transcend local boundaries, because they were designed to attend to relatively small communities, and most lacked clear mechanisms for aggregation. On the other hand, the democratization process at the microlevel took place at the same time as a recentralization and concentration of power at the level of the National Executive Branch, and more specifically in the presidency.

Intermediary mediating institutions necessary for the good functioning of democracy such as town councils consequently weakened, beginning a tendency that continued into the following stage.

The case of the CTUs illustrates the limitations of this process. Created to regulate land tenure in working-class neighborhoods, these were conceived as micro-organizations with no legal status, which had to fulfill a series of prerequisites in order to be qualified to register in an ad hoc technical office affiliated with the Republic's vice-presidency. The CTUs could not manage resources, nor were they designed to be linked to the state's intermediary levels (town councils or governorships) or associated with each other. Whenever an initiative went in that direction, the executive branch blocked them.[8]

Organizations from the middle and upper classes hardly participated in these spaces, since their basic demands were generally satisfied. During this stage, their civic action was limited to those few places where the political opposition could perform local and regional governmental functions. Contrary to the decreasing tendency of their civic actions, they lived an accelerated process of polarization and politicization, which led to some organizations joining the Democratic Coordination for Civic Action (Coordinadora Democrática de Acción Cívica). This was a platform to aggregate forces that opposed Chávez's government, which existed from 2001 until sometime after August 2004, when the organization's defeat in the recall election led to the disintegration of the Coordination (García-Guadilla 2003). During the years of high political confrontation, residents promoted neighborhood "citizens' assemblies," defined as public spaces where actors who disagreed with Chávez's project could nonetheless interact with political and intellectual leaders that opposed Chávez's government (Provea 2004). Among the organizations that became political and joined the Democratic Coordination were We Want to Choose (Queremos Elegir), the National Assembly for Education (Asamblea Nacional de Educación), and the Military Institutional Front (Frente Institucional Militar).

These middle- and upper-class civic organizations displayed forms and mechanisms of internal democracy in which people felt included and heard, and thus felt recognized as citizens. In countless interviews, participants reiterated their assessment of these forms of expression as improvements in the quality of democracy. This same democratic inclination, however, was absent when interacting with the "other," that is, the social organizations supporting the government. This lack of plurality or tolerance is an expression of the democratic deficit of these emergent forms.

Generally speaking, political parties played a secondary role in the struggle over hegemony and in these participatory processes. The parties AD and COPEI continued to decline while other new actors did not manage to replace them. Additionally, during the presidential term that ran from 2006 until 2011, the opposition's political mistakes led to the abandonment of important institutional spaces, such as the National Assembly (Asamblea Nacional, or AN). By the end of the term, political pluralism had dwindled. This contributed to the strengthening of tendencies that led to the majoritarian political system of the third stage, the political personalism behind the figure of the president, a concentration of powers in the hands of Chávez, and an erosion of the autonomy of public authorities.

Moreover, the new Constitution enshrined four different modalities for referenda, legislative initiatives, and open forums and meetings of citizens (Articles 70–74). The first referendum modality was the recall of elected public servants. The most prominent was the Coordinadora Democrática-sponsored recall referendum against the president in August 2004. Thanks in part to basically civic actions, the Constitution of 1999 had also incorporated a representation of indigenous minorities in the National Assembly (CRBV 1999, Art. 86; Van Cott 2001). Informal practices of political participation were also tried, as in the case of "street parliamentarism" (*parlamentarismo de calle*), a modality promoted by members of the AN beginning in 2006, since the assembly was left without the representation of opposition parties. By their own definition, they sought to establish popular power, taking the discussion of bills to the public parks and plazas (www.asambleanacional.gov.ve) (Gomez en EU, 28-1-2006).

Stage 3: Collective Action During Twenty-First-Century Socialism

With Chávez's reelection in December 2006, the conditions ripened for the creation of what the government called "21st-century socialism," which substituted in the official discourse for the prior guiding principle of a participatory and empowering [protagonistic] democracy. At the dawn of 2007, the president delineated a strategy for achieving this new goal. He outlined the need to create an instrument for unifying political forces called the United Socialist Party of Venezuela (Partido Socialista Unido de Venezuela, or PSUV), which required the immediate dissolution of the political parties that had supported him and their incorporation instead into one single party. Chávez announced the means to reach socialism: a renationalization of strategic industries; a new government slogan, "Homeland, Socialism or Death" (*Patria, socialismo o muerte*); and a plan that he called the "five constituent engines" (*cinco motores constituyentes*), which would serve as vehicles to achieve socialism (Chávez 2006, 2007).

On August 15, 2007, the president presented a proposal for a constitutional reform that was debated by the AN and the general public, submitted to a referendum, and defeated at the polls the following December. This rejection was the first political defeat for Chávez and his movement. As a consequence of this defeat, he provisionally suspended the plans being developed using the five engines. The new socialist model, however, would slowly creep in through other legal instruments, especially after 2009, when Chávez managed to have a constitutional amendment approved that ended term limits and in principle allowed him indefinite reelections. Between 2009 and 2010, the executive and legislative branches under Chávez's control approved a series of administrative bills, regulations, and procedures that effectively exchanged the constitutional political regime for a "revolutionary" alternative. The emergent communal state followed a Marxist-Leninist conception of the relationship between society and the state that moved away from liberal representative democracy and approximated Soviet and Cuban models.

Tendencies in the Exercise of Contentious Action

During this stage, the sociopolitical actors that supported the government as well as those who opposed it continued using CCAs to interpellate public authorities. There was a noticeable increase in their frequency. Toward the end of this period, an average of ten daily actions took place. However, violent protests decreased in these years and did not exceed 2 percent of total protests (table 13.7). Until the year 2011 Provea's annual reports counted the period of

TABLE 13.7. Violent and peaceful actions, 2006–2012

Years	Protest Actions	Daily Average	Peaceful		Violent	
				%		%
06–07	1,576	4.32	1,521	96.51	55	3.49
07–08	1,763	4.83	1,680	95.29	83	4.70
08–09	2,893	7.92	2,822	97.54	71	2.45
09–10	3,315	9.08	3,266	98.52	46	1.38
10–11	4,543	12.15	4,472	98.44	62	1.36
2012*	3,986	10.92	3,925	98.47	61	1.53

*Starting in 2012 Provea's annual reports go from January to December.

Source: Provea's annual reports.

a year from October to September. Starting in 2012, the yearly period expands over the twelve months of a single year (January–December).

The state improved its respect for citizen expression, after the setback of the first years of the period (see table 13.8). Although there was less in situ repression by law enforcement, the governmental policy to criminalize protest expanded, which meant that hundreds of citizens were charged with criminal offenses for their "crime" of protesting in public spaces (Provea 2006–12).

The motivations for protest are predominantly socioeconomic, in some years representing more than 75 percent of the total, and in others exceeding 60 percent (see table 13.9). Unlike in the previous stage, these actions took place to demand the satisfaction of promised socioeconomic rights, independent of the participants' political color. Some motivations for protest included problems with income, inefficient public management, and unfinished public works. They frequently took place in front of the Presidential Palace (Provea 2006–12). Most CCAs for civil and political rights were protests for more public safety, given the alarming increase in crime rates. Others frequently demanded their right to free speech, to due process, and to political participation (Provea 2006–12). Meanwhile, polarization continued to increase. The student movement that had remained dormant during the previous stage reemerged over the unresolved confrontation between the government and the private media. In 2007, students polarized into protests and counterprotests as the government withdrew the broadcast license of Radio Caracas Televisión (RCTV).

Weakened by their political defeats, the organized middle class that had used CCAs in the previous stage to make their claims against the state initially decreased their mobilization. Following the campaign to oppose the presi-

TABLE 13.8. Repressed peaceful protests, 2006–2012

Years	Peaceful Protests	Repressed	One in . . .
06–07	1,521	98	16
07–08	1,680	83	20
08–09	2,822	187	15
09–10	3,266	150	22
10–11	4,472	134	33
2012*	3,925	69	57

*Starting in 2012 Provea's annual reports go from January to December

Source: Provea's annual reports.

TABLE 13.9. Protests and their motivations, 2006–2012

Years	DESC	%	DCP	%
06–07	1,063	67.45	488	30.96
07–08	1,334	75.66	411	23.31
08–09	1,947	67.30	932	32.21
09–10	2,591	78.15	686	20.69
10–11	2,773	61.04	1,761	38.76
2012	2,970	75.67	955	24.33

Source: Provea's annual reports.

dential proposal for constitutional reform, however, they began to organize again and gained new mobilizing capacity. The role the student movement played to oppose the government was particularly relevant. Toward the end of this stage, these new capacities were consolidated in a process of more successful political unification expressed in the massive demonstrations and marches that took place during the different electoral periods.

For its part, the new Chavista party, PSUV, and to a lesser extent the remainder of the official political parties, continued to build a powerful machinery to mobilize the masses in support of the government's policies and electoral processes. For that purpose, they could count on public resources, which were used in violation of explicit legal mandates. This instrumental use of state resources calls into question the nature of contentious collective actions during this period.

Civic Action: Communal Councils, Communes, and the Communal State

During this stage, the government promoted civic collective actions according to the changes in its political project. The emphasis was now on the creation and expansion of CC, for their future aggregation into communes. Through this practice, the government sought a new territorial organization as the basis for a communal state following the socialist model. According to the newly enacted law, other organizations had to articulate around the CC and commit to the construction of the socialist society that the president had proposed. The CC and communes entered the recentered structure of the state, which assigned them functions for the planning and management of public policies at the local microlevel and administration of resources. They also collaborated with the Bolivarian militias and promoted forms of social economy. This scheme left little room for pluralism or autonomy.

The tendency among the organizations of the opposition has been to regroup in political parties and social movements, hoping to stop what they identify as authoritarian tendencies from the government and developing civic actions in national and international entities to denounce the government's moves. Other social organizations once again took up their specific agendas—around rural, ecological, and gender issues, among others—in their dialogue with different levels of the state. They decreased their intervention in the polarized national politics.

Final Considerations

After the collapse of a political system based on a representative democracy, both contentious and civic collective actions have mainly fostered transformations in the Venezuelan political order. They have also contributed to shaping some characteristics of today's "democracy." The analysis of this counterpoint between contentious and civic actions through these three differentiated stages lead us to recognize the strengths and weaknesses of both.

During the first stage, one can see these actions developing independently from governmental guidance. The main protagonists of civic actions were the middle-class organizations, which elaborated agendas that emphasized the aspirations of a political transformation aimed at deepening representative democracy through the mechanisms of a direct and semidirect democracy. The main protagonist of CCAs, on the other hand, was the weakly organized working class, whose actions were directed to render its socioeconomic demands visible. Both groups had aspirations that the Bolivarian Movement drew together during a process that would eventually lead to the elaboration of the Constitution of 1999. What was fruitful about this dialogue between the two forms of action was that it legitimized each of them in the following stages.

During the second stage, the relationship between these two kinds of actions differs in that contentious actions were used to confront divergent political proposals in a context where actors were highly polarized. The national government, local and regional governments, and various sociopolitical forces all embraced the CCA modality. Civic actions, on the other hand, were mainly promoted by the national government through the creation of spaces for the participation of organized working-class communities—the state's main political base—in addressing their socioeconomic rights. The new spaces reflected different conceptions of participation, which emerged from the heterogeneity among those who composed the government's coalition. During this period, the various organizations coexisted in tension with one another. The organizations of the opposition were excluded and, generally speaking, their demands were ignored. There is no dialogue or complementarity between both modalities of collective action, which translates into a permanent sociopolitical instability that reached insurrectional levels in 2002 and 2003.

The third stage shows diverse developments in the CCAs. On the one hand, as in the first stage, diverse actors used them mostly for socioeconomic reasons, revealing that the government had failed to comply with the *agenda of the poor*. On the other hand, political parties and organizations opposing the government increasingly used them as well. This produced a reaction among the officialist forces on the streets that, compared to the previous stage, featured as less violent. The CCAs' increase due to socioeconomic reasons points to a lack of management, which neither the government's participatory innovations nor its social objectives could overcome. The state, for its part, returned to the criminalization of contentious actions.

In the field of civic collective actions, the CC functioned as any other organizational form among communities, except that they operated from the government and inserted themselves within the socialist model of the communal state. The working-class organizations, weakened with regard to their autonomy and independent action, thus increasingly constituted the institutional arms of the central government and its socialist project.

With regard to the sustained struggle for hegemony, it expanded over the 1990s when these modalities of collective action were so crucial. In recent years, these sustained efforts from both the Chavista as well as the opposing sides sought to rebuild political organizations that could guarantee a long-lasting political leadership at all levels. This seems to reflect a budding awareness of the need to move beyond street actions toward actions within the state in order to reconstruct the political system as a public space. The government has sought to secure governability while the opposing forces struggle for more inclusive policy.

NOTES

1. I use this term *hegemony* in its Gramscian sense.

2. This section is based on the work of López Maya, Smilde, and Stephany (2002).

3. To understand the Venezuelan sociopolitical process from the 1990s, Chávez's ascent to power, and his political alliance with the government in 1998, see, among others, Kornblith 1998; and López Maya 2005.

4. The first annual report on the Human Rights Situation in Venezuela corresponded to the period between October 1989 and September 1990. For data preceding this period, see the database El Bravo Pueblo (BDEBP 2007).

5. In a previous work, I interpreted the struggle that developed in Venezuela since the Caracazo of 1989 as a struggle for hegemony. See López Maya (2005).

6. For a description of the MBR 200, see López Maya (2005).

7. I use here the same approach as that of Provea's annual reports. It groups protests in two large categories according to the motivations expressed by the participants themselves: protests for economic, social, and cultural rights (Derechos Económicos, Sociales y Culturales, DESC) and for political and civil rights (Derechos Civiles y Políticos, DPC).

8. This conclusion is supported by interviews with participants from several CTUs. An agreement was made with the interviewees not to share their names (López Maya 2007).

Chapter 14

BRAZIL: BACK TO THE STREETS?

GIANPAOLO BAIOCCHI AND
ANA CLAUDIA TEIXEIRA

No one could have predicted the wave of protests that shook Brazil in June 2013. Even the Free Fare Movement (Movimento do Passe Livre, or MPL),[1] the leading organization of the first demonstrations against rising bus fares in São Paulo, seemed caught off-guard as protests escalated. By month's end, there were protests in some 140 other cities around the country, with estimates of participants in the millions, earning comparisons to the Arab Spring, Occupy, and the protests in Greece and Spain. The protests of 2013 were also marked by a dizzying diversity of causes for dissatisfaction: not only bus fares and the right to mobility, but World Cup megaprojects, political corruption, poor public education, the lack of access to quality public health, and a host of other issues. Even socially conservative Brazilians made their presence felt, protesting against abortion or in favor of the reduction of criminal age. The June Protests, as they became known, were a milestone in the history of the country, dwarfing both the protests of the 1980s surrounding the country's transition to democracy and those of the 1990s that led to the impeachment of President Fernando Collor de Mello. And while the mobilizations eventually dwindled and did not end with regime change, their impact on the Brazilian political context has been decisive.

In this chapter we discuss what "Brazil's Occupy" has been about and what its implications are for the future of Brazil's democracy. We depart somewhat from other analyses of the course of events in Brazil, which have tended to focus on neoliberalism's contradictions, or even how the movement is part of a global wave of protests. Our argument is that the Brazilian protests indeed borrowed the practices and formats of Occupy, 15M, and the Arab Spring: the massive occupation of public space, a strong youth presence, and the marked use of social media. The limits of the developmentalist model of the last dozen years have certainly contributed to the dissatisfaction visible in the movement but Brazil's protests are difficult to reduce to a single logic, set of motivations, or even a symbolic target, such as the 1 percent in the United States or the dictatorships of the Arab Spring. If the global economic crisis seems to have been a spark for protests in Spain, Greece, or the United States, Brazil's protests were driven by varied causes and its ostensible spark—bus fares—multiplied into scores of causes and demands that characterized the mobilizations. As in other parts of the world, the inadequacies of representative democracy are an important part of the puzzle. But the groups that occupied Brazil's streets were plural, sometimes with completely opposing demands.

We thus explore the relationship between this movement, a very visible manifestation of what the introduction to this volume describes as the "contentious face of cultural-political struggles," with the country's very robust system of participatory democracy and its organized civil society. It is fitting to do so as one of the closing remarks of this volume, as the experiences in Brazil around participation have been so central to the debates of the Civil Society Agenda (as amply demonstrated by the various chapters in this book). The street protests expressed something uncontained and quite outside formal democratic and participatory institutions and serve as a poignant reminder of their limits. After the June protests, the country has lived a contradictory, but intense political period—social movements have taken up the banner of some of the demands in newly contestatory ways, while political conservatism has also been in the streets for the first time in a generation. As well, the political process has been unable to absorb this energy, with disaffection being the main result of the subsequent elections. After a brief discussion of the chronology of events, we discuss the motivations and consequences of the protests, before venturing some conclusions about their broader implications.

The Chronology of Events

While protests around public transportation had taken place throughout the country since at least 2002, most analysts date the beginning of the June protests to June 13. On that date, overzealous military police in São Paulo attempted to end a bus-fare protest with batons and tear gas. The sweeping arrests and rubber bullets were able to disperse much of the crowd that night, but not before images and testimonials were circulated widely, including those of journalists and bystanders being attacked. This had been the fourth and largest demonstration of the Free Fare Movement, which had been agitating since the beginning of the month against a nine-cent rise in bus fares. Outrage quickly turned to Twitter-speed mobilization, and the movement flooded the streets again on June 17, this time with over 100,000 people and with companion protests in other large cities as well. Again, the overwhelming police force only motivated protesters to escalate activities.

The notoriously conservative mainstream media in Brazil began to rapidly change its coverage at this point. From the first protests at the beginning of June, media coverage had been disparaging, always highlighting property damage and presenting the activity as a "wave of disorder." The case of José Luiz Datena, a conservative TV talk show host on TV Bandeirantes, was emblematic of this change. On the evening of June 17 he ran a live poll on his show asking if viewers supported the protests. He was surprised to see that viewers were actually sympathetic, so he ran the poll again, now by referring to the protests as a turmoil (*baderna*). "Do you support the turmoil, viewers?" he asked in the new survey. This time, viewers were even more supportive. He moderated his criticisms just as the first supportive editorials were published. By June 20, what had been calls for the repression of disruptive protesters became active support of the mobilization. Now TV Globo and its ideological print counterpart, Veja, started to present it as a patriotic movement against the corruption of the Workers' Party (Partido dos Trabalhadores, or PT), likening the protests to the impeachment of Collor. For these news sources the protests had to do with a national discontentment with the PT, corruption, bureaucracy, and high taxes.

By Friday, June 21, the country had come to a near standstill as more and more Brazilians took to the streets. If at first, in São Paulo, it had a clearly leftist, but not partisan, orientation, by this time, anticorruption and nationalist slogans were seen on the streets as well. Slogans, such as "the giant has awoken," which alluded to a popular whisky ad, coexisted with Anonymous/Guy Fawkes masks, Brazilian flags, and slogans about better public transportation. It is as if there were two simultaneous protests in Brazil: one started by the MPL, with its clarity and strategy, to which other demands were added; and another protest, more explosive and inchoate. A hasty attempt by organized social movements to show support for the national government by calling for supporters to come to the streets in well-publicized instances of violence against partisans.

The political process also took note of the protests and responded quickly. Most large cities repealed the bus fare increases. Brazil's ruling PT initially appeared to be in disarray. Its president, Rui Falcão, called for party activists to join the mobilization, while other party members—some notably referring to the mobilizations as having fascist overtones—called for people to stay away. The party's youth wing similarly called for the governing coalition to be more "daring," while some progressive politicians within the party responded with admiration to the protests.

On June 24, in a meeting with governors and mayors, President Dilma Rousseff put forward a five-point pact to concretely respond to the protests. She offered an endorsement of peaceful protests and proposals for improvements to education and health, and promised to listen to the people on the streets. One of the most notable elements was a proposal to hold a plebiscite on political reforms including completely public funding of electoral campaigns, laws to enable popular referenda on national policies, recalls of elected officials via popular vote, better access to public documents, and more serious punishment for corruption. Big media outlets argued that reforms would just direct even more public money to politicians who were already overpaid. Aided by the press, Center and Center-Right parties quickly defeated the idea of the plebiscite.

DIVIDES IN THE MOVEMENT

At first, by boldly rejecting all political parties, the June movement appeared quite distinct from Brazil's organized movements such as the landless movement, the unions, and the urban movements whose history is intertwined with that of the PT. To that effect, during the June protests, there were even attacks on activists who carried political party banners. After those attacks, the MPL released a statement that it was a nonpartisan movement, but that it was not "anti-party," a distinction that was largely lost by the mainstream media, which attempted to characterize the protests as an anticorruption, anti-political-party movement.

Traditional movements, such as the national unions or the landless movement, at first had a distant and cautious relationship with the June protests. Some organized movement leaders, from the protests' early days, expressed suspicion of the middle-class component and distrust of political parties that pervaded the June movement. Some traditional organizers also claimed right-wing manipulation in the protests and that the demonstrators were privileged people who did not understand the importance of a leftist government. Yet other organizers attempted to more centrally and visibly insert their movements into the broader wave of protests, which was initially unsuccessful.

After initially avoiding street protests, traditional social movements started to make their presence felt once again when the June movement began to dwindle in size. Several of the large unions, in concert with some nationally organized movements, called for a "National Day of Struggle" on July 11, which included a general strike. The demands—for political reform and greater spending on health and education—were consonant with the concerns of the protesters. By mid-July, the mass movement had all but fizzled, but protests now continued by specific movements throughout the country for months afterward. Brazil has seen a wave of smaller mobilizations since that time, carried out by social movements and unions that had been largely absent, or invisible, in the June protests. The Movement of Homeless Workers (Movimento dos Trabalhadores Sem Teto, or MTST) and the Movement for Housing have staged increasingly militant protests in large cities. Public school teachers in cities such as Rio had strikes and mobilizations. In support of the teachers' strikes, young people mobilized in Black Blocs devising such brazen tactics as occasionally confronting the police with stones and bottles. Another significant protest was by municipal garbage collectors, who in the middle of Carnaval 2014 went on strike, letting trash accumulate throughout the city in the middle of its most profitable tourist days.

Making Sense of the Protests

The June protests seemed to fade as quickly as they appeared. While some specific policies were changed in direct response to the protests, the vast inchoate majority of demands went unanswered. The World Cup took place, largely undisturbed; there was little progress on political reform; and the only candidate in the 2014 presidential elections to claim the mantle of the June protests, Marina da Silva, faded from view after a poor showing in the first round.

This was not the only paradox. The protests took place after a period of unprecedented growth and economic prosperity, after over a decade of Center-Left governments, social policies such as the conditional cash transfer program Bolsa Família, and commitments to dialogue and citizen participation. Brazil had had a seemingly unstoppable economic growth in the Lula years—weathering the global recession relatively well—and a long list of remarkable social achievements, such as doubling the number of college students, making real gains in affirmative action, and reducing extreme poverty by 75 percent under the PT national rule.[2] The PT has, for better or worse, become the standard-bearer of a certain kind of "pragmatic leftism" in Latin America. Now, after more than ten years of national rule, it has become common to speak of PT-style rule as combining economic growth, a market-orientation, and attention to social justice.[3] And while on certain scores, such as land redistribution and the reform of the political system, the administration has fallen short of expectations, most progressive commentators agree that national rule under the PT has represented a significant break from previous periods, appearing to chart a route of social and economic development different from free-market orthodoxies.[4]

But the puzzle is even greater. The Workers' Party is, in principle, very different from the European Social Democrats and Latin America's Old Left. The Workers' Party's history is also deeply connected to the radical democratic currents, from liberation theology to the New Unionism and the World Social Forum. What happened to the "party of social movements," which was able to translate the street mobilization into innovative institutional action and novel public policies for so long by channeling social grievances?

The Uncontained: Limits of Brazil's Participatory Democracy

The argument we explore in this chapter is that as robust, and intensive, as the institutions of participatory democracy have become in Brazil under the PT, the mobilizations point to their limits, and more broadly, to the limits of noncontentious modes of claims-making by organized civil society.

When Luiz Inácio Lula da Silva came to power, there had been much anticipation about his government. The expectation was that the administration would break with the old ways of doing politics, as well as with favor trading, a practice characterizing many government affairs in Brazil. It was hoped that the old ways of governing would be replaced by new forms of citizen participation. By the late 1990s, the phrase "PT way of governing" had become synonymous with participation, transparency, and good governance. A central component of this participation was its connection with real decision-making and a broader strategy of social transformation. Local administrations, through these participatory mechanisms, were able to develop and legitimize redistributive policies. And before acclaim for its pragmatic Left policies, the party was known as a party for its radically democratic orientation. Born under the influences of liberation theology, new social movements, and popular education, the PT was from its inception a party where activist movements could speak and where traditional leftist ideas of class politics were conjoined with policy goals. From its very first local administrations in the 1980s, the party ran governments that relied heavily on popular input from both organized and unorganized sectors.

The government has certainly kept its commitment to participation. Since Lula's victory in 2002, there have been countless instances of popular participation over every imaginable issue. From labor policy, to social assistance, to urban affairs and the environment, the national government has brought citizens and civil society alike into arenas of consultation. By one figure, over a million individual Brazilians have attended a national-level participatory forum in Brasília. Despite ignoring many of the claims formulated by social movements and organized civil society, including the creation of a national participatory budget, the Lula administration created twenty-five national new councils for citizen dialogue and revived several of the existing ones. It promoted countless public hearings, workshops and forums, and national conferences, making it difficult to overestimate the sheer institutional investment in this participation. Multiplied by local instances—nearly all cities have at least some functioning councils on various areas of service provision—a conservative guess would be that tens of millions of Brazilians have participated in some forum or another to debate their government policies.

Over the first eight years, the national administration held conferences on forty different themes, twenty-eight of which were new, including, for instance, conferences on the rights of the elderly, on cities, on the youth, on culture, on the environment, on lesbian, gay, bisexual, transvestite, transsexual (LGBTT) concerns. The best estimates assess that conferences mobilized at least 5 million participants, leading to more than 14,000 proposals and 1,100 motions. And these figures do not include myriad local efforts. Throughout the 2000s, municipalities created thousands of municipal councils to discuss various topics, and it became commonplace for cities to develop participatory master plans and participatory municipal constitutions, as well as to involve citizens in all aspects of governance. Scholars have come to the conclusion that participation became central to the legal language of the Brazilian state (Gurza Lavalle 2011).

And the administration has also certainly maintained a proximity to social movements. One striking difference between the Lula government and its predecessors was the sheer number of social movement activists in the administration, many of whom created new ministries and departments. In a survey that analyzed the origin of political appointments in the federal administration, some 45 percent belonged to labor movements and 46 percent to social movements, well above the national average (D'Araújo 2007, 44). But the administration also continued to dialogue with organized social movements through various ministries.

Despite the fact that these activists brought significant experience in participatory institutions and that there has been a commitment to participation, under the federal administration this participation has been largely divorced from decision making. The government's ability to "listen" to social movements—a much less demanding form of participation compared with earlier periods—was the way the government handled the tension between its historical links with social movements and the political compromises that characterized the national PT administration. So, as the PT abandoned its earlier understandings of what participation means, it gave way to a new model of governance based on congressional compromise and consultative practices of "listening" and "dialogue."

Thus, while social movement activists have never had so much access to government as they do now, a common refrain is that there is a lot of listening but little else, especially over issues that conflict with powerful interests. A long-awaited land reform push has been stalled; on environmental problems, the government has sided with business; on urban issues, land developers have prevailed over popular sentiment; the now-famous cash transfer program, Bolsa Família, ignored the voices of progressive antihunger activists; slum clearings under the banner of beautification for the World Cup and Olympics were never up for debate, nor was the government's apparent embrace of a dictatorship-era security apparatus. Generally speaking, there is very little meaningful participation in the economic decisions of the country or on issues of infrastructure. Participatory channels largely focus on social policies and their implementation. Transportation, for example (precisely the target of demonstrations), is not discussed in any institutional body. Some of the energy in the streets no doubt has to do with disappointment and the growing recognition that the PT, for a parcel of the population, is ultimately not that different from other political parties.

A second element is that there is a large number of people in Brazil today little moved by PT's cultural politics, its leftist discourse, or even the idea of

social movements as they function. This is especially true of a younger generation of people who did not experience the transition to democracy. For some
of the people on the streets, large, organized social movements in Brazil are
too close to the government. There is today a large gap between organized
sectors involved with the channels of the federal government dialogue and
a large uninvolved population. In the last decade, the number of university
students doubled, but most have not joined the student movement; 1.2 million low-income families now have homes but have not joined neighborhood
associations; 22 million people have joined the labor market, but the numbers
of members of unions have not increased (Pochman 2014).

And many of them feel that they have been excluded from Brazil's recent
economic development. For every significant social advance under PT—such
as ambitious affirmative action reforms—there are equally damning retreats:
today elementary public education is in shambles, and urban inequality remains extreme. Brazil's rapid development over the last several years has been a
contradictory path in which the wealthy have done extremely well while many
others groups have not. Many analysts attribute the protests to the depletion of
Brazil's model of urbanization—the lack of quality of public services and urban
rights, the lack of public spaces, the limits of consumer-based citizenship—
always reminding us that the spark for these protests was police repression
and lack of responsiveness from all levels of government. Others point to the
depletion of traditional forms of social organization. For those left behind, it
is too much to be asked to accept postponing their aspirations in the name of
an elusive and abstract progressive ideal, especially while others around them
have benefited so much.

THE CONSERVATIVE WAVE?

Finally, another uncontained element that finds little expression within participatory forums or organized movements is a political conservatism that
appeared in the protests of 2013 and continues to manifest itself. During the
June protests, a variety of conservative causes were mobilized, such as "pro-
family"/antigay causes, vague patriotic causes, and calls to lower the legal age
for criminal punishment, albeit in isolated instances. More common during
the June protests was a diffuse, "anti-political party" and anticorruption sentiment, which was taken by the mainstream media to mean anti-PT. Nonetheless, political conservatives, aided and abetted by the mainstream media, took
the protests as legitimating their various causes.

The period after the protests in Brazil has been one in which the political
discourse has clearly taken a turn. Middle-class resentment against the broader

political project of the Workers' Party has been openly expressed. Hostility against affirmative action, against the masses of the poor in the northeast who rely on income assistance (and who are thought to provide a voting block for the party), and against the "political correctness" the party stands for have now all come to the fore in unprecedented ways. This hostility has been most present in social media, but increasingly also in the mainstream media and by some politicians who have adopted shock-jock styles of presentation.

And although Dilma Rousseff of the Workers' Party was reelected, the elections of 2014 were disastrous from the point of view of the Left and of confidence in electoral democracy. While nearly 30 percent of voters cast blank ballots, less than 2 percent voted in parties to the left of the PT. And the Congress elected was whiter, richer, more Christian-fundamentalist, more law-and-order, and more sexist and homophobic than before, and is the most conservative Congress since 1964, according to analysts. There is now a sizeable "law-and-order" caucus in Congress, as well as a sizeable Christian-fundamentalist caucus, which opposes gay rights, and a very large rural caucus, which has tended to oppose land reform and indigenous rights. There were specific anti-PT mobilizations throughout the electoral campaign. But it was after the electoral victory of Dilma Rousseff that mobilizations became more organized, beginning the calls for impeachment that would eventually succeed in removing Dilma from office in 2016.

Political Reform

When Dilma Rousseff proposed a referendum on political reform, she was speaking to an issue for protesters, and one that had been stalled in Congress for many years. The point of view of the federal government seemed to be that the demonstrations signaled a huge democratic deficit, in which politicians lacked legitimacy and the population did not feel heard or respected. Rousseff's move for a referendum, and an attempt to circumvent the prerogative of Congress to call referendums, failed. Disappointment mounted among activists and alarm among analysts, who had been warning about the low quality of Brazilian democratic institutions for some time. Gabriel Cohn (2013) warned, in an interview, that Brazilians were creating a system of "perverse selection": "the more you say that politicians are worthless . . . the more you scare those who have democratic attitudes and democratic beliefs. This discourages them from the political game. You destroy the basic institutions from the inside." Marcos Nobre (2013) assumed there were two possible consequences of the demonstrations. One would be a radical reform of the political system to accommodate demands, and the other would be an ever more closed political system based on "low-intensity democracy."

The public debate on political reform of course predates the protests of 2013. In July 2004, in São Paulo, a group of organizations set up a seminar on "the meanings of democracy and participation" to evaluate, sixteen years after the Constitution of 1988, the state of the country's democracy. Participants were anxious to make sense of what the Lula government was proposing in terms of participation and democracy. After extensive discussions, a consensus emerged around the idea of political reform, understood in a broad sense, as well as around a set of specific demands about institutional reforms. The demands included not only the reform of the electoral system, but also a series of tweaks to representative democracy, trying to address decision making in society as a whole.

This whole process generated a unifying platform relying on several pillars: the strengthening of mechanisms of direct democracy (such as plebiscites), the strengthening of participatory/deliberative democracy, the improvement of representative democracy, the democratization of information and communication, and the democratization of a more transparent judiciary. Within this broad platform, there were specific proposals such as the importance of protecting public campaign financing, and closed-list elections with gender quotas. Since the beginning, activists had pursued two strategies: to mobilize society in discussion around these themes and to provoke debate in Congress. The campaign produced materials: radio and video programs, pamphlets, newspaper articles, and public debates organized all over Brazil.

After the June 2013 protests, the movement for political reform was re-energized. In November, a National Campaign for a Popular Plebiscite for a New Political System was launched. Over seventy civil society organizations and social movements signed on to an ambitious proposal for mobilization that succeeded in raising nearly 8 million signatures in September 2014. The call for reforms points to several deficiencies in Brazilian democracy: private businesses accounted for 95 percent of campaign spending in the last election; women and people of color are severely underrepresented. However, the Popular Plebiscite faced an insurmountable legal hurdle. As per Brazilian law, for plebiscites to have legal standing, they need to be called by Congress.

The need for political reform is widely shared by ordinary Brazilians who feel that their political system does not represent them. The call for reform has, for several years, oscillated between social movements and progressive members of the Workers' Party in congress and senate. But since the June protests, it has become part of a national conversation about the future of the country. What is unique now, perhaps for the first time since the country's transition to democracy, is the recognition on the part of social movements that their assumed partner in the institutions, the PT, is unable or unwilling to channel those demands.

Conclusions: Back to Street Politics?

The legacy of the protests of June 2013 in Brazil is certainly contradictory. The weeks and months after it have seen bolder and bolder expressions of a kind of conservatism that can only signal regressions in important arenas, such as indigenous rights and affirmative action. But on the other hand, some movements have been energized. The protests decisively showed that contestatory street politics can have results in ways that participatory forums and traditional democratic mechanisms cannot. As Pablo Ortellado (2013) notes, one of the greatest legacies of the demonstrations was the successful combination of clear demands and effective strategies. In fact, one of the most important legacies of the June protests was that protests in the street were actually successful in reducing bus fares almost immediately in all large Brazilian cities while bringing the idea of the "free-pass" to the middle of the political debate.

These victories were achieved, ultimately, by collective actors who remained entirely autonomous from the government. This had already existed since the country's transition to democracy, but the new element was the combination of horizontal and countercultural politics of movements with a mature sense of strategy. Since the protests, the country has seen many other mobilizations, this time from organized sectors—the landless movement, the homeless movement, the civil servant unions—which have all found renewed energy for protests and strikes. The protests showed the limits of the PT, which for many years has been seen as the only legitimate interlocutor and representative of social movements. Not only did the protests expose the limits of participatory mechanisms, but they have brought to the fore a generation of people little connected to traditional social movements, unions, or the party itself.

A final legacy has been the renewal in interest in political reform, and it is against this background that the movement for political reform continues to build momentum. The reactions of the most conservative sectors in Congress and the mainstream media have been negative, questioning the legitimacy of organized sectors to propose changes in the electoral system. We cannot predict the future, whether or not there will be broad support for political reform, much less which elements will be implemented. It is possible that conservative sectors hijack the platform so that implemented reforms do not really change anything in the existing status quo. It would not be the first time that such a thing happened in Brazil.

But we may wonder whether political reforms are enough. The proposed changes are certainly important and meaningful. It is undeniably critical to curb the influence of economic power over the electoral process, as well as to introduce mechanisms to improve access to the electoral system. But the demonstrations also lead us to reflect on other absences. Is what is missing in Brazil more participation, more debate, more voices in decision making? Does Brazil have a deficit of the Civil Society Agenda? Or is it missing something else: political projects proposing new forms of life, forms of politics beyond pragmatic compromise, and forms of struggle that evoke different utopias?

NOTES

1. The Free Fare Movement advocates the adoption of free fares in mass transit. The movement was founded in a session during the World Social Forum in 2005, in Porto Alegre, and gained prominence for its participation in the planning of the 2013 Brazilian protests.

2. The estimate comes from the Food and Agriculture Organization of the United Nations' State of Food Insecurity Report of 2014 (FAO 2014). It also notes that poverty was reduced by 65 percent in the period.

3. This has provided fodder for a number of interesting debates about the Left and Latin America's future, with the PT model being most often contrasted, favorably or unfavorably, with the Bolivarian proposals of the late Hugo Chávez. These debates turn on the prominence of market rule and the role of redistributive policies. Defenders of the current Brazilian path point to a number of its most impressive achievements: a stark reduction in poverty, newfound social mobility for the lower middle class, a doubling of the number of university students, and seemingly unstoppable economic growth.

4. There has been lively debate about how to make sense of Brazil's Center-Left project under the PT. Some of the debate is captured in Anderson (2011), Morais and Saad-Filho (2007), and Singer (2012). There are a number of additional useful, specific analyses of different aspects of national PT rule, including foreign policy (Cervo 2010) and the party itself (Hunter 2010; Samuels 2006). For more general discussions on the so-called Pink Tide of Latin America, of which Brazil's Lula is only one example, see Weyland, Madrid, and Hunter (2010).

Chapter 15

MONUMENTS OF (DE) COLONIZATION

Violence, Democracy, and Gray Zones
in Bolivia after January 11, 2007

JOSÉ ANTONIO LUCERO

Because decolonization comes in many shapes, reason wavers and
abstains from declaring what is true decolonization and what is not.
—Frantz Fanon, *The Wretched of the Earth*

Bolivia can either be a South Africa or a Zimbabwe—it's still in the balance.
—Thomas Shannon, U.S. State Department

Bolivia is one of the most contentious societies in the Americas. While it has avoided the *civil* wars (a strange term indeed) that have plagued countries such as Guatemala, Colombia, and Peru, Bolivia has had more than its share of civil and uncivil contention from the colonial period up to the present. As René Zavaleta ([1977] 1988, 81) once observed, all of the country's "centuries are marked by uprisings or rebellions, it is as if Bolivia were nothing but that which had been built between the walls of defensive barricades erected against a territory populated by the Indian masses (*la indiada*)." Yet, with the historic election of Evo Morales in 2005, arguably the first president of Bolivia to come from Indigenous and popular origins,[1] those "Indian masses" are no longer outside the barricades of dominant power. Riding a wave of popular, anti-neoliberal mobilizations (the Water, Tax, and Gas "Wars" that took place between 2000 and 2005), Evo, as he is universally known in Bolivia, and his Movement toward Socialism (Movimiento al Socialismo, or MAS) party have moved boldly in areas such as the "nationalization" of hydrocarbon revenues and in the elaboration of a new Constitution, both of which were described as being part of a broad project of "decolonization" (Hylton and Thomson 2007). Nevertheless, this project has not been without its share of conflicts. Indeed, Roberto Laserna and Miguel Villarroel (2008) note that compared with thirteen political conjunctures in Bolivia since 1970, the Evo Morales period is the third-most conflictive, coming just behind the rocky return of civilian rule and rise of hyperinflation (under the presidency of Hernán Siles, 1982–85) and the conflictual "second gas war" (Carlos Mesa, 2003–5). Since Evo's election, both supporters and opponents have staged an increasing number of marches and mobilizations, several of which have involved violent confrontations (Fontana 2013; Laserna 2007; Laserna and Villarroel 2008). This chapter examines one of those conflicts, which took place on January 11, 2007, in the city of Cochabamba.

January 11 has become one of many new tragic dates on the calendar of conflicts in Bolivia. Yet unlike the days of "black October" in the Gas War of 2003 and the violent clashes in Chuquisaca (May 24, 2008) and Pando (September 11, 2008), in which the violence was often described and decried as violence against Indigenous people, "January 11" represents a more contested moment as both MAS supporters and opponents commemorate this day as a tragic day for democracy and the nation. In paradoxical but instructive mirror-image moves, people from both pro- and anti-Morales sides point to the deaths suffered on that day as proof of the hostile intention of the other side and of the crisis of Bolivian democracy. The deaths of an Indigenous *cocalero* from the countryside and a mestizo youth from the city have subsequently been the subject of public contestations over the meanings of democracy, race, and citizenship in Cochabamba and Bolivia.[2] This chapter does not examine the causes of this conflict nor test any explanations for it. Rather, it contextualizes this conflict within a broader process of social change and examines the public transcripts of contention provided by monuments, mobilizations, and other public political performances used by pro- and antigovernment forces. Situating both the physical and interpretive struggles in Cochabamba within the larger divides in contemporary Bolivia, I suggest some lessons about decolonization and the gray zone between civil and uncivil contention in the Andes. Before entering into the Bolivian empirical context, the first section of this chapter provides a theoretical frame within which to evaluate the different commemorations of the violence by each of the opposing sides and their implications for the projects of decolonization and democratization. Drawing on the work of Frantz Fanon, I suggest that the commemoration of "January 11" has taken place in ways that reinforce rather than challenge the colonial order of things in Bolivia. While we should be cautious in not attributing too much to one particular event, these dynamics are not encouraging signs for the process of decolonizing democracy in Bolivia.

Framing Decolonization and Democratization

My use of terms such as *coloniality*, *(neo)colonial*, and *decolonization* in this chapter may strike some as unwise. Scholars such as Frederick Cooper (2005) see terms like *coloniality* as hopelessly reductive, ahistorical, and generic. In Cooper's view, coloniality, as it has been used by Aníbal Quijano (2000), Walter Mignolo (2000), and others, is a concept that "plucks" an essence of colonialism out of time and space, homogenizing the complex, actually existing workings of colonialism and decolonization in Africa, Asia, and the Americas. Although I take these objections and the concern for conceptual clarity seriously, I insist on these terms for two reasons. First, while Latin America is not "stuck" in some static past, it is important to call attention to the remarkable persistence of certain patterns of racialized exclusion and inequality that have an unmistakably colonial feel to them, patterns that have been sorely neglected by many students of democracy in Latin America. Second, in using the term *decolonization*, I do not envision any romanticized, return to precolonial times, but rather emphasize the process of resisting modes of domination that assign specific categories of people to particular positions in political economies. Thus, "decolonization, in Fanon's sense, does not prematurely signify the end of colonialism but refers to the multifaceted, ongoing project of resistance struggles that can persist . . . in the midst of simultaneous neocolonial exploitation" (Lowe 1996, 106). Accordingly, this chapter is concerned with situating a particular struggle in Cochabamba, Bolivia, and exploring if and how it fits within the dynamics that reproduce or disrupt the rigid categorical inequalities that have long been at the heart of coloniality in Bolivia. Although Bolivia's 1952 revolution offered the promise of inclusion, Indigenous people have continued to suffer economic and political marginalization. A quick numerical snapshot of that exclusion may be helpful. As the following World Bank figures show (tables 15.1 and 15.2), Indigenous people continue to be among the most disadvantaged members of society (Hall and Patrino 2006). Additionally, a United Nations Devel-

TABLE 15.1. Changes in poverty rates of Indigenous and non-Indigenous people over the 1990s: Percent change in headcount poverty rate between earliest and latest survey year

Country	Non-Indigenous	Indigenous
Bolivia (1997–2002)	8	Change of less than 0.1
Ecuador (1994–2003)	14	Change of less than 0.1
Guatemala (1989–2000)	25	-1.5
Mexico (1992–2002)	5	Change of less than 0.1
Peru (1994–2000)	3	Change of less than 0.1

Source: Hall and Patrinos 2006.

TABLE 15.2. Being Indigenous and the probability of being poor, controlling for other common predictors of poverty: Percent increase in probability of being poor, if Indigenous

Country	Early 1990s	Latest Available Year
Bolivia	16	13
Ecuador	—	16
Guatemala	11	14
Mexico	25	30
Peru	—	11

Note: Data are the marginal effects of an Indigenous indicator in a logit regression that estimates the percent by which an individual's likelihood of being poor increases as a result of being Indigenous, controlling for other factors, including age, household composition, region, employment status, and education level. These estimates were not generated for Ecuador or Peru in 1994.

Source: Hall and Patrinos 2006.

opment Programme (UNDP) study from 2004 found that opinions about Indigenous people tend to become much more negative among certain sectors of Bolivian society. In response to a question about how comfortable a respondent would feel having an Aymara or Quechua business partner, the pattern of discomfort was predictable: higher in cities, higher in the eastern lowlands, and higher among the upper-middle class (PNUD 2004).

Like many societies in the Americas, these statistical trends are experienced in everyday ways. In every major city, the geographies of privilege and exclusion are well known. For example, Zona Sur (elite) and El Alto (popular) in La Paz could hardly be more different racially or socioeconomically. Nationally, Andean (*qolla*) La Paz and lowland (*camba*) Santa Cruz are seen as the centers of the "two Bolivias," while the valleys of Cochabamba have had a reputation of being the intermediate terrain of *mestizaje* and thus held the promise of a national synthesis. National and local spatial and racial orders call to mind the famous "Manichaean" division that Frantz Fanon describes in *The Wretched of the Earth* as the very hallmark of colonialism. Thus, it is perhaps no surprise that Fanon offers some guidance in thinking through the challenges of decolonization in the Andes. Yet, it is not the production of some kind of ideal type of a colonial situation that makes Fanon a useful guide, but rather two specific elements of his thought that allow us to understand the challenges of disrupting colonial patterns.

First, there is Fanon's emphasis on the lived experience of colonialism,[3] which he explored through his work as a practicing psychiatrist and as a phenomenologically attuned social theorist. The psychological and physiological manifestations of colonialism—the work on minds and bodies of both colonizers and colonized—help remind us that colonialism is not only a structure of domination, but to borrow Raymond William's (1978) famous expression also a structure of feeling.

Second, though Fanon's analysis of colonialism often gets reduced to a discussion of Manichaean divisions and the importance of violence, more important to Fanon's approach is what Ato Sekyi-Otu (1996) calls the "dialectic of experience." The spatial Manichaeism that Fanon identifies as an important part of the colonial order of things is also meant to call attention to a thinking that keeps people and things in "their" place. Decolonization must thus be an attempt to challenge this very kind of ordering. In addressing what Fanon called "this narrow world strewn with prohibitions," Sekyi-Otu suggests that Fanon is not simply invoking the social and spatial apartheid of the colonial world, but rather, "he is speaking more profoundly of the brutally narrowed compass and categories of our moral and political arguments, reasoning, and imagination, from the moment the salient and defining feature of our being becomes our ascribed racial identity and membership" (2003, 7). Fanon's well-known ambivalence regarding negritude reflects just such a concern, the worry that for liberation struggles, the tendency to "racialize claims . . . leads African intellectuals into a dead end" (Fanon [1963] 2003, 153). Thus Fanon's advice is to avoid the reinscription of old colonial identities, and instead to search for what Nigel Gibson (1999, 419) calls opportunities "for radically new behaviour in both public and private life, a chance for cultural regeneration and creation where positive concepts of self-determination, not contingent upon the colonial status quo, are generated." In *A Dying Colonialism*, Fanon writes about one such dialectical possibility when speaking of the relationship that can emerge between outside doctors (like himself) and local peoples. After "living the drama of the people, the Algerian doctor became a part of the Algerian body. There was no longer that reticence, so constant during the period of unchallenged oppression. He was no longer 'the' doctor, but 'our' doctor" (Fanon 1965, 142).

Although often overlooked by theorists of democracy, colonial legacies and decolonizing strategies are of great importance. While minimalist, procedural definitions of democracy have long-held dominance in political science, many recent studies have noted that without understanding the political and sociological landscapes on which new political institutions are constructed, we are ill equipped to understand why democratic experiences in Latin America have often remained thin and fragile. These "proceduralist" approaches miss a central reality of many democracies in the region: a colonialist distribution of power that serves to reinforce "categorical inequalities" based on race, and reproduce forms of "decentralized despotism" in which local (and transnational) elites dominate formal and extraformal institutions (Mamdani 1996; Tilly 1999, 2004). While such dynamics are not confined to the Andes,[4] this region provides a particularly good setting to examine the persistence of neocolonial racial orders and the emergence of challenges to those orders. Guillermo O'Donnell (1993) issued an influential call to rethink studies of democratization through his metaphorical cartography of the Latin American state in which "brown areas" were those regions characterized by a very weak presence of the state understood as a set of political, bureaucratic, and legal institutions. Students of Indigenous politics in Latin America have echoed O'Donnell's argument by noting that in many parts of rural Latin America, Indigenous people find the state to be, in a popular saying, *lejano y ajeno* (distant and foreign). Thus while Indigenous communities were often excluded from national political communities, they were able to create, over time, networks of organizations and alliances that allowed them to become powerful actors in the 1990s, challenging the exclusionary and colonialist nature of neoliberal democracies (see, e.g., Van Cott 2005; Yashar 2005). Yet, these movements have also generated countermovements, as non-Indigenous sectors have not been passive in the face of challenges to their sources of privilege. This is of course not a new phenomenon, as the struggles between pro- and anti-Indigenous forces, between national power and local power, are familiar parts of the long drama of state formation. What scholars wrote about Bolivia in the 1940s could describe the aspirations of anti-Morales regional elites: "local and regional 'states' . . . undermined every centralizing and pro-Indigenous effort by the national 'state'" (Dandler and Torrico 1987, 360–61). In order to understand the clash between pro- and anti-Indigenous efforts in contemporary Cochabamba, it is important to briefly describe the tension that exists between the Andean and lowland elements of Bolivia.

Bolivia Divided

Winning a historic mandate, Evo Morales and his MAS Party promised nothing less than the "refounding" of Bolivia and began work on a long and conflict-ridden path toward a new constitutional order. In this refoundational project, as Gustafson (2010) notes, the lines of conflict were clearly drawn. On one side were the MAS and the social movements, on the other were the lowland political elites and "civic committees." In this showdown between "socials" and "civics" (borrowing Gustafson's [2010] shorthand), two important issues of contention regarded the procedures used to guide the decision making of the Constituent Assembly, the body that would (and did) draft the Constitution of 2009 and the scope and content of new autonomy provisions. Procedurally, the conflict between socials and civics was about whether a simple majority (50 percent +1) or a two-thirds majority would be required to approve the new constitutional text. The MAS had a majority, but was shy of a two-thirds majority in the assembly, and thus preferred a simple majority. The lowland civics, not surprisingly, demanded two-thirds majority rules, in order to avoid being totally shut out. In rallies throughout the country, the fraction "2/3" became a ubiquitous symbol of anti-Morales anger, expressed on T-shirts, signs, hats, and even painted on bodies.

The debate over autonomy reflected differences over how autonomy would be defined. The civics supported city-based "regional autonomy" that would give the departmental governors (or prefects) and the departmental elites considerable control over resource wealth found in the departments as well as considerable administrative and juridical power. The MAS and social movement vision about autonomy was of a different scale. Rather than endorsing or enhancing the regional distribution of wealth, the MAS promised to work for Indigenous and local autonomies that would give Indigenous people an increased voice and influence over the extraction and distribution of resource wealth.[5] Although President Morales suggested that autonomy regimes could function on various levels, each side accused the other of dividing and weakening the country. In one memorable march I saw in 2007 in La Paz, a group of older Quechua and Aymara workers loudly expressed their opposition to the Santa Cruz–style of autonomy with the following chant (that was not without its contradictions): "¡Muera Santa Cruz! ¡Que viva la unidad nacional!" (Death to Santa Cruz!

Long Live National Unity!). For the marchers, perhaps, there was no contradiction, as the autonomy idea of the civics was seen as nothing less than antinational, as seeking to create a greater distance between Cruceño identities and Andean-Indigenous ones. Common slogans (on bumper stickers and T-shirts) in Cochabamba reinforce this view: "Autonomy: Yes or Yes!" and "Santa Cruz Owes Nothing to Bolivia" (cited in Gustafson 2010).

These divisions have been performed frequently throughout the country, in parades, marches, and large gatherings (*cabildos*), and especially through the actions of new "youth" organizations (like the Cruceño Youth Union [Unión Juvenil Cruceñista, or UJC]). These performances have also spread through the Internet in dizzying arrays of video documentaries, musical videos, and blogs. While these divisions have become part and parcel of Bolivian popular cultures, they are also reflected in the official workings of electoral politics. In 2005, Evo Morales was not the only new official elected into office. For the first time, *prefectos* (or departmental governors) were also elected by popular vote (previously, they had been appointed by the president). Rubén Costas, a vocal supporter of the Cruceño autonomist project, became the first elected prefect of Santa Cruz. Meanwhile, in the department of Cochabamba, a former mayor of the city of Cochabamba and long-time rival of Evo Morales, Manfred Reyes Villa, was elected prefect. While Evo Morales won an important and a historic victory in reaching the presidency, given the new procedure for electing regional leaders, the presidential office was a weaker one than it had been for previous heads of state. Morales also found himself with a ready-made group of opponents in the regional leaders of the *media luna* region, and those enemies had an ally in Evo's own home base of support, Cochabamba, as Reyes Villa was in power and a vocal supporter of autonomy.

The events of January 11, 2007, then, were a product of these larger national conflicts. As Reyes Villa continued his campaign for autonomy (even after 65 percent of Cochabambinos rejected autonomy in a departmental referendum), the social movements began to call for Reyes Villa's ouster. As rural Cochabamba is the heart of the cocalero movement that launched Evo to national prominence, it was relatively easy to mobilize a large number of cocaleros, campesinos, and MAS supporters. They came to the city and began to ask for Reyes Villa's resignation. Marches and blockades led to confrontation between social movement organizations and the police. After one confrontation, fire was set to the departmental government building and efforts at dialogue quickly led nowhere. As Reyes Villa and Evo Morales showed little interest in compromise, anger and frustration rose within the city and the conflict now became one between *ciudadanos* (city dwellers, but also "citizens") and *campesinos* (literally, people of the countryside, but also Indigenous peasants). Young men from the city, a group called Youth for Democracy (Jóvenes por la Democracia, or JPD), were among the main protagonists in "defending their city" from the invasion of cocaleros and campesinos. Wielding baseball bats, improvised shields made of plywood, and (according to some versions of events) golf clubs, the JPD crossed police barricades and clashed with campesinos. Although many campesinos were unarmed, some had sticks and machetes and the violence raged across the city. By the end of the fighting over 200 were injured, and three people were dead.[6] January 11 (11 de enero or 11/E) has entered into the lexicon of both pro- and anti-Morales sectors as evidence of what is wrong with Bolivia. Yet, exactly what is wrong with Bolivia is the subject of extraordinary debate.

Who is to blame for the violence? What does it mean for the nation? Who are citizens in Bolivia? These questions and more are subsequently interpreted, debated, and memorialized throughout the public spaces of the city. In graffiti, signs, improvised monuments, masses, and funerals, Cochabamba became in the days after this confrontation a particular kind of "lettered city," as different factions used city walls and spaces as a canvas for expressing anxieties, fears, hatred, and political views. Family members of the fallen agree that Bolivia is divided, but disagree as to why. "We are divided," says Octavio Tica Colque. "It's the racists' fault." Christian Urresti's father tells a reporter, "We have never been so divided. It's the government's fault" (quoted in Llana 2007). The divisions at work in the description of the violence were multiple: between "socials" and "civics," *qollas* and *cambas*,[7] country and city, rich and poor, order and disorder. Let us turn to some of those "public transcripts" to see how some of these lines are being drawn and redrawn.

A Civic Death: Mourning Christian Urresti

As the dust settled after days of mounting tension and then explosive violence, people began to mourn the dead. Most of the media attention was given to the death of Christian Urresti, the seventeen-year-old *cívico* who died in the violent clashes, reportedly killed by machete and strangling, on the street corner of Mayor Rocha and Baptista, a few blocks from the main plaza. Urresti's mother asked for privacy. She told one reporter that "we are not like campesinos" who parade their dead.[8] Her calls for privacy notwithstanding, the site of Christian's death (the corner of the streets Baptista and Mayor Rocha) became almost instantly a shrine for the cause of the cívicos (see photograph in figure 15.1), and a space to challenge the government.

Figure 15.1

A shrine for Christian Urresti. Photo by José Antonio Lucero.

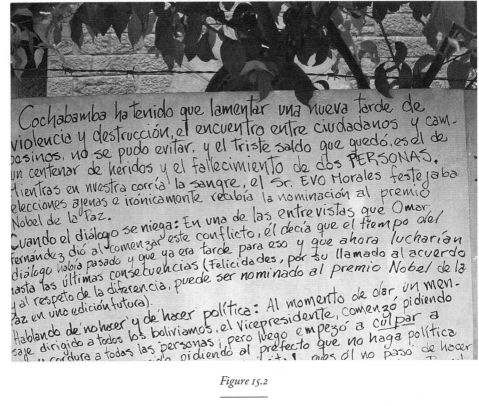

Figure 15.2

Detail of protest poster at improvised Urresti Shrine. Photo by José Antonio Lucero.

One home-made poster made the claim that Morales's Bolivia was worse than Nazi Germany. Some left long letters of thanks to Christian and exclamations of rage at the invasion of the "campesinos" who came into "our" city looking for violence. Many texts around the shrine conveyed the idea that the new policies of Evo Morales had led to this kind of violence; in one view (figure 15.2) "the clash between *campesinos y ciudadanos* was unavoidable" [el encuentro entre campesinos y ciudadanos no se pudo evitar]. Here I do not evaluate the claim of the inevitability of the conflict, but instead argue that these kinds of discourses are themselves indications of the tense racial relations in Bolivia today. It is worth quoting this comment in a bit more detail: "Cochabamba has had to face a new evening of violence and destruction, the clash between *ciudadanos* and *campesinos* was unavoidable, and the tragic balance it left was hundreds wounded two dead. While in our [city] blood was being shed, Mr. Morales was celebrating foreign elections [attending the

Figure 15.3

Comparing violence. Photo by José Antonio Lucero.

inauguration in Nicaragua] and ironically being nominated for the Nobel Peace Prize."

The text continues its indictment of Morales by mocking his announcement asking the social movements for restraint and patience:

> "I hope they will listen to me" is one of the messages of Morales. He said that Indigenous people were not vengeful, not violent (then why did they enter the city with sticks, slings and machetes?) Then he blamed others. Then he asked "he hoped" that the "social movements" would listen. As he is the leader of the Six [Cocalero] Federations of the Tropics, shouldn't they listen to their leader? Isn't it true that this violence could have been avoided? We hope that our leaders put their hands over their hearts and seek justice so that these lamentable and painful acts that hurt so many Bolivians are never repeated. May God enlighten our leader! Long live a free and united Bolivia!

This is a telling comment for many reasons. Not only does it hint at the large social and political pressure at work that transformed a political conflict between Evo and Manfred into a violent clash between Cochabambinos from town and city, but it also reveals the fractured citizenship of contemporary Bolivia so that *ciudadanos* (citizens/"city people") are placed in opposition to campesinos (as noncitizens/rural people). Morales is doubly criticized for being out of the country during this crisis and for being not a president of all Bolivians but rather the leader (and an ineffectual one at that) of the cocalero federations.

Not all the statements show the kind of restrained rage that this one seems to suggest. Some decry the death of Christian Urresti at the hands of "blood-thirsty beasts" who killed this young man in the middle of the street. Others make more hyperbolic claims, putting Evo's Bolivia in the same category as "Cuba, Iraq, Nazi Germany, Albania and the Balkans" (figure 15.3).

Yet they all converge in depicting the fallen cívico as a martyr, an interpretation that is further encouraged by the fact that at this shrine, the site of Urresti's death, is also the location of "Our Savior" Methodist Church (figure 15.4).

A few months later, after rain and wind had swept away most of these ephemeral messages of sadness and rage, a more permanent plaque was placed at this site. It reads:

> with profound gratitude to the noble
> neighbors and citizens of cochabamaba
> in the name of
> christian d urresti ferrel
> 1989–2007
> assasinated defending his city

This language has colonial echoes. *Vecinos*, the word for neighbor, during colonial times described the Spanish-descended population who lived apart from the *indios*. And Christian was memorialized for nothing less than defending "his" city from invading Indians from the countryside. A Benjaminian reading of the monument is not difficult to find: this document of Cochabambino civilization is also a monument of Cochabambino barbarism.[9] This space tells passersby that Urresti gave his life for his city and for democracy. It is a "civic" death par excellence. To return to the helpful genealogical discussion of "civil" society in this volume's introduction, this monument usefully reminds us that the "civil" of civil society can never be completely separated from the civilizing missions of colonialisms, old and new.

Figure 15.4

Civic and religious martyrdom. Photo by José Antonio Lucero.

Mourning Cocaleros

The monument making for the cocalero and campesino sectors, unsurprisingly, is very different. Choosing the Plaza de las Banderas (one of the concentrations of the protests against Manfred Reyes Villa) as the site of a memorial, social movement organizations began to erect their own monument to the fallen. As opposed to the multivocality of the Urresti shrine, where many have left their individual messages of sadness and anger, this site contains only one, with these words (as the image in figure 15.5 illustrates):

> homage to the
> fallen of 11 january 2007 and
> the 514 years of resistance of the indigenous people of
> abya yala

Figure 15.5

Cocalero monument for the fallen. Photo by José Antonio Lucero.

Instantly, differences with the Urresti monument become apparent. As opposed to the heroic individuals of the mestizo martyr, there are no individual names on this monument. The names of the fallen cocaleros Juan Tica Colque and Luciano Colque are nowhere to be seen. In their place one finds a collective subject and a historic struggle. The fallen here are placed within the frame of Indigenous resistance and anticolonialism. While this location is not heavy with the Christian religious symbolism of Urresti's monument, it does connect with Andean spirituality by choosing the Chakana, or the "Andean cross," as the main centerpiece for the monument. The construction and inauguration of the monument brought many social movement organizations (mostly from the city, but also from the countryside) together.

Controversy over the monument was inevitable. For many, like the very "invasion" of campesinos on January 11, this too was a sign of things out of place. One official suggested that proper paperwork was never filed for the building of such a monument in a public space and that it therefore had to be taken down. Once again there was a debate about the "proper" place of indigeneity in the city, a colonial legacy that is particularly tenacious in Bolivia. Yet, the decision was made by the city to let the monuments—by the civics and the socials—stand.

Despite that decision, just over six months after this monument went up, vandals tore it down, twice (Shultz 2008). The first time the monument was destroyed, the Chakana was removed from the site, prompting some social movement activists to distribute a mock "Wanted" sign via the Internet.[10] It reads:

WANTED
the chakana in honor of our dead was stolen
last monday early in the morning
—the chakana is red and 90 cm in size
—it is believed that the thief is an "hijito de papi" and
militant in youth for democracy
—if the racist mercenary is found he will be submitted to community
   justice so it better be returned
—a reward will be provided

More than a "lost" notice, this sign takes the form of a "wanted" poster, making mention of the vandals who were probably wealthy (hijitos de papi) and probably members of the Youth for Democracy. While the Chakana was never found, the monument, with its (defaced) message about the resistance of Indigenous people, was put back in its place. It stands as an emblematic reminder of the difficulties of decolonizing democracy in Bolivia.

A year after the violence in Cochabamba, members of various campesino, cocalero, and other social movement organizations gathered at the site of their monument to remember their fallen. Their speeches once again invoked centuries of struggle against "oligarchs" and more recent conflicts against the "right" (Schultz 2008). Someone also draped these words over the monument, which like the entire city had become a palimpsest recording again and again pain and struggle:

> On the 11 of January, you hurt me because you don't know me. On the 11 of January, you attacked me because you fear me. You call me ignorant because you ignore my wisdom. You call me dirty because I work and live with the land. You feel pity or shame for me, but I am the one who feeds you. Now you fight for your own miserable interests; but I fight for survival. You have started a battle you will not win. Slowly, I rediscover my own power and deconstruct yours. With my face toward the past and my back to the future, the time of the Pachakutik is coming.[11]

These references to Andean temporality (the past in Quechua is literally that which is before us, *ñawpapacha*) and to Indigenous struggle (*pachakutik* is a revolution in time and space) make clear that this is part of a long (anti) colonial story between the Self and Other, colonizer and colonized. The battle lines are drawn and violence seems to be, as the writing around Urresti's shrine declared, "inevitable." While this may sound similar to Fanon's famous chapter "On Violence," it ignores the longer Fanonian process in which violence is only productive and decolonizing if it leads to new forms of identification, of solidarity, and, in his terms, of a new humanism. These embattled words of Cochabamba's social movements, ironically written on a precarious sheet of paper, are symbols of a Manichaean social order that shows little sign of disappearing.

Conclusion: Gray Zones and Manichaean Divides

The ongoing struggles between "socials" and "civics" in Bolivia is taking place on the well-trodden discursive borderlands of civilization and barbarism, with each side finding the other on the wrong side of the divide. As both sides couch their struggles and honor their fallen in and with the language of democracy and autonomy, one can be forgiven for not knowing on which side of the civil/uncivil divide these actors are on. That very difficulty suggests that we are in that strange middle ground that Primo Levi (1989, 23) famously called "the grey zone," not reducible "to the two blocs of victims and persecutors." While Cochabamba is a very different place than the Lager concentration camp that Levi survived and theorized, there is no doubt that conceptually these conflicts are more complex than a simple case of "us" vs. "them." Javier Auyero (2006b, 2007) has made a persuasive case for attending to those gray zones where "extraordinary" violence meets "ordinary" political practices and identities. It is hard not to think of Bolivia as full of just such spaces. Indeed, writing from Bolivia, Aymara sociologist Silvia Rivera Cusicanqui has spoken of the importance of the Aymara notion of *ch'ixi*: "[Ch'ixi] is this heather gray that comes from the imperceptible mixing of black and white, which are confused by perception, without ever being completely mixed. The notion of ch'ixi, like many others (*allqa, ayni*), reflects the Aymara idea of something that is and is not at the same time. It is the logic of the included third" (2012, 105).

Rivera Cusicanqui suggests that ch'ixi also represents a gendered, feminine logic of weaving, as seen in the Andean arts of textiles and tapestries, where differences are braided; they are neither blended nor starkly separated. Rivera Cusicanqui suggests that standing in sharp contrast to the feminine praxis of weaving is the masculinist logic of the map and (as this chapter argues) the monument—a logic that delimits, marks, fixes. The conceptual utility of these gray zones and ch'ixi notwithstanding, Manichaean divisions, when performed and objectified, are important social facts. Violence and representations of violence have important political and cultural consequences.

In Bolivia, like other parts of the Americas, violence has become so commonplace that there is an emerging subfield in the study of violence, perhaps best exemplified by the excellent work of anthropologists Daniel Goldstein (2004) and Bret Gustafson (2010). In Goldstein's work on popular lynching (coincidentally also in Cochabamba, but before the meteoric rise of Evo Morales), violence is understood as having a spectacular dimension, like carnival or folkloric festivals that can serve to make claims about inclusion in often very exclusionary societies. Gustafson's more recent work on the violence experienced by the Guaraní people and the subsequent dissemination of images of wounded Guaraní bodies serves in his analysis as part of a decolonizing strategy: "Thus what were once killable or punishable bodies subjected to violence with impunity—the Guaraní—were converted through movement practice, transnational witnessing, and government legal action into collective socio-territorial formations validated by the MAS's calls for decolonizing (pluri)nationalism" (Gustafson 2010, 62).

Vice President Álvaro García Linera has made similar arguments in his response to the claim that the government creates division: "Bolivians have lived under apartheid since the founding of the country," he said. "We didn't bring these divisions but we have brought them to light" (quoted in Ghafour 2007). Violence then has been spoken about as a decolonizing strategy to the extent that it makes colonial divisions visible and brings them to the public sphere where they can be challenged.

Is there a similar lesson here in Cochabamba? Certainly this violence has helped make divisions visible and apparent. However, the lines seem to have gotten only more stark, and the categories of contention have become more rigid. Memorials like the ones this chapter has discussed can often be ineffective at creating the kind of decolonizing dialectic that Fanon described. As Tzvetan Todorov has written, commemorating the past also means simplifying it: "The discourse of commemoration is not objective at all. While history makes the past more complicated, commemoration makes it simpler, since it seeks most often to supply us with heroes to worship or with enemies to detest; it deals in desecration and consecration" (Todorov 2000, 133).

While Morales has been credited with inaugurating the "post-multicultural" moment in Bolivia (Postero 2006), the mirror-image strategies of civic and social movements that both use and claim the causes of democracy and self-determination have created a perverse dynamic in which all sides also claim victimhood. While new rounds of contention may lead to new rounds of dialogue, as long as the identities and strategies of mobilization continue to be framed in the dichotomies of the "two Bolivias," decolonization will remain an elusive ideal and the world of Bolivian politics will continue to be, as Fanon ([1963] 2003, 37–38) warned, a "narrow world strewn with prohibitions."

Postscript

This chapter was written before another tragic confrontation between government supporters and opponents, the clash in 2011 over the government's plan to build a road through the national park known as Territorio Indígena Parque Nacional Isiboro-Sécure, or TIPNIS. Unlike January 11, 2007, though, this conflict was framed not as "white" versus "Indigenous" but as one between an Indigenous president and his cocalero supporters on one side and local, lowland Indigenous protesters on the other. This conflict has been followed by government efforts to divide the most prominent Indigenous organizations, CONAMAQ and CIDOB, and expel NGOs such as the Danish organization Ibis which have historically been supporters of independent Indigenous organizing. This is not the place to examine these developments, which have already received important critical attention (Achtenberg 2014;

Albó 2014; Postero 2015). Taken together, however, the events of 2007 and 2011 show a disheartening trend toward creating an Indigenous project "from above," one that generates new Indigenous exclusions and that makes decolonization an even more elusive goal.

NOTES

1. Andrés de Santa Cruz, a late nineteenth-century president of both Peru and Bolivia, was a much earlier "Indigenous" president. Many of his contemporaries noted that Santa Cruz, son of a female *cacique*, could trace his lineage back to the Incas. Santa Cruz seldom made reference to his Indigenous origins. Others, however, made reference to his genealogy either to glorify him as a rightful Andean ruler or to discredit him as a "barbarian" (Sobrevilla Perea 2011, 14).

2. In the immediate aftermath of the violence, media reports make mention of two deaths, one from the "cocalero-campesino" sector, Juan Tica Colque, and the other from the "civic" urban sector, Christian Urresti. Later in the month, press reports confirmed that another campesino, Luciano Colque, died from a gunshot wound received on January 11.

3. As several commentators have noted, the famous chapter in *Black Skin, White Masks* on the "fact of blackness"—"L'expérience vécue du noir," would be better translated as the "lived experience of blackness."

4. On India, see Heller (2000); on Africa, see Mamdani (1996). For Latin America more broadly, see O'Donnell (1993, 1997) and Yashar (2005).

5. What autonomy actually ended up looking like is a complex question and beyond the scope of this chapter. For very useful discussions of the tensions of autonomy, especially between MAS and local communities (as well as within local communities), see the work of Cameron (2010, 2013).

6. See the January 2007 issues of *Los Tiempos* and *La Razón* for overviews of the violence.

7. *Qolla* is the term for Andeans; *camba* has sometimes been used to refer to people from the lowlands, especially people from Santa Cruz. During this conflict in Cochabamba, the term was used by campesinos to describe the Jóvenes por la Democracia, discursively linking them with the anti-Morales youth leagues in Santa Cruz.

8. She made this statement to a local television reporter (Lucero field notes).

9. "There is no document of civilization which is not at the same time a document of barbarism" (Benjamin 1969, 256).

10. The image was originally posted on Indymedia Bolivia: http://bolivia.indymedia.org/node/253. The image is no longer online but the author retains a copy on file.

11. A photograph of this sign was originally posted on http://bolivia.indymedia.org/node/4106. It is no longer available online, but the author has a copy on file.

Chapter 16

BEYOND THE CIVIL SOCIETY AGENDA?

Participation and Practices of Governance, Governability,
and Governmentality in Latin America

SONIA E. ALVAREZ

Prescribing Civic Participation

Civil society, as we have come to know it—as a civic arena, a participatory space, a policy buzzword, a moral imperative, a theoretical concept, or all of the above—has been produced through diverse means and in contradictory ways by an array of actors and discourses in and across a variety of sites and historical moments. As the preceding chapters have shown, in Latin America it was forged at the crossroads of multiple discourses and distinct cultural-political processes. "Civil society talk" can today be heard among an array of often-antagonistic inter-governmental organizations (IGO), international financial institutions (IFI), state, nonstate, government, opposition, academic, private-sector, and social movement actors. Yet despite their differing emphases and declared distinct ends, many contemporary variations of civil society talk find resonance in their advocacy of a *strikingly uniform* political agenda, one that enjoins actors who recognize themselves and/or are viewed by others as part of civil society to "participate." The Civil Society (cs) Agenda, as analyzed in this volume, presumes that participation—especially in invited participatory spaces (Cornwall, chapter 3 in this volume), participatory institutions (PIs), or what Ernesto Isunza (2006) calls "Sociogovernmental Interfaces" (*Interfaces Socioestatais*, or ISEs) that bring together state and nonstate actors—will always enhance democracy. There is a correlate proscription often implicit in this assumption: that what we call Uncivic Activism consistently undermines it.

The cs Agenda, it is important to make clear, is not (or at least is not *just*) an imposition from above; instead, as we have seen, it is a product of what Evelina Dagnino and collaborators (2002b, 2006b) have called the "perverse confluence" of radically discordant, competing cultural and political claims among a wide range of institutional and extrainstitutional actors—including many who move frequently across state/nonstate and civic/uncivic boundaries. Given its multiple origins and diverse political trajectories, moreover, it is *an agenda that social movements can also be said to have imposed upon our/themselves.* The cs Agenda is, in short, a site in which multiple political and cultural struggles about the significance of citizen involvement in public matters are waged.

The prevailing Civil Society Agenda thus represents a complex and contradictory mix of constraints and opportunities, enabling and disabling conditions (Hale 2002). If indigenous culture, as Hale and Millamán (2006, 285) suggest, has gone "from being a *battle cry* of one side in the struggle to being the *battleground* on which both sides [neoliberal policies producing the *indio permitido*, or authorized Indian, versus the radical aims of the insurrectionary Indian] meet and fight it out, activists and intellectuals alike need new analytical resources to make sense of the challenges that lie ahead," so too civic participation has become a battlefield on which *multiple and multifaceted* sides (rather than just two distinct—neoliberal versus democratic-participatory— sides) duke it out over citizenship, democracy, social, gendered, racial, sexual, environmental justice, and the like. It is therefore imperative that we work to untangle the political and discursive threads that have fashioned the treacherous texture of the contemporary cs Agenda.

It is in the spirit of seeking new analytical resources that might facilitate such disentanglings that I critically examine civil society's projected role in three (really three and a half . . .) regimes of governmental practices: "Governability," "Governance," and "Governmentality," which I refer to as G1, G2, and G3, respectively (and C-G2, for Co-Governance, that's the half). Drawing on

TABLE 16.1. Heuristics of government and participation in 3 and ½ Gs

Effects on citizen-subjects	Technologies of rule	
	Agency	*Performance*
Subjection	**G1 Governability** Producing social peace and political stability	**G3 Governmentality** Controlling populations, disciplining the "at-risk" Neoliberal (and neodevelopmentalist?) government of the social
Subjectivation	**C-G2 Co-Governance** "Governing with social movements" Producing radical democratic subjects	**G2 Governance** Producing "social capital" and civil-ized market citizens

scholarship that builds on Michel Foucault's notion of government as the "conduct of conduct," I treat these as "the organized practices through which we are governed and through which we govern ourselves" (Dean 2010, 28). I cannot, of course, pretend to do justice to the vast literature on the origins, design, composition, implementation, inclusivity, legal framework, efficacy, and other dimensions of the wide range of ISEs found in Latin America today—much of which is, in any case, addressed in several of this volume's previous chapters. I hope, instead, to explore theoretically the differing *power effects* of civil society participation in my "3 and ½ Gs," highlighting how each might work to produce distinctive political citizen-subjects. The argument I develop is represented in table 16.1, intended merely as a heuristic device and *not* as a typology of mutually exclusive categories.

Civic Participation, Practices of Government, and Technologies of Rule

GOVERNABILITY OR G1

I turn first to Governability, my G1, a notion frequently invoked by scholars, pundits, and public authorities alike in postauthoritarian Latin America. Originally deployed in the Trilateral Commission Report of 1975, "The Crisis of Democracy," and later embraced by those seeking to secure regime solidity in posttransition contexts, the notion of Governability points to political, economic, institutional, social, constitutional, and other conditions that are deemed necessary to achieve stable, though not necessarily democratic, government. The concept retains a neo-Huntingtonian bias, that is, those who deploy it tend to be more preoccupied with promoting "democratic moderation" (Crozier, Huntington, and Watanuki 1975, 113) and securing the *stability* rather than with enhancing the *quality* of democracy.

In commonsense usage, Governability is understood simply as "the capacity to govern" (Montero Bagatella 2012), or, in more social scientific terms, "conduct[ing] society through the administrative and political structures of the State, without resorting to repressive excesses or cyclical crises" (Valdés Ugalde 2008, 96). Civil society is seldom a central variable in analyses of G1. To the extent that it is considered relevant, it is because it must be self-limiting (Cohen and Arato 1992), and must not make excessive (or "unrealistic") demands on the political system. Indeed, too much participation, particularly of the uncivic variety, can result in what the Trilateral Commission referred to as a destabilizing "excess of democracy" which, in turn, "means a deficit in governability" (Crozier, Huntington, and Watanuki 1975, 173; Cruikshank 1999; Lander 2007). As a set of practices of governing, G1 accordingly aims to moderate democratic demands; to channel citizen discontent into controlled, symbolic, and often powerless "participatory" venues; and to promote civic participation in pursuit of stability.

In the early years of the *Concertación* governments of postauthoritarian Chile, for example, elites redirected the massive popular mobilization that had surged in opposition to the Pinochet dictatorship into a variety of government-sponsored participatory venues presumably to prevent an "authoritarian involution" and thereby contribute to regime stability (Ríos Tobar, Godoy Catalán, and Guerrero Caviedes 2003; Roberts 1998). During the first post-dictatorship administrations in Chile, the government adopted a dual approach toward citizen participation: "On the one hand, the government had little use for the organizations that had mobilized against authoritarian rule. But the government also had an interest in promoting participation in certain types of grassroots organizations," namely, those who could, "in a time of limited public resources and government cutbacks, deliver formerly public services" (Paley 2001, 143). Even the Socialist Party–led governments of Ricardo Lagos and Michele Bachelet arguably exhibited an "aversion to popular mobilization" and "kept organized groups at arm's length" despite their rhetorical embrace of participation (Huber, Pribble, and Stephens 2010, 80, 95).

In the wake of 2006 student protests that shook Chilean society out of its seeming complacency, Patricio Navia (2009) claims that Bachelet attempted to promote "bottom-up democracy"; but Bachelet's efforts were jeopardized when the rightist opposition associated her "commendable objective of strengthening civil society . . . with a soft hand that would bring about street demonstrations and end up undermining democracy" (332). One study of Bachelet's first government found that 143 "mechanisms of citizen participation" were recognized by administrative instances of the state, of which 76 were said to promote a *gestión pública participativa*, or participatory public administration; of the remainder, 62 corresponded to instances for "citizen information," and 7 to "strengthen civil society." Although Lagos promulgated a Ley de Participación Ciudadana (Law of Citizen Participation) and Bachelet followed suit by launching an Agenda Pro-Participación Ciudadana (Pro-Participation Citizenship Agenda) with considerable fanfare, among the 143 mechanisms studied, only 6 were found to be deliberative, that is, to have any binding decision-making power (Checa, Lagos Lira, and Cabalin 2011, 38). As Pascal Lupien maintains, "the sphere of activism [in Chile] is . . . limited by qualifiers that underscore 'responsible citizenship,' and [government] discourse suggests a relationship of cooperation, but one in which the citizen plays a subordinate role" (2015, 62).

In other G1 contexts, ISEs are also typically subordinate and "consultative"; that is, they most often purport to "give voice" or "listen" to citizens about issues relevant to particular population groups (e.g., women, indigenous peoples) or policy domains (social services). In the case of the more than 300 formal community spaces and twelve departmental commissions created by Colombia's Ley 70 for Afro-Colombian "participation," for instance, Tianna Paschel poignantly shows that "paper" and "ghost" organizations often predominate and thereby gain disproportionate governmental resources; "ritualized" forms of participation, she disturbingly concludes, have come to prevail over time (2016).

Power-empty, ritualized G1 participatory spaces aimed at redirecting or preempting "democratic excess" are today a dime a dozen in Latin America and throughout much of the Global South. As Amalia Pallares quipped during one of several Latin American Studies Association sessions we organized in relation to this project, "if I had a dollar for every Plan de Desarrollo Participativo or Participatory Development Plan that has been set up in small municipalities throughout Ecuador, I'd be a millionaire." In G1, civil society is not supposed to govern; instead, it is expected to be civic and to make demands on the system only through established institutional channels of political representation—thereby buttressing and assisting the governing work of more qualified public servants and duly-elected representatives.

Brazil became a regional leader in promoting what I once called "council democracy" (Alvarez 1997), when it was among the first to set up consultative venues for civil society participation beginning in the early 1980s under local and state governments led by Christian- and social-democratic sectors of the centrist opposition (Avritzer, chapter 2 in this volume; Baierle 1998; Friedman and Hochstetler 2002; Hochstetler 2000, 2008). Early Brazilian participatory spaces, such as the State Councils on Women's Condition, typically brought together government-appointed "representatives of civil society" and public servants to "advise" local executives on particular policy areas. Although sometimes providing venues for feminist contentions, as I shall suggest below, many G1 women's spaces within the state became sheer *simulâcros de poder*, or simulacrums of power, as Brazilian activist-intellectual Maria Bethânia Ávila aptly put it during a feminist advocacy workshop in 2005. While the first women's councils were created in response to feminist demands for a direct role in policy, *conselhos* for women, Blacks, youth, and so on proliferated throughout Brazil and other nations in the region as local politicians of all political stripes found in them convenient vehicles through which to appear responsive and "modern," even as these ostensibly participatory mechanisms were often politically marginalized, underfunded, understaffed, and stacked by representatives of civil society more beholden to their government patrons than to their putative societal constituents. Indeed, as in the case of Afro-Colombian "participation" mentioned above (see also Laó-Montes, chapter 5 in this volume), many such participatory spaces become mere political showcases and clientelistic redoubts.

GOVERNANCE OR G2

Given the generally disempowered, often manipulated, and expressly nondeliberative place prescribed for civil society participation in G1, the appearance on the scene of Governance, or G2 for our purposes, as a set of prescriptions for "new" practices of government seemed to signal progress (for overviews of that literature, see especially Grindle 2004, 2012; on Latin American debates, Zurbriggen 2014). The preoccupation, in this case, typically is proclaimed to be with both the quality *and* stability (or viability + effectiveness) of democracy. In Europe and North America, Governance's conceptual debut can largely be attributed to political science efforts to respond to neoliberalism's ascent in the 1970s and 1980s. After all, it appeared that the market, and not the state or the "political system," was to become preeminent (Bevir

2011), at the risk of disciplinary obsolescence. "Governance," Mark Bevir contends, "evokes a world in which state power is dispersed among a vast array of spatially and functionally distinct networks composed of all kinds of public, voluntary and private organisations with which the centre now interacts" (Bevir 2011, 459). This implied "the creation of new forms of networks governance—institutionalized 'interfaces' for contact between government and civil society—[which] are generally viewed as mechanisms for increasing governmental responsiveness, transparency and accountability, at the same time that they subvert the elitism and hierarchy of clientelism (and, perhaps, representative democracy more generally)" (Zurbriggen 2014, 350).

In Latin America, there has been relatively little academic debate on Governance, and the notion was mainly diffused through IFIs (Zurbriggen 2014, 345). By far the most common usage of G2 is as the right-hand man of "good," as in "*Good* Governance" (Alvarez 2001; Cornwall and Coelho 2007). Indeed, in the South of the Americas, G2 (and sometimes its C-G2 variant, as we'll see shortly) was an integral part of the so-called second-generation reforms, which recognized "the need to complement the roles and actions of the State and the market to achieve development" (Panfichi and Muñoz 2001, 11). For the World Bank, for example, "Good Governance" referred to "efficiency in public service, rule of law with regard to contracts, an effective judiciary sector, respect for human rights, a free press, and pluralistic institutional structure. The means for achieving these goals are marketization of public services, reduction of public-sector overstaffing, budgetary discipline, administrative decentralization, *and NGO participation*" (Zanotti 2005, 468, my emphasis). Governance was a policy metaphor that linked the spheres of politics and administration (Doornbos 2001, 95).

While there are étatiste approaches to G2, in much of Latin America (Good) Governance has often entailed practices of governing "without government" (Pierre 2005, 64) or "beyond the State" (Swyngedouw 2005). And here of course is where civil society comes in: "Governance-beyond-the-state refers . . . to the emergence, proliferation and active encouragement (by the state and international bodies like the European Union or the World Bank) of institutional arrangements of 'governing' which give a much greater role in policy-making, administration and implementation to private economic actors on the one hand and to parts of civil society on the other in self managing what until recently was provided or organized by the national or local state" (Swyngedouw 2005, 1992).

In G2, participation involves more than simply "listening" to civil society, but citizen engagement in ISEs still is seldom deliberative. Instead, the goal of participation is involving citizens in implementing, rather than formulating, policy—enjoining "the community" to "participate" in building stairs from the *asfalto* to the *morro*, from the wealthier and whiter city to the *favela*, for example, rather than in deciding where the stairs should go or if alternatives (an accessible winding path, a new road) might be more desirable, or if a school rather than stairs would be more in keeping with community wishes/needs (Merilee Grindle, personal communication, March 2009).

A mix of what Benjamin Goldfrank calls conservative and technocratic centrist orientations toward participation could be said to coexist under G2. For conservatives, institutions such as Participatory Budgeting (Orçamento Participativo, OP), inaugurated in PT-dominated Porto Alegre in the late 1980s, for example, are seen to "threaten the stability and even the existence of representative democracy" whereas centrist technocrats appreciate the uses of participatory technologies for "fostering 'good government,' meaning that it achieves higher levels of effectiveness and transparency, reduces poverty and eliminates corruption" (2011b, 165).

Both G2 and, as we shall see, C-G2, its progressive half-sister, deploy technologies of agency aimed primarily at folks—the permitidos—deemed capable of self-government, trustworthy enough to govern themselves. Civic, professionalized NGOs are considered to be among the most capable and thus often become the state's partners par excellence under G2. Governance, then, discursively constructs participation as invigorating citizenship and improving democracy. Significantly for purposes of the present argument, the much-studied case of the OP—first launched as a radical democratic experience by the Brazilian Workers' Party (PT) in the late 1980s—came to be held up as a quintessential example of effective Governance.

CO-GOVERNANCE OR C-G2

Indeed, perhaps some of the most "perverse confluences," again invoking Dagnino's felicitous phrase, occur today principally in the name of this G. Governance became a favorite moniker of IGOs and IFIs, which began to promote "citizen participation" in building staircases, at the same time that many of the same tropes were evident in discourses of *governar para além do Estado* (governing beyond the State) or *junto com os movimentos populares e a sociedade civil* (with popular movements and civil society) present in many versions of what Dagnino and her colleagues (Dagnino, Olvera, and Panfichi 2006b) call the *projeto democrático-participativo*, or democratic-participatory political project, such as that historically associated with the PT.

Still, it is often assumed that this progressive variant of G2—which, precisely to signal Dagnino's treacherous confluence and Hale and Millamán's confounding battleground, I label Co-Governance or C-G2—always produces democratic innovation, expanded citizenship, more equitable and sustainable development, and so on. But as much of the vast literature on the OP's implementation in Brazil (implicitly or explicitly) suggests, the *power effects* on citizen-subjects of civil society's participation in such ISEs have been mixed (for overviews, see Avritzer 2009 and chapter 2 in this volume; Goldfrank 2011a; Wampler 2007b, 2015; Baiocchi [chapter 1], Junge [chapter 4], Cornwall [chapter 3], this volume). Although the OP in C-G2 contexts sometimes can indeed "help deepen democracy," Brian Wampler cautions that such "programs can also produce weak outcomes that will not transform basic decision-making processes or allow citizens to be directly involved in policy making." Indeed, some "poorly performing" OP programs can have a negative impact on citizens and civil society groups, "which should temper calls for the widespread adoption of participatory institutions as a magic bullet" that would solve all the ills pervading the developing world (2007b, 3).

Still, as Wampler stresses, the OP started to be mainstreamed precisely "as it began to be considered a good government program as opposed to an experiment in radical democracy that would reorder the Brazilian state and society" (2007b, 29; see also Baiocchi, Heller, and Silva 2011; Goldfrank 2011a, 2011b). By the mid-2000s, the OP model of "civic participation" was supported by World Bank and UN Habitat and had been adopted in forty countries and over 250 Brazilian municipalities (Wampler 2007b, 6). Clearly, even participation inspired by C-G2 can sometimes morph into (plain old) G2, especially in a neoliberal global context, or sometimes even become simply one more dime-a-dozen G1-type empty participatory space. In an extensive study of the implementation of participatory budgeting in a number of Brazilian settings, Teixeira and Albuquerque found that "the risks of the 'domestication' of the contentious side of popular movements contained in the new institutional framework of the OP represents a challenge that is more serious the less organized is civil society. This is because the new logic of action can delegitimize more spontaneous and conflictual manifestations" (cited in Dagnino, Olvera, and Panfichi 2006b, 62)—a clear slippage of an intended C-G2 participatory mechanism toward G1.

The quest for Governability is hardly the preserve of conservative or centrist governments and parties, of course. Progressive parties also face "governability dilemmas," as Gómez Bruera suggests (2013, 4). He argues that many local PT administrations developed a "social counter-hegemonic" practice of

G1, wherein civil society's "inputs were seen as a way to solve governing problems. Participation and mobilisation were not only ideological preferences; they were also part of a strategy to alter the balance of forces within state institutions in which the elites often enjoy comparative advantages" (Gómez Bruera 2013, 4). This strategy was abandoned when the PT ascended to the presidency, as the Lula administration gradually opted for an "elite-centered" practice of G1 and "managed to keep social contestation and disruptive practices at low or manageable levels as part of a strategy to secure social governability" (4).

Gómez Bruera's detailed study of PT-civil society linkages demonstrates that this dimension of Governability was achieved less through participation and more through "engaging a number of civil society organisations in negotiations processes, by distributing a great number of jobs to their leaders, by allocating them massive state resources" (Gómez Bruera 2013, 12). "Domestication" arguably often ensued.

The discourses of the Bolivarian Revolution in Venezuela and the Citizens' Revolution in Ecuador, by contrast, still enthusiastically touted participation as a centerpiece of their C-G2 or "co-governing" practices well into the 2010s. As Lupien cogently argues, at the level of discourse, these leftist "re-foundational" regimes promoted participation based on "collective, social and active" (and, in Venezuela, protagonistic) citizenship and ascribed great importance to direct participation in local decision-making. But in both cases, the author finds that official discourse established a clear distinction between those spaces where citizens can "most effectively exercise their constitutional right to participation and the types of activities in which citizens cannot participate legitimately . . . such as protest movements and participation in organizations of civil society that do not form part of the 'collective' system" (Lupien 2015, 62). He concludes that these so-called schools of democracy make use of discursive practices to "adapt citizens to a specific model of citizenship" (Lupien 2015, 5).

GOVERNMENTALITY OR G3

In disciplining citizens such that participation is only legitimated when it occurs within government-sanctioned institutions such as Venezuela's Consejos Comunales (Communal Councils), while actively discouraging and at times even criminalizing uncivic activism critical of incumbents, some declared C-G2 participatory spaces, then, also reveal elements of what Foucault theorized as Governmentality, our G3: "forms of action and relations of power that aim to guide and shape (rather than force, control or dominate) the actions of others" (Cruikshank 1999, 4).

In the case of neoliberal governments, the range of the permitido typically is further circumscribed. Here, the CS Agenda becomes a "technology" for promoting market-led development, delivering social services, and alleviating poverty. Neoliberal G3 "governs 'through' civil society by harnessing [Civil Society Organizations' or CSOs'] expertise and ability to responsibly channel political will-formation" (Sending and Neumann 2006, 658). These rationalities of government are capillary instances of supervision and control, administered largely by "nongovernments," epitomized by the collaborative and entrepreneurial, though not-for-profit-driven, "Third Sector."

Many, if not most, of the modalities of citizen participation promoted by IFIs and IGOs have included a good dosage of G3. Typically reserved for the "disposable third," such practices of neoliberal Governmentality retain hardy doses of welfarist, statist discipline and punishment. Neoliberal G3 could be seen as promoting, as Mitchell Dean suggests, "an emergent division between *active citizens* (capable of managing their own risk) and *targeted populations* (disadvantaged groups, the 'at risk,' or the high risk) who require intervention in the management of risks" (1999, 167, emphasis in the original). "Civil-ized" citizens are invited to participate in the Third Sector, a term that indiscriminately collapses a wide array of traditional nonprofit institutions—including religious hospitals, schools, and charities—along with a range of civic, "cooperative" CSOs and NGOs. Working with the state in the "government of the social" by helping at-risk populations "help themselves," the Third Sector assists the state and compensates for the market through the volunteer, participatory efforts of a new breed of civic-minded citizens.

For the populations assisted by the civic-citizens, by contrast, participation can serve as a technique for subjection. Technologies of performance, aimed at at-risk groups, rather than technologies of agency aimed at citizens, prevail here. G3-inspired participation often entails what Dean refers to as "new formal calculative regimes," which involve "the setting of performance indicators, . . . the establishment of 'quasi-markets' in expertise and service provision, the 'corporatization' and 'privatization' of formerly public services, and the contracting-out of services, . . . all more or less technical means for locking the moral and political requirements of the shaping of conduct into the optimization of performance" (Dean 1999, 169). Although civic civil society is enjoined to participate in the nonconflictual, internally undifferentiated Third Sector, participation for the at-risk, the folks that Partha Chatterjee calls "the governed" (2006), generally consists of being administered by targeted social programs and projects that they seldom debate, much less formulate. In neoliberal G3, then, poor people's engagement is intended to be collaborative, when not passive, and "becomes viable to the extent that it can contribute greater coverage, efficiency, efficacy and lower costs in the instrumentation of public policies, especially social policy" (Rivera 2000, 108).

By the 2010s, a wide gamut of poverty-reduction schemes—such as the ubiquitous conditional cash transfer (CCTs) and microcredit programs— arguably were driven by technical calculative regimes aimed at improving performance and thereby "conducting the conduct" of the poor, and of poor women in particular (Eyben and Napier-Moore 2007; Lavinas 2013). As Wendy Hunter and Natasha Borges Sugiyama suggest, "the verdict is still out as to whether and to what extent CCTs empower women. On the one hand, the fact that payments tend to go directly to female heads of household can enhance their autonomy within the family. On the other hand, the lion's share of the burden in fulfilling conditionality requirements generally rests on mothers" (2012, 10).

G3-inspired microcredit programs produce women as permissible market citizens, transforming "at-risk" women into "entrepreneurs"—though this much-touted entrepreneurship most often entails no more than regulating and disciplining the low-wage, low-status, gender-stereotyped work—such as preparing and selling food, assembling clothing, performing day care or elder care duties—that is already performed by poor, racialized women in the informal sector (Cornwall, Harrison, and Whitehead 2007; Lind 2005; Molyneux 2008; Schild 2000). And like CCTs, such poverty relief programs are seldom "participatory" in even the most restricted of the various meanings discussed in this volume. Women beneficiaries, hardly participants, typically have to meet together regularly and check in with bureaucratic personnel to ensure they are fulfilling prescribed indicators and sustaining the expectations of a (gendered) "conduct" that will optimize their performance as mothers, market citizens, and civic community members. Although I would be the last to argue against putting money in the hands of needy women, such programs, as typically designed and implemented, actively work to produce *la mujer pobre permitida* (the permissible poor woman).

Beyond the Civil Society Agenda?

In closing, I want to underscore that many, if not most, government-linked arenas of civil society participation, even neoliberal G3-inspired ones aimed at producing market citizens, can contain elements of more than one G. We therefore need to empirically, historically, and comparatively assess and untangle particular instances of participation in terms of their G1, G2, C-G2, and G3 dimensions—rather than attempt to neatly typologize them. As I've argued, even the best-intentioned C-G2 can readily slip toward G1 or even G3, especially when the objective of governmental actors is stability or performance, respectively.

We also need to always pose the question of how G3s or G1s can be transformed into G2s (not at all a bad thing, by comparison) or even C-G2s, through political struggle or counterhegemonic practices. At least some among the scores of Brazilian women's *conselhos* created as power-empty political showcases, for instance, sometimes have provided feminist activists access to critical state resources and a modicum of influence in deliberative policy processes. Indeed, G1-inspired spaces can sometimes take on a progressive dynamic of their own and provide opportunities for more meaningful citizen involvement in the affairs of governing. After all, as Tania Li suggests—admonishing some Foucault-inspired studies of governmentality for being "anemic on the practice of politics"—"to govern means to act on the actions of subjects who retain the capacity to act otherwise" (2007, 17). To overcome this anemia, she advocates bringing together Foucault and Gramsci: "Scholars working in a Foucauldian mode have often observed the 'strategic reversibility' of power relations, as diagnoses of deficiencies imposed from above become 'repossessed' as demands from below, backed by a sense of entitlement" (2007, 26); while a Gramscian approach to what she calls "the practice of politics" would be "alert to the constellations of power in particular times and places, and the overdetermined, messy situations in which creativity arises" (27). The Civil Society Agenda, as many of the chapters in the book have tried to suggest, is riddled by such "messiness" and mined by potential "strategic reversibilities" so that even the most objectionably manipulative of G3 incarnations "may inadvertently stimulate a political challenge" (Li 2007, 26).

We therefore need not jettison wholesale the development discourse that emerged in the wake of the Washington Consensus for having irreparably *disabling*, even sinister effects, but should also engage its potentially *enabling* dimensions. Dominant discourses of Civil Society or Good Governance are *productive*. They produce new subjects, sometimes open up spaces, and foster new practices that can and have had unexpected consequences—even as they proscribe others.

Participation and decentralization are among the manifold prescriptions of the neoliberal Governance Agenda (our G2), for instance. In the case of Bolivia in the mid-1990s, a showcase of neoliberal policy at the time, a program called *Plan para Todos* included decentralization, bilingual education, and agrarian legislation, alongside privatization and other neoliberal policy measures. According to José Antonio Lucero, "The plan provided new recognition to indigenous people who could now hold political power in local municipalities, develop curricula in their own languages, and obtain titles recognizing their territories" (2008, 125). The Law of Popular Participation (1994), in turn, "transferred significant resources (20 percent of the national budget) to local municipalities and gave indigenous and popular organizations a direct role in the administration of those resources" (2008, 133–34). The political impact of these neoliberal innovations, Lucero argues, was ambivalent. On the one hand, it made Bolivian politics more "decentered and fragmented," as there were few incentives to organize supracommunally. Yet on the other, by enabling well-organized indigenous parties to take advantage of new opportunities at the local level, a nearly defunct party such as Evo Morales's MAS was able to emerge as the country's most powerful political force (135–36). "Both the critics and proponents of multicultural neoliberalism," Lucero contends, "may turn out to be right in that changes may yield real breakthroughs for the livelihood of indigenous people *and* lead to inevitable compromises with dominant power centers" (2008, 132). Our analyses of the Civil Society Agenda should attempt to expose, explore, and exploit such ambivalences in the grammar of Good Governance so as to destabilize and disrupt or perhaps interrupt rather than discard the "new development lexicon," and, emulating Morales's *cocaleros*, perhaps work to subvert it, to put it to work toward transformative ends (see Goodale and Postero 2013).

In her compelling ethnographic study of "the will to improve" that shaped governmental rationalities of development in Indonesia, Li makes a distinction that could be useful in this regard. She emphasizes the difference between "the practice of government, in which the concept of improvement [or in our case, 'civic participation'] becomes technical as it is attached to calculated programs for its realization," and what she calls "the practice of politics—the expression, in word or deed, of a critical challenge. Challenge often starts out as a refusal of the way things are. It opens up a front of struggle" (2007, 12). "Resistance," Barbara Cruikshank similarly insists, "must take the form of . . . a refusal to be what our relations to the state have made us" (1999, 121). In moving beyond the CS Agenda, then, we would have to insist on the political validity, indeed necessity, of conflict and contention in democracy, within and without participatory institutions, and refuse to always be civil-ized, well-mannered, and cooperative in relation to governing ourselves and others.

As we have seen in the preceding chapters, activists' refusal, however self-conscious, leads many to combine civic with uncivic strategies, to create and engage with innovative political spaces not authorized by public authorities, to take to the streets, block roads, shout unseemly slogans, and scream bloody murder, especially when existing "architectures of participation" all but collapse under the weight of demands for structural change and social justice. Under construction since the mid-1980s, Brazil's much-heralded "national system of participation"—involving policy councils, conferences, Participatory Budgeting, public hearings, consultations, and more—for instance, was perhaps the most extensive and highly formalized in Latin America. Yet the limitations and contradictions of Brazil's participatory institutions were singled out as one of the factors that helped trigger the massive protests that spread across over 350 Brazilian cities in 2013 (see Teixeira and Baiocchi, chapter 14). Already diagnosed to be undergoing a veritable "midlife crisis" in 2015 (Pires 2015), in the aftermath of the congressional-cum-media-orchestrated coup against (or constitutionally dubious "impeachment" of) Dilma Rousseff and the PT's dismal performance in the 2016 municipal elections, that vast participatory architecture stands on very shaky ground indeed. By the late 2010s, throughout much of Latin America and across the globe, activism of all political stripes increasingly spilled over the parameters of lo permitido. From anti-immigrant forces in Europe and the Tea Party in the United States to the "civic" coup mongers who mobilized to bring down Rousseff and the PT (and the rule of law) in Brazil—conservatives also took to the streets with growing frequency. The Civil Society Agenda's "Other," mass protest—whether civic, that is, authorized by those in power, or uncivic, either inadvertently exceeding or purposefully defying proscriptions prevailing under whichever of the Gs—appeared to have become the "new normal."

NOTE

The argument presented here was developed in dialogue with colleagues and students during various seminars and conferences held at Unicamp; UNC, Chapel Hill; the Universidad de Puerto Rico, Río Piedras; Brown University; Harvard University; UT, Austin; Rutgers University; University of Illinois, Urbana-Champaign; and several venues at the University of Massachusetts, Amherst. I thank all my interlocutors on those occasions for their provocative comments and insightful suggestions. I am especially grateful to my colleagues Barbara Cruikshank and Brian Wampler and to my fellow editors for their feedback on earlier drafts of the present chapter.

Conclusion

UNCONTAINED ACTIVISM

MILLIE THAYER AND JEFFREY W. RUBIN

In the late twentieth and early twenty-first centuries, as extractive industries expanded through Latin America's mountains and jungles and securitized states extended policing and territorial control, new structures to channel and contain dissent were layered over older ones (Amar 2013; Bebbington 2013; Bebbington et al. 2014; Gudynas 2012; Svampa 2008a). The wave of Pink Tide governments, brought to power with the help of a previous generation of social movements, sought to direct participation and protest by adopting versions of what we have called the Civil Society Agenda, incorporating their movement allies through participatory, economically inclusive, antiracist, propeasant, and women and lesbian, gay, bisexual, transgendered (LGBT)–friendly strategies consistent with evolving forms of neoliberalism (Hale 2005; Peck and Tickell 2000; Porter and Craig 2004), as well as with activists' own demands for a role in political decision-making. Toward the end of the period we examine, an emerging postneoliberal Right began to make use of these new strategies as well, combining the neoliberal model of dispossession with a strengthened regulatory state.

Our chapters show that the participatory programs enacted by leftist governments since 2000 render the world discursively so as to produce specific kinds of political subjects, as Alvarez (chapter 16 in this volume) maintains, and incite particular types of actions, those of the "permissible citizen" who lays claim to a prescribed set of rights and resources by attending meetings and working within government-sanctioned participatory spaces. Even as they offer new opportunities to activists, such programs simultaneously obscure the controlling power of the state, the "uncivil" aspects of civil society itself, and the capacity of unruly social movements to envision and enact transformative practices. The Civil Society Agenda, and the emerging neodevelopmentalist securitization regimes of which that agenda has become an integral part, act to render the *no permitido* invisible or illegitimate and to proscribe other knowledges and alternate forms of political action, increasingly fostering the criminalization of oppositional activism and protest. This process, in turn, has been given new life by right-wing movements and governments. Thus, our cases underscore not only the dual origins of participation in both neoliberal governmentality and leftist activism, but the continuing power and intertwined nature of these competing logics.

Similarly, the incorporation of identity-based demands around gender, race, sexuality, and class into state and international agendas has had ambiguous effects, as have shifts in funding on the part of international donor agencies. In the 2000s and 2010s, Latin American governments addressed injustices by channeling potentially transgressive claims into permissible programs, such as women's ministries, gay marriage legislation, state agencies dedicated to Black and indigenous affairs, and cash transfer plans. During the same period, it became increasingly difficult financially to sustain independent critical activism in Latin America, as international donor agencies retreated from a number of countries in the region, such as Brazil and Chile, that were viewed as economically viable, and nongovernmental organizations turned to states for support, through mechanisms including contracts to undertake research and implement policies.

The chapters in this book reveal/interrogate the dual aspects of Pink Tide governments, the ways they have been simultaneously invasive and inclusive, in different forms and to diverse degrees. It is this tension in the Pink

Tide that has set many of the parameters for the current turbulent period of right-wing electoral victories and rollback of progressive economic policies. In the accounts included here, policies promoting extractivism, the policing of activism, and new forms of participation combined in distinctive ways in disparate parts of the region, creating a terrain for activism that was uneven—sometimes apparently inviting, sometimes manifestly treacherous.

This book documents the outcomes for mobilization across a broad range of countries and constituencies. We find, first, *fluid, dynamic, and heterogeneous fields of contestation* in which participants adopt varied forms and degrees of engagement with one another, with hegemonic discourses, and with dominant institutions, including the state. Our contributors further illustrate activist gains: from state subsidies for the unemployed to pensions for rural women, from race- and gender-sensitive policies to greater budgetary accountability and limits on rapacious development projects. While their victories have been partial and unstable, and the risk of incorporation and repression high, Latin America's social movements have *neither* been *fully controlled* by governments nor entirely contained by regimes of neoliberal governmentality, neodevelopmentalist ambitions, or corporate incursions.

Indeed—and this is our second major finding—movements have repeatedly *overflowed the parameters of political and economic regimes and of conventional social activism*, as they have pressed their claims and struggled for room for maneuver. These overflows, we argue, have had significantly productive effects, *amplifying opportunities for engagement, and shifting social and political discourse*, though not always in the ways or to the ends that activists hoped or predicted.

In *Beyond Civil Society*, we find activists maneuvering in a multiplicity of ways among distinctive political forms, from the ostensibly civic to the unabashedly uncivic, from the permissible to the unacceptable. Some organizations, such as the Peruvian antimining activists, the Movement of Rural Women Workers (Movimento de Mulheres Trabalhadoras Rurais, or MMTR) in southern Brazil, and the Process of Black Communities (Proceso de Comunidades Negras, or PCN) in Colombia draw simultaneously on different strategies and take apparently contradictory positions toward the state, to "hold difference," as Rubin (chapter 11) puts it. Other groupings move from one approach to another across time, such as Cornwall's (chapter 3) civil society participants in "invited spaces" sponsored by the state.

In so doing, activists pour their efforts into but also transgress the bounds of the Civil Society Agenda. In Monteagudo's narrative (chapter 7), environmental protestors draw on the support of the state, but also flaunt it through local roadblocks and naked dissent in international venues. Peruvian indigenous activists described by Hoetmer (chapter 9) make use of the democratic form of the local government-sponsored community referendum (*consulta vecinal*) to challenge the development plans of the national state and mining companies. In Junge's description (chapter 4) of local experiences with participatory budgeting, we see both enthusiasm and skepticism, involvement and ambivalence. In all these cases, activism engages with but also often evades or overruns the structures designed to channel it in directions compatible with state and corporate agendas.

Activism since 2000 has overflowed not only the Civil Society Agenda, but preexisting forms of uncivic contention as well. Over the past two decades, roadblocks, workplace takeovers, *escraches* (the shaming of powerful figures outside their homes or workplaces), horizontal assemblies, mass protests, and street theater have confronted governments and powerful elites with unruly, belligerent, threatening, and at times violent actions that often secure concrete gains. Uncivic action also supported foundational leftist regimes in Venezuela and Bolivia, even as similarly belligerent tactics were taken up by opponents of those same regimes, leading to polarization that breathed new life into conventional binaries (López Maya and Lander, chapter 13; Lucero, chapter 15).

Contemporary mobilizations also overflow national borders, as in the case of the above-cited Argentinian movement against a pulp mill in Uruguay, or of the struggles and alliances along the aid chain described in Thayer's essay (chapter 8). While the transnational activism of earlier decades addressed global political issues in UN conferences, feminist gatherings or labor alliances, the cases we study here show a pragmatic grounding in local or national realities and targeted efforts to reach across borders for specific ends. This same kind of pragmatism also presses activists to push beyond the confines of assumed political orientations and preexisting organizing structures. The image of the more conventional union and political party activists struggling to be heard amidst the multivocal, cacophonous Brazilian protests described by Baiocchi and Teixeira (chapter 14) makes this point.

In other cases, we see alliances—including some of the strange bedfellows sort—being made across political locations, as in coalitions between ostensibly "uncivic" social movements and politicians in Ecuador or the discursive articulations through which Di Marco (chapter 6) finds factory workers and feminists constructing a *pueblo feminista* in Argentina. In some places and times, there is no explicit coalition, but rather parallel action by separate organizations with complementary strategies, a kind of unplanned but de facto "hard cop, soft cop" approach. Laó-Montes's discussion (chapter 5) of the field of Afro-Colombian movements that includes both black elites with links to U.S. Agency for International Development (USAID) and Afro-Latino social movements with a very different political agenda is a case in point, as are the "contentious" and the more "civic" Venezuelan mobilizations held concurrently by unaffiliated groups, which Lopez Maya and Lander detail (chapter 13), or the "pluralistic" set of Brazilian community-based movements described by Avritzer (chapter 2).

This book, then, is about overflow, about activism and protest that cannot be contained by the Civil Society Agenda, by past forms of uncivic activism, by national borders, by categories of scholarship and scholarly analysis, or by the internal structures of social movements themselves. Similarly, the dynamics of social movement activism during the Pink Tide documented in this volume, based on multiple and shifting strategies that occur simultaneously or sequentially within civil society institutions and in uncivic contention, suggest that this overflow will continue, and likely morph and expand, even as conservative governments assume power in some local and national arenas. The complex array of strategies and political forms we document here generates mobile, messy, context-contingent, sometimes ephemeral, and always productive arenas of contention, where political boundaries are continually breached and familiar categories of action from the unruly to the well behaved, the *permitido* to the *no permitido*, are confounded with one another. It is no wonder then that so many of our contributors reach for open-ended conceptions that go beyond the limits offered by the term "social movement" to describe what they see: fields, counterpublics, *pueblos*, and public spaces, constituted by a shifting and variegated set of actors. We argue that it is their diverse relations to one another, as well as to the "civic" and the permissible that often allow activists of varying political stripes to outstrip attempts at corralling them.

Is this overflow a uniquely Latin American phenomenon? Twenty-first-century activism encounters vastly different forms of governance, international intervention, and hegemonic discourse globally and takes diverse shapes as a result. In some regions, such as South Asia, governmentality may function more effectively than in our studies, while in other regions, such as parts of the Middle East and Africa, violence and sectarian conflict are today more crushing than in Latin America. Indeed, we show in these pages that many Latin American activists remain committed to progressive change within the frameworks of democratic political regimes and modernity, even as they challenge the norms upon which these political structures are based. The contribution of *Beyond Civil Society* to the study of mobilization in other parts of the world is not only its delineation of these twenty-first-century forms of Latin American activism, but also its attentiveness to the ways political challenges cross boundaries, trouble binaries, and overflow efforts to contain them. These insights may help to illuminate the appearances and trajectories—as well as the limits and contradictions—of multiple forms of social and political mobilization today, from horizontal coalitions against austerity in Spain and Greece, to feminist movements against rape in India, to emerging waves of peasant mobilization in Africa, to fundamentalist movements in the United States and beyond.

What are the outcomes of the state of affairs we describe in Latin America? What is the political excess we find being produced in our case studies? By engaging, but also exceeding, the Civil Society Agenda and other contemporary normative political prescriptions, the mobilizations described by our contributors may open new democratic spaces or defend, extend, or resignify the ones that are on offer. Participatory budgeting and other consultative processes are stretched in novel ways, international funding relationships take surprisingly reciprocal turns, territories and productive enterprises are occupied or reconfigured, internal social movement hierarchies and strategic choices are challenged, and nominally left-wing refoundational regimes find themselves being called to account by groups they assumed to be allies. Political overflow in the post-2000s conjuncture may also deepen internal tensions or splits in movements or provoke shifts away from initial goals, as when Brazilians pour into the streets of major cities in defiance of government and largely outside of organized movements, or when rural women's movements polarize over how to decide among competing political strategies or struggle to resist the norms of international funding agencies.

On another level, excess may allow activists to seek to shift the meanings that have marginalized whole categories of people, including the poor, Afro-Latin Americans, indigenous peoples, women, and LGBT communities (but also prosperous farmers, businesspeople, or right-wing politicians, earlier washed out of political—though not economic—power by the Pink Tide and now in resurgence). The discursive dimension of activist struggles means, in part, challenging (or reinscribing) hierarchies of race, class, gender, sexuality, or region, pushing back against the "social facts" that underlie the binary distinctions between who or what is permitido, and who or what is not. For some, such as indigenous populations in Peru, or Afro-descendants in Colombia, it also means making claims for alternative ontologies and epistemologies, a very old struggle made newly salient in part by the aggressively extractivist, racist, neodevelopmentalist, and capitalist paradigms that now threaten the physical, as well as spiritual, existence of these populations.

The success of counterpublics, of fields of protest, in these cultural-political conflicts has its measure in the expanding (and sometimes contracting) boundaries of lo permitido. The articulations of the *pueblo feminista*; the advances of LGBT visibility; the new racial identities constructed by diasporic, Afro-descended peoples; the tentative but persistent efforts to hold difference within rural Brazilian women's organizing; the transnational alliances around indigenous sovereignties all suggest that the border-crossing we have documented in this book between state and civil society, between the civic and the not-so-civic, between activists in very different locations within broader political fields, exceeds the capacity of both restrictive structures and confining meanings to contain contemporary Latin American political mobilizations. Such overflow reflects inventiveness and audacity, as well as tension, diffuseness, and fracture. Its results, even in the face of new right-wing political scenarios, are real, albeit deeply constrained and contingent, democratic possibilities and liberatory horizons.

References

Abers, Rebecca. 2000. *Inventing Local Democracy: Grassroots Politics in Brazil*. Boulder, CO: Lynne Rienner Publishers.

———. 2001. "From Ideas to Practice: The Partido dos Trabalhadores and Participatory Governance in Brazil." *Policy* 91 (23): 35–53.

Abers, Rebecca, and Margareth E. Keck. 2006. "Muddy Waters: Decentralization, Coordination and Power Struggle in the Brazilian Water Management Reform." *International Journal for Urban and Regional Research* 30 (3): 601–22.

Abers, Rebecca, and Luciana Tatagiba. 2015. "Institutional Activism: Mobilizing for Women's Health from Inside the Brazilian Bureaucracy." In *Social Movement Dynamics: New Perspectives on Theory and Research from Latin America*, edited by Federico M. Rossi and Marisa Von Bülow. 73–102. Burlington VT: Ashgate.

ABONG (Associação Brasileira de Organizações Nãogovernamentais). 1998. *ONGs: Um perfil, Cadastro das Associadas a ABONG*. São Paulo: ABONG.

———. 2010. *Sustentabilidade das ONGs no Brasil: Acesso a recursos privados*. Rio de Janeiro: ABONG.

Abu-Lughod, Lila. 1991. *Writing against Culture*. In *Recapturing Anthropology: Working in the Present*, ed. R. G. Fox, 137–62. Santa Fe, NM: School of American Research Press.

———. 2000. "Locating Ethnography." *Ethnography* 1 (2) 261–67.

Achtenberg, Emily. 2014. "Rival Factions in Bolivia's CONAMAQ: Internal Conflict or Government Manipulation?" *NACLA Latin America*.

Agamben, Giorgio, and Daniel Heller-Roazen. 1998. *Homo Sacer: Sovereign Power and Bare Life (Meridian: Crossing Aesthetics)*. Stanford, CA: Stanford University Press.

Albó, Xavier. 2014. "Hay un deterioro en la relación entre el Gobierno e indígenas." *Página Siete* (January 26, 2014). http://www.paginasiete.bo/nacional/2014/1/26/deterioro-relacion-entre-gobierno-indigenas-12331.html.

Alexander, J. C. 2006. *The Civil Sphere*. New York: Oxford University Press.

Alexander, Robert J. 1965. *Organized Labor in Latin America*. New York: Free Press.

Allegretti, Giovanni, and Carsten Herzberg. [August 20, 1980] 2004. "Em Lages o povo toma conta de seus assuntos." In *Participatory Budgets in Europe: Between Efficiency and Growing Local Democracy*, 28–30. Amsterdam: Transnational Institute.

Althusser, Louis. 1972. *Lenin and Philosophy, and Other Essays*. New York: Monthly Review Press.

Alvarez, Sonia E. 1993. "Deepening Democracy: Popular Movement Networks, Constitutional Reform, and Radical Urban Regimes in Contemporary Brazil." In *Mobilizing the Community: Local Politics in the Era of the Global City*, edited by Robert Fisher and Joseph Kling, 191–219. Newbury Park, CA: Sage Publications.

———. 1997. "Reweaving the Fabric of Collective Action: Social Movements and Challenges to 'Actually Existing Democracy' in Brazil." In *Between Resistance and Revolution: Cultural Politics and Social Protest*, edited by Richard G. Fox and Orin Starn, 83–117. New Brunswick, NJ: Rutgers University Press.

———. 1998. "Latin American Feminism 'Go Global': Trends of 1990s, Challenges for the New Millennium." In *Culture of Politics/Politics of Culture: Re-Visioning Latin American Social Movements*, edited by Evelina Dagnino and Arturo Escobar Sonia E. Alvarez, 293–324. Boulder, CO: Westview Press.

———. 1999. "Advocating Feminism: The Latin American Feminist NGO 'Boom.'" *International Feminist Journal of Politics* 1 (2): 181–209.

———. 2001. "Third Sector, Third Way, a Second Look: Contemporary Latin American (ist) Debates Revisited." XXIII International Congress of the Latin American Studies Association (LASA).

———. 2007. "Social Movements as Discursive Fields of Action." Unpublished manuscript.

Alvarez, Sonia E., Claudia de Lima Costa, Verónica Feliu, Rebecca J. Hester, Norma Klahn, Millie Thayer, and Cruz Caridad Bueno. 2014. *Translocalities/translocalidades: Feminist Politics of Translation in the Latin/a Américas*. Durham, NC: Duke University Press.

Alvarez, Sonia, and Evelina Dagnino. 1995. "Para Além da 'democracia realmente existente': Movimentos sociais, a nova cidadania e a configuração de espaços públicos alternativos." Paper presented at the XIX Encontro Anual da Associação Nacional de Pós-Graduação e Pesquisa em Ciências Sociais-ANPOCS, Minas Gerais.

Alvarez, Sonia E., Evelina Dagnino, and Arturo Escobar, eds. 1998a. *Cultures of Politics, Politics of Cultures: Re-visioning Latin American Social Movements*. Boulder, CO: Westview Press.

———. 1998b. "Introduction: The Cultural and the Political in Latin American Social Movements." In *Cultures of Politics, Politics of Cultures: Re-visioning Latin American Social Movements*, edited by Sonia E. Alvarez, Evelina Dagnino, and Arturo Escobar, 1–29. Boulder, CO: Westview Press.

Alvarez, Sonia E., Elisabeth Jay Friedman, Ericka Beckman, Maylei Blackwell, Norma Stoltz Chinchilla, Nathalie Lebon, Marysa Navarro, and Marcela Rios Tobar. 2002–3. "Encountering Latin American and Caribbean Feminisms." *Signs: Journal of Women in Culture and Society* 28 (2): 537–79.

Alvarez Litben, Silvia G. 2001. *De huancavilcas a comuneros: Relaciones interétnicas en la península de Santa Elena, Ecuador*. 2nd ed. Ecuador: Abya Yala CODENPE-PRODEPINE.

Alves, José C. 1998. "Baixada Fluminense: A violência na construção do poder." PhD dissertation, Sociology Department, Universidade de São Paulo.

Alves, Marcio M. 1980. *A força do povo democracia participativa em Lages*. São Paulo, Brasil: Brasiliense.

Alves, Maria Helena Moreira. 1984. "Grassroots Organizations, Trade Unions, and the Church: A Challenge to the Controlled Abertura in Brazil." *Latin American Perspectives* 11 (1): 73–102.

Amar, Paul. 2013. *The Security Archipelago: Human-Security States, Sexuality Politics, and the End of Neoliberalism*. Durham, NC: Duke University Press.

Antrobus, Peggy. 2004. *The Global Women's Movements: Origins, Issues and Strategies.* New York: Zed Press.

Arato, Andrew. 1981. "Civil Society against the State: Poland 1980–81." *Telos* 1981 (47): 23–47.

Arendt, Hannah. [1958] 2003. *La condición humana.* Buenos Aires: Paidós.

Armony, Ariel. 2004. *The Dubious Link: Civic Engagement and Democratization.* Stanford, CA: Stanford University Press.

Arrighi, Giovanni. 1999. *Chaos and Governance in the Modern World System.* Vol. 10. Minneapolis: University of Minnesota Press.

Arrighi, Giovanni, Terence Hopkins, and Immanuel Wallerstein. 1997. *Antisystemic Movements.* London: Verso.

Arturi, Carlos S. 2001. "O Debate Teórico sobre Mudança de Regime Político: O caso brasileiro." *Revista Brasileira de Ciências Sociais* 17.

Arutyunova, Angelika, and Cindy Clark. 2013. *Watering the Leaves, Starving the Roots: The Status of Financing for Women's Rights Organizing and Gender Equality.* Toronto: AWID.

Asen, Robert. 2000. "Seeking the 'Counter' in Counterpublics." *Communication Theory* 10: 424–46.

Asher, Kiran. 2009. *Black and Green: Afro-Colombians, Development, and Nature in the Pacific Lowlands.* Durham, NC: Duke University Press.

Asher, Kiran, and Diana Ojeda. 2009. "Producing Nature and Making the State: Ordenamiento Territorial in the Pacific Lowlands of Colombia." *Geoforum* 40 (3): 292–302.

Auyero, Javier. 2004. "Política, dominación y desigualdad en la Argentina contemporánea: Un ensayo etnográfico." *Nueva Sociedad* 193:133–45.

———. 2006a. "Protest in Contemporary Argentina: A Contentious Repertoire in the Making." In *Out of the Shadows: Political Action and the Informal Economy in Latin America*, edited by Patricia Fernández-Kelly and Jon Shefner, 165–93. University Park: Pennsylvania State University Press.

———. 2006b. "The Political Makings of the 2001 Lootings in Argentina." *Journal of Latin American Studies* 38 (2): 241–65.

———. 2007. *Routine Politics and Collective Violence: The Gray Zone of State Power in Argentina.* New York: Cambridge University Press.

Avritzer, Leonardo. 1994. *Sociedade civil e democratização.* Belo Horizonte: Del Rey.

———. 1995. "Transition to Democracy and Political Culture: An Analysis of the Conflict between Civil and Political Society in Post-Authoritarian Brazil." *Constellations* 2 (2): 242–67.

———. 1997. "Um desenho institucional para o novo associativismo." *Lua Nova* 39: 149–74.

———. 1998. "Civil Society in Latin America in the Twenty-First Century: Between Democratic Deepening, Social Fragmentation, and State Crisis." In *Civil Society and Democracy in Latin America*, edited by R. Feinberg, C. Waisman, and L. Zamosc. London: Palgrave Macillan.

———. 2002a. *Democracy and the Public Sphere in Latin America.* Princeton, NJ: Princeton University Press.

——. 2002b. *Democracy and the Public Space in Latin America*. Princeton, NJ: Princeton University Press.

——, ed. 2004. *A participação em São Paulo*. São Paulo: Editora UNESP.

——. 2008. *Participatory Institutions in Democratic Brazil*. Washington, DC: Woodrow Wilson Center Press.

——. 2009. *Participatory Institutions in Democratic Brazil*. Cambridge: Cambridge University Press.

Bagic, Aida. 2006. "Women's Organizing in Post-Yugoslav Countries Talking about Donors." In *Global Feminism: Transnational Women's Activism, Organizing, and Human Rights*, edited by Myra Ferree and Aili Tripp, 141–65. New York: New York University Press.

Baierle, Sergio. 1998. "The Explosion of Experience: The Emergence of a New Ethical-Political Principle in Popular Movements in Porto Alegre, Brazil." In *Cultures of Politics/Politics of Cultures: Revisioning Latin American Social Movements*, edited by Sonia E. Alvarez, Evelina Dagnino, and Arturo Escobar, 123–35. Boulder, CO: Westview Press.

Bailey, Frederick. 1983. *The Tactical Uses of Passion: An Essay on Power, Reason, and Reality*. Ithaca, NY: Cornell University Press.

Bain, Katherine. 1999. "Building or Burning Bridges: The Accountability of Trans-National NGO Networks in Policy Alliances with the World Bank." Conference on NGOs in a Global Future, Birmingham, UK.

Baiocchi, Gianpaolo. 2005a. *Militants and Citizens: The Politics of Participatory Democracy in Porto Alegre*. Stanford, CA: Stanford University Press.

——. 2005b. "Participation, Activism, and Politics: Alegre Experiment and Deliberative Democratic Theory," edited by Department of Sociology and University of Wisconsin-Madison.

Baiocchi, Gianpaolo, Patrick Heller, and Marcelo Kunrath Silva. 2011. *Bootstrapping Democracy: Transforming Local Governance and Civil Society in Brazil*. Stanford, CA: Stanford University Press.

Bair, Jennifer. 2005. "Global Capitalism and Commodity Chains: Looking Back, Going Forward." *Competition and Change* 9 (2): 153–80.

Banfield, Edward C. 1958. *The Moral Basis of a Backward Society*. Glencoe, IL: Free Press.

Batliwala, Srilatha, and Deepa Dhanraj. 2004. "Gender Myths That Instrumentalise Women: A View from the Indian Frontline." *IDS Bulletin* 35 (4): 11–18.

BDEBP. 2007. Base de datos [database] El Bravo Pueblo, Caracas, Universidad Central de Venezuela. In *Disponible en el Centro de Documentación del Cendes, Colinas de Bello Monte*.

Bebbington, Anthony. 2005. "Donor–NGO Relations and Representations of Livelihood in Nongovernmental Aid Chains." *World Development* 33 (6): 937–50.

——. 2007. *Minería y desarrollo en el Perú, con especial referencia al Proyecto Río Blanco, Piura*. Vol. 1. Lima: Instituto de Estudios peruanos.

——. 2013. "Conflicto social e instituciones emergentes: Hipótesis desde Piura, Perú." In *Industrias extractivas, conflicto social y dinámicas institucionales en al Región Andina*, edited by Anthony Bebbington. Lima: IEP Instituto de Estudios Peruanos.

Bebbington, Anthony, and Ximena S. Warnaars. 2014. "Negotiable Differences? Conflicts over Mining and Development in South East Ecuador." In *Natural Resource Extraction and Indigenous Livelihoods: Development Challenges in an Era of Globalization*, edited by Emma Gilbethorpe and Gavin Hilson, 109–28. Burlington, VT: Ashgate.

Bebbington, Anthony, Scott Guggenheim, Elizabeth Olson, and Michael Woolcock. 2006. *The Search for Empowerment: Social Capital as Idea and Practice at the World Bank*. Bloomfield, CT: Kumarian Press.

Bedford, Kate. 2009. *Developing Partnerships: Gender, Sexuality and the Reformed World Bank*. Minneapolis: University of Minnesota Press.

Benjamin, Walter. 1969. "Theses on the Philosophy of History." In *Illuminations*, edited by Walter Benjamin, Hannah Arendt, and Harry Zohn, 254–58. New York: Schocken Books.

Bennett, Jane. 2001. *The Enchantment of Modern Life: Attachments, Crossings, and Ethics*. Princeton, NJ: Princeton University Press.

Bevir, Mark. 2011. "Governance and Governmentality after Neoliberalism." *Policy and Politics* 39 (4): 457–71.

Bickham Mendez, Jennifer. 2005. *From the Revolution to the Maquiladoras: Gender, Labor and Globalization in Nicaragua*. Durham, NC: Duke University Press.

Biekart, Kees. 1999. *The Politics of Civil Society Building: European Private Aid Agencies and Democratic Transitions in Central America*. Utrecht: International Books.

Blom Hansen, Thomas, and Finn Stepputat. 2005. "Introduction." In *Sovereign Bodies: Citizens, Migrants, and States in the Postcolonial World*, edited by Thomas Blom Hansen and Finn Stepputat, 1–38. Princeton, NJ: Princeton University Press.

Bob, Clifford. 2005. *The Marketing of Rebellion: Insurgents, Media, and International Activism*. Cambridge: Cambridge University Press.

Bobbio, Norberto. 1989. "Gramsci and the Concept of Civil Society." In *Civil Society and the State: New European Perspectives*, edited by John Keane, 73–100. London: Verso.

Bonilla-Silva, Eduardo. 2001. *White Supremacy and Racism in the Post–Civil Rights Era*. Boulder, CO: Lynne Rienner.

Borras, Saturnino M. 2008. "La Vía Campesina and Its Global Campaign for Agrarian Reform." In *Transnational Agrarian Movements Confronting Globalization*, edited by Saturnino M. Borras, Marc Edelman, and Cristóbal Kay, 91–121. Hoboken, NJ: Wiley-Blackwell.

Boschi, Renato. 1987. *A arte da associação política de base e democracia no Brasil*. Rio de Janeiro: Vértice.

Boston Women's Health Course Collective. 1971. *Our Bodies, Ourselves*. Boston: New England Free Press.

Brubaker, Rogers. 2006. *Ethnicity without Groups*. Cambridge: Harvard University Press.

Bruneau, Thomas C. 1974. *O catolicismo brasileiro em época de transição*. São Paulo: Loyola.

Brysk, Alison. 2000. *From Tribal Village to Global Village: Indian Rights and International Relations in Latin America*. Stanford, CA: Stanford University Press.

Buck-Morss, Susan. 1998. "What Is Political Art?" *Private Time in Public Space inSITE* 97: 14–26.

Bullard, Robert D. 1993. "Anatomy of Environmental Racism and the Environmental Justice Movement." In *Confronting Environmental Racism: Voices from the Grassroots*, edited by Robert D. Bullard, 15–39. Cambridge, MA: South End Press.

Butler, Judith. 1997. *The Psychic Life of Power: Theories in Subjection*. Stanford, CA: Stanford University Press.

Caldeira, Teresa. 2000. *City of Walls: Crime, Segregation, and Citizenship in São Paulo*. Berkeley: University of California Press.

Calhoun, Craig. 1992. "Introduction: Habermas and the Public Sphere." In *Habermas and the Public Sphere*, edited by Craig Calhoun, 1–48. Cambridge: MIT Press.

———. 2002. "Imagining Solidarity: Cosmpolitianism, Constitutional Patriotism and the Public Sphere." *Public Culture* 14:147–71.

Cameron, John. 2009. *Struggles for Local Democracy in the Andes*. Boulder, CO: Lynne Rienner.

Cameron, John D. 2010. "Is This What Autonomy Looks Like? Tensions and Challenges in the Construction of Indigenous Autonomy in Bolivia." Meetings of the Latin American Studies Association, Toronto, October 6–9.

———. 2013. "Bolivia's Contentious Politics of 'Normas y Procedimientos Propios.'" *Latin American and Caribbean Ethnic Studies* 8 (2): 179–201.

Cameron, Maxwell A. 2009. "Latin America's Left Turns: Beyond Good and Bad." *Third World Quarterly* 30 (2): 331–48.

Cameron, Maxwell A., Eric Hershberg, and Kenneth E. Sharpe. 2014. *New Institutions for Participatory Democracy in Latin America: Voice and Consequence*. New York: Palgrave Macmillan.

Cannon, Barry, and Peadar Kirby. 2012. *Civil Society and the State in Left-Led Latin America: Challenges and Limitations to Democratization*. London: Zed Books.

Cardenas, Roosbelinda. 2012. "Green Multiculturalism: Articulations of Ethnic and Environmental Politics in a Colombian 'Black Community.'" *Journal of Peasant Studies* 39 (2): 309–33.

Casanova, José. 1994. *Public Religious in the Modern World*. Chicago: University of Chicago Press.

Castañeda, Jorge G. 1993. *Utopia Unarmed: The Latin American Left after the Cold War*. New York: Knopf.

———. 2006. "Latin America's Left Turn." *Foreign Affairs* 85 (3): 28–43.

Castro, Maria H. 1988. "Equipamentos sociais e política local no pós-64: Dois estudos de caso." *Espaço e Debates* 24:67–74.

Chalmers, Douglas A., et al. 1997. *The New Politics of Inequality in Latin America: Rethinking Participation and Representation*. Oxford: Oxford University Press.

Chandhoke, Neera. 2003. *The Conceits of Civil Society*. New Delhi: Oxford University Press.

Chatterjee, Partha. 2006. *The Politics of the Governed: Reflections on Popular Politics in Most of the World*. New York: Columbia University Press.

———. 2007. *La nación en tiempo heterogéneo y otros estudios subalternos*. Lima: CLACSO SEPHIS IEP, Instituto de Estudios Peruanos.

Chávez, Hugo Rafael. 2006. Chávez llama a conformar el Partido Socialista.

———. 2007. Juramentación del Consejo Presidencial para la Reforma Constitucional y del Consejo Presidencial del Poder Comunal. Accessed January 17, 2007. http://iucat.iu.edu/iub/8044786.

Chávez, Patricia, Tania Quiroz, Dunia Mokraniz, and María Lugones. 2011. *Despatriarcalizar para descolonizar la gestión pública*. La Paz: Vicepresidencia del Estado Plurinacional de Bolivia, Dirección de Participación Ciudadana.

Checa, Laureano, Claudia Lagos Lira, and Cristian Cabalin. 2011. "The Case of Chile during Michelle Bachelet's Administration: Citizenship Participation for Strengthening Democracy." *ARGOS* 28 (55): 13–47.

Cheretski, Isidoro. 2007. *La Politica Despues de los Partidos*. Buenos Aires: Prometeo.

CIA. 2011. *CIA World Factbook*. https://www.cia.gov/library/publications/the-world -factbook/geos/ar.html.

Clarin. 2007. Gualeguaychú y GreenPeace, Historia de un Cordial Divorcio. http:// edant.clarin.com/diario/2007/11/26/elpais/p-1549369.htm.

Clark, Cindy, et al. 2006. *Where Is the Money for Women's Rights?: Assessing Resources and the Role of Donors in the Promotion of Women's Rights and the Support of Women's Organizations*. Toronto: AWID.

Cleaver, Francis. 2001. "Institutions, Agency, and the Limitations of Participatory Approaches to Development." In *Participation: The New Tyranny?*, edited by Bill Cooke and Uma Kothari, 37–55. New York: Zed Books.

Coelho, Vera Schattan R. P. 2004. "Conselhos de saúde enquanto instituições políticas: O que está faltando." In *Participação e deliberação: Teoria democrática e experiências institucionais no Brasil contemporâneo*, edited by Vera Schattan R. P. Coelho and Marcos Nobre, 255–69. São Paulo: 34 Letras.

Cohen, Jean L., and Andrew Arato. 1992. *Civil Society and Political Theory*. Cambridge, MA: MIT Press.

Cohen, Jean L., and Joel Rogers. 1995. *Associations and Democracy*. London: Verso.

Colectivo Situaciones. 2006. "¿Hay una nueva gobernabilidad?" *La Fogata* 1. http:// www.nodo50.org/colectivosituaciones/articulos_23.htm.

Comaroff, Jean, and John L. Comaroff, eds. 2001. *Millennial Capitalism and the Culture of Neoliberalism, a Public Culture Book*. Durham, NC: Duke University Press.

Comaroff, John L., and Jean Comaroff. 1999. *Civil Society and the Political Imagination in Africa: Critical Perspectives*. Chicago: University of Chicago Press.

Conaghan, Catherine, and Carlos De la Torre. 2008. "The Permanent Campaign of Rafael Correa: Making Ecuador's Plebiscitary Presidency." *International Journal of Press/Politics* 13 (3): 267–84.

Cooke, Bill, and Uma Kothari, eds. 2001. *Participation: The New Tyranny?* London: Zed Books.

Cooley, Alexander, and James Ron. 2002. "The NGO Scramble: Organizational Insecurity and the Political Economy of Transnational Action." *International Security* 27 (1): 5–39.

Cooper, Frederick. 2005. *Colonialism in Question: Theory, Knowledge, History*. Berkeley: University of California Press.

Cornia, Giovanni, Richard Jolly, and Frances Stewart. 1987. *Adjustment with a Human Face: Protecting the Vulnerable and Promoting Growth*. New York: Oxford University Press.

Cornwall, Andrea. 2002. *Making Spaces, Changing Places: Situating Participation in Development, IDS Working Paper 170*. Brighton Institute of Development Studies (IDS).

———. 2003. "Whose Voices? Whose Choices? Reflections on Gender and Participatory Development." *World development* 31 (8): 1325–42.

———. 2004. "Introduction: New Democratic Spaces? The Politics and Dynamics of Institutionalised Participation." *IDS Bulletin* 35 (2): 1–10.

Cornwall, Andrea, and Vera Schattan P. Coelho, eds. 2007. *Spaces for Change? The Politics of Citizen Participation in New Democratic Arenas*. London: Zed Books.

Cornwall, Andrea, Elizabeth Harrison, and Ann Whitehead. 2007a. "Introduction: Feminisms in Development: Contradictions, Contestations, Challenges." In *Feminisms in Development: Contradictions, Contestations and Challenges*, edited by Andrea Cornwall, Elizabeth Harrison, and Ann Whitehead, 1–17. New York: Zed Books.

———. 2007b. "Gender Myths and Feminist Fables the Struggle for Interpretive Power in Gender and Development." In *Gender Myths and Feminist Fables: The Struggle for Interpretive Power in Gender and Development*, edited by Andrea Cornwall, Elizabeth Harrison, and Ann Whitehead, 1–19. London: Blackwell.

Cortez Ruiz, Carlos. 2004. "Social Strategies and Public Policies in an Indigenous Zone in Chiapas, Mexico." *IDS bulletin* 35 (2): 76–83.

Craske, Nikki, and Maxine Molyneux, eds. 2002. *Gender and the Politics of Rights and Democracy in Latin America*. London: Palgrave Macmillan.

CRBV. 1999. *Constitución de la Republica Bolivariana de Venezuela*. Caracas: Imprenta Nacional.

Criquillion, Ana. 2007. "Alternatives for Sustainability: The Central American Women's Fund." XXVII International Congress of the Latin American Studies Association, Montreal, September.

Crítica y Emancipación: Latin American Journal of Social Science. 2008. "Editorial: Two Moments in Latin American Social Thought." *Crítica y Emancipación: Latin American Journal of Social Science* 1 (1): 9–20.

Crozier, Michel, Samuel P. Huntington, and Joji Watanuki. 1975. *The Crisis of Democracy: Report on the Governability of Democracies to the Trilateral Commission*. New York: New York University Press.

Cruikshank, Barbara. 1999. *The Will to Empower: Democratic Citizens and Other Subjects*. Ithaca, NY: Cornell University Press.

Cruikshank, Barbara, Sonia E. Alvarez, Charles R. Hale, and Martha Balaguera Cuervo, eds. In progress. *On Protest: Comparative and Transnational Perspectives*.

Dagnino, Evelina. 1994. "Os movimentos sociais e a emergência de uma nova noção de cidadania." In *Anos 90: Política e sociedade no Brasil*, edited by Evelina Dagnino, 103–18. São Paulo: Brasiliense.

———. 1998. "Culture, Citizenship, and Democracy: Changing Discourses and Practices of the Latin American Left." In *Cultures of Politics/Politics of Cultures: Re-visioning Latin American Social Movements*, edited by Sonia E. Alvarez, Evelina Dagnino, and Arturo Escobar, 33–63. Boulder, CO: Westview Press.

———, ed. 2002a. *Sociedade civil e espaços públicos no Brasil*. São Paulo: Paz e Terra.

———. 2002b. "Sociedade civil, espaços públicos e a construção democrática no Brasil: Limites e possibilidades." In *Sociedade civil e espaços públicos no Brasil*, edited by Evelina Dagnino, 279–302. São Paulo: Paz e Terra.

———. 2003. "Citizenship in Latin America: An Introduction." *Latin American Perspectives* 30 (2): 211–25.

———. 2005. *Meanings of Citizenship in Latin America*. Brighton, UK: Institute of Development Studies.

Dagnino, Evelina, Alberto J. Olvera, and Aldo Panfichi, eds. 2006a. *A Disputa pela construção democrática na América Latina*. São Paulo: Paz e Terra.

———. 2006b. "Para uma outra leitura da disputa pela construção democrática na América Latina." In *A disputa pela construção democrática na América Latina*, edited by Evelina Dagnino, Alberto J. Olvera, and Aldo Panfichi, 13–92. São Paulo: Paz e Terra.

Damonte, Gerardo. 2007. "Minería y política: La recreación de luchas campesinas en dos comunidades andinas." In *Minería, movimientos sociales y respuestas campesinas. Una ecología política de transformaciones territoriales*, edited by Anthony Bebbington, 117–63. Lima: IEP, Instituto de Estudios peruanos.

Dandler, Jorge, and Juan Torrico. 1987. "From the National Indigenous Congress to the Ayopaya Rebellion: Bolivia, 1945–1947." In *Resistance, Rebellion, and Consciousness in the Andean Peasant World, 18th–20th Centuries*, edited by Steve J. Stern. Madison: University of Wisconsin Press.

Dangl, Benjamin. 2010. *Dancing with Dynamite: Social Movements and States in Latin America*. Oakland, CA: AK Press.

David, Evans. 1993. *Sexual Citizenship: The Material Construction of Sexualities*. London: Routledge Chapman and Hall.

Daza, Mar, Raphael Hoetmer, and Virginia Vargas. 2012. *Crisis y movimientos sociales en Nuestra América: Cuerpos, territorios e imaginarios en disputa*. Lima: Programa Democracia y Transformación Global/Coordinadora Interuniversitaria de Investigación sobre Movimientos Sociales y Cambios Político-Culturales.

Dean, Mitchell. 1999. *Governmentality: Power and Rule in Modern Society*. London: Sage.

———. 2010. *Governmentality: Power and Rule in Modern Society*. London: Sage.

de Echave C, José, Raphael Hoetmer, and Mario Palacios Panéz. 2009. *Minería y territorio en el Perú: Conflictos, resistencias y propuestas en tiempos de globalización*. Lima: Programa Democracia y Transformación Global, CooperAcción and CONACAMI.

Delamata, Gabriela. 2005. *Los barrios desbordados*. Buenos Aires: Libros del Rojas.

———. 2012. "Actualizando (localmente) el derecho al ambiente: Movilización social, activismo legal y derecho constitucional al ambiente de 'sustentabilidad fuerte' en el sector extractivista megaminero." *Papeles de Trabajo IDAES* 6 (10): 102–27.

Desai, Manisha. 2002. "Transnational Solidarity: Women's Agency, Structural Adjustment, and Globalization." In *Women's Activism and Globalization: Linking Local Struggles and Transnational Politics*, edited by Nancy A. Naples and Manisha Desai, 15–33. New York: Routledge.

Dezalay, Yves, and Bryant G. Garth. 2002. *The Internationalization of Palace Wars: Lawyers, Economists, and the Contest to Transform Latin American States*. Chicago: University of Chicago Press.

Diez, Alejandro. 2009. "Disputas por la legalidad, los derechos de propiedad y el futuro agrícola o minero de la sierra de Piura: El caso Majaz." In *Minería y conflicto social*, edited by José C. de Echave et al. Lima: IEP, Instituto de Estudios Peruanos.

Di Marco, Graciela. 2010. "Los movimientos de mujeres en la Argentina y la emergencia del pueblo feminista." *La Aljaba, segunda época* 14:51–67.

——. 2011a. *El pueblo feminista: Movimientos sociales y lucha de las mujeres en torno a la ciudadanía*. Buenos Aires: Editorial Biblos.

——. 2011b. "Claims for Legal Abortion in Argentina and the Construction of New Political Idenities." In *Feminisms, Democratization and Radical Democracy: Case Studies in South and Central America, Middle East, and North Africa*. Buenos Aires: UNSAM EDITA.

——. 2012. "Las demandas en torno a la Ciudadanía Sexual en Argentina." *SER Social* 14 (30): 210–43.

Di Marco, Graciela, and Héctor Palomino. 2003. *Movimientos sociales en la Argentina: Asambleas: La politización de la sociedad civil*. Buenos Aires: Baudino.

Doimo, Ana Maria. 1995. *A vez e a voz do popular: Movimentos sociais e participação política no Brasil pós-70*. Rio de Janeiro: Relume Dumará.

——. 2004. "Pluralidade religiosa à brasileira, associativismo e movimentos sociais em São Paulo." In *O associativismo em São Paulo*, edited by Leonardo Avritzer, 123–96. São Paulo: Editora UNESP.

Doornbos, Martin. 2001. " 'Good Governance': The Rise and Decline of a Policy Metaphor?" *Journal of Development Studies* 37 (6): 93–108.

Dover, Robert v. h., and Joanne Rappaport. 1996. "Ethnicity Reconfigured: Indigenous Legislators and the Colombian Constitution of 1991." *Journal of Latin American Anthropology* 1 (2): 2 17.

Dreifuss, René. 1982. *A conquista do estado, ação política, poder e golpe de classe*. Petrópolis: Vozes.

DuBois, W. E. B. 1989. *The Souls of Black Folk*. New York: Penguin Books.

——. [1940] 1990. *Dusk of Dawn: An Essay toward an Autobiography of a Race Concept*. New York: Harcourt, Brace and Company.

Eckstein, Susan, ed. 2001. *Power and Popular Protest: Latin American Social Movements*. Berkeley: University of California Press.

Edwards, Michael, and David Hulme. 1997. *NGOs, States and Donors: Too Close for Comfort?* New York: St. Martin's Press.

Ehrick, Christine. 1999. "Madrinas and Missionaries: Uruguay and the Pan-American Women's Movement." In *Feminisms and Internationalism*, edited by Mrinalini Sinha, Donna J. Guy, and Angela Woollacott, 62–80. Malden, MA: Blackwell.

Elyachar, Julia. 2005. *Markets of Dispossession: NGOs, Economic Development, and the State in Cairo*. Durham, NC: Duke University Press.

Encarnación, Omar G. 2003. *The Myth of Civil Society: Social Capital and Democratic Consolidation in Spain and Brazil*. New York: Palgrave MacMillan.

Encuentro Nacional de Mujeres. 2016. http://encuentrodemujeres.com.ar.

Escobar, Arturo. 1995. *Encountering Development: The Making and Unmaking of the Third World*. Princeton, NJ: Princeton University Press.

——. 2008. *Territories of Difference: Place, Movements, Life, Redes*. Durham, NC: Duke University Press.

Escobar, Arturo, and Sonia E. Alvarez, eds. 1992. *The Making of Social Movements in Latin America: Identity, Strategy, and Democracy*. Boulder, CO: Westview Press.

Escorel, Sarah. 2005. "Saúde e democracia: História e perspectivas do SUS." As Conferências Nacionais de Saúde na construção do SUS, Lima, Nísia Trinidade alli (Org).

Evans, David. 1993. *Sexual Citizenship: The Material Construction of Sexualities*. New York: Routledge Chapman and Hall.

Evers, Tilman. 1983. *Identity: The Hidden Side of New Social Movements in Latin America*. Amsterdam: Centro de Estudios y Documentación Latinoamericanos (CEDLA).

Ewig, Christina. 1999. "The Strengths and Limits of the NGO Women's Movement Model: Shaping Nicaragua's Democratic Institutions." *Latin American Research Review* 34 (3): 75–102.

Exposición de Motivos. 1999. *Constitución de la República Bolivariana de Venezuela*. Caracas: Imprenta Nacional.

Eyben, Rosalinda, and Rebecca Napier-Moore. 2009. "Choosing Words with Care? Shifting Meanings of Women's Empowerment in International Development." *Third World Quarterly* 30 (2): 285–300.

Fanon, Frantz. [1963] 2003. *Wretched of the Earth*. New York: Grove.

Feinberg, Richard, Carlos H. Waisman, and Leon Zamosc, eds. 2006. *Civil Society and Democracy in Latin America*. New York: Palgrave Macmillan.

Felski, Rita. 1989. *Beyond Feminist Aesthetics: Feminist Literature and Social Change*. Cambridge, MA: Harvard University Press.

Ferguson, James. 1994. *The Anti-Politics Machine: "Development," Depoliticization, and Bureaucratic Power in Lesotho*. Minneapolis: University of Minnesota Press.

Ferguson, James, and Akhil Gupta. 2002. "Spatializing States: Toward an Ethnography of Neoliberal Governmentality." *American Ethnologist* 29 (4): 981–1002.

Fernandes, Sujatha. 2010. *Who Can Stop the Drums?: Urban Social Movements in Chávez's Venezuela*. Durham, NC: Duke University Press.

Fisher, William F., and Thomas Ponniah. 2003. *Another World Is Possible: Popular Alternatives to Globalization at the World Social Forum*. New York: Zed Books.

Flatley, Jonathan. 2008. *Affective Mapping: Melancholia and the Politics of Modernism*. Cambridge, MA: Harvard University Press.

Fontana, Benedetto. 2006. "Liberty and Domination: Civil Society in Gramsci." *Boundary 2* 33 (2): 51–74.

Ford-Smith, Honor. 1997. "Ring Ding in a Tight Corner: Sistren, Collective Democracy, and the Organization of Cultural Production." In *Feminist Genealogies, Colonial Legacies, Democratic Futures*, edited by M. Jacqui Alexander and Chandra Talpade Mohanty, 213–58. New York: Routledge.

Forni, Pablo, and María E. Longo. 2003. *Las respuestas de los pobres ante la crisis: Las redes de organizaciones comunitarias y la búsqueda de soluciones a los problemas de las áreas periféricas de Buenos Aires*. Buenos Aires: IDICSO–Universidad del Salvador.

Foucault, Michel. 1990. *The History of Sexuality: An Introduction*. New York: Vintage Books.

———. 2003. "The Subject and Power." In *The Essential Foucault: Selections from Essential Works of Foucault, 1954–1984*, edited by Michel Foucault, Paul Rabinow, and Nikolas S. Rose. New York: New York University Press.

Fraser, Nancy. 1989. *Unruly Practices: Power, Discourse and Gender in Contemporary Social Theory*. Minneapolis: University of Minnesota Press.

———. 1997. "Rethinking the Public Sphere: A Contribution to the Critique of Actually Existing Democracy." In *Justice Interruptus: Critical Reflections on the "Post-Socialist" Condition*, edited by Nancy Fraser, 69–98. New York: Routledge.

Freeman, Carla. 2001. "Is Local: Global as Feminine: Masculine? Rethinking the Gender of Globalization." *Signs: Journal of Women in Culture and Society* 26 (4): 1007–37.

French, Jan H. 2006. "Buried Alive: Imagining Africa in the Brazilian Northeast." *American Ethnologist* 33 (3): 340–60.

Friedman, Elisabeth J., and Kathryn Hochstetler. 2002. "Assessing the Third Transition in Latin American Democratization: Representational Regimes and Civil Society in Argentina and Brazil." *Comparative Politics* 35 (1): 21–42.

Friedman, Elisabeth J., Kathryn Hochstetler, and Ann M. Clark. 2005. *Sovereignty, Democracy and Global Civil Society: State-Society Relations at UN World Conferences*. Albany: SUNY Press.

Fukuyama, Francis. 2000. *Civil Society and Social Capital*. Washington, DC: International Monetary Fund, IMF Institute.

Galletta, Ricardo. 1989. "Conselhos populares e administração petista." São Paulo: Fórum Nacional Participação Popular, Campinas.

García-Gaudillo, María P. 2003a. "Civil Society: Institutionalization, Fragmentation, Autonomy." In *Venezuelan Politics in the Chávez Era: Class, Polarization and Conflict*, edited by Steve Ellner and Daniel Hellinger, 179–96. Boulder, CO: Lynne Rienner.

———. 2003b. "Politización y polarización de la sociedad civil venezolana: Las dos caras frente a la democracia." XXIV Congreso de LASA, Dallas, March 27–29.

———. 2007. "Social Movements in a Polarized Setting: Myths of Venezuelan Civil Society." In *Venezuela: Hugo Chávez and the Decline of an "Exceptional Democracy,"* edited by Steve Ellner and Miguel Tinker Salas, 140–54. Boulder, CO: Lynne Rienner.

García Pérez, Alan. 2007. "El síndrome del perro del hortelano." *El Comercio* 28:14. http://www.justiciaviva.org.pe/userfiles/26539211-Alan-Garcia-Perez-y-el-perro-del-hortelano.pdf.

Gay, Robert. 1994. *Popular Organization and Democracy in Rio de Janeiro: A Tale of Two Favelas*. Philadelphia: Temple University Press.

Genro, Tarso. Interview with SINDPD. Accessed December 10, 2004.

Gereffi, Gary, and Miguel Korzeniewicz. 1994. *Commodity Chains and Global Capitalism*. Westport, CT: Praeger.

Ghafour, Hamida. 2007. "Anarchy in the Andes as Race Divides Bolivia." *Telegraph* (May 7). http://www.telegraph.co.uk/news/worldnews/1550601/Anarchy-in-the-Andes-as-race-divides-Bolivia.html.

Giarracca, Norma. 2007. "La tragedia del desarrollo: Disputas por los recursos naturales en Argentina." *Sociedad* 26:9–36. Buenos Aires: Editorial Prometeo.

Giarracca, Norma, and Daniela Mariotti. 2012. "Porque juntos somos muchos más: Los movimientos socioterritoriales de Argentina y sus aliados." *OSAL-CLACSO* 32:95–115. Buenos Aires: CLACSO.

Gibson, Nigel C. 1999. "Radical Mutations: Fanon's Untidy Dialectic of History." In *Rethinking Fanon: The Continuing Dialogue*, 408–46. New York: Humanity Books.

Gibson-Graham, J. K. 2006. *A Postcapitalist Politics*. Minneapolis: University of Minnesota Press.

Goldfrank, Benjamin. 2003. "Making Participation Work in Porto Alegre." In *Radicals in Power: The Workers' Party (PT) and Experiments in Urban Democracy in Brazil*, edited by Gianpaolo Baiocchi, 27–52. London: Zed Books.

———. 2011a. *Deepening Local Democracy in Latin America: Participation, Decentralization, and the Left*. University Park: Pennsylvania State University Press.

———. 2011b. "The Left and Participatory Democracy: Brazil, Uruguay, Venezuela." In *The Resurgence of the Latin American Left*, edited by Steven Levitsky and Kenneth M. Roberts, 162–83. Baltimore: Johns Hopkins University Press.

Goldman, Michael. 2005. *Imperial Nature: The World Bank and Struggles for Social Justice in the Age of Globalization*. New Haven, CT: Yale University Press.

Goldstein, Daniel M. 2004. *The Spectacular City: Violence and Performance in Urban Bolivia*. Durham, NC: Duke University Press.

Gomez, Elvia. 2006. "MVR ofrece mejores con parlamentarismo de calle." *El Universal* (January 28).

Gómez Bruera, Hernán F. 2013. *Lula, the Workers' Party and the Governability Dilemma in Brazil*. New York: Routledge.

Gómez Calcaño, Luis. 1987. *Crisis y movimientos sociales en Venezuela*. Caracas: Tropykos.

Gómez Calcaño, Luis, and Margarita López Maya. 1990. *El tejido de Penélope: La reforma del Estado en Venezuela (1984–1988)*. Caracas: Cendes-Apucv-IPP.

Goodale, Mark, and Nancy Postero. 2013. *Neoliberalism, Interrupted: Social Change and Contested Governance in Contemporary Latin America*. Stanford, CA: Stanford University Press.

Gottberg, Luis Duno. 2011. "The Color of Mobs: Racial Politics, Ethnopopulism, and Representation in the Chávez Era." In *Venezuela's Bolivarian Democracy: Participation, Politics, and Culture under Chávez*, edited by David Smilde and Daniel Hellinger, 271–97. Durham, NC: Duke University Press.

Graeber, David. 2003. "The Globalization Movement and the New New Left." In *Implicating Empire: Globalization and Resistance in the 21st Century World Order*, edited by Stanley Aronowitz and Heather Gautney, 325–38. New York: Basic Books.

Gramsci, Antonio. [1971] 1995. *Selections from the Prison Notebooks of Antonio Gramsci*. New York: International Publishers.

Grazia, Grazia de, and Ana C. Ribeiro Torres. 2003. *Experiência de orçamento participativo no Brasil: Periodo de 1997 a 2000*. São Paulo: Editora Vozes.

Grewal, Inderpal. 2005. *Transnational America: Feminisms, Diasporas, Neoliberalisms*. Durham, NC: Duke University Press.

Grindle, Merilee S. 2004. "Good Enough Governance: Poverty Reduction and Reform in Developing Countries." *Governance* 17 (4): 525–48.

———. 2012. "Good Governance: The Inflation of an Idea." In *Planning Ideas that Matter: Livability, Territoriality, Governance, and Reflective Practice*, edited by Bishwapriya Sanyal, Lawrence J. Vale, and Christina D. Rosan. 259–82. Cambridge, MA: MIT Press.

Gros, Christian. 1991. *Colombia Indigena: Identidad Cultural y Cambio Social*. Bogotá: CEREC.

Grueso, Libia, Carlos Rosero, and Arturo Escobar. 1998. "The Process of Black Community Organizing in the Southern Pacific Coast Region of Colombia." In *Cultures of Politics, Politics of Cultures: Re-visioning Latin American Social Movements*, edited by Sonia E. Alvarez, Evelina Dagnino, and Arturo Escobar, 196–219. Boulder, CO: Westview Press.

Grugel, Jean, and Pia Riggirozzi, eds. 2009. *Governance after Neoliberalism in Latin America*. New York: Palgrave Macmillan.

Gudynas, Eduardo. 2012. "Estado compensador y nuevos extractivismos: Las ambivalencias del progresismo sudamericano." *Nueva Sociedad* 237:128–46.

Gustafson, Bret. 2010. "When States Act Like Movements: Dismantling Local Power and Seating Sovereignty in Post-Neoliberal Bolivia." *Latin American Perspectives* 37 (4): 48–66.

Habermas, Jürgen. 1995. *Between Facts and Norms: Contributions to a Discourse Theory of Law and Democracy*. Cambridge, MA: MIT Press.

Hale, Charles R. 2002. "Does Multiculturalism Menace? Governance, Cultural Rights and the Politics of Identity in Guatemala." *Journal of Latin American Studies* 34 (3): 485–524.

———. 2005. "Neoliberal Multiculturalism: The Remaking of Cultural Rights and Racial Dominance in Central America." *Political and Legal Anthropology Review* 28 (1): 10–28.

———. 2006a. "Activist Research v. Cultural Critique: Indigenous Land Rights and the Contradictions of Politically Engaged Anthropology." *Cultural Anthropology* 21 (1): 96–120.

———. 2006b. *Más Que Un Indio—More than an Indian: Racial Ambivalence and Neoliberal Multiculturalism in Guatemala*. Santa Fe, NM: School of American Research Press.

Hale, Charles R., and Rosamel Millamán. 2006. "Cultural Agency and Political Struggle in the Era of the Indio Permitido." In *Cultural Agency in the Americas*, edited by Doris Sommer, 281–301. Durham, NC: Duke University Press.

Hall, Gillette, and Harry A. Patrinos. 2006. "Key Messages and an Agenda for Action." In *Indigenous Peoples, Poverty and Human Development in Latin America*, edited by Gillette Hall and Harry A. Patrinos, 221–40. Hampshire, UK: Palgrave Macmillan.

Hall, Stuart. 1986. "Gramsci's Relevance for the Study of Race and Ethnicity." *Journal of Communication Inquiry* 10 (3): 5–27.

Hanchard, Michael. 2006. *Party/Politics: Horizons in Black Political Thought*. Oxford: Oxford University Press.

Hardt, Michael. 1995. "The Withering of Civil Society." *Social Text* 45:27–44.

Harnecker, Marta. 1993a. *La alcaldía donde se juega la esperanza*. Caracas: Imprenta Municipal.

———. 1993b. *Municipio Caroní: Gobernar. Tarea de todos*. Caracas: Imprenta Municipal.

Harriss, John. 2002. *Depoliticizing Development: The World Bank and Social Capital*. London: Anthem Press.

Harriss, John, Kristian Stokke, and Olle Tornquist. 2005. *Politicising Democracy: The New Local Politics of Democratization*. Hampshire, UK: Palgrave McMillan.

Hart, Gillian. 2004. "Geography and Development: Critical Ethnographies." *Progress in Human Geography* 28 (1): 91–100.

Harvey, David. 2005. *A Brief History of Neoliberalism*. Oxford: Oxford University Press.

Heller, Patrick. 2000. "Degrees of Democracy: Some Comparative Lessons from India." *World Politics* 52 (4): 484–519.

Hemment, Julie. 2007. *Empowering Women in Russia: Activism, Aid, and NGOs*. Bloomington: Indiana University Press.

Hochstetler, Kathryn. 2000. "Democratizing Pressures from Below? Social Movements in the New Brazilian Democracy." In *Democratic Brazil: Actors, Institutions, and Processes*, edited by Peter R. Kingstone and Timothy J. Power, 162–82. Pittsburgh: University of Pittsburgh Press.

———. 2008. "Organized Civil Society in Lula's Brazil." In *Democratic Brazil Revisited*, edited by Peter R. Kingstone and Timothy J. Power, 33–53. Pittsburgh: University of Pittsburgh Press.

Hoetmer, Raphael, ed. 2010. *La resistencia de las comunidades de Ayavaca: Por el territorio, la vida, el agua y la autonomía*. Lima: Entre Pueblos.

Hoetmer, Raphael. 2013. "Minería, movimientos sociales y las disputas del futuro: Claves de lectura y pistas de reflexión-acción." In *Minería y movimientos sociales en el Perú: Instrumentos y propuestas para la defensa de la vida, el agua y los territorios*, edited by Raphael Hoetmer, Miguel Castro, Mar Daza, José de Echave C, and Clara Ruíz. Lima: Programa Democracia y Transformación Global and CooperAcción.

Hoetmer, Raphael, Miguel Castro, Mar Daza, José de Echave C, and Clara Ruíz, eds. 2013. *Minería y movimientos sociales en el Perú: Instrumentos y propuestas para la defensa de la vida, el agua y los territorios*. Lima: Programa Democracia y Transformación Global CooperAcción.

Hollway, Wendy. 1984. "Gender Difference and the Production of Subjectivity." In *Changing the Subject: Psychology, Social Regulation and Subjectivity*, edited by J. Henriques, W. Hollway, C. Urwin, C. Venn, and V. Walkerdine. London: Methuen.

Holston, James. 2009. *Insurgent Citizenship: Disjunctions of Democracy and Modernity in Brazil*. Princeton, NJ: Princeton University Press.

Hooker, Juliet. 2009. "Afro-Descendant Struggles for Collective Rights in Latin America." In *New Social Movements in the African Diaspora: Challenging Global Apartheid*, edited by Leith Mullings, 139–54. New York: Palgrave Macmillan.

Hopkins, Terence K., and Immanuel Wallerstein. 1977. "Patterns of Development of the Modern World-System." *Review (Fernand Braudel Center)* 1 (2): 111–45.

Houtzager, Peter P. 1998. "State and Unions in the Transformation of the Brazilian Countryside, 1964–1979." *Latin American Research Review* 33 (2): 103–42.

———. 2003. "Introduction: From Polycentrism to the Polity." In *Changing Paths: International Development and the New Politics of Inclusion*, edited by Peter P. Houtzager and Mick Moore, 1–31. Ann Arbor: University of Michigan Press.

Houtzager, Peter P., Adrián Gurza Lavalle, and Arnab Acharya. 2003. "Who Participates?: Civil Society and the New Democratic Politics in São Paulo, Brazil." Institute of Development Studies, Working paper series 210.

Howell, Jude, and Jenny Pearce. 2001. *Civil Society and Development: A Critical Exploration*. Boulder, CO: Lynne Rienner.

Huber, Evelyn, Jennifer Pribble, and John Stephens. 2010. "The Chilean Left in Power: Achievements, Failures and Omissions." In *Leftist Governments in Latin America:*

Successes and Shortcomings, edited by Kurt Weyland, Raúl de la Madrid, and Wendy Hunter, 77–97. New York: Cambridge University Press.

Hulme, David, and Michael Edwards. 1997. "NGOs, States and Donors: An Overview." In NGOs, States and Donors: Too Close for Comfort?, edited by David Hulme and Michael Edwards, 3–22. New York: St. Martin's Press.

Hunter, Wendy, and Natasha Borges Sugiyama. 2012. "Conditional Cash Transfer Programs: Assessing Their Achievements and Probing Their Promise." LASA Forum 43 (3): 9–10.

Hylton, Forrest, Sinclair Thomson, and Adolfo Gilly. 2007. Revolutionary Horizons: Past and Present in Bolivian Politics. New York: Verso.

IESA. 2000. Indicadores económicos y sociales tomados en febrero de.

Incite! Women of Color Against Violence. 2007. The Revolution Will Not Be Funded: Beyond the Non-Profit Industrial Complex. Cambridge, MA: South End Press.

Inkeles, Alex. 1969. "Making Men Modern: On the Causes and Consequences of Individual Change in Six Developing Countries." American Journal of Sociology 75 (2): 208–25.

Isunza Vera, Ernesto. 2006. "Interfaces socioestatais, prestação de contas e projetos políticos no contexto da transição política mexicana (dois casos para reflexão)." In A disputa pela construção democrática na América Latina, edited by Evelina Dagnino, Alberto J. Olvera, and Aldo Panfichi, 261–307. São Paulo: Paz e Terra.

Jad, Islah. 2004. "The NGOisation of the Arab Women's Movement." IDS bulletin 35 (4): 34–42.

James, C. L. R. 1989. The Black Jacobins: Toussaint L'Ouverture and the San Domingo Revolution. New York: Vintage Books.

Jelin, Elizabeth. 1990. Women and Social Change in Latin America. London: Zed Books.

Junge, Benjamin. 2012. "NGOs as Shadow Pseudopublics: Grassroots Community Leaders' Perceptions of Change and Continuity in Porto Alegre, Brazil." American Ethnologist 39 (2): 407–24.

———. 2014. " 'The Energy of Others': Narratives of Envy and Purification among Former Grassroots Community Leaders in Porto Alegre, Brazil." Latin American Research Review 49:81–98.

Keane, John. 1988a. Democracy and Civil Society: On the Predicaments of European Socialism, the Prospects for Democracy, and the Problem of Controlling Social and Political Power. London: Verso.

———. 1998b. Civil Society: Old Images, New Visions. Stanford, CA: Stanford University Press.

Keck, Margaret E. 1989. "The 'New Unionism' in the Brazilian Transition." In Democratizing Brazil: Problems of Transition and Consolidation, edited by Alfred Stepan, 252–96. New York: Oxford University Press.

Keck, Margaret E., and Kathryn Sikkink. 1998. Activists beyond Borders: Advocacy Networks in International Politics. Ithaca, NY: Cornell University Press.

Kim, David Kyuman. 2008. Melancholic Freedom: Agency and the Spirit of Politics. Oxford: Oxford University Press.

Kornblith, Miriam. 1998. Venezuela en los 90: La crisis de la democracia. Caracas: Ediciones UCV–IESA.

Koselleck, Reinhart. 2004. *Futures Past: On the Semantics of Historical Time*. New York: Columbia University Press.

Laclau, Ernesto. 2006a. *La razón populista*. Buenos Aires: Fondo de cultura Económica.

———. 2006b. "Why Constructing a People Is the Main Task of Radical Politics." *Critical Inquiry* 32 (4): 646–80.

Laclau, Ernesto, and Chantal Mouffe. 1985. *Hegemony and Socialist Strategy: Towards a Radical Democratic Politics*. London: Verso Press.

Lander, Edgardo. 2007. "Venezuelan Social Conflict in a Global Context." In *Venezuela: Hugo Chávez and the Decline of an "Exceptional Democracy,"* edited by Steve Ellner and Miguel Tinker Salas, 16–32. Boulder, CO: Lynne Rienner.

Lander, Luis E., et al. 1999. *Glosario de descriptores: Base de datos El Bravo Pueblo*. Caracas: Mimeo.

Lang, Sabine. 1997. "The NGOization of Feminism." In *Transitions, Environments, Translations: Feminisms in International Politics*, edited by Joan Wallach Scott, Cora Kaplan, and Debra Keates, 101–20. New York: Routledge.

Laó-Montes, Agustín. 2001. "Introduction." In *Mambo Montage: The Latinization of New York*, edited by Agustín Laó-Montes and Arlene M. Davila, 1–53. New York: Columbia University Press.

———. 2007. "Decolonial Moves: Trans-Locating African Diaspora Spaces." *Cultural Studies* 21 (2–3): 309–38.

———. 2008a. "Ningún ser humano es ilegal: Novísimos movimientos sociales de migrantes en los Estados Unidos." *Universitas Humanística* 66:273–300.

———. 2008b. "Reconfigurations of Empire in a World-Hegemonic Transition: The 1898 Spanish-Cuban-American-Filipino War." In *Revisiting the Colonial Question in Latin America*, edited by Mabel Moraña and Carlos A. Jáuregui, 209–40. Madrid: Iberoamericana.

Laserna, Roberto. 2007. "El caudillismo fragmentado." *Nueva Sociedad* 209:100–117.

Laserna, Roberto, and Miguel Villarroel. 2008. *38 años de conflicto social en Bolivia: Descripción general y por períodos gubernamentales*. Cochabamba: CERES/COSUDE/Instituto para la Democracia.

Laura, Zanotti. 2005. "Governmentalizing the Post-Cold War International Regime: The UN Debate on Democratization and Good Governance." *Alternatives: Global, Local, Political* 30 (4): 461–87.

Laurie, Nina, and Alastair Bonnett. 2002. "Adjusting to Equity: The Contradictions of Neoliberalism and the Search for Racial Equality in Peru." *Antipode* 34 (1): 28–53.

Lavinas, Lena. 2013. "21st-Century Welfare." *New Left Review* 84:5–42.

Leal, Pablo A. 2007. "Participation: The Ascendancy of a Buzzword in the Neo-Liberal era." *Development in Practice* 17 (4): 539–48.

Lebon, Nathalie. 1996. "Professionalization of Women's Health Groups in Sao Paulo: The Troublesome Road towards Organizational Diversity." *Organization* 3 (4): 588–609.

———. 1998. "Up the Purse's Strings: NGO Relations with Donor Agencies." PhD, Department of Anthropology, University of Florida, Gainesville.

Levi, Primo. 1989. *The Drowned and the Saved*. New York: Vintage International.

Levitsky, Steven, and Kenneth M. Roberts, eds. 2011. *The Resurgence of the Latin American Left*. Baltimore: Johns Hopkins University Press.

LGDESN. 2001. Líneas generales del Plan de Desarrollo Económico y Social de la Nación, 2001–2007. In *MINPADES*. Caracas, Venezuela.

Li, Tanya Murray. 2007. *The Will to Improve: Governmentality, Development, and the Practice of Politics*. Durham, NC: Duke University Press.

Lievesley, Geraldine, and Steve Ludlam, eds. 2009. *Reclaiming Latin America: Experiments in Radical Social Democracy*. London: Zed Books.

Lima, Nisia Trinidade, Silvia Gerschman, Flavio Coelho Edler, and Julio Manuel Suárez. 2005. *Saúde e democracia: História e perspectivas do Sistema Único de Saúde no Brasil*. Rio de Janeiro: Fiocruz.

Lind, Amy. 2005. *Gendered Paradoxes: Women's Movements, State Restructuring, and Global Development in Ecuador*. University Park: Penn State University Press.

———, ed. 2010. *Development, Sexual Rights and Global Governance*. New York: Routledge.

Llana, Sara Miller. 2007. "Autonomy Push Sparks Racial Strife in Bolivia." *Christian Science Monitor*, April 2.

López Maya, Margarita. 2003. "Hugo Chávez Frías: His Movement and His Presidency." In *Venezuelan Politics in the Chavez Era*, edited by Steve Ellner and Daniel Hellinger, 73–92. Boulder, CO: Lynne Rienner.

———. 2005. *Del viernes negro al referendo revocatorio*. Caracas: Alfadil.

———. 2006. "Venezuela 2001–2004: Actores y estrategias en la lucha hegemónica." In *Sujetos sociales y nuevas formas de protesta en la historia reciente de América Latina*, edited by Gerardo Caetano, 23–48. Buenos Aires: CLACSO.

———. 2007. "La Venezuela bolivariana y sus modalidades participativas: las MTA, OCAS y Consejos Comunales" In *Taller ESRC Innovaciones municipales en acciones públicas no gubernamentales: la GB y AL (ESRC-Universidad de Bradford)*. March 5–11, Bradford, England.

López Maya, Margarita, and Luis E. Lander. 2001. "Ajuste, costos sociales y la agenda de los pobres en Venezuela: 1984–1998." In *El ajuste estructural en América Latina: Costos sociales y alternativas*, edited by Emir Sader, 231–54. Buenos Aires: CLACSO.

López Maya, Margarita, David Smilde, and Keta Stephany. 2002. *Protesta y cultura en Venezuela: Los marcos de acción colectiva en 1999*. Buenos Aires: CLACSO, Consejo Latinoamericano de Ciencias Sociales.

Lowe, Lisa. 1996. *Immigrant Acts: On Asian American Cultural Politics*. Durham, NC: Duke University Press.

Lucero, José Antonio. 2008. *Struggles of Voice: The Politics of Indigenous Representation in the Andes*. Pittsburgh: University of Pittsburgh Press.

Lupien, Pascal. 2015. "Mechanisms for Popular Participation and Discursive Constructions of Citizenship." *Citizenship Studies* 19 (3–4): 367–83.

MacKinnon, Catharine A. 1982. "Feminism, Marxism, Method, and the State: An Agenda for Theory." *Signs: Journal of Women in Culture and Society* 7 (3): 515–44.

Madrid, Raúl L. 2008. "The Rise of Ethnopopulism in Latin America." *World Politics* 60 (3): 475–508.

Mallimaci, Fortunato, Humberto Cucchetti, and Luis Donatello. 2006a. "Caminos sinuosos: Nacionalismo y catolicismo en la Argentina contemporánea." In *El altar y el trono: Ensayos sobre el catolicismo político iberoamericano*, 155–90. Barcelona: Anthropos/Unibiblos.

Mallimaci, Fortunato, Humberto Cucchetti, and Luis Miguel Donatello. 2006b. "Religión y política: Discursos sobre el trabajo en la Argentina del siglo XX." *Estudios Sociológicos de El Colegio de México* 24 (71): 423–49.

Mamdani, Mahmood. 1996. *Citizen and Subject: Contemporary Africa and the Legacy of Late Colonialism*. Princeton, NJ: Princeton University Press.

Marquetti, Adalmir. 2003. "Participação e redistribuição: O orçamento participativo em Porto Alegre." In *A inovação democrática no Brasil*, edited by Leonardo Avritzer and Zander Navarro, 129–56. São Paulo: Cortez.

Martin, William G. 2005. "Global Movements before 'Globalization': Black Movements as World-Historical Movements." *Review (Fernand Braudel Center)* 18 (1): 7–28.

——, et al., eds. 2008. *Making Waves: Worldwide Social Movements, 1750–2005*. Boulder, CO: Paradigm Press.

Martínez Alier, Juan. 2002. *The Environmentalism of the Poor: A Study of Ecological Conflicts and Valuation*. Cheltenham, UK: Edward Elgar Publishing.

Massey, Doreen. 1994. "A Global Sense of Place." In *Space, Place, and Gender*, edited by Doreen Massey, 146–54. Minneapolis: University of Minnesota Press.

McCabe, Patricio E. 2007. "Gualeguaychú no tiene quién le escriba." *Dialéktica: Revista de Filosofía y Teoría Social* 16 (19): 127–38.

Melucci, Alberto. 1996. *Challenging Codes: Collective Action in the Information Age*. Cambridge: Cambridge University Press.

Merlinsky, Maria Gabriel. 2008. "La gramática de la acción colectiva ambiental en Argentina: Reflexiones en torno al movimiento ciudadano ambiental de Gualeguaychú y su inscripción en el espacio público." *Temas y Debates* 12 (15): 35–60.

Merry, Sally Engle. 2003. "Rights Talk and the Experience of Law: Implementing Women's Human Rights to Protection from Violence." *Human Rights Quarterly* 25 (2): 343–81.

Mignolo, Walter. 2000. *Local Histories/Global Designs: Coloniality, Subaltern Knowledges, and Border Thinking*. Princeton, NJ: Princeton University Press.

Milkman, Ruth, Stephanie Luce, Penny Lewis. 2013. *Changing the Subject: A Bottom-Up Account of Occupy Wall Street in New York City*. New York: Joseph S. Murphy Institute for Worker and Labor Studies, City University of New York. https://media.sps .cuny.edu/filestore/1/5/7/1_a05051d2117901d/1571_92f562221b8041e.pdf.

Miller, Francesca. 1990. "Latin American Feminism and the Transnational Arena." In *Women, Culture and Politics in Latin America*, edited by Emilie Bergmann, et al., 10–26. Berkeley: University of California Press.

——. 1991. *Latin American Women and the Search for Social Justice*. Hanover, NH: University Press of New England.

Miñoso, Yuderkys Espinosa, Diana Gómez Correal, and Karina Ochoa Muñoz. 2014. "Tejiendo de otro modo: Feminismo, epistemología y apuestas descoloniales en Abya Yala." Coloquio Tejiendo de Otro Modo Feminismo, Epistemología y Apuestas Descoloniales en Abya Yala, Popayán, Colombia.

Mohan, Giles. 2001. "Beyond Participation: Strategies for Deeper Empowerment." In *Participation: The New Tyranny?*, edited by Bill Cooke and Uma Kothari, 153–67. New York: Zed Books.

Mohanty, Ranjita. 2007. "Gendered Subjects, the State and Participatory Spaces: The Politics of Domesticating Participation in Rural India." In *Spaces for Change: The Politics of Citizen Participation in New Democratic Arenas*, edited by Andrea Cornwall and Vera Schattan Coelho, 76–94. London: Zed Books.

Molyneux, Maxine. 2008. "The 'Neoliberal Turn' and the New Social Policy in Latin America: How Neoliberal, How New?" *Development and Change* 39 (5): 775–97.

Molyneux, Maxine, and Sian Lazar. 2003. *Doing the Rights Thing: Rights-Based Development and Latin American NGOs*. Rugby, UK: Practical Action.

Monteagudo, Graciela. 2007. "The Autonomist Movements in a New Governmentality." In *Alternative Globalizations*, edited by Global Studies Association, 75–89. Chicago: Changemaker.

———. 2008. "The Clean Walls of a Recovered Factory: New Subjectivities in Argentina's Recovered Factories." *Urban Anthropology* 37 (2): 175–210.

———. 2011. "Politics by Other Means: Rhizomes of Power in Argentina's Social Movements." PhD diss., Anthropology, University of Massachusetts, Amherst.

Montero Bagatella, Juan Carlos. 2012. "Gobernabilidad: Validez/Invalidez o moda del concepto." *Revista Mexicana de Ciencias Políticas y Sociales* 57 (216): 9–23.

Moore, Henrietta. 1994. "The Problem of Explaining Violence in the Social Sciences." In *Sex and Violence: Issues in Representation and Experience*, edited by P. Harvey and P. Gow. London: Routledge.

Morais, Lecio, and Alfredo Saad-Filho. 2005. "Lula and the Continuity of Neoliberalism in Brazil: Strategic Choice, Economic Imperative or Political Schizophrenia?" *Historical Materialism* 13 (1): 3–23.

Moraña, Mabel, Enrique D. Dussel, and Carlos A. Jáuregui. 2008. *Coloniality at Large: Latin America and the Postcolonial Debate*. Durham, NC: Duke University Press.

Mosquera Rosero-Labbé, Claudia, and Luiz Claudio Barcelos, eds. 2007. *Afroreparaciones: Memorias de la esclavitud y justicia reparativa para negros, afrocolombianos y raizales*. Bogotá: Universidad Nacional de Colombia.

Mouffe, Chantal. 1999. "Deliberative Democracy or Agonistic Pluralism?" *Social Research* 66 (3): 745–58.

———. 1999. *El Retorno de lo Político: Comunidad, Ciudadanía, Pluralismo, Democracia Radical*. Buenos Aires: Paidós.

———. 2005. *On the Political: Thinking in Action*. New York: Routledge.

Mullings, Leith. 2009. *New Social Movements in the African Diaspora: Challenging Global Apartheid*. New York: Palgrave Macmillan.

Murdock, Donna F. 2008. *When Women Have Wings: Feminism and Development in Medellín, Colombia*. Ann Arbor: University of Michigan Press.

Nagar, Richa, and Sangtin Writers. 2006. *Playing with Fire: Feminist Thought and Activism through Seven Lives in India*. Minneapolis: University of Minnesota Press.

Navarro, Zander. 1996. "Democracia, cidadania e representação: Os movimentos sociais rurais no estado do Rio Grande do Sul, Brasil, 1978–1990." In *Política, protesto e cidada-*

nia no campo: As lutas sociais dos colonos e dos trabalhadores rurais no Rio Grande do Sul, edited by Zander Navarro, 62–105. Porto Alegre: Editora da Universidade, UFRGS.

———. 1998. "Affirmative Democracy and Redistributive Development: The Case of 'Participatory Budgeting' in Porto Alegre, Brazil (1989–1997)." Washington, DC: World Bank.

———. 2002. "'Mobilização sem emancipação': As lutas sociais dos sem terra no Brasil." In *Produzir para viver: Os caminhos da produção não capitalista*, edited by Boaventura de S. Santos, 189–232. São Paulo: Civilização Brasileira.

———. 2010. "The Brazilian Landless Movement (MST): Critical Times." *Redes* 15 (1): 196–223.

Navia, Patricio. 2009. "Top-Down and Bottom-Up Democracy in Chile under Bachelet." In *Widening Democracy: Citizens and Participatory Schemes in Brazil and Chile*, edited by Patricio Silva and Herwig Cleuren, 315–37. Leiden: Brill.

Ng'weno, Bettina. 2007. *Turf Wars: Territory and Citizenship in the Contemporary State*. Stanford, CA: Stanford University Press.

OCN (Organización de Comunidades Negras). 1996. "Movimiento negro, identidad y territorio: Entrevista con la Organización de Comunidades Negras de Buenaventura." In *Pacífico ¿Desarrollo o Diversidad?: Estado, capital y movimientos sociales en el Pacífico colombiano*, edited by Arturo Escobar and Alvaro Pedrosa, 245–65. Bogotá: CEREC y ECOFONDO.

O'Donnell, Guillermo. 1993. "On the State, Democratization and Some Conceptual Problems: A Latin American View with Glances at Some Postcommunist Countries." *World Development* 21 (8): 1355–69.

———. 1997. *Contrapuntos: Ensayos escogidos sobre autoritarismo y democratización*. Buenos Aires: Paidós.

O'Donnell, Guillermo, and Philippe C. Schmitter. 1986. *Transitions from Authoritarian Rule: Tentative Conclusions about Uncertain Democracies*. Baltimore: Johns Hopkins University Press.

Ong, Aihwa. 2006. *Neoliberalism as Exception: Mutations in Citizenship and Sovereignty*. Durham, NC: Duke University Press.

Ong, Aihwa, and Stephen Collier, eds. 2004. *Global Assemblages: Technology, Politics, and Ethics as Anthropological Problems*. Oxford: Blackwell.

Oxhorn, Philip. 1995. *Organizing Civil Society: The Popular Sectors and the Struggle for Democracy in Chile*. University Park: Penn State University Press.

———. 2003. "Social Inequality, Civil Society, and the Limits of Citizenship in Latin America." In *What Justice? Whose Justice? Fighting for Fairness in Latin America*, edited by Susan Eckstein and Timothy P. Wickham-Crowley, 35–63. Berkeley: University of California Press.

Página 12. 2006. Se Trata de una Causa Nacional. Accessed October 8, 2016. http://www.pagina12.com.ar/diario/elpais/1-62891-2006-02-10.html.

Pakkasvirta, Jussi. 2008. "From Pulp to Fiction?: Fray Bentos Pulp Investment Conflict through the Finnish Media." *Cooperation and Conflict* 43 (4): 421–46.

Paley, Julia. 2001. *Marketing Democracy: Power and Social Movements in Post-Dictatorship Chile*. Berkeley: University of California Press.

Paludo, Conceição, and Venderléia L. P. Daron. 2001. *Gênero, classe e projeto popular: Compreender mais para lutar melhor*. Passo Pundo: Gráfica Batistel.

Panfichi, Aldo, and Paula Muñoz Chirinos. 2002. "Sociedade civil e governabilidade democrática nos Andes e no Cone Sul: Uma visão panorâmica na entrada do século XXI." In *Sociedade civil e espaços públicos no Brasil*, edited by Evelina Dagnino, 303–30. São Paulo: Paz e Terra.

Paredes, Julieta. 2008. *Hilando fino: Desde el feminismo comunitario*. La Paz: CEDEC (Comunidad Mujeres Creando Comunidad).

Parker, Dick. 2007. "El desarrollo endógeno:¿Camino al socialismo del siglo XXI?" *Revista Venezolana de Economía y Ciencias Sociales* 13 (2): 59–85.

Paschel, Tianna S. 2016. *Becoming Black Political Subjects: Movements, Alignments and Ethno-Racial Rights in Colombia and Brazil*. Princeton, NJ: Princeton University Press.

Pearce, Jenny. 1997. "Between Co-option and Irrelevance? Latin American NGOs in the 1990s." In *NGOs, States and Donors: Too Close for Comfort*, edited by David Hulme and Michael Edwards, 257–74. New York: St. Martin's Press, Save the Children.

———. 2010. "Is Social Change Fundable? NGOs and Theories and Practices of Social Change." *Development in Practice* 20 (6): 621–35.

Peck, Jamie, and Adam Tickell. 2002. "Neoliberalizing Space." *Antipode* 34 (3): 380–404.

Pereira, Carlos. 1996. "A política pública como caixa de pandora: Organização de interesses, processo decisório e efeitos perversos na Reforma Sanitária Brasileira—1985–1989." *Dados* 39 (3): 63–84.

Petchesky, Rosalind P. 2003. *Global Prescriptions: Gendering Health and Human Rights*. New York: Zed Books.

Petras, James. 1997. "Imperialism and NGOs in Latin America." *Monthly Review* 49 (3): 10–27.

Petras, James, and Henry Veltmeyer. 2003. *Social Movements and State Power: Argentina, Brazil, Bolivia, Ecuador*. London: Pluto Press.

———. 2011. *Social Movements in Latin America: Neoliberalism and Popular Resistance*. New York: Palgrave Macmillan.

Picolotto, Everton Lazzaretti. 2009. "A emergência dos 'agricultores familiares' como sujeitos de direitos na trajetória do sindicalismo rural brasileiro." *Mundo Agrario* 9 (18).

Pierre, Jon. 2005. "Governance and Governability: Time, Space and Structure." In *Governing Complex Societies: Trajectories and Scenarios*, edited by Jon Pierre and B. Guy Peters, 64–79. New York: Palgrave Macmillan.

Pinto, Vladimir. 2009. "Reestructuración neoliberal del Estado peruano, industrias extractivas y derechos sobre el territorio." In *Minería y territorio en el Perú: Conflictos, resistencias y propuestas en tiempos de globalización*, edited by José de Echave C, Raphael Hoetmer, and Mario Palacios Panéz, 87–107. Lima: Programa Democracia y Transformación Global.

Pires, Roberto. 2015. "The Midlife of Participatory Institutions in Brazil." *LASA Forum* 46 (3): 28–30.

PNUD (Programa de las Naciones Unidas para el Desarrollo). 2004. *Interculturalismo y globalización: La Bolivia posible*. La Paz: Plural.

———. 2012. "Cuaderno del Informe de Desarrollo Humano Colombia 2011. Afroco-lombianos: Sus territorios y condiciones de vida." In *Report on Human Development in Colombia 2011. Afrocolombians: Their Territories and Life Conditions*. Bogotá: PNUD.

Porter, Doug, and David Craig. 2004. "The Third Way and the Third World: Poverty Reduction and Social Inclusion in the Rise of 'Inclusive' Liberalism." *Review of International Political Economy* 11 (2): 387–423.

Porto Gonçalves, Carlos Walter. 2001. *Geo-grafías: Movimientos sociales, nuevas territorialidades y sustentabilidad*. Mexico City: Siglo Veintiuno.

Postero, Nancy. 2006. *Now We Are Citizens: Indigenous Politics in Post-Multicultural Bolivia*. Stanford, CA: Stanford University Press.

———. 2010. "The Struggle to Create a Radical Democracy in Bolivia." *Latin American Research Review* 45 (4): 59–78.

Prevost, Gary, Carlos Oliva Campos, and Harry E. Vanden. 2012. *Social Movements and Leftist Governments in Latin America: Confrontation or Co-optation?* London: Zed Books.

Provea. Años Citados. Situación de los Derechos Humanos en Venezuela. Informes Anuales. Caracas: Provea.

Putnam, Robert D. 1995. "Bowling Alone: America's Declining Social Capital." *Journal of Democracy* 6 (1): 65–78.

Putnam, Robert D., Robert Leonardi, and Raffaella Nanetti. 1993. *Making Democracy Work: Civic Traditions in Modern Italy*. Princeton, NJ: Princeton University Press.

Quijano, Aníbal. 2000a. "Colonialidad del Poder, Eurocentrismo y América Latina." In *La colonialidad del saber: Eurocentrismo y ciencias sociales*, edited by Edgardo Lander, 201–46. Buenos Aires: Consejo Latinoamericano de Ciencias Sociales (CLASCO).

———. 2000b. "Colonialidad del poder y clasificación social." *Journal of World-Systems Research* 11 (2): 342–86.

———. 2000c. "Coloniality of Power, Eurocentrism, and Latin America." *Nepantla: Views from the South* 1 (3): 533–80.

Ramamurthy, Priti. 2004. "Why Is Buying a 'Madras' Cotton Shirt a Political Act? A Feminist Commodity Chain Analysis." *Feminist Studies* 30 (3): 734–69.

Rancière, Jacques. 1996. *El desacuerdo: Política y filosofía*. Buenos Aires: Nueva Visión.

———. [2003] 2009. The Future of the Image. Reprint ed. Edited and translated from the French by Gregory Elliot. London: Verso.

Redclift, Michael 1988. *Sustainable Development: Exploring the Contradictions*. London: Metheun.

Reis, Elisa. 1995. "Desigualdade e solidariedade: Uma releitura do 'familismo amoral' de Banfield." *Revista Brasileira de Ciências Sociais* 10 (29): 35–48.

Richards, Patricia. 2004. *Pobladoras, Indígenas, and the State: Conflicts over Women's Rights in Chile*. New Brunswick, NJ: Rutgers University Press.

Richardson, Diane. 2000. "Constructing Sexual Citizenship: Theorizing Sexual Rights." *Critical Social Policy* 20 (1): 105–35.

Riedel, Manfred. 1984. *Between Tradition and Revolution*. Cambridge: Cambridge University Press.

Ríos Tobar, Marcela, Lorena Godoy Catalán, and Elizabeth Guerrero Caviedes. 2003. *Un nuevo silencio feminista?: La transformación de un movimiento social en el Chile posdictadura.* Santiago: Centro de Estudios de la Mujer, Editorial Cuarto Propio.

Rivera, Marcia. 2000. "Panorama General de la Región." In *Memoria del II Seminario Regional De poderes y saberes, debates sobre reestructura política y transformación social,* edited by Development Alternatives with Women for a New Era (DAWN) and Red de Educación Popular Entre Mujeres de América Latina y el Caribe (REPEM). Montevideo: DAWN.

Rivera Cusicanqui, Silvia. 2012. "'Ch'ixinakax utxiwa': A Reflection on the Practices and Discourses of Decolonization." *South Atlantic Quarterly* 111 (1): 95–108.

Roberts, Kenneth. 1998. *Deepening Democracy?: The Modern Left and Social Movements in Chile and Peru.* Stanford, CA: Stanford University Press.

———. 2001. "La descomposición del sistema de partidos en Venezuela visto desde el análisis comparativo." *Revista Venezolana de Economía y Ciencias Sociales* 7 (2): 183–200.

Robins, Steven, Andrea Cornwall, and Bettina Von Lieres. 2008. "Rethinking 'Citizenship' in the Postcolony." *Third World Quarterly* 29 (6): 1069–86.

Robinson, Cedric J. 1997. *Black Movements in America.* New York: Routledge.

Rodrigues, Marta M. A., and Eduardo Meira Zauli. 2002. "Presidentes e Congresso Nacional no processo decisório da política de saúde no Brasil democrático (1985–1998)." *Dados* 45 (3): 387–429.

Rodríguez, Dylan. 2007. "The Political Logic of the Non-Profit Industrial Complex." In *The Revolution Will Not Be Funded: Beyond the Non-Profit Industrial Complex,* edited by Incite! Women of Color Against Violence, 21–40. Cambridge, MA: South End Press.

Rodriguez Neto, Eleutério, José Gomes Temporão, and Sarah Escorel. 2003. *Saúde: Promessas e limites da constituição.* Rio de Janeiro: FIOCRUZ.

Rojas, Jeannette S. 1996. "Las mujeres en movimiento: Crónicas de otras miradas." In *Pacífico ¿Desarrollo o diversidad?: Estado, capital y movimientos sociales en el Pacífico colombiano,* edited by Arturo Escobar and Alvaro Pedrosa, 205–19. Bogotá: CEREC ECOFONDO.

Ross, Cliff, and Marcy Rein, eds. 2014. *Until the Rulers Obey: Voices from Latin American Social Movements.* Oakland, CA: PM Press.

Rossi, Frederico M., and Marisa von Bülow, eds. 2015. *Social Movement Dynamics: New Perspectives on Theory and Practice from Latin America.* Burlington, VT: Ashgate.

Rubin, Jeffrey W. 1998. "Ambiguity and Contradiction in a Radical Popular Movement." In *Cultures of Politics, Politics of Cultures: Revisioning Latin American Social Movements,* edited by Sonia E. Alvarez, Evelina Dagnino, and Arturo Escobar, 141–64. Boulder, CO: Westview Press.

———. 2004. "Meanings and Mobilizations: A Cultural Politics Approach to Social Movements and States. *Latin American Research Review* 39, no. 3 (October): 106–42.

Rubin, Jeffrey W., and Vivienne Bennett, eds. 2014. *Enduring Reform: Progressive Activism and Private Sector Responses in Latin America's Democracies.* Pittsburgh: University of Pittsburgh Press.

Rubin, Jeffrey W., and Emma Sokoloff-Rubin. 2013. *Sustaining Activism: A Brazilian Women's Movement and a Father-Daughter Collaboration*. Durham, NC: Duke University Press.

Rzezak, Hernan Fair. 2008. "El Conflicto entre el gobierno y el campo en Argentina: Lineamientos políticos, estrategias discursivas y discusiones teóricas a partir de un abordaje multidisciplinar." *Iberóforum. Revista de Ciencias Sociales de la Universidad Iberoamericana* 3:82–106.

Sacchi, Hugo M. 1972. *El movimiento obrero en América Latina*. Buenos Aires: Centro Editor de América Latina.

Sader, Eder. 1988. *Quando novos personagens entraram em cena: Experiências, falas e lutas dos trabalhadores da Grande São Paulo (1970–80)*. São Paulo: Paz e Terra.

Sader, Emir. 2011. "Neoliberalismo versus pos-neoliberalismo: A disputa estratégica contemporânea." *Margem Esquerda* 16:123–27.

Santos, Boaventura de S. 1998. "Participatory Budgeting in Porto Alegre: Toward a Redistributive Democracy." *Politics and Society* 26 (4): 461–510.

Santos, Sônia Beatriz dos. 2009. "As ONGs de mulheres negras no Brasil." *Sociedade e Cultura* 12 (2): 275–88.

Santos, Wanderley Guilherme dos. 1979. *Cidadania e justiça: A política social na ordem brasileira*. Rio de Janeiro: Editora Campus.

———. 1987. *Crise e castigo: Partidos e generais na política brasileira*. Rio de Janeiro: Vértice Instituto Universitário de Pesquisas do Rio de Janeiro.

———. 1993. *Razões da desordem*. Rio de Janeiro: Rocco.

Sarmiento, Domingo Faustino. 1960. *Life in the Argentine Republic in the Days of the Tyrants; or, Civilization and Barbarism*. New York: Hafner Pub. Co.

Sassen, Saskia. 1996. *Losing Control?: Sovereignty in an Age of Globalization*. New York: Columbia University Press.

Saule, Nelson, Jr. 1995. "O Direito à cidade na Constituição de 1988: Legitimidade e eficácia do Plano Diretor." Unpublished master's thesis in law, Catholic University.

Sawyer, Mark Q. 2005. *Racial Politics in Post-Revolutionary Cuba*. New York: Cambridge University Press.

Schild, Veronica. 1998. "New Subjects of Rights? Women's Movements and the Construction of Citizenship in the 'New Democracies.'" In *Cultures of Politics/Politics of Cultures: Revisioning Latin American Social Movements*, edited by Sonia E. Alvarez, Evelina Dagnino, and Arturo Escobar, 93–117. Boulder, CO: Westview Press.

———. 2000. "Neo-liberalism's New Gendered Market Citizens: The 'Civilizing' Dimension of Social Programmes in Chile." *Citizenship Studies* 4 (3): 275–305.

Schmukler, Beatriz. 1995. "Las mujeres en la democratización social." *Estudos Feministas* 3 (1): 136–55.

Schneider, Sergio, and Paulo André Niederle. 2010. "Resistance Strategies and Diversification of Rural Livelihoods: The Construction of Autonomy among Brazilian Family Farmers." *Journal of Peasant Studies* 37 (2): 379–405.

Schuster, Federico, and Sebastián Pereyra. 2001. "La protesta social en la Argentina democrática: Balance y perspectivas de una forma de acción política." In *La Protesta social en la Argentina: Transformaciones económicas y crisis social en el interior del país*, edited by Norma Giarracca, 85–97. Buenos Aires: Alianza.

Sekyi-Otu, Ato. 1996. *Fanon's Dialectic of Experience*. Cambridge, MA: Harvard University Press.

———. 2003. "Fanon and the Possibility of Postcolonial Critical Imagination." Codesria Symposium on Canonical Works and Continuing Innovations in African Arts and Humanities, University of Ghana, Legos.

Selee, Andrew, and Enrique Peruzzotti. 2009. *Participatory Innovation and Representative Democracy in Latin America*. Washington, DC; Baltimore: Woodrow Wilson Center Press; Johns Hopkins University Press.

Sending, Ole Jacob, and Iver B. Neumann. 2006. "Governance to Governmentality: Analyzing NGOs, States, and Power." *International Studies Quarterly* 50 (3): 651–72.

Seoane, José A. 2002. "Argentina: La configuración de las disputas sociales ante la crisis." In *Observatorio social de América Latina (Argentina)*. Buenos Aires: Consejo Latinoamericano de Ciencias Sociales–CLACSO.

Seoane, José, and Emilio Taddei. 2003. "Movimientos sociales, conflicto y cambios políticos en América Latina." *OSAL* 9.

SGP (Secretaria-Geral da Participação). 2010. "Democracia Participativa: Nova relação do Estado com a sociedade 2003–2010." Brasília: SGP, Secretaria-Geral da Participação.

Shah, Anwar, ed. 2007. *Participatory Budgeting*. Washington, DC: World Bank.

Shankland, Alexander John Ludovic. 2010. "Sparking for the People: Representation and Health Policy in the Brazilian Amazon." Doctoral thesis (DPhil), University of Sussex.

Shills, Edward. 1991. "The Virtue of Civil Society." *Government and Opposition* 26 (1): 3–20.

Shultz, Jim. 2008. "El 11 de Enero: One Year Later." The Democracy Center. http://democracyctr.org/blogfrombolivia/el-11-de-enero-one-year-later/.

Silliman, Jael. 1999. "Expanding Civil Society: Shrinking Political Spaces—The Case of Women's Nongovernmental Organizations." *Social Politics: International Studies in Gender, State and Society* 6 (1): 23–53.

Silva, Ana A. da. 1991. *Reforma urbana e o direito à cidade*. Vol. 1. Porto Alegre: POLIS–Instituto de Estudos Formação e Assessoria em Políticas Sociais.

Silva, Eduardo. 2009. *Challenging Neoliberalism in Latin America*: Cambridge: Cambridge University Press.

Singer, André. 2012. *Os sentidos do lulismo: Reforma gradual e pacto conservador*. 276 vols. São Paulo: Companhia das Letras.

Singh, Nikhil Pal. 2005. "Black Is a Country: Race and the Unfinished Struggle for Democracy." Harvard University, Cambridge, Massachusetts.

Sitrin, Marina. 2006. *Horizontalism: Voices of Popular Power in Argentina*. Oakland, CA: AK Press.

———. 2012. *Everyday Revolutions: Horizontalism and Autonomy in Argentina*. London: Zed Books.

Sitrin, Marina, and Dario Azzellini. 2014. *They Can't Represent Us!: Reinventing Democracy from Greece to Occupy*. London: Verso Books.

Skocpol, Theda, and Morris P. Fiorina. 2004. *Civic Engagement in American Democracy*. Washington, DC: Brookings Institution Press, Russell Sage Foundation.

Slater, David, and Amerika Centrum voor Studie en Documentatie van Latijns. 1985. *New Social Movements and the State in Latin America*. [Amsterdam]; Cinnaminson, NJ: CEDLA; Distributed by FORIS Publications USA.

Sobrevilla Perea, Natalia. 2011. *The Caudillo of the Andes: Andrés de Santa Cruz*. Cambridge: Cambridge University Press.

Sommer, Doris. 2014. *The Work of Art in the World: Civic Agency and Public Humanities*. Durham, NC: Duke University Press.

Souza, Celina. 2001. "Participatory Budgeting in Brazilian Cities: Limits and Possibilities in Building Democratic Institutions." *Environment and Urbanization* 13 (1): 159–84.

Souza, Herbert José de. 1982. "Município de boa esperança: Participação popular e poder local." In *Alternativas populares da democracia: Brasil anos 80*, edited by José Alvaro Moisés, 99–120. São Paulo: Vozes.

Spalding, Hobart A., Jr. 1977. *Organized Labor in Latin America: Historical Case Studies of Urban Workers in Dependent Societies*. New York: Harper and Row.

Sperling, Valerie, Myra Marx Ferree, and Barbara Risman. 2001. "Constructing Global Feminism: Transnational Advocacy Networks and Russian Women's Activism." *Signs* 26 (4): 1155–86.

Stahler-Sholk, Richard, Glen David Kuecker, and Harry E. Vanden. 2008a. *Latin American Social Movements in the Twenty-First Century: Resistance, Power, and Democracy*. Lanham, MD: Rowman and Littlefield.

———. 2008b. "Introduction." In *Latin American Social Movements in the Twenty-First Century: Resistance, Power, and Democracy*, edited by Richard Stahler-Sholk, Glen David Kuecker, and Harry E. Vanden, 1–15. Lanham, MD: Rowman and Littlefield.

Stahler-Sholk, Richard, Harry E. Vanden, and Marc Becker, eds. 2014. *Rethinking Latin American Social Movements: Radical Action from Below*. Lanham, MD: Rowman and Littlefield.

Starn, Orin. 1999. *Nightwatch: The Politics of Protest in the Andes*. Durham, NC: Duke University Press.

Stepan, Alfred C. 1988. *Rethinking Military Politics: Brazil and the Southern Cone*. Princeton, NJ: Princeton University Press.

———. 1989. *Democratizing Brazil: Problems of Transition and Consolidation*. New York: Oxford University Press.

Stephen, Lynn. 1997. *Women and Social Movements in Latin America: Power from Below*. Austin: University of Texas Press.

Svampa, Maristella, ed. 2008a. *Cambio de época: Movimientos sociales y poder político*. Buenos Aires: CLACSO; Siglo XXI.

———. 2008b. "La disputa por el desarrollo: Territorios y lenguajes." In *Cambio de época: Movimientos sociales y poder político*, edited by Maristella Svampa. Buenos Aires: Siglo XXI.

Svampa, Maristella, and Sebastián Pereyra. 2003. *Entre la ruta y el barrio: La experiencia de las organizaciones piqueteras*. Buenos Aires: Editorial Biblos.

Swyngedouw, Erik. 2005. "Governance Innovation and the Citizen: The Janus Face of Governance-beyond-the-State." *Urban Studies* 42 (11): 1991–2006.

Tapia, Luis. 2006. *La invención del nucleo comun: Ciudadanía y gobierno multisocietal*. La Paz: Editorial Muela del Diablo.

———. 2009. "Lo político y lo democrático en los movimientos sociales." In *Democracia y teoría política en movimiento*, edited by Luis Tapia, 109–22. La Paz: Muela del Diablo Editores/CIDES-UMSA.

Tarrow, Sidney G. 1989. *Democracy and Disorder: Protest and Politics in Italy, 1965–1975.* Oxford: Clarendon Press.

Tatagiba, Luciana. 2002. "Os conselhos gestores e a democratização das políticas públicas no Brasil." In *Sociedade civil e espaços públicos no Brasil*, edited by Evelina Dagnino, 47–103. Rio de Janeiro: Paz e Terra.

Tatagiba, Luciana, and Ana C. C. Teixeira. 2006. "Democracia representativa e participativa: Complementaridade ou combinação subordinada? Reflexões sobre instituições participativas e gestão pública na cidade de São Paulo (2000–2004)." *Concurso do Clad sobre Reforma do Estado e Modernização da Administração Pública.*

Telles, Edward E. 2004. *Race in Another America: The Significance of Skin Color in Brazil.* Princeton, NJ: Princeton University Press.

Thayer, Millie. 2001. "Transnational Feminism: Reading Joan Scott in the Brazilian Sertão." *Ethnography* 2 (2): 243–71.

———. 2010. *Making Transnational Feminism: Rural Women, NGO Activists, and Northern Donors in Brazil.* New York: Routledge.

———. 2014. "Translations and Refusals: Resignifying Meanings as Feminist Political Practice." In *Translocalities/Translocalidades: Feminist Politics of Translation in the Latin/a Américas*, edited by Sonia E. Alvarez, Claudia de Lima Costa, Verónica Feliu, Rebecca J. Hester, Norma Klahn, and Millie Thayer, 401–22. Durham, NC: Duke University Press.

Thorne, Eva. 2001. "The Politics of Afro-Latin American Land Rights." XXIII International Congress of the Latin American Studies Association, Washington, DC, September 6–8.

Tilly, Charles. 2004. *Social Movements, 1768–2004.* Boulder, CO: Paradigm.

———. 2006. *Regimes and Repertoires.* Chicago: University of Chicago Press.

Tilly, Charles, and Sidney Tarrow. 2006. *Contentious Politics.* Boulder, CO: Paradigm.

Tobar, Marcela Ríos, Lorena Godoy Catalán, and Elizabeth Guerrero Caviedes. 2003. *Un nuevo silencio feminista?: La transformación de un movimiento social en el Chile posdictadura.* Santiago, Centro de Estudios de la Mujer: Cuarto Propio.

Todorov, Tzvetan. 2003. *Hope and Memory: Lessons from the Twentieth Century.* Princeton, NJ: Princeton University Press.

Trouillot, Michel-Rolph. 1995. *Silencing the Past: Power and the Production of History.* Boston: Beacon.

Tsing, Anna Lowenhaupt. 2005. *Friction: An Ethnography of Global Connection.* Princeton, NJ: Princeton University Press.

Union de Asambleas Ciudadanas. 2007. Accessed October 8 2016. http://asambleasciudadanas.org.ar/.

Urrea-Giraldo, Fernando, and Carlos Augusto Viáfara López. 2007. *Pobreza y grupos étnicos en Colombia: Análisis de sus factores determinantes y lineamientos de políticas para su reducción.* Departamento Nacional de Planeacion. Bogota, Colombia.

Urrea-Giraldo, Fernando, Carlos Augusto Viáfara López, and Mara Viveros Vigoya. 2014. "From Whitened Miscegenation to Tri-Ethnic Multiculturalism: Race and

Ethnicity in Colombia." In *Pigmentocracies, Ethnicity, Race and Color in Latin America,* edited by Edward Telles, 81–125. Chapel Hill: University of North Carolina Press.

Valdés Ugalde, Francisco. 2008. "Gobernanza e instituciones: Propuestas para una agenda de investigación." *Perfiles Latinoamericanos* 16 (31): 95–119.

Van Cott, Donna Lee. 2000. *The Friendly Liquidation of the Past: The Politics of Diversity in Latin America.* Pittsburgh: University of Pittsburgh Press.

———. 2001. "Movimientos indígenas y transformación constitucional en los Andes." *Revista Venezolana de Economía y Ciencias Sociales* 8 (3): 41–60.

———. 2005. *From Movements to Parties in Latin America: The Evolution of Ethnic Politics.* Cambridge: Cambridge University Press.

van der Schaaf, Alice. 2001. *Jeito de mulher rural: A busca de direitos sociais e da igualdade de gênero no Rio Grande do Sul.* Passo Fundo, Brazil: Editora Universidade de Passo Fundo.

Vargas Valente, Virginia. 1996. "Disputando el espacio global: El movimiento de mujeres y la IV Conferencia Mundial de Beijing." *Nueva Sociedad* 141:43–53.

———. 2003. "Feminism, Globalization and the Global Justice and Solidarity Movement." *Cultural Studies* 17 (6): 905–20.

Vila, Enrique 2003. "La política social del proyecto bolivariano: Ideas controversiales." *Revista Venezolana de Economía Ciencias Sociales* 9 (3): 111–44.

Villalón, Roberta. 2008. "Neoliberalism, Corruption, and Legacies of Contention: Argentina's Social Movements, 1993–2006." In *Latin American Social Movements in the Twenty-First Century: Resistance, Power, and Democracy,* edited by Richard Stahler-Sholk, Glen David Kuecker, and Harry E. Vanden, 253–69. Lanham, MD: Rowman and Littlefield.

Viola, Eduardo, and Scott Mainwaring. 1987. "Novos movimentos sociais: Cultura política e democracia." In *Uma revolução no cotidiano? Os novos movimentos sociais na América Latina,* edited by Ilse Scherer-Warren and Paulo Krische, 102–88. São Paulo: Brasiliense.

Vommaro, Pablo. "La producción y las subjetividades en los movimientos sociales de la Argentina contemporánea: el caso del MTD de Solano." Informe final del concurso: Movimientos sociales y nuevos conflictos en América Latina y el Caribe. Programa Regional de Becas CLACSO (2003): el caso del MTD de Solano. Buenos Aires: CLACSO-ASDI.

Wade, Peter. 1995. "The Cultural Politics of Blackness in Colombia." *American Ethnologist* 22 (2): 341–57.

———. 2004. "Ethnicity, Multiculturalism and Social Policy in Latin America: Afro-Latin (and Indigenous) Populations." ESRC seminar series on Social Policy, Stability and Exclusion in Latin America, Seminar on "Gender, Ethnicity and Identity," London, February 27.

Wampler, Brian. 2007a. "A Guide to Participatory Budgeting." In *Participatory Budgeting,* edited by Anwar Shah, 21–54. Washington, DC: World Bank.

———. 2007b. *Participatory Budgeting in Brazil: Contestation, Cooperation, and Accountability.* University Park: Pennsylvania State University Press.

———. 2015. *Activating Democracy in Brazil: Popular Participation, Social Justice, and Interlocking Institutions.* Notre Dame, IN: University of Notre Dame Press.

Wampler, Brian, and Leonardo Avritzer. 2004. "Participatory Publics: Civil Society and New Institutions in Democratic Brazil." *Comparative Politics* 36 (3): 291–312.

Warner, Michael. 2005. *Publics and Counterpublics.* New York: Zone Books.

Weffort, Francisco. 1982. "Nordestinos em São Paulo: Notas para um estudo sobre cultura nacional e cultura popular." In *A Cultura do povo*, edited by Edenio Valle, José J. Queiroz, and Carmen Cinira Macedo, 13–23. São Paulo: EDUC.

———. 1989. "Why Democracy?" In *Democratizing Brazil: Problems of Transition and Consolidation*, edited by Alfred Stepan, 327–50. New York: Oxford University Press.

Weyland, Kurt, Raúl L. Madrid, and Wendy Hunter, eds. 2010. *Leftist Governments in Latin America: Successes and Shortcomings.* New York: Cambridge University Press.

White, Sarah C. 1996. "Depoliticizing Development: The Uses and Abuses of Participation." *Development in Practice* 6 (1): 6–15.

Wickramasinghe, Nira. 2005. "The Idea of Civil Society in the South: Imaginings, Transplants, Designs." *Science and Society* 69 (3): 458–86.

Williams, Glyn. 2004. "Evaluating Participatory Development: Tyranny, Power and (Re)Politicisation." *Third World Quarterly* 25 (3): 557–78.

Winant, Howard. 2001. *The World Is a Ghetto: Race and Democracy since World War II.* New York: Basic Books.

———. 2004. *The New Politics of Race: Globalism, Difference, Justice.* Minneapolis: University of Minnesota Press.

Wolford, Wendy. 2006. "The Difference Ethnography Can Make: Understanding Social Mobilization and Development in the Brazilian Northeast." *Qualitative Sociology* 29:335–52.

———. 2010. *This Land Is Ours Now: Social Mobilization and the Meanings of Land in Brazil.* Durham, NC: Duke University Press.

World Bank. 2006. *World Development Report: Equity and Development.* Washington, DC: World Bank.

———. 2008. *Uruguay Country Brief.* Washington, DC: World Bank.

Yashar, Deborah J. 2005. *Contesting Citizenship in Latin America: The Rise of Indigenous Movements and the Postliberal Challenge.* Cambridge: Cambridge University Press.

Zanotti, Laura. 2005. "Governmentalizing the Post–Cold War International Regime: The UN Debate on Democratization and Good Governance." *Alternatives: Global, Local, Political* 30 (4): 461–87.

Zavaleta, René. [1977] 1988. *50 años de historia.* La Paz: Los Amigos del Libro.

Zibechi, Raúl. 2003. *Genealogía de la revuelta. Argentina: La sociedad en movimiento.* La Plata: Letra libre.

———. 2010. *Dispersing Power: Social Movements as Anti-state Forces.* Translated by Ramor Ryan. Oakland, CA: AK Press.

———. 2012. *Territories in Resistance: A Cartography of Latin American Social Movements.* Translated by Ramor Ryan. Oakland, CA: AK Press.

Zurbriggen, Cristina. 2014. "Governance: A Latin America Perspective." *Policy and Society* 33 (4): 345–60.

Contributors

SONIA E. ALVAREZ is director of the Center for Latin American Studies, Caribbean and Latina/o Studies and Leonard J. Horwitz Professor of Latin American Politics and Society at the University of Massachusetts Amherst. She is the author of *Engendering Democracy in Brazil: Women's Movements in Transition Politics* and coeditor of *The Making of Social Movements in Latin America: Identity, Strategy, and Democracy*; *Cultures of Politics/Politics of Cultures: Re-visioning Latin American Social Movements*; and *Translocalities/Translocalidades: Feminist Politics of Translation in the Latin/a Américas*. She has published extensively, in Spanish and Portuguese, as well as in English, with many essays written collaboratively, on topics including social movements, feminisms, NGOs, civil society, transnational activism, and democratization. Her current work focuses on the dynamics of feminist discursive fields and activist assemblages, and on the (mis)encounters of feminism and antiracism in Brazil. It forms part of a larger book project entitled *Feminisms in Movement*, forthcoming from Duke University Press.

KIRAN ASHER, grounded in two decades of field-based research in Latin America and South Asia, has published a monograph, *Black and Green: Afro-Colombians, Development, and Nature in the Pacific Lowlands* (Duke University Press, 2009). She is currently working on a theoretical and political critique of development theories and postdevelopment proposals by drawing on feminist and Marxist approaches in a postcolonial frame. From 2002 to 2013, she was associate professor of international development and social change at Clark University, Massachusetts. From 2013 to 2015, she was a senior scientist in the Forests and Livelihoods Program at the Center for International Forestry Research (CIFOR), in Bogor, Indonesia. She is now associate professor in the Department of Women, Gender, and Sexuality Studies at the University of Massachusetts Amherst.

LEONARDO AVRITZER is professor in the Department of Political Science at the Universidade Federal de Minas Gerais (UFMG), Brazil, and researcher 1 of CNPq, Brazil. Leonardo Avritzer has published extensively on civil society and participation in Brazil. He is the author of many books, among them *A moralidade da democracia*, which received the award of best book of the year in the Brazilian social sciences. He published in several journals, including *Comparative Politics, Latin America Research Review, International Journal of Regional and Urban Research, Journal of Public Deliberation,* and *Revista Dados*. He published two books in English: *Democracy and the Public Space in Latin America* and *Participatory Institutions in Democratic Brazil*. He is the current president of the Brazilian Political Science Association.

GIANPAOLO BAIOCCHI is an ethnographer interested in questions of politics and culture, critical social theory, and cities. He is associate professor of Individualized Studies and Sociology at NYU, where he directs the Urban Democracy Lab. He has written widely on Brazil and, more recently, on the United States. His last monograph, coauthored with Ernesto Ganuza, *Popular Democracy and the Paradoxes of Participation* (2016), explores the travel of policy instruments in the current moment, using the case of Participatory Budgeting. He is currently working on a book that explores the lessons of recent horizontalist movements.

ANDREA CORNWALL is professor of anthropology and international development in the School of Global Studies at the University of Sussex, where she works currently on the politics of bureaucratic activism. She has published widely on participation, gender, sexuality, and international development. Her recent publications include *The Participation Reader* (2011), *Women, Sexuality and the Political Power of Pleasure* (edited by Jolly, Cornwall, and Hawkins, 2013), *Feminisms, Empowerment and Development* (edited by Cornwall and Edwards, 2014), and *Masculinities under Neoliberalism* (edited by Cornwall, Karioris, and Lindisfarne, 2016).

GRACIELA DI MARCO directs the Center for Studies of Democratization and Human Rights and the Graduate Program in Human Rights and Social Policies at the University of San Martín. Her research combines studies of democratization, social movements, feminisms, human rights, and social policies. She is the author, among other publications, of *El pueblo feminista: Movimientos sociales y lucha de las mujeres en torno a la ciudadanía* (2011) and the coauthor of *Feminismos, democratización y democracia radical: Estudios de caso de América del Sur, Central Medio Oriente y Norte de África* (2011).

RAPHAEL HOETMER is an associate researcher at the Programa Democracia y Transformación Global in Lima (Peru), and has collaborated closely with communities affected by mining, rural social organizations, and environmentalist NGOs around the country. Hoetmer is a member of the Political Ecology Working Group of the Latin American Social Sciences Council (CLACSO) and taught at the San Marcos and Antonio Ruiz de Montoya Universities in Lima. Currently he is working on his PhD at the Institute for Social Studies in the Hague, Netherlands, on mining conflicts in Peru.

BENJAMIN JUNGE at the State University of New York at New Paltz is a cultural anthropologist with specialization in the ethnographic study of social movements, citizenship, gender, sexuality, and health. His research projects and publications to date focus on gendered experience of grassroots political participation in Porto Alegre, the complex relationships between religion and social movements in Latin America, and new forms of HIV prevention in the United States. His current, NSF-funded research examines political subjectivity among Brazil's so-called new middle class in the northeastern city of Recife.

LUIS E. LANDER is a mechanical engineer with doctoral studies in social science from the Universidad Central de Venezuela, where he is also a senior professor (emeritus) of the

Faculty of Social Science. He has been editor of *Revista Venezolana de Economía y Ciencias Sociales* and is currently director of Observatorio Electoral Venezolano. His recent publications include *Elecciones regionales del 16-D* (2013); *La sobrevenida elección de abril* (2013); *La representación proporcional y la personalización del sufragio* (2016).

————

AGUSTÍN LAÓ-MONTES teaches sociology at the University of Massachusetts Amherst, where he is also affiliated with the Center for Latin American, Caribbean and Latino Studies, as well as with the Department of Afro-American Studies. He has published extensively in the fields of Africana Studies, Decolonial Critique, the Sociology of Social Movements, Urban Sociology, and Historical Sociology. He is in the leadership of the Articulation of Afro-Descendants in Latin America and the Caribbean (ARAAC), a web of social movements across the region.

————

MARGARITA LÓPEZ MAYA is a historian and PhD in Social Sciences at the Universidad Central de Venezuela. Senior professor-researcher (retired) of the Center for Development Studies (CENDES) also of Universidad Central, Professor López Maya has been editor of *Revista Venezolana de Economía y Ciencias Sociales* and on the Board of the Latin American Social Sciences Council (CLACSO). Her recent publications include *Democracia participativa en Venezuela: Orígenes, leyes, percepciones y desafíos* (2011); *El estado descomunal* (2013); "The Political Crisis of Postchavism," *Social Justice* (2014); and "Venezuela 2014: Descontento económico y protestas," in R. Balza Guanipa, ed., *Venezuela 2015: Economía, política y sociedad* (2015).

————

JOSÉ ANTONIO LUCERO was born in El Paso, Texas, and raised on both sides of the Mexican-U.S. border. He is associate professor at the Henry M. Jackson School of International Studies at the University of Washington, with affiliate appointments in American Indian Studies, Geography, and the Comparative History of Ideas. His main research and teaching interests include Indigenous politics, social movements, Latin American politics, and borderlands. Lucero is the author of *Struggles of Voice: The Politics of Indigenous Representation in the Andes* (2008) and the coeditor of the *Oxford Handbook of Indigenous Peoples' Politics* (forthcoming).

————

GRACIELA MONTEAGUDO is a U.S.-based Argentine artist and interdisciplinary scholar-activist with training in performance; Latin American politics; philosophy; anthropology; and women, gender, and sexuality studies. She researches the unintended consequences of neoliberalism, with a focus on women in nonhierarchical, untamed social movements. Monteagudo has over fifteen years of fieldwork. She was involved in the human rights struggles in the 1980s in Argentina, and, as an artist, she helped organize numerous giant puppet protests in the streets with the anticorporate globalization movements in the United States and the United Kingdom. She also worked with the Madres de Plaza de Mayo, popular assemblies, and piquetero movements. She holds a BA from the Facultad de Filosofía y Letras of the Universidade de Buenos Aires, an MFA-IA (interdisciplinary arts) from Goddard College, and a PhD in Anthropology from the University of Massachusetts Amherst, where she is currently a lecturer.

AMALIA PALLARES is professor and director of Latin American and Latino studies and professor of political science at the University of Illinois at Chicago. She teaches courses on social movements, Latin American and Latino politics, race and ethnicity, and qualitative research methodologies. Her books include *Family Activism: Immigrant Struggles and the Politics of Non-Citizenship*, *Marcha: Latino Chicago and the Immigrant Rights Movement* (coedited with Nilda Flores Gonzalez), and *From Peasant Struggles to Indian Activism: The Ecuadorian Andes in the Twentieth Century*. She was born in Ecuador and has written extensively on Ecuadorian ethnic and regional politics.

———

JEFFREY W. RUBIN is associate professor of history and research associate at the Institute on Culture, Religion, and World Affairs at Boston University. He is the author of *Decentering the Regime: Ethnicity, Radicalism, and Democracy in Juchitán, Mexico* (Duke University Press, 1997) and coauthor of *Sustaining Activism: A Brazilian Women's Movement and a Father-Daughter Collaboration* (Duke University Press, 2013). He is coeditor of *Enduring Reform: Progressive Activism and Private Sector Responses in Latin America's Democracies* (2014) and "Lived Religion and Lived Citizenship in Latin America's Zones of Crisis" (a special issue of the *Latin American Research Review*, 2014). Rubin's research has been funded by the MacArthur Foundation, the Open Society Foundation, the American Philosophical Society, the Fulbright Program, and the Mellon-LASA (Latin American Studies Association) Seminars.

———

ANA CLAUDIA TEIXEIRA holds a PhD in social sciences from the Universidade Estadual de Campinas in Brazil. She is the author of *Identidades em construção: Organizações não-governamentais no processo de democratização* (2003). Her PhD thesis, "Beyond the Vote: A Narrative on Participatory Democracy in Brazil (1975–2010)," was awarded the 2014 National Award for best thesis in Sociology. From 2000 to 2010, she was a researcher at Polis—Institute for Research in Social Policy, and worked as coordinator of the Citizen Participation Team and executive coordinator (2006–8) at the same institution. She is presently a researcher at the Center for Research on Participation, Social Movements and Collective Action (Nepac-Unicamp). She is currently working on a project that explores the impacts of social movements on public policies in Brazil.

———

MILLIE THAYER is associate professor of sociology at the University of Massachusetts Amherst, and affiliated with the Center for Latin American, Caribbean and Latino Studies and Women, Gender, Sexuality Studies. Her book *Making Transnational Feminism: Rural Women, NGO Activists, and Northern Donors in Brazil* (2010) is an ethnography of cross-border feminist relationships. She is a coeditor of and author in *Translocalities/Translocalidades: Feminist Politics of Translation in the Latina Américas* (Duke University Press, 2014) and *Global Ethnography: Forces, Connections, and Imaginations in a Postmodern World* (2000). Her most recent project concerns the political economies of feminist movements in Brazil.

Index

Page numbers followed by *t* indicate tables.

Armony, Ariel, 12

Asamblea Popular Ambiental de Gualeguaychú (Argentina), 142–54; gender disparities
in, 149–50; horizontal organization of,
148–49; performance and protest tactics of,
142, 150–54; rhizomatic network of, 150–51

Assembly for the Right to Abortion (Argentina), 133–34

Association for Women in Development
(AWID), 171

Association of Displaced Afro-Colombians
(AFRODES), 212–13

authorized activism. *See* permitido activism

auto-governmentality (governmentality from
below), 43–44

autonomy of civil society, 14–15, 47–61; in
Brazil, 52–54, 57, 61nn3–4, 62n8; as imaginary, 64–66. *See also* interdependency of
civil society

Auyero, Javier, 158, 313

Ávila, Maria Bethânia, 321

Avritzer, Leonardo, 335

Bachelet, Michele, 319–20

Baiocchi, Gianpaolo, x–xi, 47, 53

Baixada Fluminense neighborhood association
(Brazil), 32–33

Banfield, Edward, 8

Batliwala, Srilatha, 75–76

Battle, Jorge, 145–46

Bevir, Mark, 322

"Beyond the Civil Society Agenda" project,
xi–xii

Biekart, Kees, 175n6

biopolitical projects, 145–46

Black Communities Process (PCN) (Colombia). *See* Process of Black Communities

Black Freedom Movement (U.S.), 105–8

Black Marxism, 105

Black Organization of Central America, 110

Black Panthers (U.S.), 106

Blacks. *See* Afro-Latin American movements

Black Skin, White Masks (Fanon), 315n3

Boa Esperança (Brazil), 35

Bolivarian Revolutionary Movement 200
(MBR 200) (Venezuela), 268–69, 325

Bolivia, xi, 27; black and indigenous rights
in, 108, 329; Constitution of 2009 of, 302;
decolonization context of, 13–14, 298–302;
economic inequality in, 299–300; Gas and
Water Wars of, 1–2; indigenous marginalization in, 298–302; January 11, 2007, protests
in, 296–314, 315n2; Law of Popular Participation of, 328–29; Morales's refoundational
regime of, 238–39, 253, 296–97, 302–7,
314–15, 325, 329, 334; mourning of protest
deaths in, 304–12; struggle between socials
and civics in, 5, 302–4, 312–15; TIPNIS
protests of 2011 in, 314–15; violence and
apartheid in, 303–4, 312–14, 315n7

Bônes, Gessi, 231

Boschi, Renato, 51

Botnia pulp mill (Uruguay), 145–54

Brazil, 1, 45–61; agroindustry of, 222–23, 227,
229; aid relationships of civil society in,
156–74, 175n7; ambivalence of participatory citizens in, 83–85, 91–100, 290–91;
antisystemic movements in, 18–19; black
and indigenous rights in, 111, 112, 120; black
political parties in, 107; Bolsa Família
program in, 42, 288, 290; Catholic Church
activism in, 50–51, 57–60, 62n7, 62nn9–10,
221, 223, 235, 289; conservative mobilization in, 291–92; Constitution of 1988 of,
223–25, 293; corporate philanthropy in,
176n22; de-democratization of Cabo de
Santo Agostinho in, 66–80; economy of,
49–50, 222, 236n6, 288, 295n3; emergence
of civil society in, 49–54; expansion of
citizen participation in, 41–42, 289–90;
feminist activism in, 156–57, 164–65, 172,
328; free municipal elections and opposition mayors in, 35–37; June 2013 protests
in, 235, 283–95; labor organizing in, 6–7;
Lula da Silva's presidency of, 41–42, 82–83,
87, 288–90, 293; March of Black Women
in, 13–14; Movement of Rural Women
Workers in, 21, 156–57, 164, 172, 174nn1–2,
219–36, 237n9, 333; National Constituent
Assembly proposals in, 54–57, 62nn5–6;
National Forum on Popular Participation
in Democratic and Popular Administrations of, 37–39; neighborhood associations
in, 31–34; Netherlands' aid to feminists
in, 166–69; New Social Movements in,
33–34; participatory councils in, 66–80,

289–90, 321; participatory democracy in, 31–44, 49, 63–80, 234, 288–92, 323–25, 330; political liberalization in, 51–54; Porto Alegre's citizens' participation in, 81–99; Porto Alegre's participatory budgeting in, 4, 10, 21, 37–40, 56–57, 82–83, 87–89, 93–99, 234, 323–25; rates of participation in civil society in, 48–49, 51–52, 57–60, 61n4, 62nn7–10, 289–90; revolutionary councils of, 30; rights and new citizenship demands in, 11; Rousseff's impeachment in, 330; Rousseff's reform referendum in, 292–94; rural poverty in, 222–24; state's role in civil society in, 42–43, 47–49, 52–61, 62nn7–10, 63–66, 173–74, 176n22; student movement in, 291; urban poor of, 49, 52, 222–23, 291; Varguista corporatism of, 61n3; World Cup and Olympics in, 283, 287, 290

Brazilian Worker's Party. *See* Workers' Party
Bread for the World, 161
Brubaker, Roger, 251
Bush, George W., 104

Cabo de Santo Agostinho (Brazil), 63–80; creation of inclusive health council in, 67–71; de-democratization of health council of, 71–80; learning democracy in, 70
Caldera, Rafael, 265
Camaño, Eduardo, 138–39n2
Campaign of 500 Years of Indigenous, Black and Popular Resistance, 108
Canadian International Development Agency (CIDA), 9
Carrión, Pintado, Magdiel, 185
Carrozo, Evangelina, 150
casi permitido activism, 241–42. *See also* intersection of civil and uncivic activism
Catholic Church: activism in Brazil of, 50–51, 57–60, 62n7, 62nn9–10; activism in Colombia of, 205; in Argentina, 126, 132–33, 135, 138, 139–40nn13–15, 151, 154; discourse on sexuality of, 132–33; liberation theology of, 30, 31, 221, 223, 235; in Venezuela, 270
Central Labor Trade Union (CUT) (Brazil), 54
Centro das Mulheres do Cabo (Brazil), 68
Chandhoke, Neera, 65
Chango, Marco, 255
Carmichael, Stokely, 105–6

Chatterjee, Partha, 12, 22, 326
Chávez, Hugo, xi, 172, 238–39, 253, 295n3; Bolivarian Movement of, 268, 325; first presidential term of, 262, 268–76; recall referendum on, 262, 269–70, 275–76; second presidential term of, 262–63, 276–80. *See also* Venezuela
Cheah, Pheng, 163
Chile: antisystemic movements in, 18–19; Concertación governments of, 319–20; copper production in, 188; gay/lesbian movements in, 16; student protests in, 2, 236n1, 320
ch'ixi, 313
Cisneros, Daniel, 255
Cisneros, Patricio, 240, 242–44, 247, 255–56
citizen participation. *See* participatory democracy
civil society, 46, 316–30; autonomy, interdependency, and state power in, 34, 47–61, 77–80; co-governance and, 317, 318t, 323–25, 327–28; contemporary tripartite model of, 46–47, 61n2; effects of voluntary association on, 52–54; focus on the poor in, 45–49, 52–53; governability and, 317–21, 327–28; governance and, 317, 318t, 321–23, 327–28; governmentality and, 317, 318t, 325–28; Gramscian formulation of, 7, 10, 12–13, 46, 202–3; gray zone with uncivic activism of, 4–5, 17–18, 21–23, 99, 312–15, 329–30, 333–37; market-based aid relationships in, 156–74; multiple actors of, 2, 316–17; oppositional spaces (counterpublics) in, 11, 14, 17, 21–22, 170–72, 175n18, 225–26, 336–37; originary dualist model of, 45–46, 61n1; political elite guidance of, 256–57. *See also* intersection of civil and uncivic activism
Civil Society Agenda, xi, 1–23, 316–18, 327–33; absorption by hegemonic assumptions of, 2–3, 34, 47–61, 77–80, 200, 317; Afro-Latin American movements and, 114–16; ambiguity of, 12–13; co-optation by neoliberalism of, 12, 83–84, 104, 112–14, 200–203, 317, 325–27, 331–32; dominant scholarly constructs of, 5–6, 83–85, 99, 162–64; genealogy of, 5–7; language of decolonization in, 13–15, 195; North Americanized conceptions of, 7–11, 317, 321–23; post-Washington

cultural studies, ix–x
Cultures of Politics/Politics of Cultures (Alvarez, Dagnino, and Escobar), x

Dagnino, Evelina, ix, 10, 11; on Civil Society Agenda actors, 317, 323–24; on new citizenship, 34; on outsourcing of social movements, 64
Darío Santillán Front (FDS) (Argentina), 136
Datena, José Luiz, 285
Dean, Mitchell, 326
De Angelis, Alfredo, 152–53
decolonization, 13–15, 298–302
de la Rúa, Fernando, 1, 123
De la Torre, Carlos, 245
del Castillo, Jorge, 188
Democratic Action (AD) (Venezuela), 265, 276
Democratic Coordination for Civic Action (Venezuela), 275
Department for International Development (DFID) (UK), 9
development organizations. *See* intergovernmental organizations; international financial institutions; nongovernmental organizations
Dhanraj, Deepa, 75–76
Diadema (Brazil), 36
Di Marco, Graciela, 16–19, 334
DuBois, W. E. B., 105
Duhalde, Eduardo, 127, 138–39n2
Durán Ballén, Sixto, 253
Durban process, 3, 110–14, 118. *See also* Third World Conference against Racism and Related Forms of Discrimination
Dutra, Olívio, 56
A Dying Colonialism (Fanon), 300–301

Ecclesiastic Base Communities (CEBs), 31
Ecuador, xi, 238–57; anti-provincialization forces in, 240, 244; black and indigenous rights in, 108, 112, 120; decolonization language of, 14; implementation of participatory methodologies in, 245, 320, 325; indigenous uprising of 1990 in, 1, 108; integrated civil and uncivic activism in, 240–42; mining activities in, 181; politics of class and ethnicity in, 249–52; refounda-

tional politics of, 238–39, 252–54, 256, 325; Santa Elena's provincialization movement in, 239–57; spatialized politics of class and ethnicity in, 242; traditional constructions of regions of, 242
Erundina, Luiza, 38
Escobar, Arturo, 22, 155n1, 202, 206–7, 209
ethnicity-based demands. *See* identity-based demands
European Community, 176n22
Evans, David, 134

Facundo: Civilización y Barbarie (Sarmiento), 6
Fajardo, Fausto, 243, 244
Falcão, Rui, 286
Falconí, Jessica, 252
Fals Borda, Orlando, 13
Fanon, Frantz, 119; on decolonization of knowledge, 13; on ongoing project of decolonization, 298–301, 314; on spatial experience of colonialism, 300, 315n3
Farabundo Martí National Liberation Front (FMLN) (El Salvador), 30
Farm Women (Brazil), 224, 226. *See also* Movement of Rural Women Workers
Feliu, Verónica, x
Felski, Rita, 17, 174n5
feminist activism, 3; on abortion rights, 130, 133–38, 140n15; in Argentina's popular feminism, 124–38, 144, 334; in Brazil, 156–57, 164–65, 172, 328; funding relationships of, 165–66; heterogeneous collective identity in, 130–32, 135–38, 140n17; oppositional spaces (counterpublics) of, 11, 14, 17, 21–22, 170–72, 175n18, 225–26, 336–37; on sexual citizenship, 129–30, 134, 139n10; in shadow commodity chains, 170–71. *See also* identity-based demands
feminist theory, 163–64, 166
Fifth Republic Movement (MVR), 266–67
Fiorina, Morris, 78–79
First Inter-American Women's Congress of 1947, 19
Fondo Centroamericano de Muheres (Nicaragua), 172
Ford Foundation, 114, 161, 176n22
Fortaleza (Brazil), 36
Fortuyn, Pim, 167

Forum for Reproductive Rights (Argentina), 133–34

Foucault, Michel: on governmentality, 318, 325, 328; on operations of power, 12; on spaces of power, 80, 153

Fourth Encounter of Afro-descendants for Revolutionary Transformation in Latin America and the Caribbean (Venezuela), 119

Fracasso, Vera, 227–28

Fraser, Nancy, 17, 174n5

Free Fare Movement (MPL) (Brazil), 283, 285–87, 295n1

Free Trade of the Americas Agreement (FTAA), 86

Frente Negra Brasileira, 107

Front for a Country in Solidarity (FREPASO) (Argentina), 123

Front for the Sustainable Development of the Peruvian Northern Border (FDSFNP), 182, 186–87, 192, 193, 196, 198n15

Fujimori, Alberto, 180, 195

Fundação Getúlio Vargas, 39

Fundo Elas (Brazil), 172

Garcia, Jesus "Chucho," 104

García Gonzales, Melanio, 182

García Linera, Álvaro, 313–14

García Pérez, Alan, 179, 180, 197

Garía, Alan, 193

Garvey, Marcus, 105

gay/lesbian (LGBTTTI) movements, 16, 124, 133, 136

gender: in horizontal organizations, 148–50; in perceptions of the WSF, 91–93; in uncivic claiming of citizenship, 97–99. See also feminist activism; identity-based demands

"General Guidelines for the Economic and Social Development of the Nation 2001–2007" (Venezuela), 273

Gibson, Nigel, 300

Gibson-Graham, J. K., 18

Gilberto Murillo, Luis, 212–13

the global, 18

globalization. See neoliberalism

glyphosate, 155n6

Goldfrank, Benjamin, 323

Goldstein, Daniel, 313

Gomes, Elias, 67–68, 71

Gómez Bruera, Hernán, 324–25

Gómez Vílchez, Luis, 193

Gonzabay, Dionicio, 240, 242–44, 247, 255–56

Goodale, Mark, 12

good governance programs, 9–10, 40–42, 321–25. See also participatory democracy

governability, 317–21, 327–28

governance, 317, 318t, 321–23, 327–28

governmentality, 317, 318t, 325–28

Gramsci, Antonio, 46; civil society formulation of, 7, 10, 12–13, 46; on conjunctural analysis, 202–3; on peaceful revolution, 121n7, 210; on political practice, 328

Greek Indignados, 231, 236n1, 283–84

Greenpeace, 150, 152

Grewal, Inderpal, 12

Grueso, Libia, 206–7, 212

Guatemala, 7, 8, 108

Gustafson, Bret, 302, 313

Gutiérrez, Lucio, 252

Hague Tribunal, 154

Haiti, 18

Hale, Charles, 115, 202, 317, 324

Hall, Stuart, 202–3

Harcourt, Wendy, x

Hardt, Michael, 12–13

Harriss, John, 9

Herbalife, 221, 229–30

Herrera Racho, Remberto, 182

Hester, Rebecca, x

Hoetmer, Raphael, 3, 4, 14, 16, 19, 334

Honduras, 118

Hopkins, Terrence, 159, 162, 164

Houtzager, Peter: on mutuality of civil society and government, 78–79; on participation rates in São Paulo civil society, 48, 58, 60, 61n4, 62nn7–8

Humala, Ollanta, 180, 193

Human Development Report, 40

human rights. See rights and social-justice discourses

Hunter, Wendy, 327

identity-based demands, 4, 331–32; on abortion rights, 130, 133–38, 140n15; in Argentina, 124–38; for black and indigenous rights,

61n2, 108–9, 111, 112, 120, 199–201, 203, 206–7, 213–14, 217n2; of Brazil's MMTR, 220–22; in Ecuador's Santa Elena provincialization movement, 242, 251–52, 256–57; of new social movements, 108–9; oppositional spaces (counterpublics) of, 11, 14, 17, 21–22, 170–72, 174n5, 175n18, 225–26, 336–37; permitido activism and, 3–4, 332; on sexual citizenship, 129–30, 134, 139n10; transnational movements on, 18–21, 108–9; in uncivic activism, 15–18, 97–99, 137–38, 144; UN Durban Conference on, 110–14, 121n6, 213. *See also* rights and social-justice discourses

indio permitido, 14, 24n4

Institutional Renewal Party of Social Action (PRIAN) (Ecuador), 240, 253

Inter-American Development Bank (IADB), 8, 10, 110–14, 119

interdependency of civil society, 14–15, 34, 47–61; in Brazil, 41–43, 47–49, 52–61, 62nn7–10, 64–66, 173–74; limits on oppositionality and, 65–66; in making and unmaking of civil society, 66–80

intergovernmental organizations (IGOs), 2, 7–11, 114, 118, 316

international financial institutions (IFIs), 2, 7–11, 110, 316; aid architecture of, 159–62; bilateral aid programs of, 19; co-option of civil society and, 12, 83–84, 104, 112–14; good governance agendas of, 9–10, 40–42, 321–25; post-Durban rhetoric on race of, 111–14; power relationships of, 20; structural adjustment programs of, 9–10, 19, 28, 143–47, 180, 205–6

International Labor Organization Accord, 206

International Monetary Fund (IMF), 19

intersection of civil and uncivic activism, 1–5, 329–30, 333–37; ambivalent participatory citizens in, 83–85, 91–100, 290–91; in Argentina Asamblea Popular Ambiental de Gualeguaychú, 142–54, 334; in Bolivia's protest of January 11, 2007, 296–315; in Brazil MMTR's movement-in-democracy, 219–36; ch'ixi logic of, 313; in Ecuador's Santa Elena provincialization movement, 240–42, 254; as gray zone, 4–5, 17–18, 21–23, 99, 312–14; inventive strategies in, 4–5, 331–37; in Peru's

anti-mining referendums, 179–96; in Venezuela's contentious public space, 261–81

Isunza, Ernesto, 317

Jad, Islah, 64

James, C. L. R., 105

John Paul II, Pope, 62n10

Juana Azurduy-Barrios de Pie Collective (Argentina), 136

Junge, Ben, 4, 334

Justicialist (Peronist) Party (Argentina), 123, 151, 152

Keck, Margaret E., 24n3

Kirchner, Cristina Fernández de, 23

Kirchner, Néstor, 145, 147–54

Klahn, Norma, x

Laclau, Ernesto, 31, 138, 139n11

Lages (Brazil), 34–35, 36

Lagos, Ricardo, 319–20

Lander, Luis E., 3, 335

Laó-Montes, Agustín, x–xi, 3, 4, 14, 17, 335

Laserna, Roberto, 297

Lavalle, Adrián Gurza, 48, 58, 60, 61n4, 62nn7–8

Law for Direct, Universal, and Secret Election of Governors of 1989 (Venezuela), 267–68

Law of Black Rights (Colombia), 111, 199–202, 206–8, 213–14, 320–21

Law of Citizen Participation (Chile), 320

Law of Communal Councils of 2006 (Venezuela), 274

Law of Lands of 2001 (Venezuela), 274

Law of Popular Participation (Bolivia), 328–29

Law on Violence against Women and the Family of 1998 (Venezuela), 268

League of Revolutionary Black Workers (U.S.), 106

Leal, Pablo, 28

Levi, Primo, 312–13

Li, Tania, 328–29

liberation theology, 30, 31, 221, 223, 235, 289

Lima Costa, Claudia de, x

Lista Violeta, 151

Lopes, Clovis, 81–83

López Maya, Margarita, 3, 335

Lucero, José Antonio, 3, 5, 14, 329

Lugo, Fernando, 23

Lula da Silva, Luiz Inácio, 41–42, 82–83, 87, 288–90, 293, 325. *See also* Brazil; Workers' Party

Lumumba, Patrice, 119

Lupien, Pascal, 320, 325

MacArthur Foundation, 161

Macías, Eduardo, 245, 247

MacKinnon, Catherine, 149–50

Madera de Guerrero (Ecuador), 257n2

Majaz Company, 180, 182, 188–89, 191–92, 194–95, 197n3

The Making of Social Movements in Latin America (Escobar and Alvarez), ix

Manhattan Company, 183

market-based aid relationships. *See* aid relationships

Marx, Karl, 202

Meek, Gregory, 104

Menem, Carlos, 123, 155n2

Merino, Beatriz, 193

Mexico: antisystemic movements in, 18–19; black and indigenous rights in, 108; expansion of civil society in, 7; student protests in, 2; trade union organization in, 6; workers' councils of, 30; Zapatista movement, 7, 144

microcredit programs, 158, 327

Mignolo, Walter, 298

Military Institutional Front (Venezuela), 275

Millamán, Rosamel, 317, 324

mining, 179–96

Ministry of Energy and Mining (MinEM) (Peru), 181–82

Mockus, Antanas, 27

modernization theory, 8

Mohanty, Ranjita, 63

Monteagudo, Graciela, 3, 16, 17, 19, 333–34

Monterrico Metals, 181, 182, 197n8

Morales, Evo, xi, 5, 238–39, 253, 296–307, 314–15, 329; decolonization language of, 13; indigenous origins of, 296–97, 314, 315n1

Morales, Soledad, 123

Moreira Alves, Maria Helena, 33

Mothers in Pain (Argentina), 123

Mothers of the Plaza de Mayo, 133–34, 151

Motta, Carlos Carmelo, 50

Mouffe, Chantal, 69

Movement for Housing (Brazil), 287

Movement of Argentinian Workers (MTA) (Argentina), 123

Movement of Homeless Workers (MTST) (Brazil), 287

Movement of Landless Rural Workers (MST) (Brazil), 1, 51, 54, 221, 226, 231, 235, 236nn3–4, 287

Movement of Neighborhood Associations (MAB) (Brazil), 32–33, 43

Movement of Peasant Women (MMC), 227, 230, 236n2

Movement of Rural Women in Struggle (MMAL) (Argentina), 123

Movement of Rural Women Workers (MMTR) (Brazil), 21, 156–57, 164, 172, 174nn1–2, 219–36, 237n9, 333; affective dimensions of, 234–35; civil society agenda approaches of, 227–28; formation of, 221–24; fragmentation of, 227–32; marketing of Herbalife by, 221, 229–30; as movement-in-democracy, 219–22, 230–36, 236n1, 237n12; national alliance of, 227, 236n2; rights-based agenda of, 223–26; social and economic context of, 222–24, 236n6; structure of, 226; tactics of, 225; uncivic mobilizations of, 227, 229–30, 232; women's pharmacy collectives of, 228

movements-in-democracy, 219–36, 236n1; affective dimensions of, 234–35; Brazil's MMTR and, 220–36; horizontal diversity and lack of consensus in, 232–36, 237n12; promotion of progressive reform with, 220, 235–36; risks of fragmentation of, 230–32

Movements of Unemployed Workers (MTD) (Argentina), 2, 15, 124–27, 129–32, 139n5, 139n12, 142, 153

Movement toward Socialism (MAS) (Bolivia), 297, 302–4, 329

Movimiento Nacional Cimarrón (Colombia), 204, 208–9, 213

Movimiento País (Ecuador), 255

multiple strategies of movements. *See* intersection of civil and uncivic activism

Municipalist Party (PM) (Ecuador), 255

National Afro-Colombian Students Collective (CEUNA) (Colombia), 117
National Alpargatista Army of Liberation, 151, 154, 155n8
National Assembly for Education (Venezuela), 275
National Campaign for a Popular Plebiscite for a New Political System (Brazil), 293–94
National Campaign for the Right to Legal, Safe, and Free Abortions (Argentina), 134, 136–38
National Confederation of Agricultural Workers (CONTAG) (Brazil), 236n3
National Confederation of Peruvian Communities Affected by Mining (CONACAMI), 186, 192, 193
National Congress of Afro-Ecuadorian Peoples, 120
National Consortium for Reproductive and Sexual Rights (CONDERS) (Argentina), 133–34
National Forum on Popular Participation in Democratic and Popular Administrations (FNPP), 37–39
National Movement for Urban Reform (MNRU) (Brazil), 54, 55–56
National Movement of People Affected by Dams (MAB) (Brazil), 236n3
National Women's Encounters (ENMs) (Argentina), 131–34, 138, 144, 154, 155n4
Navia, Patricio, 320
Nebot, Jaime, 256–57
negros escogidos, 14, 24n4, 115–16, 120
neighborhood associations, 31–34, 51–52. *See also* participatory democracy
neoliberal governments, 325–27; of Argentina, 146–48, 153; biopolitical projects of, 145–46; of Colombia, 214–17; co-optation of Civil Society Agenda by, 12, 83–84, 104, 112–14, 200–203, 317, 325–27, 331–32; IFI promotion of, 19–20; impact of unruly civil action on, 3, 15–18; modified forms of, 145, 162, 167, 172, 176n20; North Americanized conceptions of civil society in, 7–11, 321–25; participatory democracy in, 28–29; of Peru, 190, 194–95; poverty-reduction schemes of, 327; trademarked democracy of, 200; transnational institutions of, 110

neoliberalism: capitalist globalization of, 14, 20, 108–10; coloniality of power in, 195, 198n14; corporate economic citizenship in, 189; economic development paradigms of, 83, 159–62; governance networks in, 321–23; market discourses of, 19; market-oriented aid relationships of, 166–69, 173–74; multicultural discourses of empowerment of, 14, 15–16, 110, 199, 202–3; Pan-Africanist formulations of, 104, 117–18; racial order of, 301; structural adjustment programs and, 9–10, 19, 28, 40, 143–47, 180; subaltern spaces of, 200–203; supranational institutions of, 194–95; uncivic activism in response to, 141–54
Netherlands, 162, 166–69, 175n8, 175nn12–16, 176n21
Network of Afro-Latin American and Caribbean Women, 110
New Left parties, 7
New Social Movements, 33–34, 77, 108–9
Nicaragua, 108
Noboa, Alvaro, 240
Nobre, Marcos, 292–93
nongovernmental organizations, 10, 15, 19–20; competition for funds among, 165–66, 168, 173; funding of, 10, 161, 162t, 169, 173–74; institutionalization (NGO-ization) of, 20, 64, 110, 112–14, 159, 163; market-based aid relationships of, 156–74; professionalization of, 161–62, 165–66; scholarly analysis of, 162–64; solidarity aid regime of, 160. *See also* aid relationships
no permitido activism, 3–4, 332. *See also* uncivic activism
North American conception of civil society, 7–11; good governance approach of, 9–10, 321–25; intermediation of NGOs in, 10, 322–23
North American Free Trade Agreement (NAFTA), 108

Obama, Barack, 107, 119
Occupy Wall Street, 233, 235, 236n1, 283–84
O'Donnell, Guillermo, 301
Olvera, Alberto, 10
ONECA, 118
Organic Law for Elections and Political Participation of 1998 (Venezuela), 268

Organic Law on Town Council Governance of 1989 (Venezuela), 267–68

Organization of American States (OAS), 114

Organization of People's Neighborhoods and Black Communities of the Chocó (OBAPO), 204, 207–9, 212

Ortega, Daniel, 23

Ortellado, Pablo, 294

Our Bodies, Ourselves (Boston Women's Health Course Collective), 165

overflows of activism, 23, 220, 235, 333–37. *See also* intersection of civil and uncivic activism

Oxfam UK, 161

Palacios, Alfredo, 240

Pallares, Amalia, 3, 4, 16, 320

Pan-Africanism, 116; of the 1930s, 105; neoliberal formulations of, 104, 117–18

Panfichi, Aldo, 10

Parsons, Talcott, 8

participatory budgeting: as governmentality from below, 43–44, 323; local experiments in, 34–35, 43; official discourses on, 93–94; Porto Alegre (Brazil) model of, 4, 10, 21, 37–40, 56–57, 82–83, 87–89, 93–99, 234, 323–25; promotion and diffusion of, 40–41

participatory democracy, 2, 27–44, 320, 332; adoption into mainstream governance of, 28–29, 40–41, 49, 64–71, 288–92; agency of subjective participants in, 84–85, 332; ambivalence of participants in, 83–85, 91–100, 290–91; of Brazil's municipal and regional councils, 66–80, 289–90, 321, 330; free municipal elections and, 35–37; in good governance paradigms, 40–42, 321–25; interdependency with the state of, 41–43, 47–49, 52–61, 64–66, 173–74, 175n6; liberation theology and, 30, 31; making and unmaking of democratic space in, 66–80, 234; movements-in-democracy and, 219–36; normative scholarly assumptions of, 83–85, 99, 162–64; in popular local administrations, 34–40; populist logic of, 29–31, 43; radical-democratic logic of, 30–31, 35–37, 43; social movement origins of, 28; Venezuela's innovations in, 273–76, 325; women's mobilization in, 75–76

participatory methodologies, 245

Partido do Frente Liberal (PFL) (Brazil), 71

Partido Independiente de Color (Cuba), 107

Partido Popular Socialista (PPS) (Brazil), 67–70

Partido Revolucionario Institucional (PRI) (Mexico), 6

Partido Social Cristiano (PSC) (Ecuador), 243, 253–54, 256, 257n2

Patrick, Deval, 107

Paschel, Tianna, 320

Pastore, Elenice, 228

Patriotic Pole (Britain), 262

Patriotic Society (SP) (Ecuador), 240

Peasant Movement from Santiago (MOCASE) (Argentina), 123

People's Permanent Court, 182

permitido activism, 3–4, 332

Perón, Juan, 6, 30

Peru: anti-mining protest in, 182–83, 187; black and indigenous rights in, 108; constitutional rights of citizens in, 185–86, 190–91; expansions of mining in, 180–81; Law on Free and Informed Prior Consultation in, 194; Ministry of Energy and Mining of, 181–82; neoliberal capitalism in, 190, 194–95; repression of dissidence in, 182, 190–95, 197n7, 198n12; structural adjustment program in, 180; Territorial Zoning Code of, 194

Peru's Río Blanco mine referendum, 179–96, 333–34; civil society's objectives in, 193–95; eco-territorial framework of, 181, 183–87, 193, 195–96; heterogeneous network of mining opponents and, 186–87, 189–90, 195–96; nonbinding status of, 197n2; official discrediting of, 188–91, 193, 198n10; repression and criminalization of dissidence in, 182, 190–95, 197n7, 198n12; results of, 183, 184t; successful organization and execution of, 187–93, 198n9

Petchesky, Rosalind, 163

Petras, James, 163

Pink Tide, xi, xv, 10, 23, 105, 119; Civil Society Agenda of, 12, 24n1, 27, 331–33, 335–36; modified neoliberalism of, 145, 162t, 172, 176n20

Pinoargote, Jimmy, 251

Pinochet, Augusto, 319

piqueteros (Argentina). *See* Movements of Unemployed Workers

334; of Bolivia's January 11, 2008, protests, 296–315; of Brazil's June 2013 protests, 235, 283–95; of Brazil's MMTR, 227, 229–30, 232; claiming of citizenship with, 97–99; collective subjectivity of identity-based demands in, 15–18, 97–99, 332; of conservative activists, 330; of Ecuador's Santa Elena provincialization movement, 240–41, 246–49, 254; gray zone with civil activism of, 4–5, 17–18, 21–23, 99, 219–36, 312–14, 329–30, 333–37; impact on neoliberal governments of, 3, 15–18; as politics by other means, 143; in Venezuela's contentious public space, 261–81. *See also* intersection of civil and uncivic activism

UN Development Programme (UNDP), 9, 28, 40, 298–99

UN Habitat, 324

United Assembly of Citizens (UAC), 143

United Nations (UN), 114, 160. *See also* Third World Conference against Racism and Related Forms of Discrimination

United Peasant Association of the Atrato River (ACIA) (Colombia), 204–5

United Socialist Party of Venezuela (PSUV), 276–79

United States: black conservatism in, 107; black Freedom Movements of, 105–8, 116; color-blind racism of post-racial society in, 107; conservative activism in, 330; Durban response by, 121n6; imperialist project of, 104, 114; Pan-Africanism in, 105; Plan Columbia anti-drug campaign of, 211–12

Universidad Nacional del Litoral (Argentina), 151

University of the Santa Elena Peninsula (UPSE), 242, 243

UN Women/ONU Mulheres, 176n22

Urban Latin America (URB-AL) network, 40

Uribe, Álvaro, 104, 211, 214

Urresti, Christian, 304–9, 315n2

Uruguay: antisystemic movements in, 18–19; biopolitical project in, 145–46; Botnia pulp mill in, 145–54; IMF's structural adjustment program for, 145–47; neoliberal economic policies of, 145–47, 153–54

U.S. Agency for International Development (USAID), 8, 28, 103, 119, 335; imperialist goals of, 114; on participatory democracy, 40, 83–84; post-Durban rhetoric on race of, 111–14

U.S. Congressional Black Caucus, 114, 212

Van Cott, Donna Lee, 215

Vargas, Getúlio, 6, 61n3

Venezuela: black and indigenous rights in, 108, 112, 276; black political activism in, 104, 119–20, 335; Bolivarian Movement in, 268, 325; Caracazo of 1989 of, 1, 261, 263; Catholic Church of, 270; Chávez regime in, 172, 238–39, 253, 262–63, 268–80, 295n3, 334; collective civic action in, 261–81; Communal Councils of, 10, 262–63, 274, 279–80, 325; Constitution of 1999 of, 269, 273, 276, 277; Fifth Republic Movement in, 266–67; National Assembly of, 276; opening of political space in, 267–76; participatory innovations in, 273–76; petro-dollars and patronage in, 265–66; polarized responses to Chávez's government in, 262, 269–72, 275–80; post-neoliberal right in, 2; poverty rates in, 266; Presidential Recall Referendum of, 262, 269–70, 275–76; protest repression rates in, 270–71, 278; socialist communal state in, 262–63, 276–80; women's movement in, 268; working-class politics of the streets in, 262–68

Vera, Otto, 255

Verba, Sidney, 8, 52

Via Campesina, 226

Vienna Business Summit of 2006, 150

Villarroel, Miguel, 297

Wade, Peter, 202, 214

Wallerstein, Immanuel, 159, 162, 164

Wampler, Brian, 40, 324

Warner, Michael, 234

Washington Consensus, 3–4, 108, 328

Weffort, Francisco, 162

We Want to Choose (Venezuela), 275

Wickramasinghe, Nira, 5

Williams, Raymond, 300

Winant, Howard, 116, 121n9

"Women and the Politics of Place" (WPP) project, x